Advance Praise for
Fact-Checking the Fact-Checkers

"This is THE definitive book exposing the fact-checking industry as an arm of the liberal media. After revealing how the industry acts to further censorship, Matt Palumbo then extensively proves that no one knows less about the facts than the self-proclaimed fact-checkers."
— DAN BONGINO, Host of *The Dan Bongino Show and Unfiltered*

"Matt Palumbo's deeply researched book shows why the public doesn't trust the media's self-appointed 'fact checkers.' Their name trumpets their neutrality. The reality is sadly different. All too often, their goal is to advance a partisan agenda and do it more effectively by feigning non-partisan independence. Palumbo rips off the mask."
— CHARLES LIPSON, Peter B. Ritzma Professor Emeritus, University of Chicago

"In this substantive and gripping exposé, Matt Palumbo pulls back the curtain on the so-called fact-checking industry. This book vividly documents the dishonesty and incompetence of the cabal that big tech companies have chosen to be the arbiters of truth."
— JAMES D. AGRESTI, President of Just Facts

FACT-CHECKING ☑
— THE —
FACT-CHECKERS ☒

HOW THE LEFT HIJACKED AND WEAPONIZED THE FACT-CHECKING INDUSTRY

MATT PALUMBO

Liberatio
Protocol

A LIBERATIO PROTOCOL BOOK
An Imprint of Post Hill Press
ISBN: 978-1-63758-820-8
ISBN (eBook): 978-1-63758-821-5

Fact-Checking the Fact-Checkers:
How the Left Hijacked and Weaponized the Fact-Checking Industry
© 2023 by Matt Palumbo
All Rights Reserved

Cover Design by Conroy Accord

Post Hill Press
New York • Nashville
posthillpress.com

Published in the United States of America
1 2 3 4 5 6 7 8 9 10

To the incompetent fact-checkers,
for without them this book would not exist

TABLE OF CONTENTS

INTRO AND ACKNOWLEDGMENTS

I had two main goals when I began writing this book: to expose the fact-checking industry for the fraud that it is and to provide an archive of their errors extensive enough to discredit them once and for all.

A casual political observer may take the "fact-checker" label at face value. But the entire industry (with little exception) serves as a Trojan horse to justify censorship for the political left. The first chapter of this book, which accounts for nearly a third of it, gives a comprehensive overview of the history of the fact-checking industry, how we know for a fact that it's biased, and what its real goals are.

The rest of the book is rapid-fire fact-checking of fact-checkers, which I wrote as individual essays. The only exception is the last chapter, which is in long-form essay format, and tackles what I believe to be the most consequential stories the fact-checkers got wrong. As I began going through my own work, it became evident that fact-checker incompetence fell into categories, which became the basis for many of the chapters. Like most of my books, none of them need to be read in chronological order, and the table of contents names each essay within every chapter specifically to make it easier for anyone who wants to jump around.

A book of this nature is naturally research-heavy and would have been nowhere near as extensive without additional help.

While performing my own original research, I was blessed to have a number of friends who regularly sent me anything they thought could possibly help assist in writing the book, including Bryan W. White of PolitiFact Bias (who also helped with editing an early draft of this book), Capital Research's Parker Thayer, MetaFactGroup, Katie Sweeney, James Agresti, and Joseph Vazquez from the Media Research Center.

Lastly, my friends Samuel Gautsch and Michelle Kelly also helped in going through earlier drafts of the book to find any potential readability issues and also caught another five hundred typos.

PART 1

THE FACT-CHECKING INDUSTRY

Having had many personal entanglements with the so-called fact-checkers over the years, it was only a matter of time before this book was written out of spite.

For the past five years, I've semi-regularly been writing articles on the theme of "fact-checking the fact-checkers." Even without actively searching for bad fact-checks to refute, the volume of misinformation from those claiming to debunk it was large enough to make it impossible to ignore.

In the past year, mostly out of frustration from seeing the most incompetent people in politics be heralded as truth-tellers, I began actively documenting every example of fact-checker incompetence I could find to eventually present and expose the industry in the book you're now reading. My fact-checks of those supposed fact-checkers are all contained in the second part of this book, but first, it needs to be explained who exactly the fact-checkers are, how they operate, how we know they're (extremely) biased, and how they wield so much power over the national narrative.

Even in the absence of a book documenting their partisanship and sloppy fact-checks, most people, especially those right of center, have wised up to their bias.

A Rasmussen poll ahead of the 2016 election found that only 29 percent of likely voters believe the media's fact-checkers, while 62 percent believe that they're skewed to "help candidates they support."[1]

Similarly, the Pew Research Center did polling on how Republicans and Democrats view fact-checkers in 2019 as they're increasingly used to

---

1   "Voters Don't Trust Media Fact-Checking." Rasmussen Reports, September 30, 2016, https://www.rasmussenreports.com/public_content/politics/general_politics/september_2016/voters_don_t_trust_media_fact_checking.

drive the national conversation.[2] Only 28 percent of Republicans believe that fact-checkers deal with both sides fairly, compared to 70 percent who think they're biased. Democrats trust fact-checkers 69 percent to 29 percent, and Independents are split 51 percent to 47 percent.[3]

While fact-checking itself is nothing new, it was throughout the Trump presidency that the media escalated the use of supposed "fact-checks" to backdoor censorship against dissenting voices. Due to the role that fact-checkers play on social media, once something is "fact-checked" by them, the issue is treated as settled. Anyone who repeats a claim on major social media platforms that's been supposedly refuted by these de facto arbiters of truth will find their post slapped with a warning telling them that they've shared misleading or false information, with a fact-check article attached purporting to justify it.

On Facebook specifically, accounts that are fact-checked have their pages restricted so that future posts don't appear as often in the feeds of their followers. Pages can also risk losing the ability to monetize their content as a result.

This kills two birds with one stone for the censor, having both the effect of limiting the spread of information that goes against the cathedral and spreading a preferred narrative.

For better or for worse, nearly half of the country gets some or most of their news from one social media platform or another, with Facebook as the king, accounting for where 31 percent of the American public gets at least part of their news from.[4]

The rise of advocacy fact-checkers has not-coincidentally coincided with the decline of journalism, an industry whose employees are disproportionately liberal. Weekly newspapers lost more than half their workforces from 1990 to 2017, shedding a quarter of a million jobs. As jobs in journalism shrunk, journalists rebranding themselves as fact-checkers rose. In 2014, there were forty-four fact-checking organizations in the U.S.—and by June 2021, there were 341. More fact-checking organiza-

2   Walker, Mason, and Jeffrey Gottfried. "Republicans Far More Likely Than Democrats to Say Fact-Checkers Tend to Favor One Side." Pew Research Center, June 27, 2019, https://www.pewresearch.org/fact-tank/2019/06/27/republicans-far-more-likely-than-democrats-to-say-fact-checkers-tend-to-favor-one-side/.

3   Ibid.

4   Walker, Mason, and Katerina Eva Matsa. "News Consumption Across Social Media in 2021." Pew Research Center, September 20, 2021, https://www.pewresearch.org/journalism/2021/09/20/news-consumption-across-social-media-in-2021.

tions were added in the year prior to June 2021 (fifty-one new groups) than existed in 2014.[5] A headline from Harvard University's Nieman Lab says it all: "Publishers hope fact-checking can become a revenue stream. Right now, it's mostly Big Tech who is buying."

The *Washington Post*'s fact-checker Glenn Kessler famously began a running tally of their fact-checks during the Trump administration, eventually claiming that President Trump had made 30,000+ false statements during his presidency.[6] The "30,000 lies" figure was perfect for the headlines—and also the result of poor reasoning and methodological trickery.

Illustrating the subjective nature of fact-checking, one such example of Trump's supposed lies included his statement that "my job was made harder by phony witch hunts, by 'Russia, Russia, Russia' nonsense." This single true statement and variants of it account for at least 227 of the "lies" on their list. Jokes, sarcasm, and examples of obvious hyperbole also dominate the list, and each time they're repeated, they're counted as an additional "lie" to further the appearance of mass dishonesty.[7]

Uncoincidentally, Kessler decided to stop maintaining a running presidential fact-check database after Biden's first one hundred days in office.[8]

The bias is further evident in what Kessler sees as worthy of examining. In one bizarre column, Kessler, who is the great-grandson of Jean Baptiste August Kessler, an oil executive responsible for the growth of the Royal Dutch Shell Company (now Shell Oil), and the grandson of industrialist Geldolph Adriaan Kessler, decided to fact-check how difficult Republican senator Tim Scott's family "really" had it living in the Jim Crow south.

---

5   Siegel, Jacob. "Invasion of the Fact-Checkers." *Tablet Magazine*, January 1, 2022, https://www.tabletmag.com/sections/news/articles/invasion-fact-checkers.

6   Kessler, Glenn, et al. "Trump's false or misleading claims total 30,573 over 4 years." *Washington Post*, January 24, 2021, https://www.washingtonpost.com/politics/2021/01/24/trumps-false-or-misleading-claims-total-30573-over-four-years/.

7   Hemingway, Mark. "No, Trump Hasn't Made 20,000 'False or Misleading' Claims." *Buffalo News,* September 16, 2020, https://buffalonews.com/news/national/govt-and-politics/no-trump-hasnt-made-20-000-false-or-misleading-claims/article_cc0abf55-7146-5d93-95e6-b2ac11166210.html.

8   Richardson, Valerie. "Washington Post shuts down presidential fact-checking database after 100 days of Joe Biden." *Washington Times,* April 27, 2021, https://www.washingtontimes.com/news/2021/apr/27/washington-post-shuts-down-presidential-fact-check/.

Contrary to their job title, the role of the fact-checker is to simply provide cover for liberal media narratives, the media being an industry to which they themselves belong. One notable recent example of national significance was when then–New York governor Andrew Cuomo was heralded as a champion in fighting the COVID-19 pandemic in its early days, while Florida's governor, Ron DeSantis, was portrayed as taking a "do nothing" approach by resisting crushing lockdowns and questionable mask science. In this case, even objectively true statements weren't safe from the fact-checkers. In July 2020, PolitiFact's Tom Kertscher fact-checked the counter-narrative claim that "Florida is doing over five times better than New Jersey and New York in COVID-19 deaths per million people" by acknowledging that the claim was 100 percent true at the time of writing, but saying that things could change in the future, so they rated it "Mostly False."[9]

While the numbers are subject to change (and are now closer, but Florida still has fewer deaths per capita despite a larger elderly population), this is a statement that deserves a "Mostly True" rating with a caveat that they're subject to change. It's these sorts of unfair ratings that reveal the "fact-checker's" role in silencing a contrary narrative—especially when you consider the mental gymnastics required to admit something is true before rating it "Mostly False." This is common enough that I've devoted an entire chapter titled "Adventures in Mental Gymnastics" to this entire theme of fact-checking.

Nothing is truly too absurd to check as long as it's coming from a Republican. My favorite fact-check of all time came from the *Mercury News*, which fact-checked Trump's obviously-not-literal claim that if you stacked up the one thousand burgers he'd bought to cater an event at the White House, they'd pile up "a mile high." That produced a headline you can't help but just laugh at: "FACT CHECK: At two inches each, a thousand burgers would not reach one mile high." [10]

Thank God they cleared that up.

9   Palumbo, Matt. "Politifact Botches Another Fact Check on New York vs. Florida Coronavirus Deaths." Bongino, August 4, 2020, https://bongino.com/politifact-botches-another-fact-check-on-new-york-vs-florida-coroanvirus-deaths.

10   *Washington Post.* "Breaking down Trump's extravagant, $3,000, 300-sandwich celebration of Clemson University." *Mercury News,* January 15, 2019, https://www.mercurynews.com/2019/01/15/president-trumps-extravagant-3000-300-sandwich-celebration-of-clemson-university/.

In some cases it's impossible not to get the impression that the conclusions of the fact-checkers are determined before they're even written. One such example comes from when the fact-checkers rallied to defend Joe Biden against accusations that he had eulogized a Klansman—which he did at the 2010 funeral of Robert Byrd. The eulogy was broadcast live on CSPAN and can be found easily online.[11]

To downplay the incident, the fact-checkers decided to nitpick Byrd's job description. The fact-checkers instead combed through the depths of social media to find any random person making a less true version of the "Biden eulogized a Klansman" claim and then seized on that version of it. In this case, it turned out that some people on social media wrongly said that Biden eulogized a Grand Dragon in the KKK, which gave the fact-checkers exactly what they needed to spin the truth.

The Associated Press fact-checker rated the claim that Biden eulogized a Klansman "Partly false" because while "Biden did eulogize Sen. Robert C. Byrd when he died… Byrd was not a 'grand wizard' in the Ku Klux Klan. He was a member of the KKK in the early 1940s but later renounced his affiliation with the hate group." They continue: "As a young man in West Virginia, Byrd recruited members to a local KKK chapter and was elected to the post of 'exalted cyclops' according to his 2005 autobiography," the AP informs us. [12] The "exalted cyclops" is the head of a local Klan chapter, making it a relatively high ranking position within the organization, and the AP makes no mention of this, nor do they mention that Byrd also held the title of Kleagle (recruiter).[13]

Amazingly, *USA Today*'s Ella Lee provided the same defense: "Fact check: Photo shows Biden with Byrd, who once had ties to KKK, but wasn't a grand wizard," read her headline for an article that mostly focused on Byrd later denouncing the Klan and arguing that he had a good record on race relations in a fact-check that borders on PR.[14]

---

11 "Vice President Biden Eulogizes Senator Byrd." CSPAN, July 2, 2010,
    https://www.c-span.org/video/?c4454847/vice-president-biden-eulogizes-senator-byrd.
12 Joffe-Block, Jude, and Marcos Martínez Chacón. "Biden did not eulogize former
    KKK 'grand wizard.'" Associated Press, October 10, 2020, https://apnews.com/
    article/fact-checking-afs:Content:9545480195.
13 Schumpeter. "The Exalted Cyclops." *The Economist*, June 30, 2010,
    https://www.economist.com/schumpeter/2010/06/30/the-exalted-cyclops.
14 Lee, Ella. "Fact check: Photo shows Biden with Byrd, who once had ties to KKK,
    but wasn't a grand wizard." *USA Today*, June 16, 2020, https://www.usatoday.com/
    story/news/factcheck/2020/06/14/fact-check-biden-isnt-kkk-grand-wizard-photo/
    3183887001/.

Reuters published a similar fact-check of the "grand wizard" claim and even noted that Barack Obama and Bill Clinton also spoke at the funeral in an attempt to normalize it—as if that's not damning to them too.[15]

This also raises some obvious questions, such as how it is that every major fact-checker chose to check the same "truth-adjacent" claim just to distract from the truth. To point out the blatantly obvious, how do you suppose they would've rated such a claim if it were Donald Trump (or any Republican) in the same situation? Would they bother to explain that the person later renounced their beliefs? Would they spend hundreds of words humanizing a former Klansman? To ask such a question is to answer it.

These brief bouts of insanity you've read so far are just a preview of what's coming ahead in this book. Admittedly, when I began writing this book, I expected to find one major error for every fifty or so fact-checks I reviewed. As it turns out, I overestimated their competence by at least a factor of ten.

But before I dig into that, it's worth reviewing who the major players in this battle are, who is backing them, and how we know their goal is to rewrite reality in favor of the prevailing liberal narrative.

POLITIFACT

PolitiFact takes the cake as the worst of the faux fact-checkers, and has rightly garnered a reputation for being the most clearly biased in favor of the left.

PolitiFact originated as a project out of the *Tampa Bay Times* (then the *St. Petersburg Times*) and *Congressional Quarterly* in 2007, both of which are owned by the Poynter Institute. The *Tampa Bay Times* endorsed Hillary Clinton in 2016 and Joe Biden in 2020.

Journalist Bill Adair founded PolitiFact and accepted a Pulitzer for that work in 2009. He then created the International Fact-Checking Network (IFCN) in 2015 (which was launched by the Poynter Institute), which has the claimed goal of monitoring fact-checkers.

---

15   Reuters Staff. "Fact check: Robert Byrd, eulogized by Joe Biden at funeral, was not KKK grand wizard." Reuters, October 7, 2020, https://www.reuters.com/article/uk-factcheck-byrd-eulogy-biden-kkk-grand/fact-checkrobert-byrdeulogized-by-joe-bidenat-funeralwas-notkkkgrandwizard-idUSKBN26S2EE.

The *St. Petersburg Times* Washington Bureau Chief was appointed to be the first PolitiFact editor, and he was succeeded by the current editor, Angie Drobnic Holan, in 2013.

PolitiFact rates statements with their "Truth-O-Meter" scale, which ranges from "True" to "Pants on Fire."

In an interview with the *Pacific Standard*, Adair admitted that the fact-checking process is subjective. "Yeah, we're human. We're making subjective decisions. Lord knows the decision about a Truth-O-Meter rating is entirely subjective. As Angie Holan, the editor of PolitiFact, often says, the Truth-O-Meter is not a scientific instrument." [16]

But they'll frame their checks as scientific fact anyway.

Adair also explained that his vision is to develop fact-checking to the point where it can be automated. "Ultimately, my vision is that you get instant fact-checking when you're watching a major speech, when you're watching cable news, when you're watching a political convention, a debate, whatever—the goal is that the fact-check pops up on the screen and says, *Hey that thing that the senator just said is false*." Much of the implementation of fact-checks is already automatic and has countless flaws exposed later in this chapter.

In a 2019 op-ed for the *Columbia Journalism Review*, Adair argued that bias is good, despite what "conservative critics" who "wrongly suggest that bias in journalism is always bad" have to say. "In fact, bias in journalism is good. It just needs to be labeled and understood," Adair argues. He categorized bias on a scale rating from "objective news" to "opinion," which is pictured below. [17]

---

16 Schulson, Michael. "An Interview with the Founder of PolitiFact, During a Season of Distorted Reality." *Pacific Standard*, August 1, 2017, https://psmag.com/news/an-interview-with-the-founder-of-politifact-during-a-season-of-distorted-reality.

17 Adair, Bill. "Bias is good. It just needs a label." *Columbia Journalism Review*, August 29, 2019, https://www.cjr.org/opinion/bias-journalism.php.

The Continuum of Journalism

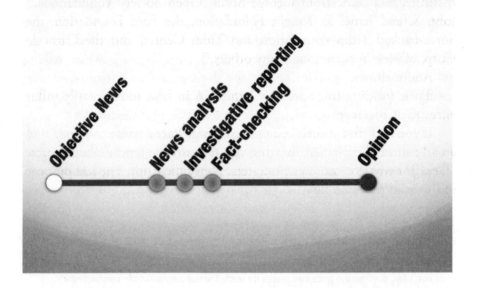

Interestingly, "fact-checking" is right at the center between objectivity and opinion—signaling it's one type of reporting where the facts can be twisted and that Adair approves of it.

In May 2021, PolitiFact hosted a virtual festival called "United Facts of America: A Festival of Fact-Checking" that included CNN's Brian Stelter and Christiane Amanpour, MSNBC's Charlie Sykes, Virginia Democrat senator Mark Warner, and Dr. Anthony Fauci. At the event, Editor in Chief Angie Holan praised Democrat billionaire Craig Newmark, who has been a major financial backer of the site and supported Biden's 2020 campaign (among many other liberal causes).

At the festival, Amanpour complained about objectivity: "[objectivity] is not about taking any issue, whether it be about genocide, or the climate, or U.S. elections, or anything else happening around the globe—COVID, for instance—and saying, 'Well, on the one hand, and on the other hand,' and pretending there is an equal amount of fact and truth in each basket..."[18] This comment came a mere three days before

---

18   Taibbi, Matt. "'Fact-Checking' Takes Another Beating." TK News by Matt Taibbi, May 24, 2021, https://taibbi.substack.com/p/fact-checking-takes-another-beating.

PolitiFact was forced to update their not-objective article dismissing the Wuhan lab leak hypothesis.

Major funding from PolitiFact's parent organization, the Poynter Institute, has come from George Soros' Open Society Foundations,[19] John S. and James L. Knight Foundation, the Ford Foundation, the Soros-backed Tides Foundation and Tides Center, and the Carnegie Corp. of New York, among many others.[20]

And it shows.

Their funding from Soros is Exhibit A in how money easily influences their coverage.

If you ever find yourself Googling George Soros' name, you may find an ad from PolitiFact encouraging you to learn the "truth" about Soros. "George Soros does not pay protesters. Here's the truth. The real purpose of the 'paid protester' myth."

When you click through, you're brought to a fact-check of a claim from Candace Owens that Soros is "funding the chaos" in Minneapolis via the Open Society Foundations (this was during the 2020 George Floyd riots).[21]

Fact-checker Emily Venezky predictably rates Owens' claim "False" while acknowledging that Soros donated $33 million to organizations "that have worked with Black Lives Matter or worked to raise awareness

---

19 The Poynter Institute. "$1.3 Million in Grants from Omidyar Network, Open Society Foundations Will Expand Poynter's International Fact-Checking Network." PRNewswire, June 29, 2017, https://www.prnewswire.com/news-releases/13-million-in-grants-from-omidyar-network-open-society-foundations-will-expand-poynters-international-fact-checking-network-300481553.html.

20 Lucas, Barbara Joanna. "Dishonest Fact-Checkers." Capital Research Center, March 10, 2017, https://capitalresearch.org/article/dishonest-fact-checkers/.

21 Venezky, Emily. "No, George Soros and his foundations do not pay people to protest." PolitiFact, June 1, 2020, https://www.politifact.com/factchecks/2020/jun/01/candace-owens/no-soros-and-foundation-do-not-pay-people-protest/.

during the Ferguson-related protests." She then tries to hedge that admission: "However, they had never given money to groups for the express purpose of organizing protests with the movement," as if BLM wasn't going to use the funds for whatever they want regardless.

The purpose of the article is simply to downplay the role of Soros in degrading law and order in the U.S. Whether or not Soros is funding protesters in the exact manner in the exact city that Candace is stating is almost irrelevant when we're talking about a man who has spent $40 million funding far-left prosecutors nationwide, all of which implement soft-on-crime policies and favor defunding police departments.

In a similar vein, PolitiFact's Yacob Reyes wrote an article downplaying Soros' funding of Black Lives Matter–adjacent groups. When Candace Owens, citing the same data as Venezky, said that Soros "injected $33 million into Black Lives Matter," Reyes rated the claim "False" because the groups weren't official BLM groups. They were just groups that shared a virtually identical ideology and engaged in the same kind of disruptive activities.[22]

Soros' network sees the major fact-checkers as allies, as proven by a leaked concept paper for George Soros' Open Society Foundations from the liberal (and Soros-funded) New America Foundation that praised PolitiFact, FactCheck.org, and the *Washington Post* fact-checker specifically for their role in the 2008 and (then forthcoming) 2012 election and argued that they should be amplified,[23] describing the emergence of fact-checking sites as "one of the few bright spots" in the media landscape.[24]

Soros himself has copied the strategy of pushing censorship by crying disinformation. In early 2022, Soros and fellow leftist billionaire Reid Hoffman (known for co-founding LinkedIn) founded the hilariously Orwellian-named "Good Information Inc." The company has the stated mission of "tackling misinformation" (which they'll presumably do by spreading misinformation), and is led by former Democratic strategist Tara McGowan, whose firm ACRONYM was known for epically botch-

---

22   Reyes, Yacob. "Soros' alleged support of Black Lives Matter resurges on social media." PolitiFact, April 18, 2022, https://www.politifact.com/factchecks/2022/apr/18/facebook-posts/soros-alleged-support-black-lives-matter-resurges-.

23   "The Pursuit of Facts Project: A Concept Paper for the Open Society Institute." New America Foundation, February 8, 2011, https://www.danielpipes.org/rr/tab-03-extreme-polarization-and-breakdown-in-civic-discourse.pdf, 22.

24   Ibid, 20.

ing running the 2020 Iowa caucus.[25] Their advisory board membership includes Nandini Jammi, an activist who once wrote an article for the National Crime Prevention Council complaining that punishments were too harsh for youth sex offenders.[26]

Heading into the 2022 midterms, in an open letter signed by eleven other leftist groups, the Soros-funded Leadership Conference on Civil and Human Rights called on Big Tech CEOs to take "immediate" action to spread so-called "voting disinformation" to "help prevent the undermining" of democracy. The signatories had received a combined $30.3 million from Soros in just a four-year period.[27]

While this book is U.S.-centric, it's worth noting that with all things Soros, his reach extends globally in this regard.

As the Hungarian publication Remix documented, as of mid-2020, of the eleven Facebook-approved fact-checking organizations for Central and Eastern Europe, eight are funded by Soros. As is the case for the U.S., these fact-checking groups are largely critical of the political right in those countries.[28] For nearly the entirety of Central and Eastern Europe, Soros-backed groups have a virtual monopoly on fact-checking.

That the left's biggest political donor sees the fact-checkers worth funding is itself strong evidence of their bias—and there's plenty more where that came from.

How We Know PolitiFact Is Biased

The existence of bias at PolitiFact has been studied and analyzed many times over the years—and all with the same result.

25 Fischer, Sara. "Billionaires back new media firm to combat disinformation." Axios, October 26, 2021, https://www.axios.com/2021/10/26/soros-hoffman-disinformation-tara-mcgowan.

26 Palumbo, Matt. "Soros-Backed Activist Nandini Jammi Argued for Lesser Punishments for Young Sex Offenders." Bongino.com, December 18, 2021, https://bongino.com/soros-backed-activist-nandini-jammi-argued-for-lesser-punishments-for-young-sex-offenders.

27 Vazquez, Joseph. "Soros Gave $30M to Groups Urging Censorship of So-Called Disinfo Before Midterms." NewsBusters, October 14, 2022, https://www.newsbusters.org/blogs/business/joseph-vazquez/2022/10/14/breaking-soros-gave-30m-groups-urging-censorship-so-called.

28 Cody, John. "George Soros funds 8 out of 11 of Facebook's fact-checking organizations in Central and Eastern Europe." Remix, May 27, 2020, https://rmx.news/article/exclusive-george-soros-funds-8-out-of-11-of-facebook-s-fact-checking-organizations-in-central-and-eastern-europe/.

That so-called fact-checkers are just biased left-wing gatekeepers is obvious to anyone who's followed their track record, and PolitiFact in particular has done a poor job of concealing its partisanship. In one case they assigned different ratings to nearly identical statements based on the ideology of the person making them. When Ron Paul (a libertarian who was a registered Republican at the time) and Jim Webb (a Democrat) made nearly identical statements about the U.S. lacking income taxes prior to 1913, they received different rulings from the site. Ron Paul's statement was only determined to be "Half True,"[29] while Webb's was "Mostly True."[30]

RON PAUL

Says the U.S. federal income tax rate was 0 percent until 1913.

— *PolitiFact Texas* on *Tuesday, January 31st, 2012*

JIM WEBB

"We did not even have a federal income tax in this country until 1913."

— *PolitiFact Virginia* on *Monday, August 24th, 2015*

In one amusing case of reality slapping them in the face, PolitiFact initially rated Obama's first-term campaign promise that "if you like your health-care plan, you can keep your health-care plan" claim as "True."[31]

---

29   Ashford-Grooms, Meghan. "Ron Paul says federal income tax rate was 0 percent until 1913." PolitiFact, January 31, 2012, https://www.politifact.com/factchecks/2012/jan/31/ron-paul/ron-paul-says-federal-income-tax-rate-was-0-percen/.

30   Gorman, Sean. "Jim Webb Says U.S. didn't have income taxes until 1913." PolitiFact, August 24, 2015, https://www.politifact.com/factchecks/2015/aug/24/jim-webb/jim-webb-says-us-didnt-have-income-taxes-until-191/.

31   Holan, Angie Drobnic. "Obama's plan expands existing system." PolitiFact, October 9, 2008, https://www.politifact.com/factchecks/2008/oct/09/barack-obama/obamas-plan-expands-existing-system/.

PolitiFact would later have to reevaluate that claim, which they determined to be the "Lie of the Year" in 2013.[32]

Both the article rating Obama's "if you like your plan you can keep your plan" lie true and the one years later rating it the "Lie of the Year" were written by the same person, PolitiFact Editor in Chief Angie Drobnic Holan. She made no mention of her own positive evaluation of the lie while penning her 2013 "Lie of the Year" article where she admitted that "Obama's promise was impossible to keep."[33]

But she didn't realize that years prior?

The RealClearPolitics Fact Check Review reviewed 434 articles from PolitiFact and found that 15 percent of their "fact-checks" are really "opinion-checks."[34]

A University of Minnesota School of Public Affairs survey of all five hundred statements that PolitiFact rated in January 2010 through January 2011 found that of ninety-eight statements they rated "False," seventy-four were from Republicans.[35]

The Center for Media and Public Affairs at George Mason University found in a 2013 study that in the first four months of Obama's second term, PolitiFact flagged Republicans as being dishonest at three times the rate of Democrats.

The Media Research Center's (MRC) Tim Graham noted of the report:

> Even while the Obama scandals piled up—from Benghazi to the IRS to the DOJ phone-records scandals—Republicans are still being flagged as worse than Democrats, with 60 percent of the website's selective claims rated as false so far [in May 2013] compared to 29 percent of their Democratic statements—a 2 to 1 margin.

---

32   Holan, Angie Drobnic. "Lie of the Year: 'If You Like Your Health Care Plan, You Can Keep It.'" PolitiFact, December 12, 2013, https://www.politifact.com /article/2013/dec/12/lie-year-if-you-like-your-health-care-plan-keep-it/.

33   Ibid.

34   Zeiser, Bill. "Snopes and Editorializing Fact Checks." RealClearPolitics, July 18, 2018, https://www.realclearpolitics.com/articles/2018/07/ 18/snopes_and_editorializing_fact_checks_137551.html.

35   Ostermeier, Eric. "Selection Bias? PolitiFact Rates Republican Statements as False at 3 Times the Rate of Democrats." Smart Politics, February 10, 2011, https://smartpolitics.lib.umn.edu/2011/02/10/selection-bias-politifact-rate/.

As for the entire four months, PolitiFact rated 32 percent of Republican claims as "False" or "Pants on Fire," compared to 11 percent of Democratic claims—a 3 to 1 margin. Conversely, Politifact rated 22 percent of Democratic claims as "entirely true" compared to 11 percent of Republican claims—a 2 to 1 margin.

A majority of Democrat statements (54 percent) were rated as mostly or entirely true, compared to only 18 percent of Republican statements. By contrast, a majority of Republican statements (52 percent) were rated as mostly or entirely false, compared to just 24 percent of Democrat arguments.[36]

Meanwhile, statements by Republicans were rated entirely false ("False" or "Pants on Fire") twice as often as Democrats (29 percent vs. 15 percent). At the time Graham reported on this study, the "Pants on Fire" page on PolitiFact's website displayed eighteen false claims by Republicans and two by Democrats.

The Federalist's Matt Shapiro ran the numbers in December 2016 and further confirmed that there really is a double standard when it comes to how PolitiFact evaluates claims.[37]

After evaluating thousands of PolitiFact articles and assigning their ratings a score ranging from 0 ("True") to 5 ("Pants on Fire"), he found that Democrats had an average rating of 1.8, which is between "Mostly True" and "Half True." The average Republican rating was 2.6, which is between "Half True" and "Mostly False." "Mostly False" was the most common rating given to Republicans, and they ranked Hillary Clinton as the second-most honest politician.[38]

When it came to the worst possible ruling, "Pants on Fire," Donald Trump accounted for half of those ratings. But even with Trump excluded, PolitiFact has a penchant for giving Republicans that rating which indicates they were caught in an outrageous, bald-faced lie,

---

36   Graham, Tim. "Study Reveals Republicans Lie More…Or That Politifact Has a Serious Liberal Bias Problem." MRC NewsBusters, May 29, 2013, https://www.newsbusters.org/blogs/nb/tim-graham/2013/05/29/study-reveals-republicans-lie-moreor-politifact-has-serious-liberal.

37   Shapiro, Matt. "Running the Data On PolitiFact Shows Bias Against Conservatives." The Federalist, December 16, 2016, https://thefederalist.com/2016/12/16/running-data-politifact-shows-bias-conservatives/

38   lol

while when Democrats make false claims, PolitiFact will be able to find some semblance of truth within the claim so that they only have to rate it "Mostly False" or "Half True." During the 2012 election season, PolitiFact assigned Mitt Romney nineteen "Pants on Fire" ratings, while ALL Democrats combined received twenty-five "Pants on Fire" ratings from 2007 to 2016.[39]

Are we to believe that Romney was a more egregious liar during the 2012 campaign season than all Democrats over nearly a decade? That's about as believable as the claim that Hillary Clinton was the second-most honest politician in America.

Speaking of Hillary, a Media Research Center analysis during the 2016 election found that PolitiFact gave its "Pants on Fire" rating to Trump fifty-seven times, compared to only seven times to Hillary Clinton, the woman who played a role in creating a conspiracy theory that Russia was behind a secret plot to elect her opponent. Trump's statements received "False," "Mostly False," or "Pants on Fire" ratings 77 percent of the time, compared to only 26 percent for Hillary.[40]

As the 2016 presidential race was in its endgame, from September to Election Day, Republicans received the "Pants on Fire" ranking twenty-eight times, half of which went to Trump, while Democrats only got that ranking four times, one of which went to Hillary.[41]

The inconsistencies in ratings are everywhere—and while they aren't as explicit as fact-checking a nearly identical claim and giving it a different rating, they aren't hard to miss.

The obvious bias has only continued into the Biden era.

During Joe Biden's first one hundred days in office, PolitiFact evaluated only thirteen of his claims while evaluating 106 others in defense of him. [42]

Of the thirteen Biden statements, eight were some sort of falsehood, but not one earned him a "Pants on Fire" rating. Of the 106 fact-checks

---

39   Shapiro, "Running the Data."

40   Bozell, L. Brent, and Tim Graham. "Brent Bozell: The Liberal Tilt at PolitiFact." *Investor's Business Daily*, June 30, 2016, https://www.investors.com/politics/columnists/brent-bozell-the-liberal-tilt-at-politifact/.

41   Ibid.

42   Graham, Tim. "STUDY: PolitiFact's 8 Times as Likely to Defend Biden Than Check His Facts." MRC NewsBusters, May 4, 2021, https://www.newsbusters.org/blogs/nb/tim-graham/2021/05/04/study-politifacts-8-times-likely-defend-biden-check-his-facts.

of claims about Biden, ninety-one were "Mostly False," and twenty-four were "Pants on Fire."[43]

There wasn't exactly a shortage of false claims they could've evaluated, as even the *Washington Post*'s fact-checker (Glenn Kessler) had concluded that Biden told seventy-eight lies that earned a "Four Pinocchios" rating by that time (but then, as mentioned previously, announced that he would be discontinuing the database of Biden falsehoods during his first one hundred days in office). "Pinocchios" are awarded to false claims in the *WaPo* fact-checker, with more "Pinocchios" indicating a more false claim.

This was just the beginning of PolitiFact treating the Biden presidency with kid gloves.

According to the MRC's Graham, after reviewing Biden's first year, the same pattern held. Biden was fact-checked forty times by PolitiFact his first year, while his critics were checked 230 times. Excluding the aforementioned first one hundred days, Biden was checked twenty-eight times, compared to 124 fact-checks of his critics. While nearly half of Biden fact-checks were "Mostly False" or worse, 201 of the 230 claims from his critics (87.4 percent) were rated the same. Only three statements from Biden's critics were rated "True." PolitiFact also didn't assign a single "Pants on Fire" rating to any of Biden's comments, of which he's only received six since they launched in 2007. As Graham puts it, "Biden can say the evacuation from Afghanistan was an 'extraordinary success', and the Republicans are pushing 'Jim Crow on steroids' [by supporting election integrity laws] and there will be no fact checks."[44]

By contrast, many of the "Pants on Fire" ratings for Biden's critics were claims laughably pointless to fact-check. This included fact-checking claims such as "Biden is computer generated," debunking photoshopped pictures of Biden sniffing people (though there are plenty of real ones), and refuting a report that Biden was handed a "vile of blood" from a child on a walk back to the White House.[45] (Similarly, over at Snopes,

---

43   Ibid.

44   Graham, Tim. "STUDY: PolitiFact Is Almost 6 Times More Likely to Defend Biden Than Check His Facts." MRC NewsBusters, January 27, 2022, https://newsbusters.org/blogs/nb/tim-graham/2022/01/27/study-politifact-almost-6-times-more-likely-defend-biden-check-his.

45   Ibid.

they've gone as far as to get to the bottom of whether or not Biden really pooped his pants while on a trip in Rome.)[46]

Similar to the example given with Ron Paul and Jim Webb's nearly identical statements on the income tax, PolitiFact's bias leads to inconsistent standards in fact-checking. In one case, PolitiFact's writers couldn't even agree with one another on what it means to "cut" government spending.

PolitiFact rated Republican claims during the 2012 election that Obama had cut Medicare by $700 billion as "False" because it wasn't an outright $700 billion cut but a $700 billion reduction in future spending.[47]

Meanwhile, in a fact-check defending Britain's National Health Service (NHS) against criticism from Donald Trump, PolitiFact reported that "while the NHS has lost funding over the years, the march that took place was not in opposition to the service, but a call to increase funding and stop austerity cuts towards health and social care."[48] They were referring to Trump mistaking a pro-NHS protest for an anti-NHS protest, but the relevant point here is that NHS had *not* seen their budget cut; it was a cut in future spending.

It's a common trick for politicians to frame reductions in increases in spending as cuts, and PolitiFact was able to correctly identify this in the former example yet also apply it inconsistently in the latter depending on the party of those being fact-checked. An entire chapter titled "Fact-Checkers vs. Fact-Checkers" documents just how inconsistently standards are applied among the major fact-checkers depending on who is speaking.

Running Up the Score

One tactic PolitiFact uses to help create the perception of an abundance of Republican lies relative to others is re-fact-checking similar claims over and over again to boost the number of falsely rated comments they make.

---

46   Evon, Dan. "Did Biden Poop His Pants in Rome?" Snopes, November 1, 2021, https://www.snopes.com/fact-check/did-biden-poop-his-pants-in-rome.

47   Holan, Angie Drobnic. "Checking the facts on the $700 billion Medicare 'cut.'" PolitiFact, August 20, 2012, https://www.politifact.com /article/2012/aug/15/checking-facts-700-billion-medicare-cut/.

48   Soellner, Mica. "Donald Trump wrongly suggests British don't love their health care system." PolitiFact, February 8, 2018, https://www.politifact.com/factchecks/2018/ feb/08/donald-trump/donald-trump-wrongly-suggests-british-dont-love-th/.

By the end of 2016, PolitiFact devoted six separate fact-checks to Trump denying he ever supported the Iraq War, five on voter fraud claims, and seven to his comments on Obama's birth certificate.[49]

Examining the biggest lies of Hillary Clinton showed a different pattern. Her statements about not sending classified info in her emails got two fact-checks, her statement about landing in Bosnia under sniper fire got one, and her false claim that the FBI said she was truthful about her emails got one. In the 2016 election cycle, PolitiFact also tended to fact-check people making claims about a particular Hillary Clinton statement instead of fact-checking her own statement itself.[50]

In one attempt to defend Hillary's lie that she was named after Sir Edmund Hillary, PolitiFact concluded that she wasn't, but that it was possible Hillary's parents lied to her about it when she was young, so they rated this claim "Half True."[51]

But when it was Mitt Romney on the campaign trail, PolitiFact issued five separate fact-checks to his claim that Obama had "apologized" for America. They did the opposite for Obama, with PolitiFact running six columns defending the former president's claim that if you liked your health-care plan, you can keep your health-care plan—which, as mentioned earlier, later became their own "Lie of the Year" in 2013.[52]

PolitiFact inconsistently awards and justifies these "repeat" fact-checks.

After VP Kamala Harris lied in a February 2021 Axios interview that the Biden administration had to "start from scratch" on COVID-19 vaccine distribution, The Federalist's Tristan Justice reached out to PolitiFact to ask why they hadn't written anything on the claim. PolitiFact Editor in Chief Angie Holan said that the claim wasn't fact-checked because White House Chief of Staff Ron Klain made the same false statement in January, which was checked as "Mostly False." [53]

49   Shapiro, Matt. "How PolitiFact Slants Its Truth Ratings Against Republicans." The Federalist, December 29, 2016, https://thefederalist.com/2016/12/29/politifact-slants-truth-ratings-republicans/.

50   Ibid.

51   Jacobson, Louis. "Did Hillary Clinton lie about being named after Sir Edmund Hillary?" PolitiFact, July 19, 2016, https://www.politifact.com/factchecks/2016/jul/20/mitch-mcconnell/did-hillary-clinton-lie-about-being-named-after-si/.

52   Shapiro, "How PolitiFact Slants."

53   Justice, Tristan. "PolitiFact Not Very 'Interested' in Fact-Checking Vice President." The Federalist, February 17, 2021, https://thefederalist.com/2021/02/17/politifact-not-very-interested-in-fact-checking-vice-president/.

At the time of that Axios interview, PolitiFact hadn't published a single fact-check of Harris since September 2020, over a month before the election. When Holan was asked if she thought Harris hadn't made any falsehoods since September, she said that they were just not interested in fact-checking her. "We've always been more interested in fact-checking the president than the vice president."

Yet over at PolitiFact, even low-profile Republicans were seen as more worthy of fact-checking than the most influential Democrats. While VP Harris didn't get fact-checked heading into an election, PolitiFact was fact-checking Republican Marco Rubio nearly every month since a year before he was elected to the Senate.

As The Federalist's Shapiro explains:

> Rubio was fact-checked as many times before he took office than long-time senator and erstwhile Senate Majority Leader Harry Reid has been checked in his entire career. Before he even started his presidential campaign Rubio was fact-checked 10 times more than Democrat Sen. Elizabeth Warren has been during her tenure [as of December 2016].

> Before he even announced his run for president, PolitiFact had checked Rubio more times (87 fact-checks) than they had checked Clinton during her entire 2008 presidential run (83 fact-checks). It seems over-eager to check a four-year junior senator more than a presidential candidate, vice president, Senate majority leader, and speaker of the House.

> Nor was Rubio alone in this. Before he ran for president, Sen. Ted Cruz was fact-checked 46 times, more than any Democratic senator we checked. House Speaker Paul Ryan was fact-checked nearly twice as often as former House Speaker Nancy Pelosi, even if you take out every single fact check from the time period in which he was the Republican vice presidential nominee. Michelle Bachmann (remember her? Three-term congresswoman who placed sixth in the Iowa caucus) was fact-checked a stunning 51 times, nearly as many times as governor, senator, and vice presidential candidate Tim Kaine.[54]

---

54   Shapiro, "How PolitiFact Slants."

And if that looks like they're targeting Republicans, the timing of when they dialed up the heat on certain candidates during the 2016 presidential cycle is the smoking gun.

When comparing the ratings on a month-to-month basis during the 2016 election cycle, PolitiFact had mostly rated Cruz and Trump as equally dishonest during the Republican primary until Cruz dropped out, clearing the path for Trump as the nominee. That month PolitiFact hit Trump with five "Pants on Fire" ratings, five "False" ratings, and three "Mostly False." While he and his main challenger were portrayed as equally dishonest when they were competing, once Trump became the only threat, PolitiFact ramped up their negative coverage to portray him as Pinocchio on steroids.

A PolitiFact Insider Speaks Out

Brian Riedl is a Senior Fellow at the Manhattan Institute and worked with PolitiFact in 2007 after they had just launched. Riedl ended up quitting over the site's open left-wing bias. He was a go-to source for facts for PolitiFact (and not a fact-checker himself) while he was also working as an economics expert at the conservative Heritage Foundation.

Riedl told the Daily Wire that "Conservatives have a right to be suspicious of PolitiFact because their reporters openly shared their biases with their sources. They would start with a rating and then ask their sources for ammunition to justify a preset rating. It was brazen."

Riedl says that his reputation as a conservative critical of George W. Bush got him attention from the media. He explained:

> I had established a pretty notable reputation in Washington for pummeling President Bush for runaway spending, and it got me a lot of media love at the time — that I was a Heritage Foundation employee who was criticizing a Republican president. For a lot of reporters, the best source is a conservative willing to trash Republicans. They came to me and basically thought that because I had criticized Bush so much on runaway spending, that I would provide a veneer of bipartisan credibility by trashing republicans in their fact-checking.

When I started criticizing Obama for the same thing a few years later, suddenly all the reporters didn't like me.[55]

Riedl said that bias at PolitiFact was out in the open, and reporters would explicitly ask for quotes negative towards Republicans. He added that on one occasion he was asked if he knew any "outrageous" comments from Republicans that would be worth writing about.

Riedl says fact-checkers would go "expert shopping," and that it was common for them to ask him for facts, only to then disagree with him and leave his comments out of their articles. "They were employing double standards. They were using straw men. They were presetting the rating before they talked to people. And their response was if you are not going to give us the ammunition and arguments we want, then we'll find someone else who will."[56]

He said, in conclusion:

> Through the years, I have continued to follow their ratings, and a lot of the same people are still there — and their ratings are a joke. They make huge elementary factual mistakes in their fact checks. It's all motivated reasoning.
>
> When you read their fact checks, it is painfully obvious that they often decided on the rating first and backward reasoned their way through intellectual logical backflips, trying to come up with any way to justify the rating. They're a joke.[57]

It's no coincidence that given their bias in the fact-checking process, most of the people who read PolitiFact hold left-wing views—hardly something you'd expect if they were an unbiased arbiter of truth.

Liars List Lies of the Year

Every year, PolitiFact holds a "Lie of the Year" poll that their readers pick, which itself reveals the biases of their audience.

---

55   Pearce, Tim. "Meet the Former Politifact Source Who Quit over Left-Wing Bias: 'Wanted Me to Help Them Nail Republicans.'" The Daily Wire, May 11, 2022, https://www.dailywire.com/news/meet-the-former-politifact-fact-checker-who-quit-over-left-wing-bias-wanted-me-to-help-them-nail-republicans.

56   Ibid.

57   Ibid.

In 2020, 51 percent of PolitiFact's readers said that the "Lie of the Year" was that the 2020 election was rigged, while another 41 percent picked "lies about the coronavirus."[58]

In 2019, 53 percent of readers said the "Lie of the Year" should be Donald Trump's statement that "There has never been, ever before, an administration that's been so open and transparent." In second place with 16 percent of the vote was Trump's statement that "the first so-called second hand information 'Whistleblower' got my phone conversation almost completely wrong."[59]

In 2018, 36 percent of readers picked the "Lie of the Year" as Trump's statement that "the Democrats want to invite caravan after caravan of illegal aliens into our country. And they want to sign them up for free health care, free welfare, free education, and for the right to vote."[60]

In 2017, 56 percent of readers picked Trump's (true) statement that "this Russia thing with Trump and Russia is a made-up story. It's an excuse by the Democrats for having lost an election that they should've won" as the "Lie of the Year."[61]

It's for that reason many liberal lies that have become canon go unchecked.

In 2009, PolitiFact chose "death panels" as the "Lie of the Year," a hyperbolic term used to highlight the rationing that tends to arise when there's greater government control of health care. Sarah Palin helped popularize the use of the term. While we all understand rhetoric and hyperbole, PolitiFact doesn't and rated this claim the "Lie of the Year" because the government didn't set up literal panels of death.[62]

58   Valverde, Miriam. "2020 Lie of the Year Readers' Choice poll results."
      PolitiFact, December 17, 2020, https://www.politifact.com/article/
      2020/dec/17/2020-lie-year-readers-choice-poll-results/.
59   Holan, Angie Drobnic. "2019 Lie of the Year Readers' Poll results."
      PolitiFact, December 16, 2019, https://www.politifact.com/
      article/2019/dec/16/2019-lie-year-readers-poll-results/.
60   Holan, Angie Drobnic. "2018 Lie of the Year Readers' Poll results."
      PolitiFact, December 11, 2018, https://www.politifact.com/
      article/2018/dec/11/2018-lie-year-readers-poll-results/.
61   Holan, Angie Drobnic. "2017 Lie of the Year Readers' Poll results."
      PolitiFact, December 12, 2017, https://www.politifact.com/
      article/2017/dec/12/2017-lie-year-readers-poll-results/.
62   Holan, Angie Drobnic. "PolitiFact's Lie of the Year: 'Death panels.'"
      PolitiFact, December 18, 2009, https://www.politifact.com/
      article/2009/dec/18/politifact-lie-year-death-panels/.

Palin was referring to one specific panel, the Independent Payment Advisory Board, which would advise the government on cutting costs by determining which treatments were the most efficient. The existence of this council isn't even mentioned in PolitiFact's article.

In 2012, PolitiFact rated Mitt Romney the biggest liar (not coincidentally because he was running for president and thus public enemy number one to them).[63]

Jon Greenberg initially reviewed Romney's claim that Obama "sold Chrysler to Italians who are going to build Jeeps in China at the cost of American jobs" and gave it a "Pants on Fire" rating.[64] Romney's claim was later elevated to "Lie of the Year" status.

He was responding to a Romney presidential ad, where a narrator says, "Obama took GM and Chrysler into bankruptcy and sold Chrysler to Italians who are going to build Jeeps in China. Mitt Romney will fight for every American job."

The entirety of the fact-check is contingent on whether the ad was talking about moving *all* production to China or part of it.

Greenberg claims that Romney mischaracterizes the sale of Chrysler to Fiat because it's something they wanted to do before Obama took office—which is irrelevant because, by Greenberg's own admission, "Obama created an auto task force and in March, the task force told Chrysler to cut a deal with Fiat or be cut off from further government loans. In early April, Chrysler filed for bankruptcy and at the same time, announced an alliance with Fiat."

He also mentions that Chrysler HQ has denied the accusations, stating that "Jeep has no intention of shifting production of its Jeep models out of North America to China."

It would be only one month after PolitiFact selected Romney's claim to be 2012's "Lie of the Year" that Chrysler announced a deal to build jeeps in China.[65]

---

63   Holan, Angie Drobnic. "Lie of the Year: the Romney campaign's ad on Jeeps made in China." PolitiFact, December 12, 2012, https://www.politifact.com/article/2012/dec/12/lie-year-2012-Romney-Jeeps-China/.

64   Greenberg, Jon. "Mitt Romney says Obama's Chrysler deal undermined U.S. workers." PolitiFact, October 30, 2012, https://www.politifact.com/factchecks/2012/oct/30/mitt-romney/mitt-romney-obama-chrysler-sold-italians-china-ame/.

65   "It's Official: Jeep Will Build Models in China." CBS Sacramento, January 22, 2013, https://www.cbsnews.com/sacramento/news/its-official-jeep-will-build-models-in-china/.

And just like that, another "Lie of the Year" turned out to be anything but.

The Federalist's Mark Hemingway began a back-and-forth with PolitiFact, and in one exchange, they rationalized their ruling as follows:

> Our story focused on the clear message of the Romney campaign's ad, that jobs in the United States were being moved to China, or perhaps that Jeep was moving its entire operations to China. That is not the case and has never been the case.

The "perhaps" proves that PolitiFact is simply debunking an interpretation of the ad, which never states that Chrysler would be moving *all* production to China and never said that they would be outsourcing *existing jobs*.

Then, incredibly, PolitiFact admits to Hemingway that Romney's statements could be literally true, stating:

> The Romney campaign was crafty with its word choice, so campaign aides could claim to be speaking the literal truth, but the ad left a false impression that all Jeep production was being moved to China.[66]

But only PolitiFact is getting crafty with their word choice, as the only way they can rate the statements in the ad false is by creating their own "implications."

Very Fine Fact-Checkers: PolitiFact Spreads One of the Biggest Media Lies of Trump's First Year

One form of unofficial fact-check that PolitiFact publishes are called "in context" articles that don't have any rating attached, and read like "explainer" style articles on a topic.

In one such article titled "In Context: Donald Trump's 'very fine people on both sides' remarks," Editor in Chief Holan fails to correct the widespread lie that Donald Trump called white supremacists in Charlotteville, Virginia, "very fine people." This same article would later be cited by a different PolitiFact writer to further spread the lie.

---

66   Hemingway, Mark. "PolitiFact Concedes Their 'Lie of the Year' is the 'Literal Truth.'" *Washington Examiner*, January 18, 2013, https://www.washingtonexaminer.com /weekly-standard/politifact-concedes-their-lie-of-the-year-is-the-literal-truth.

Holan's article opens: "We wanted to look at Trump's comments in their original context. Here is a transcript of the questions Trump answered that addressed the Charlottesville controversy in the days after it happened."[67]

Despite presenting the article as an "explainer," Holan merely provides a full transcript of the exchange with no commentary on what exactly we're supposed to glean from it. The only bolded words in the entire transcript are Trump saying, "Excuse me, excuse me. They didn't put themselves—**and you had some very bad people in that group, but you also had people that were very fine people, on both sides**," but the words providing the clarifying context, that Trump was not talking about white supremacists with that comment, aren't bolded.

If presented honestly, the relevant part of the nearly three-thousand-word transcript would look like the following:

> **Reporter:** The neo-Nazis started this. They showed up in Charlottesville to protest—
>
> **Trump:** Excuse me, excuse me. They didn't put themselves— and you had some very bad people in that group, but you also had people that were **very fine people, on both sides**. You had people in that group. Excuse me, excuse me. I saw the same pictures as you did. You had people in that group that were there to protest the taking down of, to them, a very, very important statue and the renaming of a park from Robert E. Lee to another name.
>
> **Reporter:** George Washington and Robert E. Lee are not the same.
>
> **Trump:** George Washington was a slave owner. Was George Washington a slave owner? So will George Washington now lose his status? Are we going to take down—excuse me, are we going to take down statues to George Washington? How about Thomas Jefferson? What do you think of Thomas Jefferson? You like him?[68]

---

67   Holan, Angie Drobnic. "In Context: Donald Trump's 'very fine people on both sides' remarks (transcript)." PolitiFact, April 26, 2019, https://www.politifact.com /article/2019/apr/26/context-trumps-very-fine-people-both-sides-remarks/.

68   This did end up happening on multiple occasions during the 2020 George Floyd riots.

Reporter: I do love Thomas Jefferson.

Trump: Okay, good. Are we going to take down the statue? Because he was a major slave owner. Now, are we going to take down his statue? So you know what, it's fine. You're changing history. You're changing culture. **And you had people—and I'm not talking about the neo-Nazis and the white nationalists—because they should be condemned totally. But you had many people in that group other than neo-Nazis and white nationalists. Okay? And the press has treated them absolutely unfairly.**

Now, in the other group also, you had some fine people. But you also had troublemakers, and you see them come with the black outfits and with the helmets, and with the baseball bats. You had a lot of bad people in the other group.

Even in presenting the full transcript, Holan presented it in such a way to prevent the reader from stumbling upon the true context.

PolitiFact's Sophie Austin and Louis Jacobson themselves spread the Charlottesville lie in a 2020 fact-check, writing: "As president in 2017, Trump said there were 'very fine people, on both sides,' in reference to neo-Nazis and counter-protesters in Charlottesville, VA."[69] Their source for the claim is the aforementioned "in context" article that proves the opposite to anyone who carefully reads it.

This was arguably the biggest lie about Trump during his first year in office (besides the Russia hysteria) and one that practically became canon in the media.

And the fact-checkers helped canonize it.

In addition to misrepresenting the facts, PolitiFact is fine with their own conclusions being misrepresented so long as the misrepresentation supports a left-wing position, as was the case with one of their fact-checks that California Governor Gavin Newsom shared.

The article in question was from PolitiFact's Chris Nichols, who fact-checked the claim that "there are at least twice as many licensed firearm dealers in California as there are McDonald's," rating the claim "True."

---

69   Jacobson, Louis, and Sophie Austin. "The long history of racism in the US presidency." PolitiFact, July 27, 2020, https://web.archive.org/web/20210212214136/https://www. politifact.com/factchecks/2020/jul/27/joe-biden/long-history-racism-us-presidency/.

PolitiFactCalifornia Retweeted

Gavin Newsom @GavinNewsom · Jul 19
In a break from the GOP Convention --> FACT: It's easier to get a gun than a Happy Meal in California.

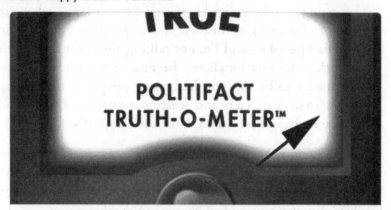

It's no Whopper: Licensed gun dealers outnumber McDonald's abo...
Gun control advocates make a lot of claims about how easy it is to get a firearm in America. "We flood communities with so many guns that it is e...
politifact.com

↩   ⟲ 79   ♡   ♥ 100   •••

"It's no Whopper: Licensed gun dealers outnumber McDonald's about 2-to-1 in California," he wrote.[70]

This attempt at creative writing doesn't really work because the Whopper is a Burger King product, not McDonald's, but nonetheless, Nichols is referring to the number of Federal Firearms Licenses (FFL) outstanding in California, which he correctly quoted as double the number of McDonald's in the state.

But having an FFL doesn't make one a gun salesman. Nearly anyone can get an FFL03 license, but for the license to actually be useful, one would need an additional Certificate of Eligibility from the DOJ.[71]

---

70   Nichols, Chris. "It's no Whopper: Licensed gun dealers outnumber McDonald's about 2-to-1 in California." PolitiFact, July 19, 2016, https://www.politifact.com/factchecks/2016/jul/19/safety-all-initiative/its-no-whopper-licensed-gun-dealers-outnumber-mcdo/.
71   "Gun Dealers in California." Giffords, September 15, 2021, https://giffords.org/lawcenter/state-laws/gun-dealers-in-california/.

California leads the nation in McDonald's locations with 1,190 stores[72]—while one directory of gun shops by state turns up forty-six results for California.[73]

That aside, Newsom invented a claim out of this fact-check and tweeted out Nichols' article with the caption "…FACT: It's easier to get a gun than a Happy Meal in California," a false claim that's bizarre to see him make considering he himself runs the state.

Instead of correcting the governor for incorrectly reporting the conclusion of their already flawed fact-check, PolitiFact instead approvingly retweeted Newsom's post from one of their accounts.[74]

Even if we were to wrongly interpret PolitiFact's data about FFL permits as meaning that there are more gun sellers than McDonald's in California, even that wouldn't justify the conclusion that it's easier to get a gun in California than visit a restaurant that's open to the general public.

Procuring a Happy Meal simply requires one visit a McDonald's with some cash or a credit card. To obtain a firearm in California, which the pro-gun control Giffords Law Center ranks as having the strictest gun laws in America,[75] would require:[76]

- Being twenty-one years old (for a handgun) or eighteen (for a rifle or shotgun)

- Being subject to a Personal Firearms Eligibility Check (background check), which has a $20 fee (enough money to buy about thirty chicken nuggets at my local McDonald's) and can take sixty days to process

- Possessing a Firearm Safety Certificate, which requires one to pass a thirty-question written test administered by DOJ-

72   "Number of McDonalds stores in the United States in 2022." August 1, 2022, https://www.scrapehero.com/location-reports/McDonalds-USA/.
73   "Results in California." Gun Shop Directory, August 7, 2022, https://gunshop.directory/california/p:4.
74   Hoy, Matthew. "Abetting Gavin Newsom's Big Lie." Hoystory, July 27, 2016, https://hoystory.com/2016/07/abetting-gavin-newsoms-big-lie/.
75   "Annual Gun Law Scorecard." Giffords, https://giffords.org/lawcenter/resources/scorecard/?scorecard=CA.
76   "Licensing in California." Giffords, September 15, 2021, https://giffords.org/lawcenter/state-laws/licensing-in-california/.

certified instructors, which has a $25 fee, enough to buy twenty-five large Coca-Colas.

- Completing Dealer Record of Sale paperwork with the firearms dealer

- Not having a history of mental illness or chronic alcoholism or having ever had a felony DUI

- Waiting ten days before a firearm can be released to you

- Not being able to purchase more than one handgun per month

The merit and faults of these steps aside, it's more than a bit more excessive than the process to purchase a Big Mac. That PolitiFact sees this sort of "bumper-sticker-slogan" style of thinking as acceptable is more embarrassing than the lie itself.

Poynter Institute Bias

Of those who publicly express their views over at PolitiFact's parent, the Poynter Institute, all express views favorable to the left.

In one cringe-inducing article published by Poynter by Alex Sujong Laughlin (who also writes for the *Washington Post, New York Times*, and Buzzfeed), she argues that journalists would be trusted more if they were openly biased in favor of the left.

In the article, Laughlin writes of her experience at the 2016 Democratic National Convention, recalling how she went in with the goal of not showing any emotion because she had press credentials and knew that a photo of her laughing or crying would go viral on social media and harm the credibility of her employer.

However, that plan was quickly derailed by what can only be described as a religious experience sparked by the sight of Hillary Clinton, of all people! She wrote, unironically:

> The sensory shock of it—the loud shatter, the thunderous applause, the music—shook something loose in me. I slipped into the emotion of the moment. I let myself drift on the experience while Clinton thanked the delegation for helping her put the "biggest crack in that glass ceiling yet." The camera panned away and showed a little girl at her side.

"And if there are any little girls out there who stayed up late to watch, let me just say: I may become the first woman president, but one of you is next."

I already had tears in my eyes, but that's when I broke. I ripped off my lanyard, stuffed it into my tote bag, sat down on the bleacher, and sobbed.

It was less about Clinton and more about what her nomination symbolized—about what the moment symbolized. When I watch the video back, I'm less moved by her presence than the images of the crowd responding to her and absorbing the enormity of what they'd accomplished. After the grueling campaign season watching Trump glide closer and closer to the Republican nomination by speaking to what felt like America's cruelest natures, to be in a room filled with women of all ages, queer people, and people of color who were interested in working together to protect my rights and the rights of people I loved was a powerful reminder that a plural and liberal coalition could exist, and that it did exist. It was a moment of optimism after months of horror.[77]

"I lost access to all objectivity, if I had any to begin with," Laughlin concluded the story about her ascension to cloud nine.

The rest of the article went on to argue that it's more important than ever to not be objective in the wake of *Roe v. Wade* being overturned, and then Laughlin checks off a number of boxes by bringing up the plights of interns, women of color, queer people, transgender people, Asian Americans, George Floyd, "victims" of ICE raids, and people who died from COVID-19. Only a random January 6 mention is needed to complete the progressive bingo board.

Further demonstrating the alternate reality they live in, when Jen Psaki departed the White House, the Poynter Institute published an article with the hilarious, reality-defying headline "Jen Psaki's legacy? One of the best press secretaries ever."

---

77   Laughlin, Alex Sujong. "It's possible to be a journalist and a human."
      The Poynter Institute, June 28, 2022, https://www.poynter.org/business-
      work/2022/journalism-objectivity-roe-scotus-social-media/.

Among the nuggets of comedy gold is the following passage declaring that "Psaki has restored honor, dignity and class to the White House briefing room after four years of Donald Trump press secretaries, who seemed more interested in picking fights and criticizing the media than effectively communicating that administration's policies and agenda."[78]

Every fact-checker actively participates in the fact-free culture of the modern left, where even facts as basic as the reality of gender are called into question. In one fact-check where PolitiFact's Linda Qiu rated "Mostly False" an ad from the 2016 Ted Cruz campaign (but not Sen. Cruz himself), which stated that Donald Trump believes "a grown man pretending to be a woman should be allowed to use the woman's restroom," a larger percentage of the article was spent virtue signaling on transgender issues than actually disproving the claim from the Cruz campaign.

While not a biologist, Qiu declares here that biological men can be women, though we're not given much explanation on how exactly such an impossible feat would be pulled off. "It's not accurate to say that transgender women are men. Though there isn't universal agreement on this point, medical experts typically agree that a transgender person is someone who identifies differently from their assigned sex at birth. In short, a transgender woman is a woman and not 'a grown man pretending to be a woman,'" Qiu wrote.[79] She ended up editing that paragraph out of her article after many in conservative media began making fun of it, but not because she had any concerns about factual accuracy.[80]

A year prior, PolitiFact's W. Gardner Selby rated Senator Cruz's claim that the "federal government is going after school districts, trying to force them to let boys shower with little girls" as "False" in a fact-check that quotes one expert who argues that this isn't true because transgender peo-

78   Jones, Tom. "Jen Psaki's legacy? One of the best press secretaries ever." The Poynter Institute, May 12, 2022, https://www.poynter.org/commentary/2022/jen-psakis-legacy-one-of-the-best-press-secretaries-ever/.

79   The article was updated before any version of it was saved to the Wayback Machine, but NewsBusters has the original quote. Bozell, Brent, and Tom Graham. "Transgender 'Fact' and Fantasy." NewsBusters, April 30, 2016, https://newsbusters.org/blogs/nb/brent-bozell/2016/04/30/bozell-graham-column-transgender-fact-and-fantasy.

80   The catalyst for the update seems to be this article: Griswold, Alex. "PolitiFact Rules It's Now Objectively False to Call Transgender Women Men." Mediaite, April 26, 2016, https://www.mediaite.com/online/politifact-rules-its-now-objectively-false-to-call-transgender-women-men/.

ple are the identity they identify as,[81] much like how Selby and company are only fact-checkers because they identify as such.

Poynter Admits They're Policy Advocates

The Poynter Institute was widely mocked after it published a series of tips for journalists on how to cover "red flag" laws that enable gun confiscation so that they could better advocate for them.

"Beware of misinformation about red flag laws, including critics who say they lack due process, which is not accurate. Another false claim is that the laws allow people with a grudge, such as an ex-spouse, to take guns away," PolitiFact captioned their tweet sharing their article.[82]

How can they be trusted to accurately fact-check anything that relates to red flag laws, when this is what they're tweeting about it?

Poynter relies on the supposed expertise of Jennifer Mascia, a founding staff member at The Trace, which was created with seed money from the nation's largest gun control advocacy group, Everytown for Gun Safety, Dr. Garen Wintemute, who believes California's gun laws are a model for the rest of the country, and Johnny Magdaleno, a courts reporter with bylines in a handful of left-wing rags.[83]

The only explanation of what a red flag law is comes from Mascia, who says they're merely "a tool to separate someone from their guns in a time of crisis." Zero perspectives were offered on how such laws could be misused, but that's to be expected from partisans disguising themselves as fact-checkers.

In Senate testimony from David B. Kopel before the Judiciary Committee, he asserted that in Connecticut, 23 percent of gun confiscation orders are wrongly issued against innocent people and were overturned, and a study in Marion County, Illinois, produced similar results (29 percent).[84] But because Poynter has already picked a side in

81   Selby, W. Gardner. "Ted Cruz incorrectly says government trying to force boys and girls to shower together." PolitiFact, December 4, 2015, https://www.politifact.com/factchecks/2015/dec/04/ted-cruz/ted-cruz-incorrectly-says-obama-forcing-boys-and-g/.

82   PolitiFact. June 13, 2022, https://twitter.com/politifact/status/1536557140768342017.

83   Sherman, Amy, and Hana Stepnick. "As the Senate considers funding red flag laws, tips for journalists about the laws." The Poynter Institute, June 13, 2022, https://www.poynter.org/reporting-editing/2022/what-are-red-flag-laws-what-to-know.

84   "Red Flag Laws: Examining Guidelines for State Action. Written Testimony of David B. Kopel." United States Senate Judiciary Committee, March 26, 2019, https://www.judiciary.senate.gov/imo/media/doc/Kopel%20Testimony1.pdf

the debate, this easily obtainable information didn't make its way into its article.

While the fact-checker publicly admitted their stance here, as you read more of their work it becomes increasingly clear they've done the same privately on all the other issues they claim to be fact-finding for.

SNOPES

Of all the major fact-checkers, Snopes has the longest presence and is the closest to being a household name. The site garnered immense popularity in the late 1990s and early 2000s as a sort of "go-to" site to check urban legends and claims made in chain emails. The site was originally called "Urban Legends Reference Pages" before being changed to "Snopes," which was the screenname of the site's cofounder David Mikkelson (the other founder being his then-wife Barbara Mikkelson).

For all my criticism of the fact-checking industry, Snopes was good at this style of fact-checking, though it's not exactly like it takes a genius to debunk Bigfoot sightings and hysterical emails. It was only when Snopes ventured into political fact-checking that it deservingly became a laughingstock.

Snopes almost entirely employs leftists, as was revealed by a review of their staff after Facebook announced that Snopes would be a fact-checking partner for the social media site. The partnership ended in 2019 after two years.

Two of Snopes' fact-checkers joined after working for the far-left publication Raw Story.[85]

One of them, Arturo Garcia, was also editor-at-large for Raw Story. When Trump floated launching his own media network in 2016, Garcia said it should be called "White Entertainment Television."[86]

The other, Bethania Palma Markus, also previously wrote for Raw Story and is a "contributing writer" to the far-left Truth-Out.org, which is a nonprofit working to "spur the revolution in consciousness and inspire the direct action that is necessary to save the planet and humanity." She also supported France's decision to censor advertisements where models

---

85   Pfeiffer, Alex, and Peter Hasson. "Snopes, Which Will Be Fact-Checking For Facebook, Employs Leftists Almost Exclusively." The Daily Caller, December 16, 2016, https://dailycaller.com/2016/12/16/snopes-facebooks-new-fact-checker-employs-leftists-almost-exclusively/.

86   Ibid.

were "too skinny." When a Boston University professor was criticized for racist tweets calling college-aged white men a "population problem," Markus defended them as "not actually racist" because they were directed at white people (and also apparently doesn't know what the word "racist" means).[87]

Snopes' managing editor (at the time) Brooke Binkowski, previously worked for CNN, CBS, NPR, and Qatar's faux-progressive version of Al Jazeera, AJ+, and believes that "the only thing most of the GOP is selling these days is reactionary misogynistic and racist disinformation narratives."[88]

Another Snopes fact-checker, Kim LaCapria, says that Republicans are "repressive" and "afraid of female agency" and called the Tea Party "Teahadists."[89]

Their bias isn't remotely disguised after changing publications. Snopes writer David Emery captioned one fact-check debunking a fake Trump quote with, "Incredibly, some people actually think they have to put words in Trump's mouth to make him look bad."[90] Even debunking a falsehood about Trump, they editorialize that he's still the bad guy in all this regardless.

Snopes has had its fair share of controversies over the years. David Mikkelson, the site's cofounder who owns half the company, had fifty-four of his articles retracted after allegations of plagiarism against him were investigated. While Snopes claims to check the facts, it doesn't check the originality of its own content.

The internal review found possible problems with 140 articles. Mikkelson stole heavily from the websites of the *Guardian*, *Los Angeles Times*, *New York Times*, CNN, NBC, BBC, and more, and used their content for Snopes articles that fell into the "breaking" and "odd" sections of the website.[91]

Mikkelson's pseudonym was Jeff Zarronandia, which Brooke Binkowski explained was because "he used to write about topics he knew would get

---

87   Ibid.
88   Binkowski, Brooke. June 1, 2022, https://twitter.com/brooklynmarie/
      status/1532090102712741890.
89   Pfeiffer and Hasson, "Snopes, Facebook's New Fact-Checker."
90   Ibid.
91   Jones, Dean Sterling. "The Co-Founder of Snopes Wrote Dozens Of Plagiarized
      Articles For The Fact-Checking Site." BuzzFeed News, August 27, 2021, https://www.
      buzzfeednews.com/article/deansterlingjones/snopes-cofounder-plagiarism-mikkelson.

him hate mail under that assumed name. Plus it made it appear he had more staff than he had." The Zarronandia byline was eventually changed to "Snopes staff."[92]

The "biography" page for Jeff Zarronandia now reads, "Jeff Z. is a defunct pseudonym created by Snopes.com cofounder David 'Snopes' Mikkelson. Regrettably, this pseudonym is tied to a considerable number of retracted stories due to plagiarism and poor attribution."[93]

Mikkelson attributed his errors to a "lack of formal journalism experience," even though most of us understand by middle school what plagiarism is. But he doesn't appear too naïve by Binkowski's description of why the plagiarism occurred. "He would instruct us to copy text from other sites, post them verbatim so that it looked like we were fast and could scoop up traffic, and then change the story in real time. I hated it and wouldn't tell any of the staff to do it, but he did it all the time," she explained.[94]

Two other employees told Buzzfeed that copying and rewriting content was part of his strategy to drive traffic. "Taking credit for other people's work" was "part of his model," one said anonymously.[95]

Internal Slack (chat) messages also suggest that plagiarism was part of the business. He wrote in one message from January 2016: "Usually when a hot real news story breaks (such as a celebrity death), I just find a wire service or other news story about it and publish it on the site verbatim to quickly get a page up. Once that's done, then I quickly start editing the page to reword it and add material from other sources to make it not plagiarized."[96]

In two emails from 2014 and 2015, Mikkelson instructed staff to "pop over to one of our competitor sites (urbanlegends.com or hoax-slayer.com), pick something out that they've recently published that we haven't covered," and then "rewrite it just enough to avoid copyright infringement."[97]

As the goal of fact-checking is to protect the prevailing liberal narrative, even satire wasn't safe from Snopes' so-called fact-checks.

---

92   Ibid.
93   "Jeff Zarronandia." Snopes, https://www.snopes.com/jeff-zarronandia/.
94   Ibid.
95   Ibid.
96   Ibid.
97   Ibid.

The Babylon Bee launched as a Christian-conservative version of The Onion, which it's now nearly as big as in terms of web traffic. Some of its satirical articles have done such a good job of mocking the insanity of the modern left that they've proved prophetic. Examples include "California Lets Men Into Women's Prisons" (2017), "Church Avoids Coronavirus Restrictions by Installing Slot Machines" (2020), "Biden Administration Deploys Elite Squad of TikTok Influencers to Stop Taliban" (2021), and "California School System to Feature Mandatory 2nd Grade Field Trips to Gay Bars" (2019), among many, many others.

And to protect the left from mockery, Snopes began "fact-checking" the Bee in 2019, writing dozens of articles "debunking" jokes. Thanks to the joke police over at Snopes, they've informed us that Alexandria Ocasio-Cortez didn't really make an appearance on *The Price Is Right* and guess that everything is free[98] and that Democrats didn't really force Brett Kavanaugh to subject himself to DNA testing to prove he's not related to Hitler.[99]

USA Today has jumped in on the "fact-checking satire" bandwagon too, to assure readers that it's not true that Biden sold Alaska back to Russia "so we can start drilling oil there again."[100]

In one case where the Bee's article "CNN Purchases Industrial-Sized Washing Machine to Spin News Before Publication" was deemed "false by Snopes" and censored, leading to the Bee having to appeal to Facebook. Facebook claimed to have rectified the "mistake," but the Snopes fact-check still appeared under their article. Facebook did claim to have ended threats of demonetization as a result of this faux fact-checking, however.[101] Snopes made no effort to fact-check that one.

Snopes justified protecting liberals from being made fun of by saying too many people were mistaking the Bee for legitimate news, which is

98 Evon, Dan. "Did U.S. Rep. Ocasio-Cortez Repeatedly Guess 'Free' on TV Show 'The Price Is Right?'" Snopes, April 15, 2019, https://www.snopes.com/fact-check/ocasio-cortez-price-is-right/.

99 Emery, David. "Did Democrats Demand That Brett Kavanaugh Submit to a DNA Test to Prove He's Not Actually Hitler?" Snopes, September 5, 2018, https://www.snopes.com/fact-check/democrats-demand-kavanaugh-dna-test/.

100 Field, Chris. "USA Today fact-checks clearly satirical Babylon Bee report that Biden sold Alaska to Russia." Blaze Media, March 10, 2022, https://www.theblaze.com/furnace/usa-today-fact-checks-clearly-satirical-babylon-bee-report-that-biden-sold-alaska-to-russia.

101 Hagstrom, Anders. "Facebook Is STILL 'Fact Checking' Christian Satire Article After Saying It Was A 'Mistake.'" The Daily Caller, March 2, 2018, https://dailycaller.com/2018/03/02/facebook-fact-check-babylon-bee/.

odd, because the banner on the Bee's website literally reads "fake news you can trust." The Bee fired back at Snopes with their own article, titled "Concerning Survey Finds Too Many People Believe Snopes Is A Legitimate Fact-Checking Website."[102]

This came amid a media environment where the pitchforks were out for the Bee, with the *New York Times* having recently blasted them as a "far-right misinformation site" that "trafficked in misinformation." They eventually walked back those allegations in the face of legal threats, which goes to show how flimsy the allegations are, especially in a country like the U.S. where it's difficult to successfully sue for libel.[103]

OTHER MAJOR PLAYERS

PolitiFact, Snopes, and the *Washington Post*'s Glenn Kessler account for the majority of the content in the "fact-checking the fact-checkers" section of this book, but the other players are worth profiling too to expose the role they play in strengthening the left's censorship apparatus.

Lead Stories is among the most prolific fact-checkers policing content on Facebook, and their staff reveals them to practically be a CNN offshoot that unfortunately hasn't yet gone the way of CNN Airport, CNN+, Brian Stelter, and Chris Cuomo.

About a quarter of Lead Stories' staff has donated to Democrats according to FEC data—and zero have donated to Republicans. Lead Stories chairman and founder Perry Sanders donated $3,700 to Hillary Clinton's 2016 presidential campaign, and Obama's 2008 campaign (among other donations to Democrats).

One writer, Gina Smith, donated ninety-nine times to Democrat campaigns and was taken off of doing political stories after that was reported in an exposé by the National Pulse. Lead Stories Editor in Chief Alan Duke insisted, "We have a rule that you cannot have donated to political candidates. We have a hard-and-fast rule and when we find out

---

102   "Concerning Survey Finds Too Many People Believe Snopes Is a Legitimate Fact-Checking Website." The Babylon Bee, August 21, 2019, https://babylonbee.com/news/concerning-survey-finds-too-many-people-think-snopes-is-a-real-fact-checking-website.

103   Roth, Madeline. "NY Times Corrects Story After Legal Threat, Admits Babylon Bee Is 'Satirical Website' and Not 'Misinformation.'" The Wrap, June 14, 2021, https://www.thewrap.com/new-york-times-correction-babylon-bee-satirical-website-misinformation/.

that that happens, we have to react to that."[104] Yet no one else at the company who made political donations has been punished for it.

At least half of Lead Stories' staff have been affiliated with CNN and have a combined one hundred years of experience there between them. The site's editor in chief and cofounder, Alan Duke, worked at CNN for nearly thirty years as a reporter and editor. Lead Stories' senior editor, Monte Plott, was a news editor at CNN for over a decade.[105] The site's other founder, who makes editorial decisions, Maarten Schenk, lives in Belgium.

The site's former managing editor, Eric Ferkenhoff, implied that Donald Trump is a white nationalist on Twitter.[106]

The National Pulse's Natalie Winters unearthed social media posts from Lead Stories' senior editor Leslie Lapides after the site's founder and editor in chief, Alan Duke, repeatedly denied allegations of left-wing bias. On four occasions, Lapides tweeted in support of an activist campaign targeting advertisers listed on Breitbart News in an attempt to bankrupt the website. In other tweets, she's encouraged various members of Congress to launch an investigation into Trump's financial ties to Russia and declared, "RESISTANCE IS PATRIOTIC"[107] (but only when Republicans are in charge).

Lead Stories disclosed in its application to join the International Fact-Checking Network (IFCN) that it offers its Trendolizer engine (software that flags internet activity as it starts to trend) on a commercial basis and that the DNC and DCCC have both requested access and pay $350 a month for it.[108]

Another group, FactCheck.org, was created by the nonprofit Annenberg Public Policy Center at the University of Pennsylvania in 2003.

---

104   Staff Writer. "SCALP: Facebook's Fact Checker Says They Removed Staff After National Pulse Exposé." The National Pulse, July 20, 2021, https://thenationalpulse.com/2021/07/20/facebook-fact-checker-national-pulse-scalp/.

105   Winters, Natalie, and Raheem Kassam. "EXCLUSIVE: Facebook's Fact-Checker 'Lead Stories' is Staffed by Exclusively Democrat Party Donors, CNN Staffers, And 'Defeat Trump' Activists." The National Pulse, June 18, 2020, https://thenationalpulse.com/2020/06/18/facebook-lead-stories-democrat-donors-cnn/.

106   Ferkenhoff, Eric. February 11, 2016, https://twitter.com/EricFerk/status/697741144965455872.

107   Winters, "Editor for 'Unbiased' Facebook."

108   "Lead Stories." International Fact-Checking Network, https://www.ifcncodeofprinciples.poynter.org/application/public/lead-stories/CD36E717-3ACD-8CD1-3326-85E744D72DF2.

Initially, it was mainly funded by the Annenberg Foundation (which had given it over $87 million from 2004 to 2016), but it now takes donations.[109]

Its cofounder Brooks Jackson said the site was born out of frustration that journalists had with the media's supposedly unfair coverage of former presidential candidate and tank enthusiast Michael Dukakis, something they were still frustrated with over a decade and a half later for some reason. Jackson has been a journo for the Associated Press, *WSJ*, and CNN. He was recruited to run FactCheck.org by Annenberg Public Policy Center director Kathleen Hall Jamieson, who previously served on the board of the George Soros–funded Center for Public Integrity.

Jackson ran the site until 2013, when it was handed over to former *Philadelphia Inquirer* and *USA Today* writer Eugene Kiely. Jackson has since been director emeritus.

Differing from other major fact-checkers, FactCheck.org doesn't employ the sort of "Truth-O-Meter" or Pinocchio ratings system that PolitiFact and the *Washington Post*, respectively, do. Instead, it presents a disputed claim and then what they say is the "full story," making them more similar to PolitiFact's "explainer"-style articles.

And seemingly everyone else in the liberal media has joined the fact-checking game, too, including the Associated Press, Reuters, Huffington Post, and *USA Today*, among many others that have launched their own fact-checking arms.

Big Tech companies have not only relied on these fact-checkers who share their ideological proclivities for narrative enforcement, they actively seek it out.

Of the $8.1 million that the tech industry workers donated to presidential candidates in 2016, 95 percent went to Hillary Clinton. In Silicon Valley specifically, it was 99 percent.[110] The figures were similar for Biden in 2020.[111]

Over at Facebook, four days after Trump defeated Hillary Clinton, CEO Mark Zuckerberg announced that his company would be working to combat fake news but urged caution about Facebook becoming "arbi-

109   Ibid.
110   Hasson, Peter J. *The Manipulators: Facebook, Google, Twitter, and Big Tech's War on Conservatives*. Regnery Publishing, 2020, 15.
111   Schleifer, Theodore, and Rani Molla. "Silicon Valley is spending millions more for Joe Biden than it did for Hillary Clinton." Vox, October 30, 2020, https://www.vox.com/recode/2020/10/30/21540616/silicon-valley-fundraising-donald-trump-joe-biden-analysis.

ters of truth ourselves." The types of fake news that were being targeted at this time were in the most literal sense—such as fake stories about a certain candidate getting arrested, dying, or being quoted saying something damning they never said.[112]

Mark Zuckerberg himself personally resisted calls for social media policing, reasonably calling it a "pretty crazy idea" that the results of the 2016 election were altered by misleading internet posts. But that didn't last for long. Zuckerberg eventually backed down upon facing an "internal insurgency," where Facebook employees started a task force to examine the company's role in pushing fake news and Zuckerberg's apparent evasion of responsibility.[113]

The International Fact-Checking Network (IFCN) penned an open letter to Zuckerberg on November 16, 2016, making a sales pitch for their services while attempting to make it look like they were concerned about facts. "We believe that Facebook should start an open conversation on the principles that could underpin a more accurate news ecosystem on its news feed. The global fact-checking community is eager to take part in this conversation. Many of our organizations already provide training in fact-checking to media organizations, universities and the general public. We would be glad to engage with you about how your editors could spot and debunk fake claims."[114] The letter was signed by twenty fact-checking organizations.

The next month, Facebook announced that the IFCN would be their main partner as part of a new fact-checking initiative to clean up the platform.

The IFCN acts as the "high body" for the dozens of fact-checking organizations under its umbrella, which unite under a shared code of principles, and their mission "to bring together the growing community of fact-checkers around the world and advocates of factual information in the global fight against misinformation." Among the most well-known organizations that are affiliated with the IFCN are the Associated Press

---

112   Hasson, *The Manipulators*, 30.

113   Smith, Lee. "How Facebook Ate the News: Mark Zuckerberg, America's Public
        Enemy No. 1." *Tablet Magazine*, June 21, 2017, https://www.tabletmag.com/
        sections/news/articles/zuckerberg-public-enemy-no-1.

114   The International Fact-Checking Network. "An open letter to Mark
        Zuckerberg from the world's fact-checkers." The Poynter Institute,
        November 17, 2016, https://www.poynter.org/fact-checking/2016/an-
        open-letter-to-mark-zuckerberg-from-the-worlds-fact-checkers/.

fact-checker, FactCheck.org, The Dispatch fact-checker, the *Washington Post* fact-checker, and PolitiFact.[115]

According to the IFCN's founding director Alexios Mantzarlis (who now works at Google), "fact-checkers are no longer a fresh-faced journalistic reform movement; they are wrinkly arbiters of a take-no-prisoners war for the future of the internet."[116]

The IFCN was launched in 2015 as a division of the Poynter Institute, PolitiFact's parent. Poynter's funding comes from Silicon Valley tech companies, leftist philanthropic organizations, and the U.S. government. IFCN's initial funding came from the National Endowment for Democracy (backed by the U.S. State Department), the Omidyar Network, Google, Facebook, the Bill & Melinda Gates Foundation, and George Soros' Open Society Foundations.

Finding evidence of bias within the IFCN is as simple as picking a random employee's name from their website and looking them up.

One of the IFCN's "certifiers" responsible for reviewing which organizations can join is American University journalism professor Margot Susca. She's certified nineteen fact-checking organizations, including AP Fact Check, Check Your Fact, Lead Stories, The Dispatch, and the *Washington Post* Fact Checker.

Susca has shared tweets claiming that racism is "embraced by nearly half of" the American electorate and called herself part of Hillary Clinton's "team." In May 2020, she appeared on the state propaganda network Russia Today and described how hard it is for her to be objective in the age of Trump. "It's hard for me to be an objective observer of this presidential administration when for years now they have continuously tried to delegitimize and marginalize news reporters for doing their constitutionally protected job," she stated in an interview, where she also blasted Kayleigh McEnany as a liar and praised the *Washington Post* and Russia Today.[117]

---

115   "Verified Signatories of the IFCN Code of Principles." International Fact-Checking Network, https://www.ifcncodeofprinciples.poynter.org/signatories.

116   Mantzarlis, Alexios. "Fact-checkers are no longer a fresh-faced movement. They're fighting for the future of the internet." The Poynter Institute, June 20, 2018, https://www.poynter.org/fact-checking/2018/fact-checkers-are-no-longer-a-fresh-faced-movement-theyre-fighting-for-the-future-of-the-internet/.

117   Gottschalk, Jonah. "'Nonpartisan' Facebook Fact-Checking Arbiter Trashed Republicans on Russian Propaganda Outlet." The Federalist, December 14, 2020, https://thefederalist.com/2020/12/14/facebooks-nonpartisan-fact-checking-arbiter-trashed-republicans-on-russian-propaganda-outlet/.

In early 2022, the Democratic National Committee released a nearly five-thousand-word action plan for aggressively implementing censorship under the guise of "combating online misinformation."[118] The DNC recommends social media platforms promote what they determine to be "authoritative" news sources, and positively reference Facebook's partnership with the IFCN, only complaining that it hasn't scaled "to the size of the site's misinformation problem."

But before I get too far ahead of myself, it was in January 2018 that Zuckerberg announced that Facebook's algorithm would get two changes to help boost "trusted" news outlets while suppressing their competitors. Facebook claimed they determined trustworthiness by a two-question poll asking if a user had heard of a publication before and whether or not they trusted it.[119]

At a tech conference in February 2018, former NBC and CNN anchor and current Facebook executive Campbell Brown said they'd be boosting "quality" news sources regardless of name recognition. "So much of the best journalism today is being done by smaller, more niche, more focused journalists who aren't going to have the brand recognition. To me, this is the future of journalism. This is where the experts are gonna be."

The changes overwhelmingly benefited left-wing outlets. NewsWhip, a social media engagement tracking website, explained in April 2018:

> The changes could be divided into two fairly distinct camps: engagement boosts for mainstream news outlets such as CNN and NBC, and declines for smaller, politically-focused sites and entertainment publishers.
>
> Looking at individual sites, it's clear that some names, namely CNN, the New York Times, the Guardian, BBC News and the Washington Post, all posted dramatic increases in their interaction counts. CNN was up 30.1 percent, and the New York Times, although with less engagements, was up by 48 percent. Increases of this magnitude had not been seen in a long time.

---

118 "DNC Recommendations for Combating Online Misinformation: Comparative Social Media Policy Analysis." Democratic National Committee, https://democrats.org/who-we-are/what-we-do/disinfo/comparative-social-media-policy-analysis/.

119 Hasson, *The Manipulators*, 34.

As usual, plenty of these sites saw viral hit stories in March which had the effect of boosting their overall totals for the month. But the effect of a rise in average engagements on stories could also be seen for many sites, including NPR and CNN, which grew its average interaction count from 4,982 in February to 7,010 in March.[120]

As for the losers, the conservative Western Journal fell from 20.5 million interactions in January (fourth overall) to 9.1 million in March (22nd). Ben Shapiro's Daily Wire fell from 18.6 million to 15 million over the same time period.[121]

Tech website The Outline published a similar report in March 2018 that the biggest losers were conservative and right-wing publishers such as Breitbart, Fox News, and the Gateway Pundit. Many websites were decimated by the change, with Independent Journal Review becoming a shell of what it was and suffering mass layoffs in February 2018. The libertarian-conservative Rare ceased publication and laid off its staffers in March 2018, and sold itself to Open Media Group.[122]

While testifying before the Senate Commerce and Judiciary committees in April 2018, Mark Zuckerberg explained the "learning process" that led him to take action against, among other things, "fake news" that has the ability to change the outcomes of elections:

> Overall, I would say that we are going through a broader philosophical shift in how we approach our responsibility as a company. For the first 10 or 12 years of the company, I viewed our responsibility as primarily building tools, that if we could put those tools in people's hands, then that would empower people to do good things.
>
> What I think we have learned now across a number of issues, not just data privacy but also fake news and foreign interference in elections, is that we need to take a more proactive role and a broader view of our responsibility. It is not enough to just build tools; we need to make sure that they are used for

---

120   "Facebook engagement trends in March: the winners and losers." NewsWhip, April 12, 2018, https://www.newswhip.com/2018/04/facebook-engagements-march-2018/.
121   Ibid.
122   Hasson, *The Manipulators*, 35.

good. And that means that we need to now take a more active view in policing the ecosystem and in watching and kind of looking out and making sure that all of the members in our community are using these tools in a way that is going to be good and healthy.[123]

As literal fake news sites died out after the election cycle came to a close, the purpose of these fact-checkers shifted their justification for "fact-checking" away from debunking stories invented out of thin air. Zuckerberg wrote in a November 2018 post titled "A Blueprint for Content Governance and Enforcement" that they have a "broader social responsibility to help bring people closer together—against polarization and extremism. The past two years have shown that without sufficient safeguards, people will misuse these tools to interfere in elections, spread misinformation, and incite violence."[124]

During his testimony, Zuckerberg also said that Facebook would be manipulating the type of content that people see going forward.

> One of the biggest issues social networks face is that, when left unchecked, people will engage disproportionately with more sensationalist and provocative content. This is not a new phenomenon. It is widespread on cable news today and has been a staple of tabloids for more than a century.
>
> …
>
> The category we're most focused on is click-bait and mis-information.
>
> …
>
> One common reaction is that rather than reducing distribution, we should simply move the line defining what is acceptable. In some cases this is worth considering, but it's important to remember that won't address the underlying incentive

---

123   "S.Hrg. 115-683 — Facebook, Social Media Privacy, and the Use and Abuse of Data." U.S. Congress, April 10, 2018, https://www.congress.gov/event/ 115th-congress/senate-event/LC64510/text?s=1&r=59.

124   Hasson, *The Manipulators*, 31.

problem, which is often the bigger issue. This engagement pattern seems to exist no matter where we draw the lines, so we need to change this incentive and not just remove content.

I believe these efforts on the underlying incentives in our systems are some of the most important work we're doing across the company. We've made significant progress in the last year, but we still have a lot of work ahead.

By fixing this incentive problem in our services, we believe it'll create a virtuous cycle: by reducing sensationalism of all forms, we'll create a healthier, less polarized discourse where more people feel safe participating.[125]

As the Daily Caller's Peter Hasson points out, there was never any inquisition against clickbait headlines when it came to the left. Clickbait *Washington Post* headlines like "A dad longed to spend Christmas with his flight attendant daughter. He found a clever way" and "The 10 weirdest celebrity apologies of 2018, from a cemetery selfie to a very awkward tweet" remained unaffected by Facebook's changes.[126]

As always, the enforcement of the rules is more important than the rules themselves.

With the algorithm changes in place, on December 15, 2018, Facebook announced it was partnering with five outside fact-checkers: PolitiFact, ABC News, FactCheck.org, the Associated Press, and Snopes, all of which lean left. Facing allegations of bias, Facebook later added the conservative Daily Caller and the neoconservative *Weekly Standard*. After the *Weekly Standard* went bust, Facebook added The Dispatch, which was founded by alumni from the *Standard*.

Later in 2020, Facebook created an "oversight board," which they claim its members "were chosen for their expertise and diversity," and "must not have actual or perceived conflicts of interest that could compromise their independent judgement and decision making." We're also

---

125 Constine, Josh. "Facebook Will Change Algorithm to Demote 'Borderline Content' That Almost Violates Policies." TechCrunch, November 15, 2018, https://techcrunch.com/2018/11/15/facebook-borderline-content/.

126 Hasson, *The Manipulators*, 32.

assured that they all "have expertise in, or experience advocating for, human rights."[127]

Of the twenty members of Facebook's oversight board, eighteen have ties to George Soros' Open Society Foundations (OSF).[128]

Among those with the most direct connection to the Soros network are Afia Asantewaa Asare-Kyei, a program manager for the OSF in West Africa; Nighat Dad, the executive director of the OSF-funded Digital Rights Foundation; Ronaldo Lemos, the cofounder of the Soros-backed Institute for Society and Technology; Michael McConnell, head of the OSF-funded Constitutional Law Center; Julie Owono, head of Internet Sans Frontieres, which is a member of the Soros-backed Global Network Initiative; Alan Rusbridger of the OSF-funded Committee to Protect Journalists; Andras Sajo, one of the cofounders of Soros' Central European University; and Helle Thorning-Schmidt, who is on the board of the OSF-funded European Council of Foreign Relations, and a trustee at the OSF-funded International Crisis Group, where Soros himself sits on the board.

As the *Columbia Journalism Review* calls it, there is an entire sector of "fact-checking philanthropy" funded by Google, Facebook, and nonprofits. In 2018, forty-one out of forty-seven fact-checking organizations were part of or affiliated with a media company, which fell to thirty-nine in 2019, indicating that their association with traditional outlets is weakening.[129]

While Facebook doesn't disclose how much it pays its fact-checkers, Snopes reported $100,000 in earnings from them in 2018 and $406,000 in 2018. FactCheck.org said they earned $188,881 in 2018, and $242,000 in 2019.[130]

---

127 Overly, Steven, and Alexandra Levine. "Facebook announces first 20 picks for global oversight board." Politico, May 6, 2020, https://www.politico.com/news/2020/05/06/facebook-global-oversight-board-picks-240150.

128 Attkisson, Sharyl. "Facebook's Fact-Check Board Gets a Lot of 'Likes' from Soros." RealClearInvestigations, August 4, 2020, https://www.realclearinvestigations.com/articles/2020/08/04/factcheck_sidebar_factcheck_sidebar_factcheck_sidebar_factcheck_sidebar__124710.html.

129 Bell, Emily. "The Fact-Check Industry." *Columbia Journalism Review*, Fall 2019, https://www.cjr.org/special_report/fact-check-industry-twitter.php.

130 Ibid.

Facebook itself (or at least its parent company) announced that it too will be joining the fact-checking industry in August 2022, with Meta announcing that they would be building an artificial intelligence program to fact-check all 6.5 million Wikipedia articles—a recipe for disaster.[131]

Google started a fact-checking nonprofit called First Draft at the beginning of the 2016 election cycle. In addition to being supported by Google, it's supported by the Ford Foundation and George Soros' Open Society Foundations. One of the group's original organizers, Alastair Reid, constantly shares leftist propaganda and anti-American rhetoric on his social media feeds. The group has also uncritically spread misinformation, such as directing readers to the bogus story that Trump told "people to drink bleach" to fight COVID-19.[132]

An eighty-five-page internal memo was circulated by Google in March 2018 titled "The Good Censor," which informed employees on the virtues of censorship. In the memo,[133] which was leaked by Breitbart, Google explains that the tech industry is adapting its stance towards censorship in direct response to the "anxiety of users and governments." The memo concludes that "tech firms have gradually shifted away from unmediated free speech and towards censorship and moderation." The memo tries to spin censorship as a positive because it makes "online spaces safer."[134]

This is their philosophy—and it had already been put into practice to the detriment of conservative outlets. A year prior, Google began displaying fact-checks on publications in their results, which overwhelmingly targeted conservative sites.

When a certain publication is Googled, a "card" with info about them would appear on the right side of the search result. That includes a "reviewed" claims tab that includes past fact-checks directed at claims made on that particular website.

131　Bates Ramirez, Vanessa. "Meta Is Building an AI to Fact-Check Wikipedia—All 6.5 Million Articles." SingularityHub, August 26, 2022, https://singularityhub.com/2022/08/26/meta-is-building-an-ai-to-fact-check-wikipedia-all-6-5-million-articles/.

132　Attkisson, "Investigating the Prevalence."

133　Bokhari, Allum. "The Good Censor - GOOGLE LEAK." Scribd, https://www.scribd.com/document/390521673/The-Good-Censor-GOOGLE-LEAK#from_embed.

134　Hasson, *The Manipulators*, 13.

The Daily Caller's is pictured below:

As it turns out, Google is just as bad at attaching fact-checks to publications as fact-checkers are at writing them.

One of the fact-checks attached to the Daily Caller's Google page in the search results (pictured above) purports to refute a Daily Caller article claiming that Special Counsel Robert Mueller only hired Hillary Clinton supporters for his special counsel, but the article doesn't claim that he did. The faux "fact-checked" Daily Caller article was reporting on a specific Clinton donor that Mueller hired.[135]

As explained earlier about social media's fact-checking process, Google also uses automatic fact-checking techniques that rely on algorithms to attach fact-checks specific to one particular claim from a particular source to anywhere else that may have repeated or made a similar

---

135   Ibid.

claim. Google did not disclose its use of automatic fact-checking in its documentation about its "fact-checking" feature.[136]

Another faux fact-check that Google attached came from Snopes and claimed to refute a Daily Caller article reporting that a "transgender woman raped a young girl in a women's bathroom because bathroom bills were passed." Yet the Daily Caller article this supposedly refuted doesn't mention a bill or any legislation at all. It just reports on the incident.[137]

Another fact-check was of a tongue-in-cheek article mocking a writer at *The Atlantic* who tried to racialize a solar eclipse. "The Atlantic, a once-great magazine, has determined that Monday's total eclipse of the sun fails to affect enough black people," writer Eric Owens quipped.[138] For some reason, Snopes decided to fact-check the snark, which just re-summarized the article Owens was mocking.

Almost exclusively conservative outlets got this treatment. As the Daily Caller's Eric Lieberman found after some digging:

> ...a review of mainstream outlets, as well as other outlets associated with liberal and conservative audiences, shows that only conservative sites feature the highly misleading, subjective analysis. Several conservative-leaning outlets like TheDC are "vetted," while equally partisan sites like Vox, ThinkProgress, Slate, The Huffington Post, Daily Kos, Salon, Vice and Mother Jones are spared.
>
> ...
>
> Big name publications like The New York Times, The Washington Post, and the Los Angeles Times are even given a column showcasing all of the awards they have earned over the years.[139]

---

136   Lurie, Emma, and Eni Mustafaraj. "'Highly Partisan' and 'Blatantly Wrong': Analyzing News Publishers' Critiques of Google's Reviewed Claims." *Proceedings of the 2020 Truth and Trust Online Conference (TTO 2020)*, 2020, https://par.nsf.gov/biblio/10278902.

137   Ibid.

138   Owens, Eric. "The Eclipse Is Racist Because It Fails to Affect Enough Black People, the Atlantic Suggests." The Daily Caller, August 20, 2017, https://dailycaller.com/2017/08/20/the-eclipse-is-racist-because-it-fails-to-affect-enough-black-people-the-atlantic-suggests/.

139   Lieberman, Eric. "Google's New Fact-Check Feature Almost Exclusively Targets Conservative Sites." The Daily Caller, January 9, 2018, https://dailycaller.com/2018/01/09/googles-new-fact-check-feature-almost-exclusively-targets-conservative-sites/.

Lieberman missed a number of left-wing publications that did have the "fact-checking" feature, but they were all fringe websites you've probably never heard of. Mainstream left-wing publications were absent.

While mainstream conservative websites such as Breitbart, the Daily Caller, The Federalist, *Commentary Magazine*, and Bearing Arms make the list, not a single mainstream left-wing publication is censored in the same way.

The only left-wing publications that get flagged tend to be those that fall into the literal fake news category and push hyper-partisan narratives, such as the widely ridiculed Occupy Democrats and Palmer Report.

Bias or Accuracy	List of websites to which Google assigned a reviewed claims tab (ordered by Alexa Rank)
Right	Breitbart, the Daily Caller, the Daily Wire, World Net Daily, the Gateway Pundit, the Federalist, Free Republic, the Conservative Treehouse, OAN Network, Big League Politics, the Political Insider, FrontPage Magazine, American Greatness, American Renaissance, Bearing Arms, Red State Watcher, Truthfeed, 100 Percent Fed Up, Freedom Outpost, Commentary Magazine, the Millenium Report, VDARE, Sparta Report, En Volve, Conservative Fighters, Silence is Consent, America's Freedom Fighters, Freedom Daily, American News, American Conservative Herald, the New York Evening
Left	Upworthy, Palmer Report, Democratic Underground, Counterpunch, Right Wing Watch, Bipartisan Report, True Activist, OpEdNews, American Herald Tribune, Occupy Democrats, Egberto Willies, If You Only News, American News X, Resistance Report

Source: National Science Foundation[140]

---

140   Lurie and Mustafaraj, "'Highly Partisan.'"

One story at The Federalist mentioned, "Another woman, Eileen Wellstone, claimed Clinton raped her while he was at Oxford University in the 1960s," which resulted in them getting a Snopes fact-check attached to their publication's "reviewed claims."

The Snopes article attached debunks the claim that Bill Clinton was expelled from Oxford over the alleged rape—a claim that the Federalist article doesn't make. The Federalist mentioned the alleged incident, not that it was linked to an expulsion. Yet, just mentioning her name was enough to trigger a fact-check and, in this case, one that doesn't even check the right claim.[141]

Claim: Bill Clinton was expelled from Oxford University for raping a British classmate named Eileen Wellstone. See Example(s)

Claimed by: The Federalist

Fact check by Snopes.com: Unproven

Fact Check Crime Bill Clinton Was Expelled from Oxford Over a Rap...
https://www.snopes.com/bill-clin...

In another case, The Federalist reported on an Abe Lincoln statue being vandalized in Chicago and noted that it came against the backdrop of activists wanting to tear down memorials of anyone connected to the Confederacy (of which Lincoln himself was no fan).

---

141   Harsanyi, David. "Google's New 'Fact-Checker' Is Partisan Garbage."
      The Federalist, January 10, 2018, https://thefederalist.com/2018/01/10/
      googles-new-factchecker-is-partisan-garbage/.

> **Claim:** A bust of Abraham Lincoln was vandalized in Chicago in protest of confederate statues.
>
> **Claimed by:** The Federalist
>
> **Fact check by Snopes.com:** Unproven
>
> ---
>
> FACT CHECK: Was a Bust of Abraham Lincoln Vandalized in...
> https://www.snopes.com/lincoln...

The Federalist article doesn't make any explicit connection between those protesters and whoever vandalized the Lincoln statue. But a Snopes fact-check still got attached to the article to debunk the claim that the statue was vandalized in protest of confederate statues, which they rated "unproven." Again, The Federalist never said they were.

Google ended up discontinuing this feature amid criticism of its numerous flaws—but has since only gone into overdrive and added fact-checks to search results,[142] and pledged over $13 million to the Poynter Institute as part of their new "Global Fact Check Fund" launching in 2023.[143]

NEWSGUARD

NewsGuard serves a similar purpose as the fact-checkers, providing a service that claims to rate the credibility of news information and to track misinformation. They offer a downloadable browser extension that gives websites different "trust" ratings on a scale of 100. The service also gives a "nutritional label" based on whether the site has a reputation for publish-

---

142   "Find fact checks in search results." Google Search Help, https://support.google.com/websearch/answer/7315336?hl=en.

143   Jaeger, Jarryd. "Google, YouTube spend MILLIONS to launch Global Fact Check Fund." The Post Millennial, November 29, 2022, https://thepostmillennial.com/google-youtube-spend-millions-to-launch-global-fact-check-fund.

ing false content, avoids deceptive headlines, corrects or clarifies errors, "gathers and presents information responsible," and discloses ownership, among other criteria.

NewsGuard claims to have reviewed news sources that account for 95 percent of online engagement.

They were founded in 2018 by journalist Steven Brill and media executive L. Gordon Crovitz.

On July 17, 2021, NewsGuard praised White House press secretary Jen Psaki after she called for a government-media partnership to fight what they considered to be disinformation the day before. Psaki stated, admitting that this was already happening to some extent:

> It shouldn't come as any surprise that we're in regular touch with social media platforms — just like we're in regular touch with all of you and your media outlets — about areas where we have concern, information that might be useful, information that may or may not be interesting to your viewers.
>
> You all make decisions, just like the social media platforms make decisions, even though they're a private-sector company and different, but just as an example.
>
> So we are regularly making sure social media platforms are aware of the latest narratives dangerous to public health that we and many other Americans seeing — are seeing across all of social and traditional media. And we work to engage with them to better understand the enforcement of social media platform policies.[144]

NewsGuard was enthused, writing, "When NewsGuard offered Facebook our data on websites that spread misinformation at the start of the pandemic—they didn't want it. Picking fights with [the president of the United States] won't fix the misinformation epidemic—working collaboratively will. Our door is open."[145]

---

144   "Press Briefing by Press Secretary Jen Psaki, July 16, 2021." The White House, July 16, 2021, https://www.whitehouse.gov/briefing-room/press-briefings/2021/07/16/press-briefing-by-press-secretary-jen-psaki-july-16-2021/.

145   Magness, Phillip W., and Ethan Yang. "Who Fact Checks the Fact Checkers? A Report on Media Censorship." American Institute for Economic Research, August 11, 2021, https://www.aier.org/article/who-fact-checks-the-fact-checkers-a-report-on-media-censorship/.

Much like the traditional fact-checkers, the "disinfo screeners" at NewsGuard have chosen a side.

A review from economic historian Phil Magness found NewsGuard falls short of their own professed standards:

> Most of the company's fact checkers lack basic qualifications in the scientific and social-scientific fields that they purport to arbitrate. NewsGuard's own track record of commentary—particularly on the COVID-19 pandemic—reveals a pattern of unreliable and misleading claims that required subsequent corrections, and analysis that regularly conflates fact with opinion journalism in rendering a judgement on a website's content. Furthermore, the company's own practices fall far short of the transparency and disclosure standards it regularly applies to other websites.[146]

For over a year prior to the Biden administration and other experts suddenly giving consideration to the Wuhan lab leak theory for the origin of COVID-19 after previously denouncing it as conspiratorial, NewsGuard penalized websites for even pondering the hypothesis. "There is no evidence that the Wuhan Institute of Virology was the source of the outbreak, and genomic evidence has found that the virus is '96% percent identical at the whole-genome level to a bat coronavirus,'" wrote NewsGuard's "Deputy Director of Health" John Gregory to an offending website in early 2020. Gregory also contacted a medical news site that ran the headline "Coronavirus may have leaked from China's highest biosafety lab" to demand a retraction.[147]

Even after new evidence came out favoring the lab leak hypothesis, Gregory remained adamant that "the lab leak theory remains unsubstantiated and under investigation." Regardless, in late June 2021, NewsGuard issued at least twenty-one separate corrections to ratings where websites were dinged for reporting on the lab leak theory, though, having provided ratings to 7,500 websites, it's likely they failed to correct many more than they did correct.[148]

The libertarian-leaning American Institute for Economic Research (AIER) was targeted by Gregory with a seemingly hostile message that

---

146   Ibid.
147   Ibid.
148   Ibid.

complained about AIER describing themselves as nonpartisan because they criticized Biden in an article accusing him of not being more trustworthy on corruption than any other Washington bureaucrat, and another article of theirs argued that Biden, Fauci, and Nancy Pelosi don't care about policies that destroy the nuclear family, educational system, and other pillars of our society.

Yet Gregory could've just typed Trump's name into the search bar on AIER's website and found articles with titles such as "The Economic Policy Failures of the Trump Administration," "The Surreal Logic of Trump's Trade Deal," "Trump's American Greatness Also Political Paternalism," and "Trump Cutting the Budget? Don't Believe It," among dozens of other articles criticizing Trump.

Another issue with NewsGuard's review of AIER had to do with the Great Barrington Declaration, which was an open letter sponsored by AIER and published in October 2020 from infectious disease epidemiologists and public health scientists concerned with the consequences of lockdowns, instead favoring focused protection.

The declaration was authored by Dr. Martin Kulldorff, a professor of medicine at Harvard, Dr. Sunetra Gupta, an epidemiologist and professor at Oxford University, and Jay Bhattacharya, a professor at Stanford Medicine school, epidemiologist, and health economist.[149]

Gregory claimed that none of the three had ever published peer-reviewed research about the COVID-19 pandemic at the time they had published the declaration, a false claim also repeated by PolitiFact in their criticism of the declaration.[150] But Jay Bhattacharya had published research that appeared in the *Journal of the American Medical Association* in May 2020.[151]

Most of NewsGuard's review of the declaration is based on a statement from the former U.K. health secretary Matt Hancock, a politician with no formal scientific or medical training, who has never published peer-reviewed research about the COVID-19 pandemic and believes that herd immunity wouldn't be achieved even if everyone got COVID-

---

149 "Great Barrington Declaration." Great Barrington Declaration, https://gbdeclaration.org/.
150 Putterman, Samantha. "PolitiFact - Great Barrington herd immunity document widely disputed by scientists." PolitiFact, October 27, 2020, https://www.politifact.com/factchecks/2020/oct/27/facebook-posts/great-barrington-herd-immunity-document-widely-dis/.
151 Magness, Phillip. "Email from Phillip W. Magness." NewsGuard, July 1, 2021, https://www.newsguardtech.com/feedback/publisher/aier-org/.

19. NewsGuard also cited blogger Nafeez Ahmed, a 9/11 truther who writes about conspiracy websites and promoted an unfounded conspiracy about the declaration that it was funded by Charles Koch in coordination with the British Ministry of Defense and the proprietor of a hotel resort in Wales. [152]

This is in contrast to the standards outlined by NewsGuard co-CEO Brill, who says that their judgments are only based on "sources who are experts."

Gregory didn't correct other errors, such as claiming that the Barrington Declaration "argued that face masks should be eliminated for people at lower risk of severe illness of death from COVID-19"—but the declaration doesn't mention mask policy. It focuses on lockdowns and school closures.

In another case in November 2019, NewsGuard contacted the website RealClearInvestigations (RCI) to question its use of anonymous sources in revealing the identity of the "whistleblower" that sparked the Ukraine-related impeachment of President Trump. Noting how normalized relying on anonymous sources has become in the Trump era, RCI responded to ask NewsGuard if they were reaching out to the *New York Times*, *Washington Post*, CNN, NBC, or Buzzfeed for relying on anonymous sources, to which NewsGuard didn't respond to comment.[153]

Like the entirety of the media it's supposed to keep in check, NewsGuard was on the wrong side of the Hunter Biden laptop story, which they initially labeled a Russian hoax. Cofounder Brill told CNBC after the laptop story broke, "My personal opinion is there's a high likelihood this story is a hoax, maybe even a hoax perpetrated by the Russians again."[154]

Unlike the major fact-checking organizations, NewsGuard at least lives up to its name in that it's a guard for the left's news.

---

152 Ibid.

153 Attkisson, Sharyl. "Investigating the Prevalence of Left-Leaning 'Fact-Checkers.'" The Daily Signal, August 10, 2020, https://www.dailysignal.com /2020/08/10/investigating-the-prevalence-of-left-leaning-fact-checks/.

154 Bokhari, Allum. "NewsGuard Ultimate Fake News Humiliation: 'Fact-Checking' Org's Co-Founder Called Hunter Biden's Laptop a 'Hoax.'" Breitbart, March 17, 2022, https://www.breitbart.com/tech/2022/03/17/newsguard-ultimate-fake-news-humiliation-fact-checking-orgs-co-founder-called-hunter-bidens-laptop-a-hoax/.

THE DISINFORMATION RACKET

The separation of fact-checker and state fully collapsed during the second year of the Biden administration, when they moved from encouraging Big Tech censorship[155] to creating their own de facto Ministry of Truth.

On April 27, 2022, the Department of Homeland Security announced the creation of a new advisory board, the "Disinformation Governance Board," and Nina Jankowicz was named executive director of the new board.

Jankowicz was previously a "disinformation fellow" at the Wilson Center and adviser to the Ukrainian Foreign Ministry as part of the Fulbright Public Policy Fellowship (then known as the "Fulbright-Clinton Public Policy Fellowship" until 2018, when Hillary Clinton's name was dropped from it).[156] Jankowicz wrote two books: *How To Lose The Information War: Russia, Fake News, and the Future of Conflict* and *How to Be a Woman Online: Surviving Abuse and Harassment, and How to Fight Back.*

She, like all others in the disinformation industry, has a lengthy history of spreading disinformation herself.

During the Trump years, Jankowicz boosted tweets and reports about Trump's nonexistent "collusion with Russia," all of which are now thoroughly discredited, often with her added commentary in the vein of "Wow. This is serious!" to lend credibility to the shared article.

In one tweet, she linked to an article from Slate journalist Franklin Foer that originated the lie that Trump Tower had been communicating with the Russian Alfa Bank, calling it "her worst nightmare." [157] Hours after Foer's article was published on October 31, 2016, Hillary Clinton released a public statement that "computer scientists have apparently uncovered a covert server linking the Trump Organization to a Russian-based bank."

155   Patteson, Callie. "Psaki calls for censorship of Instagram, Facebook: 'Too much power.'" *New York Post*, September 24, 2021, https://nypost.com/2021/09/24/psaki-calls-for-censorship-of-instagram-facebook/.

156   Morello, Carrol. "Hillary Clinton's name vanishes from State Department fellowship." *Washington Post*, March 20, 2018, https://www.washingtonpost.com/world/national-security/clintons-name-vanishes-from-state-department-fellowship/2018/03/19/ebe0c61c-2938-11e8-bc72-077aa4dab9ef_story.html

157   Dunleavy, Jerry. "Biden disinformation chief Nina Jankowicz pushed Trump-Russia collusion claims." *Washington Examiner*, May 9, 2022, https://www.washingtonexaminer.com/news/biden-disinfo-chief-nina-jankowicz-pushed-trump-russia-collusion-claims.

And it was all fiction—the FBI investigated the Alfa Bank server and, in February 2017, concluded that no such communication link with Trump Tower existed.[158]

In 2021, Foer admitted that he sent his Slate story to Fusion GPS (a firm that worked with the Clinton campaign and funded the bogus Christopher Steele dossier) the day before it was published,[159] and it was revealed during the 2022 trial of former Hillary Clinton lawyer Michael Sussmann that Hillary personally signed off on spreading the Alfa Bank lie.[160] Jankowitcz herself has sung Steele's praises.[161]

In October 2020, Jankowicz insanely claimed the Hunter Biden laptop was a "product of the Trump campaign" and the discovery of the laptop at a repair shop was a "fairytale." Jankowicz also peddled a letter signed by dozens of "intelligence officials" claiming the Biden laptop bore all the hallmarks of "Russian disinformation," which turned out to be untrue.[162]

Jankowicz ridiculed claims that COVID-19 is a lab-made virus or that funds granted through the NIH and Anthony Fauci were ultimately used to create the virus. She does offer mealy-mouthed "we don't really know the origins, but 'experts agree' the virus was not man-made" excuses.[163] The phrase "experts agree" is cliché in the disinformation industry, with the so-called experts usually handpicked ideologically when quoted for comment.

158 Scarborough, Rowan. "FBI file disproves Trump-Alfa Bank link." *Washington Times*, October 21, 2021, https://www.washingtontimes.com/news/2021/oct/21/fbi-file-disproves-trump-alfa-bank-link/.

159 Flood, Brian, and David Rutz. "Slate journalist sent draft of story to Fusion GPS about possible link between Trump, Russian Bank: Indictment." Fox News, September 17, 2021, https://www.foxnews.com/media/slate-journalist-story-fusion-gps-trump-russian-bank.

160 Turley, Jonathan. "How the Sussmann trial revealed Hillary Clinton's role in the Alfa Bank scandal." The Hill, May 21, 2022, https://thehill.com/opinion/judiciary/3496659-how-the-sussmann-trial-revealed-hillary-clintons-role-in-the-alfa-bank-scandal/.

161 Dunleavy, Jerry. "Biden 'disinformation' chief a Trump dossier author fan and Hunter Biden laptop doubter." *Washington Examiner*, April 28, 2022, https://www.washingtonexaminer.com/news/bidens-disinformation-chief-is-trump-dossier-author-fan-and-hunter-laptop-doubter.

162 Ibid.

163 Dunleavy, Jerry. "Biden 'disinformation' chief's criticisms of lab leak theory were boosted by CCP." *Washington Examiner*, April 29, 2022, https://www.washingtonexaminer.com/news/biden-disinformation-chiefs-criticisms-of-lab-leak-theory-were-boosted-by-ccp.

Later in March 2021, Jankowicz reported that the intelligence community "has a high degree of confidence that the Kremlin used proxies to push influence narratives, including misleading or unsubstantiated claims about President Biden, to U.S. media, officials, and influencers, some close to President Trump. A clear nod to the alleged Hunter laptop."[164]

Jankowicz played a role in the Integrity Initiative, as was revealed by Revolver's Darren Beattie who describes it as the most "explosive and aggressively censored national security leaks of the century."[165]

The initiative was a government-funded NGO founded in 2015 that engaged in political meddling and covert influence operations in Western countries. Funders included the U.K.'s Foreign, Commonwealth, and Development office, NATO, and the U.S. State Department. The key takeaway here is that they advanced their propaganda under the false pretense of "fighting disinformation."[166]

Jankowicz's name appeared in a 2018 leak as a member of the inner core of the U.K.'s branch of the initiative and was specifically dedicated to combating supposed Russian interference. Another name leaked with Jankowicz's was Ben Nimmo, who, at the time, worked for a subsidiary of the Atlantic Council (also funded by the U.K. Commonwealth Office, NATO, and State Department) called the Digital Forensic Research Lab. The lab claims to have "operationalized the study of disinformation by exposing falsehoods and fake news." As of writing, Nimmo now works at Facebook to fight "influence operations."[167]

Amid an uproar over the Biden administration creating what was widely labeled a "Ministry of Truth," the Disinformation Governance Board was "paused" after only three weeks, and Jankowicz submitted her resignation.[168]

---

164 Jankowicz, Nina. March 16, 2021, https://twitter.com/wiczipedia/status/1371889543582990336.

165 "Busted: Biden's 'Minister of Truth' Nina Jankowicz Participated in Secret NATO-Funded Cabal to Subvert Western Democracies Using Disinformation as Cover." Revolver, May 16, 2022, https://www.revolver.news/2022/05/biden-minster-of-truth-nina-jankowicz-and-the-secret-nato-funded-cabal-to-subvert-western-democracies-using-disinformation-as-cover/.

166 Ibid.

167 Ibid.

168 Lorenz, Taylor. "How the Biden administration let right-wing attacks derail its disinformation efforts." *Washington Post*, May 18, 2022, https://www.washingtonpost.com/technology/2022/05/18/disinformation-board-dhs-nina-jankowicz/.

Mayorkas announced that during the pause, members of the Homeland Security Advisory Council would be conducting a review. A co-leader of the review was DHS Secretary Michael Chertoff, who also pushed the lie that the Hunter Biden laptop was disinformation in November 2020.[169]

Jankowicz personally blamed disinformation for the board's implosion while complaining to MSNBC's Chris Hayes after her resignation, before describing herself as "reasonable and nuanced" and claiming to not be partisan.[170]

During an appearance on CNN's *Reliable Sources* with Brian Stelter after the board was shelved, she described disinformation as a "democratic problem" and was eventually asked about criticisms that she herself has spread disinformation, though Stelter didn't mention anything in particular for her to respond to.

Jankowicz responded by saying that she's been accused of spreading disinformation about Hunter Biden's laptop back in October 2020 (by falsely branding it disinformation), and she claimed that she herself wasn't endorsing the allegations that the laptop was bogus but simply sharing comments made during one of the presidential debates.[171] In the tweet she's referring to, she was reacting to the presidential debate, writing at the time "Biden notes 50 former natsec officials and 5 former CIA heads that believe the laptop is a Russian influence op. Trump says 'Russia, Russia, Russia.'"[172]

Yet just twelve hours before that tweet, Jankowicz shared a *TIME* magazine article that she said had cast "yet more doubt on the provenance of the NY Post's Hunter Biden story," which nukes the excuse she gave herself on CNN.[173]

Never before had one such story generated so many calls for immediate censorship. Twitter banned users entirely from posting the *New York*

169   Dunleavy, Jerry. "Mayorkas misled under oath about DHS disinfo board, GOP senators charge." *Washington Examiner*, June 10, 2022, https://www.washingtonexaminer.com/news/senate/biden-disinformation-board-mayorkas-misled-senators-hawley-grassley.

170   Key, Pam. "Jankowicz: 'Ironic' Disinformation Board Killed by Disinformation." Breitbart, May 18, 2022, https://www.breitbart.com/clips/2022/05/18/jankowicz-ironic-disinformation-board-killed-by-disinformation/.

171   Reliable Sources. "Jankowicz: Disinformation 'is a democratic problem.'" CNN Business, https://edition.cnn.com/videos/business/2022/07/10/a2.cnn.

172   Jankowicz, Nina. October 22, 2020, https://twitter.com/wiczipedia/status/1319463138107031553.

173   Jankowicz, Nina. October 22, 2020, https://twitter.com/wiczipedia/status/1319251093298302976.

Post's article that broke the Hunter Biden laptop story, while Facebook reduced promotion of the story in people's newsfeeds to the point where the story was de facto banned from the platform. And the FBI played a role.

During an appearance on Joe Rogan's podcast, Meta (Facebook's parent company) CEO and founder Mark Zuckerberg revealed that Facebook algorithmically censored the Hunter Biden laptop story before the 2020 presidential election came, after the FBI warned them about supposed "Russian disinformation."

When asked by Rogan about censorship of the laptop story, Zuckerberg revealed that "the FBI, I think, basically came to us, some folks on our team, and was like hey, just so you know, you should be on high alert. We thought that there was a lot of Russian propaganda in the 2016 election. We have it on notice that basically there's about to be some kind of dump that is similar to that. So just be vigilant."[174] It was after this meeting that they began censoring the story.

Documents released by Senators Josh Hawley and Chuck Grassley would later expose more about the Disinformation Governance Board's true mission. It was learned that the DHS had planned for the board's creation as early as September 2021, with a letter to Secretary Alejandro Mayorkas detailing the proposed structure of the board. The letter listed "serious homeland security risks" that included "conspiracy theories" about the validity of elections (specifically mentioning those who questioned the 2020 results and those involved in January 6), "disinformation" about the origin of COVID-19, and information questioning the efficacy of COVID-19 vaccines and masks.[175]

Another document had notes about a meeting between Under Secretary for HHS Strategy, Policy, and Plans Robert P. Silver and two Twitter executives with the objective of discussing a "public-private" partnership between the DHS and Twitter, and informing Twitter executives of the DHS's work on misinformation.[176]

---

174   The Joe Rogan Experience. "Episode #1863 - Mark Zuckerberg." August 2022, https://open.spotify.com/episode/51gxrAActH18RGhKNza598.

175   Nightingale, Hannah. "REVEALED: 'Ministry of Truth' formed to fight 'conspiracy theories' regarding COVID-19, 2020 election, domestic violent extremism." The Post Millennial, June 9, 2022, https://thepostmillennial. com/revealed-ministry-of-truth-formed-to-fight-conspiracy-theories-regarding-covid-19-2020-election-domestic-violent-extremism.

176   Ibid.

When Press Secretary Karine Jean-Pierre was pressed by Fox News' Peter Doocy in May about what changed to make the Biden administration pause the board, she replied that the DHS's "work across several administrations that addresses disinformation that threatens the security of the country is critical and will continue. So that work is going to continue."[177]

The board mutated quickly, and the following month, Vice President Kamala Harris announced the launch of a White House "task force" to stop "gendered disinformation" and abuse online. A memo released by the White House railed against "gender disinformation" and indicated that they would be "developing programs and policies to address online harassment, abuse, and disinformation campaigns targeting women and LGBTQI+ individuals who are public and political figures, government and civic leaders, activists, and journalists in the United States and globally."[178]

Another reporter asked, "On a background call last night, we were told that it's going to be different from the Disinformation Governance Board and that it's going to focus on illegal conduct online, but the memo creating it was a little bit broader and mentioned—and I'm quoting from the document, quote, 'Online harassment, abuse, and disinformation campaigns targeting women and LGBTQI+ individuals who are public and political figures.' Can you clear the disinformation charges—"

Jean-Pierre then opted to plead ignorance. "So, I would need to talk to her team. I was not on the background call. So that specific language that you're—you're providing to me, I would just have to check in with her. I would also encourage you to check—to check as well with her—her team. I can't say more because I—I wasn't on the background call."[179]

Much like her predecessor, she never circled back on that.

---

177   Schwartz, Ian. "WH's Karine Jean-Pierre on Disinformation Board: It's Paused, But 'The Work Doesn't Stop.'" RealClearPolitics, May 18, 2022, https://www.realclearpolitics.com/video/2022/05/18/karine_jean-pierre_on_disinformation_board_its_paused_but_the_work_doesnt_stop.html.

178   "Memorandum on the Establishment of the White House Task Force to Address Online Harassment and Abuse." The White House, June 16, 2022, https://www.whitehouse.gov/briefing-room/presidential-actions/2022/06/16/memorandum-on-the-establishment-of-the-white-house-task-force-to-address-online-harassment-and-abuse/.

179   "Karine Jean-Pierre Can't Say How Kamala's New 'Task Force' Is Different from Biden Ministry of Truth." Grabien, https://grabien.com/story.php?id=382221.

As it turns out, the work the Disinformation Governance Board was to carry out is, and already was, being carried out by Cybersecurity and Infrastructure Security Agency (CISA), which is part of the DHS.

Prior to the 2020 election, Twitter, Facebook, Reddit, Discord, Wikipedia, Microsoft, LinkedIn, and Verizon Media were meeting on a monthly basis with the FBI, CISA, and other government representatives as part of an initiative to "handle misinformation" during the election.[180]

In September 2022, it was learned that the Biden White House had been colluding with Big Tech to censor so-called misinformation on COVID-19. In emails resulting from a lawsuit filed by Missouri attorney general Eric Schmitt and Louisiana attorney general Jeff Landry, it was revealed that the censorship apparatus includes over fifty Biden administration officials across over a dozen agencies, including in "the White House, HHS, DHS, CISA, the CDC, NIAID, and the Office of the Surgeon General...the Census Bureau, the FDA, the FBI, the State Department, the Treasury Department, and the U.S. Election Assistance Commission."[181]

In one email, surgeon general Vivek Murthy is contacted by a senior Facebook official about a meeting they just had to "better understand the scope of what the White House expects from us on misinformation going forward." The same Facebook official emailed the HHS to thank them about meeting to discuss the measures Facebook was implementing to address so-called COVID-19 misinformation, which included the mass censorship and removal of pages and certain individuals from their platform. Emails showed that Facebook regularly relied on input from the CDC before making a decision to censor a user or story.[182]

The CDC proposed monthly "pre-debunking" meetings with Facebook, and "be on the lookout" calls with other major social networks.[183]

As truly defined, "misinformation" was simply anything that went counter to the Biden administration's narrative, and the censorship stretched beyond potential falsehoods. In one email chain, a White House

---

180 Klippenstein, Ken, and Lee Fang. "Truth Cops: Leaked Documents Outline DHS's Plans to Police Disinformation." The Intercept, October 31, 2022, https://theintercept.com/2022/10/31/social-media-disinformation-dhs/.

181 Winters, Natalie. "Biden White House Colluded With Big Tech To Censor COVID Info, Emails Prove." The National Pulse, September 1, 2022, https://thenationalpulse.com/2022/09/01/emails-show-federal-government-colluded-on-covid-censorship/.

182 Ibid.

183 Ibid.

official reached out to Facebook to ask them to remove an Anthony Fauci parody account.[184]

In February 2022, Microsoft executive Matt Masterson (a former DHS official) texted DHS director Jen Easterly, "Platforms have got to get comfortable with gov't. It's really interesting how hesitant they remain." In a meeting the next month, FBI official Laura Dehmlow warned of the "threat of subversive information on social media" undermining support for the U.S. government.

Dehmlow, a Democrat donor, was also one of the FBI agents who "briefed" Facebook to convince them that the Hunter Biden laptop story was Russian disinformation.[185]

The Departments of State and Homeland Security worked with a consortium called the Election Integrity Partnership that included four private firms that they awarded with millions of dollars for censoring millions of social media posts they alleged contained misinformation about the 2020 election.[186]

The four organizations included the Stanford Internet Observatory, the University of Washington's Center for an Informed Public, the Atlantic Council's Digital Forensic Research Lab, and the social media analytics firm Graphika, and amounted to a precursor to the Disinformation Governance Board. This work was done in consultation with CISA.

The four groups created a "concierge-like service" in 2020 that allowed federal agencies to file requests that certain online story links and social media posts get either censored or otherwise flagged by Big Tech companies. Among the Big Tech platforms that collaborated with the EIP are Facebook, Twitter, Google, TikTok, Reddit, NextDoor, Discord, and Pinterest.[187]

---

184   Ibid.
185   Ross, Chuck. "FBI Officials Who Briefed Facebook on Hunter Biden Story Are Dem Donors." Washington Free Beacon, October 10, 2022, https://freebeacon.com/democrats/fbi-officials-who-briefed-facebook-on-hunter-biden-story-are-dem-donors/.
186   Piper, Greg, and John Solomon. "Outsourced censorship: Feds used private entity to target millions of social posts in 2020." Just the News, September 30, 2022, https://justthenews.com/government/federal-agencies/biden-administration-rewarded-private-entities-got-2020-election.
187   Center for an Informed Public, Digital Forensic Research Lab, Graphika, & Stanford Internet Observatory (2021). "The Long Fuse: Misinformation and the 2020 Election." Stanford Digital Repository: Election Integrity Partnership, https://stacks.stanford.edu/file/druid:tr171zs0069/EIP-Final-Report.pdf, 12.

Three left-wing groups—the Democratic National Committee, Common Cause, and the NAACP—were also "empowered like the federal agencies to file tickets seeking censorship of content." A DHS-funded collaboration called the Elections Infrastructure Information Sharing and Analysis Center also had access.

A report from the consortium revealed that they flagged over 4,800 URLs that were shared nearly twenty-two million times just on Twitter. From September to November, their staff worked twelve- to twenty-hour shifts "with 'monitoring intensif[ying] significantly' the week before and after Election Day." In total, 72 percent of the tickets they processed related to what they decided constituted "delegitimization of the election."[188]

Among the things the government submitted tickets for removal were articles that cast doubt on the reliability of mail-in voting, and other election integrity–related issues from a right-wing perspective. According to John Solomon and Greg Piper:

> The consortium achieved a success rate in 2020 that would be enviable for baseball batters: Platforms took action on 35% of flagged URLs, with 21% labeled, 13% removed and 1% soft-blocked, meaning users had to reject a warning to see them. The partnership couldn't determine how many were downranked.[189]

In addition to social media posts, the consortium targeted right-leaning news organizations. The twenty most common domains flagged in incidents included Fox News, the *Epoch Times*, the *New York Post*, Zero Hedge, Just the News, The National Pulse, the Geller Report, National File, the *Washington Times*, the *Washington Examiner*, and journalist Sara Carter's website (sarahcarter.com).[190] While the *Washington Post* and *New York Times* also were cited often in incidents, it was because the EIP used them as sources for fact-checking, not targeting them for censorship like the aforementioned domains.[191]

---

188 Ibid, vi.
189 "Outsourced censorship: Feds used private entity to target millions of social posts in 2020."
190 "The Long Fuse: Misinformation and the 2020 Election," 189.
191 Ibid, 190.

They also identified what they considered to be the twenty-one most prominent spreaders of misinformation on Twitter, which included Donald Trump and Donald Trump Jr., Sean Hannity, Ric Grenell, James O'Keefe, Mark Levin, Charlie Kirk, Eric Trump, Tom Fitton, and James Woods, among others.

The fact-checking resources the EIP relied on included Snopes, PolitiFact, *USA Today*, the *Washington Post*, and CNN (in that order), who were cited a combined 925 times.[192]

CONGRESS PRESSURES TECH GIANTS TO CENSOR

Because the First Amendment prohibits the government from restricting speech, the Biden administration is attempting to backdoor censorship by having Big Tech implement it. As Glenn Greenwald points out, it is unconstitutional for the government to explicitly pressure private companies to censor, but it's unclear where exactly that line is.

Jen Psaki openly called for collusion with Big Tech to censor the administration's opposition while serving as press secretary, at one point during a July 2021 briefing admitting that the White House was "flagging" Facebook posts containing so-called "COVID misinformation" for the platform to censor. Psaki admitted, "We are in regular touch with the social media platforms and those engagements typically happen through members of our senior staff and also members of our COVID-19 team" adding that the surgeon general had conveyed that this was a big issue.[193]

When Twitter's Jack Dorsey and Mark Zuckerberg were summoned to testify on March 25, 2022, by the House Energy and Commerce Committee, the committee's chair and two chairs of the subcommittee wrote in a joint statement that the hearing was due to "falsehoods about the COVID-19 vaccine" and "debunked claims of election fraud." As always, it's only supposed misinformation that goes counter to the regime narrative that they're upset about.

They added that "these online platforms have allowed misinformation to spread, intensifying national crises with real-life, grim consequences for public health and safety," and that "this hearing will continue

---

192 "The Long Fuse: Misinformation and the 2020 Election. Stanford Digital Repository," 35.

193 Nelson, Steven. "White House 'flagging' posts for Facebook to censor over COVID 'misinformation.'" *New York Post*, July 15, 2021, https://nypost.com/2021/07/15/white-house-flagging-posts-for-facebook-to-censor-due-to-covid-19-misinformation/.

the Committee's work of holding online platforms accountable for the growing rise of misinformation and disinformation."[194]

In the wake of Elon Musk's acquisition of Twitter near the end of 2022, Musk began releasing what he called the "Twitter Files," revealing internal communications that exposed Twitter acting as a censorship subsidiary of the FBI. The revelations included that the FBI's San Francisco field office regularly sent lists of accounts to Twitter they wanted banned (some of which were joke accounts), that the CIA sent similar lists to Twitter, that the FBI was in "intense" communication with Twitter ahead of the release (and then Twitter's censorship of) the Hunter Biden laptop story, and that Twitter aided the Pentagon's online psyop campaigns.[195]

HOW THE FACT-CHECKING INDUSTRY FUELS ONLINE CENSORSHIP OF CONSERVATIVES

As has been emphasized many times already, the true purpose of fact-checking is to serve as a rubber stamp for censorship—and it works.

The *New York Times* reported in the aftermath of the 2020 election that Facebook would be taking even more steps to curtail right-wing sites:

> Employees proposed an emergency change to the site's news feed algorithm, which helps determine what more than two billion people see every day. It involved emphasizing the importance of what Facebook calls 'news ecosystem quality' scores, or N.E.Q., a secret internal ranking it assigns to news publishers based on signals about the quality of their journalism.
>
> ...The change was part of the 'break glass' plans Facebook had spent months developing for the aftermath of a contested election.[196]

---

194   Greenwald, Glenn. "Congress Escalates Pressure on Tech Giants to Censor More, Threatening the First Amendment." Substack, February 20, 2021, https://greenwald.substack.com/p/congress-escalates-pressure-on-tech.

195   Taibbi, Matt. "Capsule Summaries of all Twitter Files Threads to Date, With Links and a Glossary." Substack, January 4, 2023, https://taibbi.substack.com/p/capsule-summaries-of-all-twitter.

196   Roose, Kevin, and Sheera Frenkel. "Facebook Struggles to Balance Civility and Growth." *New York Times,* November 24, 2020, https://www.nytimes.com/2020/11/24/technology/facebook-election-misinformation.html.

According to unnamed sources quoted by the *Times*, the tools Facebook developed mostly affect right-leaning content, and they'd be making permanent some information control mechanisms designed solely for the 2020 election.

That's been made evident, given the experiences of high-profile conservatives and libertarians such as Mark Levin, Dan Bongino, Candace Owens, and John Stossel. Even when the fact-checkers don't have the facts on their side, they've learned to nitpick in a way to justify the censorship they desire.

In one case, Levin posted an article headlined, "'America is dead'— Joe Biden actually said this at his Iowa rally," days before the 2020 election, and the post was slapped with a fact-check by Facebook, attaching a PolitiFact article for supposed context.[197]

The PolitiFact article gives context that Biden was actually talking about the coronavirus death toll, not the death of the country. This would be much-needed context if it wasn't the case that the article Levin linked to correctly quotes Biden as speaking about COVID-19, making this fact-check completely pointless.[198]

In other words, PolitiFact effectively "fact-checked" a headline they didn't like, even though the contents of the fact-check were already clarified in the article they were fact-checking.

In another case, in September 2020, Levin was flagged for sharing a post from The Federalist's Sean Davis that read: "BREAKING: On July 26, 2016, U.S. intel authorities learned that Russian intel knew of Hillary Clinton's plans to cook up a scandal alleging that Trump was working with Russia. Obama was personally briefed on Russia's knowledge of Clinton's plans."[199]

The report was based on a letter from Director of National Intelligence John Ratcliffe from September 29, 2020. In that letter, Ratcliffe notes that the information *could* be Russian disinformation and that the

---

197   "'America Is Dead' – Joe Biden Actually Said This at His Iowa Rally." The Right Scoop, October 30, 2020, https://therightscoop.com/america-is-dead-joe-biden-actually-said-this-his-iowa-rally/.

198   O'Rourke, Ciara. "No, Joe Biden didn't say America is dead." PolitiFact, October 31, 2020, https://www.politifact.com/factchecks/2020/oct/31/blog-posting/no-joe-biden-didnt-say-america-dead/.

199   Davis, Sean. September 29, 2020, http://web.archive.org/web/20201003012110/https://twitter.com/seanmdav/status/1311023271400402947.

claims regarding Hillary Clinton are alleged.[200] However, on the same day, Ratcliffe later issued a statement clarifying that "this is not Russian disinformation and has not been assessed as such by the Intelligence Community."

Lead Stories' Alan Duke took issue with Davis and wrote up a fact-check that only cites a single source. That single source is a tweet from Rachel Cohen, a communications director for Democrat senator Mark Warner. In the tweet, Cohen said that the letter is Russian disinformation,[201] and Duke just takes their word for it. No level of evidence is too flimsy when it tells the fact-checker what they want to hear.

Duke eventually updated the article with Ratcliffe's denial that the claim was Russian disinformation, but left his analysis unchanged, with the headline still reading "DNI Letter On Russian Intel From July 2016 Does NOT Show 'Russia Hoax' Was 'Hillary's Plan.'" Clinton's former campaign manager Robby Mook testified in the 2022 trial of Michael Sussmann mentioned earlier that she approved her campaign's plans to spread a bogus claim that there was a backchannel between Trump Tower and the Russian bank Alfa Bank. We also now know for certain that on July 28, 2016, then–CIA director John Brennan briefed then-president Obama on Hillary Clinton's plan to tie Trump to Russia as "a means of distracting the public from her use of a private email server."[202]

So desperate are the fact-checkers to dispel any narrative damaging to the Democrat establishment that they'll even fact-check things that haven't happened yet.

When Donald Trump suggested in a May 2020 tweet that California's mail-in ballots would be "substantially fraudulent," Twitter flagged the post for containing "potentially misleading information about voting

---

200   Ratcliffe, John. "Letter to Sen. Graham Declassification of FBI's Crossfire Hurricane Investigations." Committee on Judiciary, September 29, 2020, https://www.judiciary.senate.gov/imo/media/doc/09-29-20_Letter%20 to%20Sen.%20Graham_Declassification%20of%20FBI's%20Crossfire%20 Hurricane%20Investigations_20-00912_U_SIGNED-FINAL.pdf.

201   Duke, Alan. "Fact Check: DNI Letter on Russian Intel from July 2016 Does NOT Show 'Russia Hoax' Was 'Hillary's Plan.'" Lead Stories LLC, September 29, 2020, https://leadstories.com/hoax-alert/2020/09/fact-check-dni-letter-on-russian-intel-from-july-2016-does-not-show-russia-hoax-was-hillarys-plan.html.

202   Turley, Jonathan. "How the Sussmann trial revealed Hillary Clinton's role in the Alfa Bank scandal." The Hill, May 21, 2022, https://thehill.com/opinion/judiciary/3496659-how-the-sussmann-trial-revealed-hillary-clintons-role-in-the-alfa-bank-scandal/.

processes and have been labeled to provide additional context around mail-in ballots."[203]

Trump's tweet read, "There is NO WAY (ZERO!) that Mail-in ballots will be anything less than substantially fraudulent. Mail boxes will be robbed, ballots will be forged & even illegally printed out & fraudulently signed. The Governor of California is sending Ballots to millions of people, anyone." He added that anyone "living in the state, no matter who they are or how they got there, will get one. That will be followed up with professions telling all of those people, many of whom have never even thought of voting before, how, and for whom, to vote. This will be a Rigged Election. No way!"

Even though it's impossible to fact-check something that hasn't yet happened, Twitter's fact-checkers gave it a try and assured us that "there is no evidence that mail-in ballots are linked to voter fraud." That came just after the U.S. government sent millions of stimulus checks to dead people, but pondering that they'd similarly drop the ball on mail-in ballots was too much for the fact-checkers.

Underneath Trump's tweet, Twitter added a disclaimer that reads: "Get the facts about mail-in ballots." The disclaimer claims, "Trump falsely claimed that mail-in ballots would lead to 'a Rigged Election.' However, fact-checkers say there is no evidence that mail-in ballots are linked to voter fraud" and links to articles from the *Washington Post*, CNN, and NBC calling Trump's claim "unsubstantiated"—because they say so, and we'll have to take their word for it.

The "fact-checks" are based on conflating mail-in voting with absentee voting (which the fact-checkers are arguing isn't susceptible to fraud). As the *Wall Street Journal*'s Dustin Volz wrote on Twitter: "There was an error in Twitter's fact check of Trump's vote-by-mail tweets, underscoring the challenge social media platforms face trying to arbitrate truth. It was corrected after an elections professional notified the company (and me) about the mistake."[204]

Not only was Twitter comparing two different types of voting, the same day of that botched fact-check, news broke that a West Virginia USPS employee was charged with attempted absentee ballot application

203   White, Chris. "Twitter Fact-Checks Trump For The First Time After He Claims Mail-In Ballots Will Be 'Fraudulent.'" The Daily Caller, May 26, 2020, https://dailycaller.com/2020/05/26/donald-trump-twitter-fact-check-mail-ballot/.

204   Volz, Dustin. May 26, 2020, https://twitter.com/dnvolz/status/1265490148613066753.

fraud.[205] Which is odd, because the fact-checkers declared mere hours earlier that such behavior was impossible.

Seemingly nothing is exempt from a fact-check. When Hillsdale College began advertising a course through Facebook on Executive Director of the World Economic Forum Klaus Schwab and the Great Reset, a "false information" tag was added to their advertisement, displaying a fact-checking reading, quite amusingly, "FACT CHECK: Fact Check: 'The Great Reset' Is NOT A Secret Plan Masterminded By Global Elites To Limit Freedoms And Push Radical Policies."[206] They're technically right in that it's not secret—as the man spearheading it, Klaus Schwab literally has published a book called *The Great Reset*.

The Media Research Center (MRC) has been tracking censorship through its "CensorTrack" data, and found that across seven Big Tech platforms (Facebook, Twitter, YouTube, Instagram, TikTok, LinkedIn, and Spotify), there were over 144 million times flagged that social media users had information hidden from them in just the first quarter of 2022.[207]

They call this "secondhand censorship," which they define as the number of times that users on social media have information blocked from them. In the case of Trump being banned from Twitter, his ninety million followers missed out on his average of eighteen daily posts, or secondhand censorship of over 1.6 billion times.[208]

The biggest censors, according to its data, are Facebook, YouTube, and Twitter.

The bar for what's censorable is on the floor. Among the cases the MRC documented is conservative host Matt Walsh being suspended from Twitter for tweeting the true statement that the greatest female Jeopardy champion, best female college swimmer, and first four-star admiral in the U.S. public health service are men. On transgender-related issues, the

---

205 "West Virginia mail carrier charged with attempted absentee ballot application fraud." WHSV 3, May 26, 2020, https://www.whsv.com/content/news/Pendleton-County-mail-carrier-charged-with-altering-absentee-ballot-requests-570777221.html.

206 Hayward, Steven. "The 'Fact Checkers' Come for Hillsdale." Powerline, August 17, 2022, https://www.powerlineblog.com/archives/2022/08/the-fact-checkers-come-for-hillsdale.php.

207 Bradley, Brian, and Gabriele Pariseau. "The Secondhand Censorship Effect: The Real Impact of Big Tech's Thought-Policing." NewsBusters, July 20, 2022, https://www.newsbusters.org/blogs/free-speech/brian-bradley/2022/07/20/secondhand-censorship-effect-real-impact-big-techs.

208 Ibid.

MRC noted twenty-two cases of notable figures being censored, resulting in nearly twelve million cases of secondhand censorship.[209]

Anything that went counter to the narrative on COVID-19 was also quickly censored. YouTube kicked Dan Bongino off for questioning the efficacy of masks by quoting studies casting doubt on them. His Facebook page has also been flagged for sharing similar information, resulting in secondhand censorship affecting users nearly 1.8 million times in just the first quarter of 2022.[210] As is evident in many of the "fact-checks" that his page has been slapped with, the censors' conclusion was determined before their reasoning.

Posts from the Dan Bongino Facebook page routinely dominate the list of the most shared posts on the platform and, as such, have made him a prime target for the fact-checkers whose mission is to prevent the proliferation of conservative narratives. PolitiFact's CEO Angie Drobnic Holan even singled Bongino out for blame in an article complaining about how PolitiFact reporters face "online harassment," which in this context means people making fun of their laughable fact-checks when they're mocked and exposed. In doing so, she comes just short of admitting that they specifically target his page for faux fact-checks.[211]

In some cases, posts are flagged for claims they didn't even make.

Bongino posted a video to his page in May 2022 where he reacted to a video of Pfizer's CEO talking about microchips in pills that was recorded in 2018. Bongino made it clear that the video was years old and that CEO Albert Bourla was speaking about a drug for schizophrenia. In the video, Bourla talks at a World Economic Forum event about how they have an FDA-approved drug that contains a digital sensor that can track whether people are taking their medicine.

While many others shared the clip of Bourla's comments online and gave incorrect context, trying to make it seem like he was talking about Pfizer's COVID-19 antiviral pill, Bongino didn't present it as such and explicitly stated, "Now to be clear, this clip is often misconstrued and labeled wrong. [Bourla is] not talking about a COVID pill, he's talking about a schizophrenia pill. What I'm trying to tell you is…they can invent a pill that does that if they choose—I put that clip in there to

---

209   Ibid.

210   Ibid.

211   Holan, Angie Drobnic. "PolitiFact reporters face online harassment; we keep fact-checking anyway." PolitiFact, June 13, 2022, https://www.politifact.com/article/2022/jun/13/politifact-reporters-face-online-harassment-we-kee/.

show you that the technology is out there if something were to happen in the future more severe than monkeypox or COVID, the technology is out there and being developed to implement this surveillance future where these pills can actually talk back."

And despite that, the video was slapped with a fact-check by Facebook from FactCheck.org claiming the video was "missing context." "FDA-Approved 'Electronic Pill' Isn't Evidence That COVID-19 Vaccine 'Microchip' Conspiracy Is 'Proven,'" read the article headline that in no way contradicts the contents of the video.[212]

Among the most ridiculous cases where Bongino's posts were branded false was one article headlined, "Pelosi Admits Dems Have Been Trying to Impeach Trump for the Last 'Two and a Half Years.'"[213] The article quoted Pelosi directly and even includes video of her saying as much, but because she hasn't literally been carrying out an impeachment process for the past two and a half years, the claim was rated false.

On another occasion, Bongino's page was fact-checked by Lead Stories after linking to an article reporting on Nancy Pelosi quoting a National Counterintelligence and Security Center report that concluded China would rather Biden win the 2020 U.S. presidential election.[214]

The report stated: "We assess that China prefers that President Trump—whom Beijing sees as unpredictable—does not win reelection. China has been expanding its influence efforts ahead of November 2020 to shape the policy environment in the United States, pressure political figures it views as opposed to China's interests, and deflect and counter criticism of China."[215]

Nancy Pelosi quoted the report to CNN's Dana Bash, telling her, "The Chinese…what they said is [that] China would prefer [Biden]. Whether

212   Dan Bongino Show Clips. "Latest 'Fact-Check' on My Page Proves Fakebook Has Hit Rock Bottom." Rumble, May 27, 2022, https://rumble.com/v16btw1-latest-fact-check-on-my-page-proves-fakebook-has-hit-rock-bottom.html?mref=16emn&mrefc=93.

213   Team Bongino. "Pelosi Admits Dems Have Been Trying to Impeach Trump for the Last 'Two and a Half Years.'" Bongino, December 12, 2019, https://bongino.com/pelosi-admits-dems-have-been-trying-to-impeach-trump-for-the-last-two-and-a-half-years/.

214   Frankel, Jeremy. "Pelosi Says the Quiet Part Out Loud: 'China Would Prefer Joe Biden.'" Bongino, August 10, 2020, https://bongino.com/pelosi-says-the-quiet-part-out-loud-china-would-prefer-joe-biden.

215   Marquardt, Alex, et al. "Intelligence community's top election official: China and Iran don't want Trump to win reelection, Russia working to 'denigrate' Biden. CNN, August 8, 2020, https://edition.cnn.com/2020/08/07/politics/2020-election-russia-china-iran/index.html.

they do, that is their conclusion. That they would prefer Joe Biden."[216] In response to this setup, Lead Stories fact-checker Sarah Thompson grasps at straws, arguing that just because China wants Trump to lose doesn't mean they want Biden to win. Does she think China was hoping the libertarian candidate would finally make a showing?[217]

Creators Fight Back with Lawsuits—Fact-Checkers Cave

John Stossel found himself at the whims of the fact-checkers when he published video reports challenging the dominant narrative on issues pertaining to climate change.

Stossel's first run-in with the fact-checkers came after he posted a video called "Government Funded Fires," where he argued that forest management and excessive regulation are bigger causes of wildfires than climate change. When California governor Gavin Newsom's state was experiencing massive wildfires in 2020, Newsom blamed climate change.

In his report, Stossel pointed out that well-managed forests that conduct prescribed burns don't have the same out-of-control fires.

But the fact-checkers didn't agree, with one fact-checker called Climate Feedback labeling Stossel's claims "misleading."

Specifically, they incorrectly quote Stossel as stating, "Forest fires are caused by poor management. Not by climate change"[218]—but that's not even what Stossel said. He said poor management, such as not performing prescribed burning, was a greater variable than climate change and, at one point, states in the video, "Climate change has made things worse, California has warmed three degrees over fifty years."[219] The fact-checkers couldn't even quote him correctly, much less rebut him.

Stossel emailed Climate Feedback's editor Nikki Forrester to appeal the fact-check, but she didn't respond. However, two of the three scien-

216   Staff Writer. "WATCH: Pelosi Confirms 'China Would Prefer Joe Biden.'" The National Pulse, August 9, 2020, https://thenationalpulse.com/2020/08/09/china-prefers-biden/.

217   Thompson, Sarah. "Fact Check: Nancy Pelosi Did NOT 'Confirm China Would Prefer Joe Biden.'" Lead Stories, August 11, 2020, https://leadstories.com/hoax-alert/2020/08/fact-check-nancy-pelosi-did-not-confirm-china-would-prefer-joe-biden.html.

218   Forrester, Nikki. "Climate change, forest management and several other causes contribute to wildfire severity and total area burned in the western United States." Climate Feedback, September 16, 2020, https://climatefeedback.org/claimreview/climate-change-forest-management-and-several-other-causes-contribute-to-wildfire-severity-and-total-area-burned-in-the-western-united-states/.

219   "Government Fueled Fires." Stossel in the Classroom, November 2, 2020, https://stosselintheclassroom.org/government-fueled-fires/.

tists listed as "reviewers" of Stossel's claim on Climate Feedback's article did, and it further revealed just how fraudulent the fact-checking process is.[220]

One of the men listed as a "reviewer" was Swansea University professor Stefan Doerr, who told Stossel he never even watched his video in question. "If this is implying that we have reviewed the video, this is clearly wrong. There is something wrong with the system," he told Stossel, adding that the video was probably flagged solely because Stossel interviewed Michael Shellenberger (who climate alarmists tend to dislike) in it.

Another Climate Feedback reviewer, Director of Climate and Energy at the Breakthrough Institute Zeke Hausfather, told Stossel that he hadn't seen the video either. "I certainly did not write a Climate Feedback piece reviewing your statement."

After watching the video, Hausfather told Stossel he "didn't necessarily think" Climate Feedback's rating was accurate, explaining, "While there's plenty of debate on how much to emphasize forest management vs. climate change, your piece clearly discussed that both were at fault here."

After Stossel spoke to those two reviewers, Climate Feedback's editor finally responded to him with an email telling him he could appeal the fact-check, which he did, and then they still refused to revise it. The experts cited to fact-check Stossel didn't even agree with the fact-check's conclusions, yet Science Feedback stood by their work.

Just over a year after Stossel published his video, Governor Newsom signed legislation to promote more prescribed burning in the state.[221]

Stossel wasn't alone here. Any "contrarian" information in debates related to science, a field dependent on debate to advance, is censored. Other examples include the following:

- Journalist John Tierney had an article he wrote for *City Journal* flagged where he argued that masking children can be harmful and cited complaints from over ten thousand parents, which he acknowledged isn't a random sample. The post was dinged by Science Feedback, who said the post was

---

220   "Fake Fact-Checking." Stossel TV, October 7, 2020, https://www.johnstossel.com/fake-fact-checking/.

221   Smith, Hayley. "Newsom signs fire law paving way for more prescribed burns." *Los Angeles Times,* October 7, 2021, https://www.latimes.com/california/story/2021-10-07/newsom-signs-fire-law-paving-way-for-more-prescribed-burns.

"partly false" because the study wasn't a random sample. The study later passed peer review.[222]

– Science Feedback rated the COVID-19 lab leak theory "incorrect" in February 2020, arguing that "scientific evidence indicates virus that causes COVID-19 infection is of natural origin, not the result of human engineering," as if it would even remotely be possible to know such a thing less than three months after we even became aware of what COVID-19 was.[223]

– Environmentalist Michael Shellenberger was flagged for arguing that climate change won't bring about the apocalypse and that we're not in a "sixth mass extinction." Climate Feedback said he was incorrect, citing a study from the Intergovernmental Science-Policy Platform on Biodiversity and Ecosystem Services (IPBES), which they say found the planet is being "pushed…towards a sixth mass species extinction." But a chair of IPBES told Shellenberger, "We don't say that [we're in a sixth great extinction]." A mass extinction would require 50 percent to 75 percent of all species to go extinct.[224]

– Bjørn Lomborg, known as the "skeptical environmentalist," was censored for noting that rising temperatures save net lives because cold weather kills more people than warm weather. Lomborg pointed to statistics showing that since 1990 heat deaths have remained flat while deaths from cold have nearly been cut in half. Science Feedback rated the claim "unsupported."

222 Tierney, John. "This Article Is 'Partly False.'" *City Journal,* May 17, 2021, https://www.city-journal.org/facebook-and-its-fact-checkers-spread-misinformation.

223 Teoh, Flora. "Scientific evidence indicates virus that causes COVID-19 infection is of natural origin, not the result of human engineering." Science Feedback, March 5, 2020, https://sciencefeedback.co/claimreview/scientific-evidence-indicates-virus-that-causes-covid-19-infection-is-of-natural-origin-not-the-result-of-human-engineering/.

224 "Climate Feedback Unscientifically Confuses 'Disasters' & Weather Events & Endorses Pseudoscientific Claim That We Are in a 'Sixth Mass Extinction.'" Environmental Progress, July 6, 2020, https://environmentalprogress.org/big-news/2020/7/6/climate-feedback-unscientifically-confuses-disasters-amp-weather-events-amp-endorses-pseudoscientific-claim-that-we-are-in-a-sixth-mass-extinction.

Reason Magazine's Robby Soave also had a dust-up with the fact-checkers at Science Feedback, who flagged him only to later admit that he was right.

Soave wrote an article titled "The Study That Convinced the CDC To Support Mask Mandates in Schools Is Junk Science," which discredited a CDC report claiming that countries without school mask mandates had 3.5 times more COVID-19 outbreaks than counties without them. CDC director Rochelle Walensky became fond of quoting the "3.5 times" figure in the media.

Soave's article was based largely on one authored by David Zweig in *The Atlantic,* and he summarizes Zweig's arguments that the study had numerous flaws, such as including many schools in its data set that weren't even open during the time the study was examining. It also didn't control for vaccination status, defined an "outbreak" as two or more cases, and didn't say if the transmission originated at school, amid other issues. He also quoted some scientists who do believe masks work and think that they may be needed in schools in certain scenarios but nonetheless found the CDC's study to be completely meaningless due to its many flaws.[225]

When Soave's article was posted to Facebook, it was flagged with the declaration that it contains "false information checked by independent fact-checkers." Attached was an article by Science Feedback titled "Multiple scientific studies suggest that masking can help limit transmission of SARS-CoV-2 in schools, contrary to claim in Federalist article."[226]

The attached "fact-check" was written in response to an article from The Federalist, not Soave's, and it "fact-checks" a claim Soave's article never made. Nothing in the Scientific Feedback article contradicts a single thing Soave said, which was specific to mask *mandates,* not the efficacy of masks themselves. Once again, the fact-checkers aren't even fact-checking what is being claimed.

Despite Zweig's article at *The Atlantic* (known as a left-wing publication) sharing the same findings the libertarian *Reason* and conserva-

---

225 Soave, Robby. "The Study That Convinced the CDC to Support Mask Mandates in Schools Is Junk Science." *Reason Magazine,* December 17, 2021, https://reason.com/2021/12/17/study-masks-in-schools-junk-science-cdc-walensky/.

226 Freedhoff, Yoni. "Multiple scientific studies suggest that masking can help limit transmission of SARS-CoV-2 in schools, contrary to claim in Federalist article." Science Feedback, August 27, 2021, https://sciencefeedback.co/claimreview/multiple-scientific-studies-suggest-that-masking-can-help-limit-transmission-of-sars-cov-2-in-schools-contrary-to-claim-in-federalist-ron-desantis/.

tive Federalist did, the former didn't get flagged by Science Feedback and Facebook. This fact-check being mismatched (it was used to flag an article from *Reason* but was written to respond to an article from The Federalist) indicates that it was an automatic fact-check, so reveals bias that a left-wing publication like *The Atlantic* wouldn't get picked up by the algorithm but a right-leaning outlet making an identical claim would.

Soave eventually contacted both Facebook and Science Feedback, the latter of which admitted that the article was flagged erroneously, and the "false information" label was removed. "We have taken another look at the Reason article and confirm that the rating was applied in error to this article," they wrote. "The flag has been removed. We apologize for the mistake."

But they'll do it again, and again.

Since these bogus "fact-checks" restrict how often his posts are seen by his followers and potentially damage his reputation, Stossel decided to sue Facebook. Facebook's lawyers defended themselves by admitting its fact-check labels count as mere opinion.

Facebook's lawyers argued that Climate Feedback isn't necessarily their responsibility, and that "the labels themselves are neither false nor defamatory; *to the contrary, they constitute protected opinion* [emphasis mine]."[227]

Stossel's lawsuit highlighted another questionable fact-check from Climate Feedback in response to a video he did on climate alarmism that expressed skepticism over claims that hurricanes are getting stronger, that sea level rise poses a "catastrophic" threat, and that humans will be unable to "cope with the fallout."[228]

In one part of the video, Stossel talks about a panel discussion that included a professor of climatology, a former president of the American Association of State Climatologists, and an astrophysicist. The panel acknowledged that sea levels were rising, shared data that sea levels were rising, and discussed how carbon dioxide can also be a beneficial fuel for crops. Stossel narrates that many scientists on the "climate alarmist" side were invited to join the panel discussion, but none came. Stossel concludes the video, "It's confusing when there are so many serious people

---

227 "Stossel V. Meta Platforms Inc. Et Al., 5:2021cv07385, N.D. Cal. (2022)." 26 July 2022, https://unicourt.com/case/pc-db5-stossel-v-facebook-inc-et-al-1026537.

228 "Stossel V. Meta Platforms Inc. Et Al., 5:2021cv07385 , N.D. Cal. (2022)." http://climatecasechart.com/wp-content/uploads/sites/16/case-documents/2021/20210922_docket-521-cv-07385_complaint-1.pdf.

[on the other side of the debate] who are so worried. I wish there was a real debate. Why won't the other side debate?"[229]

After being shared on Facebook, Stossel's video was slapped with a "Partly False Information" warning and an accompanying Climate Feedback article was attached to it titled "Video promoted by John Stossel for Earth Day relies on incorrect and misleading claims about climate change."[230]

The article doesn't identify any falsehoods in Stossel's reporting and instead criticizes his "reasoning" and "overall scientific credibility."

One scientist on the panel in Stossel's video states that "[sea levels have] been rising for approximately 20,000 years"—a fact that Stossel's lawsuit notes is backed up by Climate Feedback's own data.

Instead of saying the claim is false, Science Feedback targets "perceived implications" and argues the true statement is "imprecise and misleading, as it implies sea levels have continued rising since then and current sea level rise is just a continuation of past natural fluctuations."

One of the scientists who analyzed the video for Climate Feedback confirmed as much. Per the lawsuit:

> In the interview, Stossel expressed his frustration with being labeled as "partly false" for reciting true facts, and asked what was wrong with stating, for example, that there has been no significant observed trends in hurricane strength over the past century.
>
> In response, [the scientist] Brown opined "I think it's wrong that you were criticized for saying that. The IPCC [Intergovernmental Panel on Climate Change], they don't claim that [hurricanes] are increasing, they don't claim that droughts are increasing, they don't claim that floods are increasing." When Stossel again asked Brown why Defendants had labeled the Alarmism Video "partly false," Brown stated

229   "Are We Doomed?" Stossel in the Classroom, January 29, 2020,
       https://stosselintheclassroom.org/are-we-doomed/.
230   Vincent, Emmanuel. "Video promoted by John Stossel for Earth Day relies on
       incorrect and misleading claims about climate change." Climate Feedback, April
       21, 2021, https://climatefeedback.org/evaluation/video-promoted-by-john-stossel-
       for-earth-day-relies-on-incorrect-and-misleading-claims-about-climate-change/.

"[y]ou get…flagged for downplaying that [climate change is] a problem at all…it's a tonal thing, I guess."

Following the interview, Brown emailed Stossel stating that "[t]he problem is the omission of contextual information rather than specific 'facts' being 'wrong'."[231]

The lawsuit cites data finding that Climate Feedback performs negative fact-checks of content by people stating that climate change is a manageable problem three times more often than they perform negative fact-checks on climate alarmists. They argue, as I do, that the "fact-checking" process is just to justify censorship:

Defendants' "fact-check" process is nothing more than a pretext used by Defendants to defame users with impunity, particularly when Defendants disagree with the scientific opinions expressed in user content. Often, the pretext appears to be invoked based on implicit or explicit viewpoint biases.[232]

And thanks to this lawsuit, we know that they are, in their own words, truly just opinion checkers.

Similar to Stossel's case, fighting back with a lawsuit scored Candace Owens a victory in exposing the poor work of the fact-checkers after PolitiFact flagged a video of hers as false.

Candace streamed a video to her Facebook page on November 13, 2020, where she explained how Biden is not president-elect until the congressional certification of votes cast by the Electoral College.

"Joe Biden is literally and legally not the President-elect. So why is the media pretending he is?" Owens captioned the video.

While the U.S. Constitution doesn't explicitly state a date for when one becomes president-elect, it's widely assumed that it's after the certification of votes (on January 6), in accordance with the Twelfth Amendment.

In the video, she states, "Joe Biden is not the president elect. This information cannot be fact-checked because this is the truth. They cannot take that off, they cannot censor that. It is a fact."

---

231   "Stossel V. Meta Platforms Inc. Et Al., 5:2021cv07385 , N.D. Cal. (2022)." http://climatecasechart.com/wp-content/uploads/sites/16/case-documents/2021/20210922_docket-521-cv-07385_complaint-1.pdf.
232   Ibid.

And it is the truth, but PolitiFact still rated her claim "False," leading to Facebook restricting the video and prompting legal action from Owens.

Granted, nearly everyone uses the term "president elect" once a winner is announced in a presidential election, as absent an act of God, that person always goes on to become president. But Owens is still correct here, and it didn't take long for PolitiFact to cave, issue a correction, and retract their fact-check.

On November 25, PolitiFact announced they would be revising their ruling. "Correction: PolitiFact originally labeled this video false in our capacity as a third-party fact-checker for Facebook," PolitiFact said. "On Nov. 20, an appeal to that decision was made on behalf of Ms. Owens. PolitiFact approved the appeal on Nov. 20, determined that a correction was appropriate, and removed the false rating."[233]

When they cave that fast, how much confidence could they possibly have had in their own analysis to begin with?

ELON MUSK AND THE FUTURE OF FACT-CHECKING

Since finishing the first draft of this book, Elon Musk completed his acquisition of Twitter, among the consequences of which included a complete overhaul of the fact-checking process on the platform.

In mid-2021 Twitter previously rolled out a program called "Birdwatch," which it purported to be a "community based approach" for fact-checking. On paper, the system would work by allowing users to identify information they believe to be misleading, and then provide additional commentary and sources. That additional commentary would be attached to the tweet it was written in response to as a sort of "warning label," and then users can vote on if it's helpful context, and if users decide it isn't, it'll be removed.

It was a novel idea, and if this sort of "wisdom of the crowds" approach to fact-checking were applied without bias, it should, in theory, lead to the most accurate fact-checking. After all, any attempt at inserting political bias would have to withstand criticism from potentially millions of others who know better. This would also be a perfect way to fact-check fact-checking publications, as their obviously bogus spin would have to

---

233   Owens, Candace. November 26, 2020, https://www.facebook.com/politifact/
        posts/pfbid028khmYJ5CDshieiuP7kYazRF7s36779uJzkRWPHRbsyv84Nh
        Uuh4VcYQ8qqT7aYUpl.

withstand scrutiny for once and would lose their status as the "final say" on truth, at least on one platform. In any world with fact-checkers, the question of "who fact-checks the fact-checkers" will always remain, and this approach answers that question with "everyone."

Bias and unequal enforcement of the rules initially prevented this from happening, and the Birdwatch feature was never used to correct lies and errors beneficial to the left.

Only after the Musk takeover was the program actually allowed to flourish, and it showed what an equal platform for fact-checking looks like.

When the White House boasted that Social Security would be seeing its largest increase in 10 years, and credited Biden for that, a fact-check was attached to the tweet pointing out that the record increase is because benefits are linked to inflation, and have been since 1972.

The White House ✔
@WhiteHouse

•••

Seniors are getting the biggest increase in their Social Security checks in 10 years through President Biden's leadership.

> 🔘 Readers added context they thought people might want to know
>
> Seniors will receive a large Social Security benefit increase due to the annual cost of living adjustment, which is based on the inflation rate. President Nixon in 1972 signed into law automatic benefit adjustments tied to the Consumer Price Index. Pub. L. No. 92-336 (1972).
> ssa.gov/history/1972am...
>
> ---
>
> Do you find this helpful?   (Rate it)

Context is written by people who use Twitter, and appears when rated helpful by others. Find out more.

4:45 PM · Nov 1, 2022 · The White House

When Biden boasted of manufacturing job gains "on my watch," a note was attached pointing out that he was conflating "regaining lost jobs with creation of new jobs that never existed before."

Joe Biden ✔ **@JoeBiden · 21h** •••

⚑ **United States government official**

We lost over 180,000 manufacturing jobs under the last guy.

We've created 700,000 manufacturing jobs on my watch.

> ◎ **Readers added context they thought people might want to know**
>
> The Tweet is conflating regaining lost jobs with creation of new jobs that never existed before.
>
> washingtonpost.com/politics/2022/...
>
> ---
>
> Do you find this helpful?   ⟨ **Rate it** ⟩

Context is written by people who use Twitter, and appears when rated helpful by others. Find out more.

When Biden pointed to fifty-five corporations that he said made a combined $40 billion and paid no federal income taxes, and claimed that his "Inflation Reduction Act" would end this, a note was attached explaining that his legislation would only lead to fourteen of those fifty-five companies paying more in taxes.

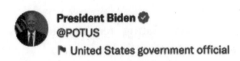

President Biden ✔
@POTUS
⚑ United States government official

Let me give you the facts.

In 2020, 55 corporations made $40 billion. And they paid zero in federal taxes.

My Inflation Reduction Act puts an end to this.

◎ **Readers added context they thought people might want to know**

The Inflation Reduction Act imposed a minimum tax on corporations with average pre-tax earnings greater than $1 billion.

reuters.com/markets/us/how...

crsreports.congress.gov/product/pdf/IF...

Out of the 55 corporations the tweet references, only 14 had earnings greater than $1 billion and would be eligible under Biden's tax law.

washingtonpost.com/politics/2021/...

itep.org/55-profitable-...

Do you find this helpful?   (Rate it)

Context is written by people who use Twitter, and appears when rated helpful by others. Find out more.

And after Biden tried to claim credit for capping insulin prices at $35 a month, a note was attached pointing out that this is only for people on Medicare, and wouldn't even apply to seniors on private insurance.

President Biden ✅
@POTUS
⚑ United States government official
     •••

Some seniors pay $400 a month for insulin. It's ridiculous.

Thanks to the Inflation Reduction Act, we're capping that cost at $35 a month.

◎ **Readers added context they thought people might want to know**

While the Inflation Reduction Act capped insulin costs at $35 for individuals on Medicare, it did not cap costs for seniors on private insurance or anyone under the age of 65.

wfyi.org/news/articles/...

Out of the 8.4 million Americans who take insulin, only 3.3 million are covered by Medicare.

marketwatch.com/story/insulin-...

Do you find this helpful?   (**Rate it**)

Context is written by people who use Twitter, and appears when rated helpful by others. Find out more.

7:25 PM · Oct 29, 2022 · The White House

    The system was hardly being weaponized against them. Musk himself has been fact-checked by the feature on multiple occasions, and countless Republican officials have been dinged by the system too. All that changed is that the rules applied to everyone.

    There is no perfect method of fact-checking since everyone is prone to error, but this approach to fact-checking has the potential to be the least error prone. And as you're about to read, no one is more prone to error than the fact-checkers.

PART 2

FACT-CHECKING THE FACT-CHECKERS

BRIEF BLUNDERS

For as deceptive as the fact-checkers usually are, sometimes their errors aren't from malice but just plain incompetence.

NOT ALL—JUST MOST: THE CASE OF DEMOCRAT CONTROL OF AMERICA'S MOST VIOLENT CITIES

The *Washington Post*'s Philip Bump decided to try to fact-check a statement from Donald Trump that "you hear about certain places like Chicago and you hear about what's going on in Detroit and other—other cities, all Democrat run. Every one of them is Democrat run. Twenty out of 20. The 20 worst, the 20 most dangerous are Democrat run."[234]

Bump responded with two charts, with one showing overall violent crimes in America's twenty most dangerous cities, and pointed out that two of them are run by Independents and one is run by a Republican.

Those figures are useless however, as crime figures have to be adjusted for population. In a second chart (pictured directly above), Bump's own data shows that on a per capita basis, none of the twenty most violent cities were run by Republicans (and nineteen, or 95 percent, are run by Democrats).

It also must be noted that there was a zero percent chance that the mayors of Springfield, Missouri, or San Antonio, Texas, were going to be a Republican or Democrat because both cities have nonpartisan mayoral elections. Despite that, the *Post* article is titled, "Trump keeps claiming that the most dangerous cities in America are all run by Democrats. They aren't." But in 100 percent of cities with partisan mayors, they are.

---

234 Bump, Philip. "Trump keeps claiming that the most dangerous cities in America are all run by Democrats. They aren't." *Washington Post*, June 25, 2020, https://www.washingtonpost.com/politics/2020/06/25/trump-keeps-claiming-that-most-dangerous-cities-america-are-all-run-by-democrats-they-arent/.

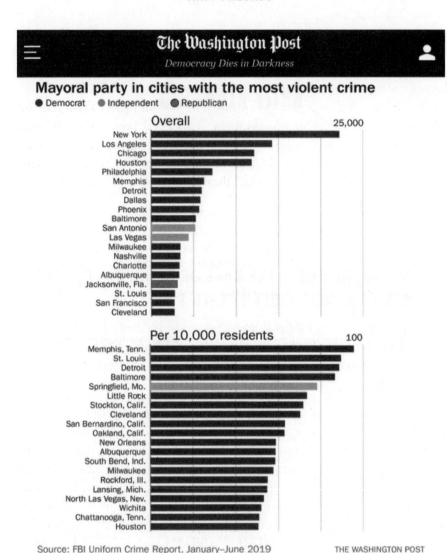

The Washington Post
Democracy Dies in Darkness

Mayoral party in cities with the most violent crime

● Democrat ● Independent ● Republican

Overall — 25,000

New York
Los Angeles
Chicago
Houston
Philadelphia
Memphis
Detroit
Dallas
Phoenix
Baltimore
San Antonio
Las Vegas
Milwaukee
Nashville
Charlotte
Albuquerque
Jacksonville, Fla.
St. Louis
San Francisco
Cleveland

Per 10,000 residents — 100

Memphis, Tenn.
St. Louis
Detroit
Baltimore
Springfield, Mo.
Little Rock
Stockton, Calif.
Cleveland
San Bernardino, Calif.
Oakland, Calif.
New Orleans
Albuquerque
South Bend, Ind.
Milwaukee
Rockford, Ill.
Lansing, Mich.
North Las Vegas, Nev.
Wichita
Chattanooga, Tenn.
Houston

Source: FBI Uniform Crime Report, January–June 2019   THE WASHINGTON POST

POLITIFACT CONFUSES TWO GOVERNMENT AGENCIES WHILE ATTEMPTING TO DEFEND DR. FAUCI

PolitiFact attempted to correct a story, and, in the process, confused two different government agencies and fact-checked the wrong claim.

Writer and filmmaker Leighton Woodhouse caught the error, which was made when PolitiFact tried to correct a post on the White Coat Waste Project Facebook page. The project has the goal of ending taxpayer-funded animal experiments and recently ran an ad about Morgan Island in South Carolina, where lab monkeys are bred for the National Institutes of Health (NIH). The island is also known as "Monkey Island" because of that.[235]

PolitiFact's Facebook account jumped in the comments section on the ad to post a fact-check article from the Associated Press. "Dr. Anthony Fauci was not involved in the research on monkey's described here, which was conducted in a different division of the National Institutes of Health from the one in which Fauci works," they wrote, linking to the AP article.

 PolitiFact ✔ · Follow
Dr. Anthony Fauci was not involved in the research on monkeys described here, which was conducted in a different division of the National Institutes of Health from the one in which Fauci works, Associated Press fact-checkers found. https://apnews.com/article/fact-checking-151646750074

 Fauci had no involvement in study on monkey threat responses
apnews.com

The AP article, which was from October 2021, long before this White Coat Waste Project ad was even made, specifically addresses the claim that "Fauci's experiments include one that magnified terror in the brains of monkeys and subjected them to frightening stimuli," and concludes that "'Dr. Fauci, director of the National Institute of Allergy and Infectious Diseases (NIAID) is not involved and has never been involved in this study,' NIMH's press team said in an emailed statement. 'Additionally, the study was not funded by NIAID.'" (NIMH is the National Institute of Mental Health.)

But there was one glaring problem: The Associated Press' fact-check *had nothing to do with Monkey Island*.[236] It appears that the PolitiFact just saw the word "monkeys" in the headline, found a fact-check that con-

235 Litterst, Isabel. "SC congresswoman accuses national organization of testing on monkeys for research." WTGS, December 16, 2021, https://fox28media.com/news/local/sc-congresswoman-accuses-national-organization-of-testing-on-monkeys-for-research.

236 Swenson, Ali. "Fauci had no involvement in study on monkey threat responses." Associated Press, October 26, 2021, https://apnews.com/article/fact-checking-151646750074.

tained both the words "Fauci" and "monkeys," and assumed they were the same. The White Coat Waste Project never alleged involvement from the NIMH in the first place.

Woodhouse explained:

> PolitiFact "debunked" our ad by pointing to an article that disputed *an entirely different claim.* The AP article wasn't about the South Carolina island. The claims in our ad are accurate, demonstrable and not in dispute.
>
> This is one of many reasons why all the calls for social media monitoring for "disinformation" are short-sighted, ridiculous, and self-serving for those who call for it. The monitors aren't only plainly politically biased; they're also incompetent.[237]

After being caught with their pants down, PolitiFact revised their initial comment: "*EDIT: We previously commented on this post with unrelated information. We regret the error."

As for the initial claims about Monkey Island, journalist Cassandra Fairbanks looked into the story last year and received confirmation from NIAID of the story:

> The island has been managed for the National Institute of Allergy and Infectious Diseases by Charles River Laboratories, one of the largest suppliers of laboratory animals in the world, since 2007.
>
> "The island is currently owned by the South Carolina Department of Natural Resources and leased by Charles River Laboratories, Inc., as part of a contract with NIAID. The nonhuman primates raised on Morgan Island are owned by NIAID," NIAID confirmed in their email.
>
> According to federal spending databases, a total of $13.5 million of a potential $27.5 million contract has been given to Charles River Laboratories to maintain the monkey island colony since March 2018. A sizable chunk of those funds,

---

237 Woodhouse, Leighton. May 18, 2022, https://twitter.com/lwoodhouse/status/1527130440577867776.

$8.9 million, was paid by Dr. Fauci's division (NIAID) of the NIH.[238]

No wonder PolitiFact just gave up.

A POINTLESS FACT-CHECK OF TED CRUZ ON THE BIBLE WORD COUNT

Just as you saw how being 95 percent right will get you the liar's treatment from the *Washington Post*'s Philip Bump pages earlier, the *Post* also awards a sort of "true but who cares" rating for when people they don't like make true statements.

WaPo fact-checker Michelle Ye Hee Lee decided to fact-check a claim from Senator Ted Cruz, found that it was true, then decided that despite it being true, it doesn't matter that much.

Cruz had stated during a speech in 2015: "On tax reform, we, right now, have more words in the IRS code than there are in the Bible—not one of them as good." Lee concedes that "Cruz is correct on the comparison of the words in both texts. But"—and then nine hundred words later, she decides that "this is a nonsense fact, something that is technically correct but ultimately meaningless."

When John Nolte reached out to *WaPo*'s Kessler to ask if the *WaPo* had ever employed this kind of fact-check where they eschew a "nonsense fact" against a Democrat, which is just opinion, Kessler only replied that he disagreed that Lee's opinion reporting was opinion.[239]

SNOPES DEFENDS THEMSELVES AS "TRUE IN SPIRIT"

In 2018, Snopes spectacularly botched the fact-check of a viral meme of a photo of Donald Trump and GOP lawmakers following the House's vote to repeal Obamacare in 2017.

---

238 Fairbanks, Cassandra. "EXCLUSIVE: Fauci's NIAID Confirms They Own All Monkeys Bred on South Carolina Island to Be Tortured." TIMCAST, November 23, 2021, https://timcast.com/news/exclusive-faucis-niaid-confirms-they-own-all-monkeys-bred-on-south-carolina-island-to-be-tortured/.

239 Treacher, Jim. "'Fake but Accurate' Has a New Friend, Courtesy of WaPo: 'Nonsense Fact.'" The Daily Caller, March 13, 2015, https://dailycaller.com/2015/03/13/fake-but-accurate-has-a-new-friend-courtesy-of-wapo-nonsense-fact/.

In the image, thirty-four people pictured standing around Trump are marked with a red X over their face, with a caption claiming, "Everyone with an X has since been voted out of Congress." The meme was put together by progressive campaign strategist Nicholas Kitchel.

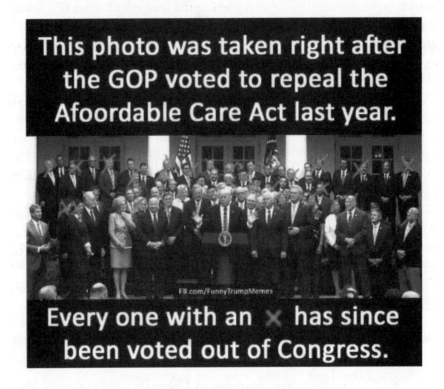

And it was laughably false.

One of the women with an "X" over her face was Seema Verma, who never served in Congress. Ron DeSantis was also pictured with an "X" over his face—but he resigned from Congress to focus on his campaign for governor of Florida, which he won. Others with the "X" included Tom Price, who resigned in 2017 over reports he took chartered flights at the expense of the U.S. taxpayer, and Blake Farenthold, who also left Congress over ethical issues, not backlash to his vote on the Obamacare repeal. Twelve actual congresspeople that were marked with the "X" went on to win reelection.[240]

240   Larsen, Emily. "FACT CHECK: A Viral Image Wildly Mischaracterizes Which GOP Congressmen Were Voted Out in 2018." Check Your Fact, November 21, 2018, https://checkyourfact.com/2018/11/21/fact-check-viral-image-x-gop-voted-out-2018/.

In another act of sloppiness, two Republicans who did lose their seats were pictured but didn't get the "X." Only one person who actually lost their race correctly was labeled with an "X."[241]

Kitchel eventually acknowledged the "several errors" with his claims (which is generous phrasing considering the image had more falsehoods than truth to it).[242]

Amazingly, despite the person who created the meme acknowledging that it was bogus, Snopes' Bethania Palma fact-checked the image three months after that...and rated it as being accurate!

Palma claimed that "in the meme, red 'X' marks were drawn through the faces of 33 lawmakers who purportedly were rejected by voters in the 6 November 2018 midterm elections." For an unknown reason, when Palma presents the image of the lawmakers in her article, it's cropped so tightly as to exclude one of them, hence her count of 33 in the photo as opposed to 34.

She continues: "Although memes are frequently grossly inaccurate, this one got the general idea correct. By our count, at least 34 Republican legislators who voted to repeal or partially repeal Obamacare will not be returning to Congress when the new session begins in January 2019."[243]

As partly already explained, there are numerous glaring problems here with her analysis, including the following:

- Palma mischaracterizes or misidentifies the image as only being of lawmakers.

- A legislator not returning to Congress does not mean they were voted out of office.

- Only three people in the image with an "X" over their faces lost their reelection bids, and they were Republicans in blue states (California, New Jersey, and New York). Another Republican, Robert Pittenger, lost his Republican primary contest, but the Republican Party held the seat.[244]

---

241 Ibid.

242 Kitchel, Nicholas. November 17, 2018, https://twitter.com/nicholaskitchel/status/1063975020186218496.

243 Palma, Bethania. "Did 33 Republicans Who Voted to Repeal Obamacare Lose Their Congressional Seats?" Snopes, December 6, 2018, https://www.snopes.com/fact-check/gop-obamacare-repeal-election/.

244 Larsen, "FACT CHECK: A Viral Image Wildly Mischaracterizes Which GOP Congressmen Were Voted Out in 2018."

The meme was a total disaster, as was Snopes' defense of it after its creator already admitted it was wrong.

When reached out to for comment from the Daily Caller, Snopes decided to pretend there was some ambiguity as to who was even being photographed, and added a line reading that "the persons actually pictured in the accompanying photograph are difficult or impossible to identify" rather than just admit they got it wrong. One moment they were claiming to have authoritatively fact-checked the image—and now they're pretending to have trouble examining it.

Snopes cofounder David Mikkelson defended the fact-check in an email to the Caller on the basis that the "overall point offered" by the image is still true, that "33 Republican members of Congress who voted to repeal the ACA lost their seats." In other words, "true in spirit" is an acceptable fact-checking rating. And he's not even right about that, as the "overall point" of the image was to argue that Republicans who voted to repeal Obamacare lost their races as a result of their vote.[245] Mikkelson is admitting that the overall point isn't true while telling us that it's true because of its overall point.

MOSTLY PEACEFUL JIHADISTS

In one *WaPo* fact-check, we're told that there's apparently an acceptable number of terrorists to let into the country.

In 2017, Senior Adviser to the President Stephen Miller cited a list of seventy-two immigrants arrested on terror-related charges since 9/11 to bolster the case for Trump's immigration ban. All seventy-two arrestees are from the seven countries affected by the travel ban, and thirty-three were convicted on "serious" terror crimes.[246]

In response, *WaPo*'s fact-checker Michelle Ye Hee Lee argued that it's just not that big of a deal, ignoring the thirty-three convicted of "serious" terror offenses and downplaying the activities of the others. One of the arrestees she tries to humanize is Siavosh Henareh, who she presents as

245   Hasson, Peter. "Snopes, Fact-Checker For Facebook And Google, Botches Fact Check." The Daily Caller, December 6, 2018, https://dailycaller.com/2018/12/06/snopes-facebook-google-fact-check/.

246   Stoltzfoos, Rachel. "WaPo Fact Check: Letting A Few Terrorists Into The Country Is No Big Deal." The Daily Caller, February 13, 2017, https://dailycaller.com/2017/02/13/wapo-fact-check-letting-a-few-terrorists-into-the-country-is-no-big-deal/.

"merely" trafficking heroin on behalf of Hezbollah, not participating in terrorism himself. Yet two of Henareh's friends were charged in connection to trafficking drugs—and weapons for Hezbollah.

Another person downplayed by Lee is a man who wired $200,000 to what he thought was Hezbollah (but was an undercover agent).

Lee must think that there's an acceptable level of terrorism, as she says this list simply isn't enough evidence to justify the claim that immigrants from that country pose a potential terror threat.

ANOTHER L FOR THE FACT-CHECKER INDUSTRIAL COMPLEX

In response to an internet meme stating that Democrats have introduced impeachment articles against every Republican president since Eisenhower, Snopes' Dan Evon rated this claim "Mostly False" because articles of impeachment weren't introduced against President Gerald Ford, and thus Democrats only introduced articles of impeachment against five of six GOP presidents since Eisenhower.[247]

Only in the world of fact-checking are "Mostly True" statements this routinely deemed to be "Mostly False."

EVEN WHEN THEY'RE RIGHT, THEY'RE WRONG: POLITIFACT SCREWS UP AN OTHERWISE FINE FACT-CHECK

As the Notre-Dame Cathedral in France was being devastated by a fire in April 2019, theories about the cause of the fire swirled online as it was still burning.

An image began circulating of two men smiling amid a sea of mourners, which was presented in some corners of the internet as evidence of Muslims cheering the building's destruction online.

PolitiFact's Ciara O'Rourke did a reverse image search and found that the image appeared elsewhere on the website Sputnik, a news agency run by the Russian government that's no stranger to publishing fake and exaggerated news.

---

247 Evon, Dan. "Have Democrats Tried to Impeach Every GOP President Since Ike?" Snopes, September 27, 2019, https://www.snopes.com/fact-check/dems-impeach-gop-presidents/.

O'Rourke pointed out that there's no evidence of the men in the photo being Muslim (and even Sputnik never claimed they were—people online just made their own inference from the photo).[248]

Had she stopped there, nothing would be wrong. But even when the fact-checkers get something right, they find a way to screw up.

O'Rourke added, based off a single person's opinion, that Sputnik had fabricated the image and digitally inserted the two men in front of it, which Sputnik denied. O'Rourke then doubled down and pointed out that Sputnik is a known source of false information.

But even Russian propaganda sites aren't as deceptive as PolitiFact.

The Associated Press tracked down the two men in the photo to interview them about the torrent of online abuse they received. They explained that they were architecture students and wanted to see what was going on with their own eyes, and one said the only reason they were smiling was that as they were going under security tape, it caught his face, which they laughed at.[249]

In a follow-up article, after it turned out the image was not doctored, O'Rourke spends 1,300 words explaining just how increasingly difficult it is becoming to tell if photos are doctored or not, which begs the question of why she alleged one was in the first place.

FACT-CHECKER SOMEHOW UNSURE WHETHER POLICE REDUCE CRIME OR NOT

USA Today's fact-checker Daniel Funke turned criminologist for a day and casted doubt on the well-established link between fewer police and more crime.[250]

Funke's fact-check specifically responded to a social media post that claimed "twelve major cities broke homicide records this year. They are ALL led by Democrat Mayors. That is what happens when you defund the police."

248 O'Rourke, Ciara. "Facebook posts wrongly claim photo shows 'Muslims laughing while Notre Dame is burning.'" PolitiFact, April 16, 2019, https://www.politifact.com/factchecks/2019/apr/16/viral-image/photo-muslims-laughing-front-notre-dame/.

249 Banet, Rémi. "'How could we rejoice in the Notre-Dame fire?' Two victims of online hate share their story." AFP Fact Check, May 6, 2019, https://factcheck.afp.com/how-could-we-rejoice-notre-dame-fire-two-victims-online-hate-share-their-story.

250 Funke, Daniel. "Fact check: No evidence defunding police to blame for homicide increases, experts say." *USA Today*, January 28, 2022, https://www.usatoday.com/story/news/factcheck/2022/01/28/fact-check-police-funding-not-linked-homicide-spikes-experts-say/9054639002/.

Funke acknowledges that "between 2019 and 2020, the U.S. recorded its highest increase in the national homicide rate in modern history. And in 2021, 12 cities did break their annual homicide records," while glossing over that it's also true that those twelve cities have Democrat mayors. The only point that Funke refutes is that not all twelve cities defunded the police, which he then uses to justify titling his article, "No evidence defunding police to blame for homicide increases."

While the homicide rate rose nearly 30 percent in 2020, the largest year-over-year increase since at least 1905,[251] the gain was even more pronounced in many of the major cities that defunded police, including Portland, which saw a 530 percent increase in their murder rate, Austin a 74 percent increase, New York a 56 percent increase, and Chicago a 54 percent increase.[252]

Funke then surprisingly calls into question whether police help that much at all.

He quotes one criminologist at the University of California-Irvine who told him that she's not aware of any data that illustrates the effect of reducing the police on homicide rates and that older research suggests there isn't a definitive conclusion.

That there's anything resembling a debate among criminologists over if police reduce crime or not is an invention of Funke—hence why he could only find one person to quote to give this impression (and didn't quote anyone who represents the consensus opinion that more police do reduce crime).

To quote one summary of just a sampling of the existing research:[253]

> In a 2005 paper, Jonathan Glick and Alex Tabarrok found a clever instrument to measure the effects of officer increases through the terrorism "alert levels" that were a feature of the early to mid-aughts. During high-alert periods, the Washington, DC, police force would mobilize extra officers, especially in

251 Gramlich, John. "What we know about the increase in U.S. murders in 2020." Pew Research Center, October 27, 2021, https://www.pewresearch.org/fact-tank/2021/10/27/what-we-know-about-the-increase-in-u-s-murders-in-2020/.

252 O'Donnell, Dan. "New FBI Data Proves 'Defund the Police' was a Deadly Mistake." MacIver Institute, September 29, 2021, https://www.maciverinstitute.com/2021/09/new-fbi-data-proves-defund-the-police-was-a-deadly-mistake/.

253 Yglesias, Matthew. "The case for hiring more police officers." Vox, February 13, 2019, https://www.vox.com/policy-and-politics/2019/2/13/18193661/hire-police-officers-crime-criminal-justice-reform-booker-harris.

and around the capital's core, centered on the National Mall. Using daily crime data, they found that the level of crime decreased significantly on high-alert days, and the decrease was especially concentrated on the National Mall.

Stephen Mello of Princeton University assessed the Obama-era increase in federal police funding. Thanks to the stimulus bill, funding for Clinton's Community Oriented Policing Services (COPS) hiring grant program surged from about $20 million a year in the late-Bush era to $1 billion in 2009. The program design allowed Mello to assess some quasi-random variation in which cities got grants. The data shows that compared to cities that missed out, those that made the cut ended up with police staffing levels that were 3.2 percent higher and crime levels that were 3.5 percent lower. This is an important finding because not only does it show that more police officers leads to less crime, but that actual American cities are not currently policed at a level where there are diminishing returns.

A larger historical survey by Aaron Chalfin and Justin McCrary looked at a large set of police and crime data for midsize to large cities from 1960 to 2010 and concluded that every $1 spent on extra policing generates about $1.63 in social benefits, primarily through fewer murders.

Steven D. Levitt (of *Freakonomics* fame) found from analyzing four studies on the impact of police presence and crime that a 10 percent increase in the size of a police force should result in between a 3 to 7 percent reduction in crime.[254] The aforementioned Jonathan Glick also published a study in 2015 that estimated regular patrols from the University of Pennsylvania Police Department were associated with a 60 percent reduction in crime.[255]

The most recent notable study on the matter was published in 2020 at the National Bureau of Economic Research and separated its results by race, finding that in areas with serious crime, it takes the hiring of ten

---

254   Guze, Jon. "More Cops, Less Crime." John Locke Foundation, March 17, 2022, https://www.johnlocke.org/more-cops-less-crime-2/.

255   Ibid.

to seventeen police officers to stop one additional homicide by year and that the impact is twice as big per capita for black victims.[256]

And more cops would be welcome. Even before the "defund the police" movement push that began in mid-2020, it was still the case that the U.S. employed 35 percent fewer police officers per capita than the world average.[257]

GINGRICH GETS IT RIGHT: FACTCHECK.ORG'S FLAWED FOOD-STAMP CLAIM

In response to Newt Gingrich's claim that "more people have been put on food stamps by Barack Obama than any president in American history" in January 2012, FactCheck.org's Brooks Jackson fact-checked the claim just months before it did become true, and then ignored when it did.

Jackson wrote:

> Gingrich would have been correct to say the number now on food aid is historically high. The number stood at 46,224,722 persons as of October [2011], the most recent month on record. And it's also true that the number has risen sharply since Obama took office.
>
> But Gingrich goes too far to say Obama has put more on the rolls than other presidents. We asked the U.S. Department of Agriculture's Food and Nutrition service for month-by-month figures going back to January 2001. And they show that under President George W. Bush the number of recipients rose by nearly 14.7 million. Nothing before comes close to that.
>
> And under Obama, the increase so far has been 14.2 million. To be exact, the program has so far grown by 444,574 fewer recipients during Obama's time in office than during Bush's.[258]

In addition to making an apples-to-oranges comparison between Obama (who had been in office for three years at that point) and Bush

---

256 Ibid.
257 Tabarrok, Alex. "Underpoliced and Overprisoned, revisited." Marginal Revolution, June 11, 2020, https://marginalrevolution.com/marginalrevolution/2020/06/underpoliced-and-overprisoned-revisited.html.
258 Jackson, Brooks. "Newt's Faulty Food-Stamp Claim." FactCheck.org, February 5, 2012, https://www.factcheck.org/2012/01/newts-faulty-food-stamp-claim/.

(who had been in office for eight), Jackson misread the statistics, as there were 14.55 million participants added to SNAP under Bush, compared to 14.46 million under Obama at that point, which is only ninety thousand fewer people.[259]

Or phrased differently, in three years Obama added 99.3 percent of what Bush added to the SNAP rolls in eight years.

Jackson did give himself some wiggle room and added that "it's possible that when the figures for January 2012 are available they will show that the gain under Obama has matched or exceeded the gain under Bush." However, he makes it clear he believes that the number on food stamps will likely go down in the future.

The only update on his article reads, "Update, Feb. 5: Revised USDA data released in February [2012] showed the downward trend continued for a second straight month in November [2011], when the number of persons getting food stamps was 134,418 fewer than it had been at the peak."[260]

There was no update when data was released for July 2012 showing 46,681,833 on food stamps, vindicating Gingrich.[261]

Meanwhile, CNN admitted that Gingrich's claim was true but rated it as "True, but incomplete," because they disagreed with his assessment that it was Obama's fault.[262]

THE NINTH CIRCUS

In early 2017, PolitiFact's Lauren Carroll rated Sean Hannity's unquestionably true statement that the U.S. Ninth Circuit Court of Appeals is "the most overturned court in the country" false.[263]

---

259   Roy, Avik. "The Ten Worst Fact-Checks of the 2012 Election." *Forbes*, November 5, 2012, https://www.forbes.com/sites/aroy/2012/11/05/the-ten-worst-fact-checks-of-the-2012-election/.

260   Jackson, "Newt's Faulty Food-Stamp Claim."

261   Halper, Daniel. "Record High Enrollment for Food Stamps: 46,681,833." *Washington Examiner*, October 16, 2012, https://www.washingtonexaminer.com/tag/barack-obama?source=%2Fweekly-standard%2Frecord-high-enrollment-for-food-stamps-46-681-833.

262   Smith, Matt. "Gingrich half-off on food stamps." CNN, January 17, 2012, https://www.cnn.com/2012/01/17/politics/truth-squad-gingrich-food-stamps/index.html.

263   Carroll, Lauren. "No, the 9th Circuit isn't the 'most overturned court in the country,' as Hannity says." PolitiFact, February 10, 2017, https://www.politifact.com/factchecks/2017/feb/10/sean-hannity/no-9th-circuit-isnt-most-overturned-court-country-/.

Carroll reviewed the stats from 2010 to 2015 and found that the Supreme Court reversed 79 percent of cases from the Ninth Circuit, which made it the third most reversed court by percentage.

In calculating those percentages, Carroll had to look up the number of Ninth Circuit cases overturned and the total number of cases appealed to the SCOTUS—yet the numerator in her equation doesn't get a mention.

And that's because had Carroll mentioned them, she would've had to admit that from 2010 to 2015, the Ninth Circuit was overturned by the SCOTUS seventy-seven times—while the next highest (the Sixth Circuit) was overturned twenty-eight times—and that the Ninth Circuit had the most cases overturned every year.[264]

The overturned decisions by circuit courts from 2010 to 2015 were as follows:

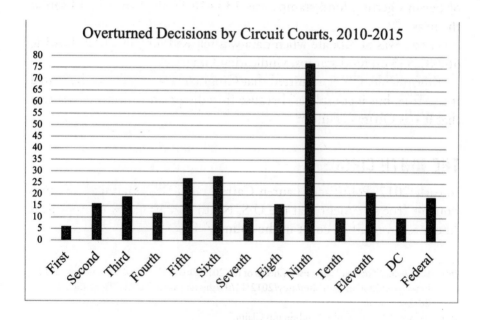

As can be gleaned from the chart above, the Ninth Circuit is indeed the most overturned court in the nation.

264 Hemingway, Mollie. "4 Recent Examples Show Why No One Trusts Media 'Fact Checks.'" The Federalist, February 21, 2017, https://thefederalist. com/2017/02/21/4-recent-examples-show-why-no-one-trusts-media-fact-checks/.

PETE BUTTIGIEG AND THE CASE OF RACIST ROADS

In its most transparent act to save a Democrat from embarrassment to date, after Pete Buttigieg made the case that asphalt was part of systemic racism, the *Washington Post* was there to defend him…and then reverse course after they realized they were wrong.

In line with the Democrats' "everything is racist" approach to public policy, Buttigieg said at a press conference, with a straight face: "If a highway was built for the purpose of dividing a white and a black neighborhood, or if an underpass was constructed such that a bus carrying mostly Black and Puerto Rican kids to a beach, or would have been, in New York, was designed too low for it to pass by, that that obviously reflects racism that went into those design choices."

As conservatives roasted Buttigieg for the comical and borderline cartoonish picture he painted, the *WaPo*'s Glenn Kessler said that the claims were backed up by a book on urban developer Robert Moses called *The Power Broker*. Kessler quoted the following passage to defend Buttigieg:

> [Robert Moses] began to limit access by buses; he instructed Shapiro to build the bridges across his new parkways low -- too low for buses to pass. Bus trips therefore had to be made on local roads, making the trips discouraging, long and arduous. For Negroes, who he considered inherently 'dirty,' there were further measures. Buses needed permits to enter state parks; buses chartered by Negro groups found it very difficult to obtain permits, especially to Moses's beloved Jones Beach; most were shunted off to parks many miles further on Long Island.[265]

Kessler learned of the passage from his colleague Philip Bump, who wrote an entire article defending Buttigieg that quoted from *The Power Broker*.[266]

Then, two days later, Kessler suddenly realized it was BS and tweeted out: "ADDENDUM: Experts increasingly doubt this story," which was

265 Kessler, Glenn. November 8, 2021, https://twitter.com/GlennKesslerWP/status/1457809268971868162.

266 Bump, Philip. "And this is why it's useful to talk about historical examples of institutionalized racism." *Washington Post*, November 8, 2021, https://www.washingtonpost.com/politics/2021/11/08/this-is-why-its-useful-talk-about-historic-examples-institutionalized-racism/.

accompanied by an article he wrote explaining that it turns out this story about roads and bridges "has largely been debunked."[267]

He also admitted that he was wrong to do a "knee-jerk" defense of Buttigieg accusing infrastructure of racism.

There's no word on if your local overpass is sexist or homophobic, however.

FACT-CHECK OF VIRGINIA LT. GOV. WINSOME SEARS DEBUNKED BY FACTS

Lieutenant Governor of Virginia Winsome Sears said in an interview on January 17, 2022, "We know last year the Loudoun County School Board spent about $300,000—that's real money, that's going-to-jail money—to bring CRT [critical race theory] in some form or fashion to the school system."

Her comment came as some proponents of critical race theory propaganda in schools tried to deny that it was already present in them.

PolitiFact's Warren Fiske rated Sears' statement "Mostly False," writing:

> Sears has a little ground beneath her. In 2020, the school system paid a consultant $34,167 to conduct seminars for senior officials on critical race theory and equity training. But that sum is almost nine times less than the $300,000 Sears claims. We asked her office three times how she came up with the figure and did not get an answer. It appears that she has greatly overstated the cost of the seminars.[268]

As is always the case with PolitiFact, they missed something.

The Daily Caller's education reporter Chrissy Clark found proof that Loudoun County did indeed spend over $300,000 on critical race theory–related materials in the form of seven payments to Equity

267 Kessler, Glenn. "Robert Moses and the saga of the racist parkway bridges." *Washington Post*, November 10, 2021, https://www.washingtonpost.com/politics/2021/11/10/robert-moses-saga-racist-parkway-bridges/.

268 Fiske, Warren. "Did Loudoun County, Va. schools pay 'about $300,000' for critical race theory training?" PolitiFact, January 24, 2022, https://www.politifact.com/factchecks/2022/jan/24/winsome-sears/did-loudoun-county-va-schools-pay-about-300000-cri/.

Collaborative LLC, a consulting firm that helps disseminate CRT propaganda in public schools.[269]

A picture of the line-item spending is as follows:[270]

Invoice Date	PO Number	Initiator	Supplier	Supplier N	GL Date	Date Invoice Receiv	Invoice Num	Invoice Amount
8/20/2018		Von Ehren, Ms	THE EQUITY COLLABORATIVE LLC	134120	9/1/2018	9/7/2018 0:00	197	6,000.00
6/11/2019	45557	Varley, Ms. Ani	THE EQUITY COLLABORATIVE LLC	134120	6/11/2019	6/18/2019 0:00	227	242,000.00
9/24/2019		Bache, Mrs. Su	THE EQUITY COLLABORATIVE LLC	134120	9/25/2019	9/24/2019 0:00	230	25,000.00
11/24/2019	48977	Barron, Mrs. Ta	THE EQUITY COLLABORATIVE LLC	134120	12/1/2019	12/30/2019 0:00	235	25,000.00
11/24/2019	49490	Schamus, Ms. I	THE EQUITY COLLABORATIVE LLC	134120	12/1/2019	12/10/2019 0:00	234	22,000.00
3/19/2020	50037	Washington, N	THE EQUITY COLLABORATIVE LLC	134120	4/1/2020	4/29/2020 0:00	244	68,333.00
6/9/2020	50037	Hernandez, Mr	THE EQUITY COLLABORATIVE LLC	134120	6/9/2020	6/9/2020 0:00	246	34,167.00

Equity Collaborative's website says they specialize in "equity" coaching: "Our goal is to help organizations develop their own capacity to create educational equity and social justice by addressing bias and oppression. Tackling bias and oppression requires solutions beyond the technical approaches of implementing policies and 'best' practices."[271] One past seminar they've held is titled "Introduction to Critical Race Theory."[272]

HotAir's John Sexton noted that Parents Defending Education (the source for the payment figures) "actually split the district's spending into two categories, $34,000 for Equity Collaborative training including CRT and another $314,000 for EQ "training."[273] It could be that PolitiFact is trying to only count the $34k as explicitly CRT related, while the rest is CRT adjacent.

The only thing Sears got wrong was the time frame—the wasteful $300,000+ spending in question began in 2019; it wasn't only spent last year. Regardless, that hardly justifies the "Mostly False" rating PolitiFact gave her statement.

269　Clark, Chrissy. January 25, 2022, https://twitter.com/chrissyclark_/status/1486005872316891139.

270　"Consultant Report Card." Parents Defending Education, https://defendinged.org/report/the-equity-collaborative/.

271　"About The Equity Collaborative." The Equity Collaborative, https://theequitycollaborative.com/about-the-equity-collaborative/.

272　Almanzán, Jaime, et al. "Introduction to Critical Race Theory." The Equity Collaborative, https://theequitycollaborative.com/wp-content/uploads/2020/05/Intro-To-Critical-Race-Theory.pdf.

273　Sexton, John. "PolitiFact's fact-check of Va Lt. Gov. appears to have missed something (Update)." HotAir, January 25, 2022, https://hotair.com/john-s-2/2022/01/25/politifacts-fact-check-of-va-lt-gov-appears-to-have-missed-something-n443959.

POLITIFACT ON GUN CONTROL: "LET'S MAKE SOMETHING CLEAR: THE NAZIS DID DENY GUNS SPECIFICALLY TO JEWS. BUT..."

In one fact-check that has to be read to be believed, PolitiFact's Samantha Putterman, who has an undergraduate degree in "journalism and media studies," opined on World War II to inform us all that while it is true that the Nazis disarmed the Jews, that doesn't matter because guns are supposedly useless in her mind, and she thinks they would've been killed anyway, offering no reason for why that is.[274]

"No, gun control regulation in Nazi Germany did not help advance the Holocaust," began her article that was fact-checking viral social media posts suggesting that gun control laws in Nazi Germany "created or exacerbated the genocide of Jews."

In an incredible paragraph, Putterman writes:

> *Let's make something clear: The Nazis did deny guns specifically to Jews. But,* [emphasis mine] given the size of their forces and their methods of confiscation and extermination, this is a trivial factor. The notion that it would have made any difference is unreasonable.

She continues, making the opposite point she thinks she is:

> On Nov. 11, 1938, the Regulations Against Jews' Possession of Weapons was issued. Under it, Jews living under the Third Reich were forbidden to own or possess any form of weapons, including truncheons, knives, firearms and ammunition.

> But the Nazis had already been raiding Jewish homes by then, and the Anti-Defamation League, an organization founded to fight anti-Semitism, explained in 2013 that "the small number of personal firearms in the hands of the small number of Germany's Jews (about 214,000) remaining in Germany in 1938 could in no way have stopped the totalitarian power of the Nazi German state."

---

274 Putterman, Samantha. "No, gun control regulation in Nazi Germany did not help advance the Holocaust." PolitiFact, April 8, 2019, https://www.politifact.com/factchecks/2019/apr/08/viral-image/no-gun-control-regulation-nazi-germany-did-not-hel/.

Unless Putterman possesses a time machine, she is effectively imagining how a hypothetical scenario would go in her head and presenting it as a fact-check. In what world would zero guns be preferable to 214,000 of them against an enemy?

This was hardly the first fact-check that relied on omniscience.

Also writing for PolitiFact, Audrey Bowler examined the question of whether or not George Washington would've been an ally to the modern-day gun-rights movement, and concluded that he wouldn't have been. In addition to fact-checking hypothetical past acts of armed resistance, the fact-checking industry has also advanced to fact-checking the hypothetical opinions of dead people.[275]

BILL AND THE BROADS

During the second presidential debate between Donald Trump and Hillary Clinton, in the wake of the infamous *Access Hollywood* tape scandal, Trump ripped Bill Clinton's treatment of women, saying, "He [Bill Clinton] was impeached, he lost his license to practice law, he had to pay an $850,000 fine to one of the women."

The Associated Press' fact-checker came to the Clintons' rescue. In a one-paragraph fact-check, the AP wrote:

> THE FACTS: Trump's facts are, at best, jumbled. In 1998, lawyers for Bill Clinton settled with former Arkansas state employee Paula Jones for $850,000 in her four-year lawsuit alleging sexual harassment. Clinton did not acknowledge wrongdoing in the settlement. But Trump erred in describing the legal consequences of that case. In a related case before the Arkansas State Supreme Court, Clinton was fined $25,000 and his Arkansas law license was suspended for five years. Clinton also faced disbarment before the U.S. Supreme Court, but he opted to resign from the court's practice instead of facing any penalties.[276]

---

275   Bowler, Audrey. "Did George Washington offer support for individual gun rights, as meme says?" PolitiFact, February 20, 2015, https://www.politifact.com/factchecks/2015/feb/20/facebook-posts/did-george-washington-offer-support-individual-gun/.

276   The Associated Press, "AP FACT CHECK: Trump says Bill Clinton lost law license." *Seattle Times*, October 9, 2016, https://www.seattletimes.com/nation-world/nation-politics/ap-fact-check-trump-says-bill-clinton-lost-law-license/.

But as NewsBusters' Tom Blumer points out, the AP flubbed their timeline.[277]

— In April 1999, District Judge Susan Webber Wright found Bill Clinton in contempt for "intentionally false testimony" in the Paula Jones sexual harassment trial and fined him over $90,000.

— In May 2000, an Arkansas Supreme Court committee determined that Clinton "should be disbarred for 'serious misconduct' in the Paula Jones case and began the court proceeding to strip him of his law license." Almost no one besides Clinton himself and his lawyer genuinely believed that the state's Supreme Court would fail to follow the committee's recommendation.

— "On January 19, 2001, Clinton agreed to a five-year suspension of his law license and a $25,000 fine in order to avoid disbarment and to end the investigation of Independent Counsel Robert Ray," which was formalized the next day.

Clinton then had to pay an $850,000 settlement in the Paula Jones lawsuit, which is more than the $750,000 she sought.

As Blumer explains, "Based on the Lewinsky-related lies Clinton told during depositions in the suit that had been dismissed, Jones was in a position to revive the case with a reasonable chance of winning and establishing for the record that Clinton had lied about the sexual imposition involved in her case. No reasonable person believes that the settlement establishes anything other than Clinton's determination to keep that from happening."[278]

To recap, Trump said Bill Clinton was impeached, lost his license to practice law, and was ordered to pay an $850,000 fine. Bill Clinton was indeed impeached, lost his law license for five years, and then never applied for it again (thus meaning he's lost his ability to practice law since then), and was fined $850,000.

But you wouldn't know that if you listened to the AP jumble the facts.

277   Blumer, Tom. "Stupid AP Fact Check Says Trump Was Wrong in Saying Bill
       Clinton 'Lost' His Law License." NewsBusters, October 14, 2016,
       https://www.newsbusters.org/blogs/nb/tom-blumer/2016/10/14/stupid-ap-
       fact-check-says-trump-was-wrong-saying-bill-clinton-lost.
278   Blumer, "Stupid AP Fact Check Says Trump Was Wrong."

POLITIFACT FACT-CHECKER LEARNS HIS EMPLOYER IS SOURCE OF CLAIM HE'S TRYING TO DEBUNK

In what was then just the latest example of a PolitiFact fact-checker stepping on a rake, reporter Yacob Reyes reached out to Ron DeSantis' press secretary, Christina Pushaw, for comment on his claim that almost 60 percent of outstanding student loan debt is graduate school debt.

"Hello, I am writing a fact-check on a quick deadline following Gov. Ron DeSantis claim: 'The student debt that it out there, almost 60% of it is graduate school debt.' If you would like to provide supporting material for the claim, I would need to hear by 9 p.m. Meanwhile, I'll be continuing my own research and interviews," he wrote in an email to Pushaw.

The quote from DeSantis was, "This student debt that's out there, almost 60% of it is graduate school debt. These are people like doctors and lawyers, people that are getting Masters' and Ph. D's and all this other stuff."[279]

It's unclear how much research Reyes had done at the time of the email, as the source of DeSantis' claim was the Poynter Institute, which employs Reyes as a staff writer.[280]

Pushaw fired back at Reyes: "Hi Yacob, your own employer, Poynter, recently published research about this topic finding that 56% of outstanding student debt is owed by households that hold graduate degrees. I think 56% qualifies as 'almost 60%.' Thanks."

The Poynter article in question, published one day before Reyes emailed Pushaw for comment, noted that:

> The foundation of that argument that debt forgiveness would benefit richer white Americans is found in the fact that people working in higher-income positions—for example, doctors and lawyers—took on a significant amount of student debt attending graduate and post-graduate school. The Brookings Institute says 56% of the outstanding student debt is owed by households that hold graduate degrees.

---

279 Gancarski, A.G. "Gov. DeSantis says it's 'wrong' for the feds to forgive student loan debt." Florida Politics, April 29, 2022, https://floridapolitics.com/archives/520558-desantis-loan/.

280 "Yacob Reyes." The Poynter Institute, https://www.poynter.org/author/yacob-reyes/.

The Federal Reserve Bank of New York spelled this out in a study that shows lower-income households would not benefit nearly as much as higher-income households.[281]

There is a difference between 56 percent of outstanding student debt *being exclusively from graduate debt* and 56 percent of outstanding debt being from people *who attended graduate school* (which includes debt accumulated from undergraduate too), and interpreting DeSantis' comment as the former is the entire basis for which Reyes rates DeSantis' claim "Mostly False" while saying that his statements "contained an element of truth."

While the phrasing from DeSantis certainly could be interpreted as the former, are we to believe that DeSantis thinks that doctors and lawyers only have graduate school debt but zero undergraduate debt? That seems unlikely.

Despite this misfire, Reyes has yet to top his historic feat in mental gymnastics from just months earlier, where he attempted to fact-check Maria Bartiromo's statement that "we have doubled our oil imports from Russia in the last year." He rated her claim "Mostly False," stating, "The U.S. did not double oil imports from Russia in the last year." Then two paragraphs into his article, Reyes writes, "*The U.S. did double the amount of crude oil imported from Russia last year.* But Russia accounts for only about 3% of overall U.S. crude oil imports in 2021 [emphasis mine]."[282]

BORDER ENCOUNTERS VS. BORDER CROSSINGS

In fact-checking Jeff Sessions' statement in 2016 that "there are about 350,000 people who succeed in crossing our borders illegally each year," PolitiFact's Miriam Valverde confuses two different measurements of border activity in her rebuttal.

She rated Sessions' statement, which is about those *who succeeded in crossing the border*, as "False." Yet her analysis is of something entirely different: how many people *are apprehended* at the border. She writes:

281   Tompkins, Al. "Can and will Biden cancel student debt for 43 million Americans?" The Poynter Institute, May 2, 2022, https://www.poynter.org/reporting-editing/2022/can-and-will-biden-cancel-student-debt-for-43-million-americans/.

282   Reyes, Yacob. "The U.S. did not double oil imports from Russia in the last year." PolitiFact, February 28, 2022, https://www.politifact.com/factchecks/2022/feb/28/maria-bartiromo/us-did-not-double-oil-imports-russia-last-year/.

In fiscal year 2015, Border Patrol tallied 337,117 apprehensions nationwide, a decrease from 486,651 in fiscal year 2014 — and almost 80 percent below apprehension peaks in 2000, according to the federal report.

...sources point to apprehension levels hovering around Sessions' 350,000 estimates, though they also find such numbers to be in decline.

...

But Sessions said that 350,000 "succeed in crossing our border." The apprehension numbers represent people who did not succeed.[283]

While it is impossible to know for sure the exact number who successfully enter the U.S. illegally, apprehensions are used as a proxy for successful border crossings.

One study published in 2013 by the Council on Foreign Relations found the relationship to be roughly one successful crossing for one apprehension.[284] In that case, we can consider 337,117 to be "about 350,000 people," like Sessions stated.

The *WaPo*'s Kessler ran a similar fact-check of the claim, quoting the 2015 figures and citing experts to paint a picture of declining apprehensions[285]—a picture that would be destroyed entirely in the Biden era.

THE *WASHINGTON POST'S* GLENN KESSLER PROVES UNPROPHETIC ON THE BIDEN BORDER CRISIS

In the early days of the Biden administration, the *Washington Post* helped democracy die in the darkness by downplaying the border crisis. In

283 Valverde, Miriam. "Sen. Jeff Sessions wrongly says 350,000 people succeed in crossing the border every year." PolitiFact, July 19, 2016, https://www.politifact.com/factchecks/2016/jul/19/jeff-sessions/senator-jeff-sessions-says-about-350000-people-suc/.

284 Plumer, Brad. "Study: The U.S. stops about half of illegal border crossings from Mexico." *Washington Post*, May 13, 2013, https://www.washingtonpost.com/news/wonk/wp/2013/05/13/study-the-u-s-stops-about-half-of-illegal-border-crossings-from-mexico/.

285 Kessler, Glenn, and Michelle Ye Hee Lee. "Fact-checking the first day of the 2016 Republican National Convention." *Washington Post*, July 19, 2016, https://www.washingtonpost.com/news/fact-checker/wp/2016/07/19/fact-checking-the-first-day-of-the-2016-republican-national-convention/.

March 2021, columnist Jennifer Rubin wrote of the crisis, "[T]here has been no surge of arrivals outside the normal fluctuation of migration." This came after statistics revealed that thirty thousand unaccompanied minors crossed the border the month prior, more than the number for the entirety of 2020.[286]

In May 2021, *Post* fact-checker Glenn Kessler himself shared an article to his Twitter he ought to have fact-checked that was published in the *Post*, titled, "There's no migrant 'surge' at the U.S. southern border. Here's the data." The headline was later changed to "The migrant 'surge' at the U.S. southern border is actually a predictable pattern."[287]

The article claims that January–April are "surge" months for illegal immigration, and the surge will naturally fall off.

But illegal immigration did not fall off, and fiscal year 2021 (ending September 20, 2021) ended up seeing a record 1.7 million illegals encountered, the highest number recorded since at least 1960.[288] Encounters continued to surge in the month that followed, with no month recording fewer encounters than for that month the prior year.

In 2022, border encounters eclipsed the FY 2021 total by June (with nearly three months left in the fiscal year),[289] and fiscal year 2022 ended with nearly 2.4 million encounters.[290]

286 Kaminsky, Gabe. "WaPo Fact-Checker Mum On Jennifer Rubin's False Claim That There Is 'No Surge' At Border." The Federalist, March 25, 2021, https://thefederalist.com/2021/03/25/wapo-fact-checker-mum-on-jennifer-rubins-false-claim-that-there-is-no-surge-at-border/.

287 Graham, Tim. "OOPS: WashPost 'Fact Checker' Promoted Un-Factual 'There's No Migrant Surge' Article." NewsBusters, March 26, 2021, https://www.newsbusters.org/blogs/nb/tim-graham/2021/03/26/oops-washpost-fact-checker-promoted-un-factual-theres-no-migrant.

288 Sullivan, Eileen, and Miriam Jordan. "Illegal Border Crossings, Driven by Pandemic and Natural Disasters, Soar to Record High." *New York Times*, October 22, 2022, https://www.nytimes.com/2021/10/22/us/politics/border-crossings-immigration-record-high.html.

289 Blankley, Bethany. "More than 2 million illegal border encounters so far in fiscal 2022." Just the News, July 16, 2022, https://justthenews.com/nation/states/center-square/fiscal-year-through-june-more-2-million-encounters-southern-border

290 U.S. Customs and Border Protection, "Southwest Land Border Encounters."

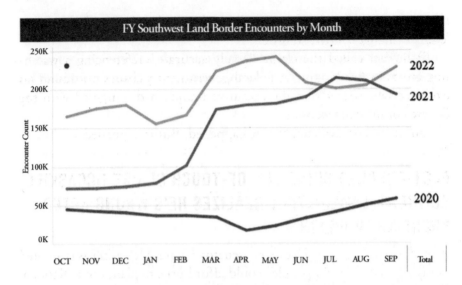

Chart Source: U.S. Customs and Border Protection[291]

This was hardly the first time that Kessler had tried to downplay a border crisis. When Trump said during his 2016 Republican nomination acceptance speech that "the number of new illegal immigrant families who have crossed the border so far this year already exceeds the entire total from 2015," Kessler admitted that Trump was right. But then he dismissed the statistic as "cherry picked" because that surge wasn't as severe as the surge in FY 2012–2014. Thus, the past awfulness of Obama on the border was used to downplay his then-current awfulness.[292]

THERE'S NO EVIDENCE IT HAPPENED, BUT IT HAPPENED

Kamala Harris alleged during her debate with then-VP Mike Pence that the Trump administration censored the website of the Senate Committee on Environment and Public Works to edit out the phrase "climate change."

Harris said, "I served, when I first got to the Senate, on the commit-tee that's responsible for the environment. Did you know, this adminis-

---

291   "Southwest Land Border Encounters." U.S. Customs and Border
       Protection, July 15, 2022, https://www.cbp.gov/newsroom/stats/
       southwest-land-border-encounters?language_content_entity=en.
292   Vaughan, Jessica M. "Fact Checkers Can't Handle the Truth." Center for Immigration
       Studies, July 25, 2016, https://cis.org/Vaughan/Fact-Checkers-Cant-Handle-Truth.

tration took the word 'science' off the website? And then took the phrase 'climate change' off the website?"

PolitiFact called the claim "largely accurate," referencing a watchdog group's work looking at federal government websites but found no evidence whatsoever that the executive branch had tampered with the Senate committee's website.[293]

So, there's no evidence that it happened. But it happened.

FACT-CHECKER SPINS OUT-OF-TOUCH CLAIRE MCCASKILL COMMENT, IMMEDIATELY REALIZES HE'S WRONG AFTER PRESSING "PUBLISH"

After former Missouri Democrat senator Claire McCaskill was quoted as saying that "normal people" could afford private planes in a National Republican Senatorial Committee ad, PolitiFact's Louis Jacobson jumped to her defense to help pretend she didn't say something so embarrassingly out of touch.

Jacobson took aim at an ad from the Senate Leadership Fund that quoted McCaskill as saying that, which he claims is out of context.

"Did McCaskill really say that 'normal people can afford private plans?' Jacobson asks. No — the ad leaves out the lead-in question from an audience member that prompted the remark."

Jacobson tracked down video from the town hall where McCaskill made the remark, elaborating: "It doesn't show the full town hall—or even the full comment that McCaskill was replying to—but it shows enough to undermine the ad's argument."

The transcript of the eighteen-second clip he located in question captured the following exchange:

> **Audience member:** You know, that's one thing the United States has that nobody else has, is the freedom to fly around and be affordable where a normal person can afford it.

> **McCaskill:** Will you remind them when they come after me about my husband's plane? That normal people can afford it.

---

293   PolitiFact Staff. "Fact-checking the 2020 vice presidential debate, Kamala Harris vs. Mike Pence." PolitiFact, October 7, 2020, https://www.politifact.com/article/2020/oct/08/fact-checking-2020-vice-presidential-debate-kamala/.

Jacobson concludes from the remarks, "One can argue with the wisdom of making this wisecrack. But it doesn't appear that McCaskill said that 'normal people can afford' private planes."[294]

After publishing his article, Jacobson was then sent the full town hall video, which destroyed the entire premise of his fact-check, and a correction now appears:

> Initially, we published this fact-check with a rating of False, because based on the video available, it did not appear that McCaskill was talking about private planes. After publication, we received more complete video of the question-and-answer session between McCaskill and a constituent that showed she was in fact responding to a question about private planes, as well as a report describing the meeting. We re-assessed the evidence, archived the original version here, and published the version you see here with a new rating of Half True. We apologize for the error.[295]

But even the revision from "False" to "Half True" is inappropriate.

The justification for the initial "False" rating was that: "The footage in the ad leaves out the lead-in comment that prompted McCaskill's remark. The full footage makes it clear that McCaskill is echoing an audience member's observation about how the US commercial aviation system is available to a 'normal person'—not saying that ordinary Americans can afford private planes."

In the revised article, the justification for the "Half True" rating is: "She said those words, but the footage in the ad leaves out both the lead-in comment that prompted McCaskill's remark and the laughter that followed it. The full footage makes it clear that McCaskill was wrapping up a policy-heavy debate with a private-aviation manager and with a riff using the airport manager's words. In context, she was referring to 'normal' users of private planes, as opposed to 'normal' Americans more generally."

How is "normal users of private planes" for newspeak?

---

294   "Original version of fact-check of Senate Leadership Fund ad about Claire McCaskill." PolitiFact, October 16, 2018, https://www.politifact.com/mccaskillarchived/.

295   Jacobson, Louis. "Did Claire McCaskill say normal people can afford a private plane?" PolitiFact, October 17, 2018, https://www.politifact.com/factchecks/2018/oct/17/senate-leadership-fund/did-claire-mccaskill-say-normal-people-can/.

THAT DEPENDS ON WHAT THE MEANING OF THE WORD "AND" IS...

After President Joe Biden announced that his selection criteria for SCOTUS justice Stephen Breyer's replacement were "black" and "woman," Sean Hannity observed that "there's never been a president [before Joe Biden] that has made race and gender the defining factor [for a Supreme Court nomination]," which PolitiFact's Bill McCarthy rated "False."[296]

McCarthy points to quotes from Donald Trump and Ronald Reagan vowing to put women on the Supreme Court. He also quotes a Harvard professor who says that Antonin Scalia's Italian background was a positive factor in Reagan's selection of him.

Thus, it becomes evident this entire fact-check is dependent on McCarthy not understanding the difference between the words "or" and "and."[297]

Hannity said that no other president has made both race *and* gender the deciding factor in a SCOTUS pick, while McCarthy's response was to state that presidents have made race *or* gender deciding factors, which is not what Hannity claimed.[298]

Making matters more absurd, McCarthy includes an eye-roll-inducing quote from some social justice warrior Harvard Law School assistant professor arguing that every president from 1789 to 1967 made race a factor in the decision-making process by "refusing to nominate anyone other than a white man."

FACT-CHECKING A COMIC STRIP (AND FAILING)

For some reason, PolitiFact's Monique Curet decided to fact-check an internet meme mocking a particular absurdity in the transgender culture

---

296 McCarthy, Bill. "Joe Biden isn't first to prioritize race, gender in picking SCOTUS nominee, as Sean Hannity claimed." PolitiFact, January 28, 2022, https://web.archive.org/web/20220131155721/https://www.politifact.com/factchecks/2022/jan/28/sean-hannity/joe-biden-isnt-first-prioritize-race-gender-pickin/.

297 Thanks to Bryan W. White for tipping me off to this one: "PolitiFact doesn't know the meaning of 'and'?" PolitiFact Bias, January 31, 2022, https://www.politifactbias.com/2022/01/politifact-doesnt-know-meaning-of-and.html.

298 Ibid.

war: that children aren't trusted to do much of anything yet can make decisions in regard to life-altering surgeries.[299]

The post imitated a *Family Circus* comic strip, illustrating a conversation between a father and son that reads:

> **Son:** Can I have a cigarette?
>
> **Father:** No, you're 5.
>
> **Son:** Can I have a beer?
>
> **Father:** No, you're 5.
>
> **Son:** Can I drive the car?
>
> **Father:** No, you're 5.
>
> **Son:** Can I take hormones and change my sex?
>
> **Father:** Sure! You know best!"

Curet tells us that there's nothing to worry about here because children are usually at least ten years old before they take puberty blockers and sixteen before they take hormone treatment—in which case they'd still be too young to have a cigarette, drink a beer, or have a full driver's license.

SOMETIMES A DEMOCRAT IS JUST A DEMOCRAT

Snopes' Kim LaCapria decided to look into whether or not the Orlando Pulse Nightclub shooter, Omar Mateen, a registered Democrat and son of a man who was seen attending a Hillary Clinton campaign rally,[300] was really a Democrat.

The claim is neither true nor false, according to LaCapria, but rather a "mixture." Why? Because LaCapria questions whether Mateen being a registered Democrat proves he's a Democrat.

---

299   Curet, Monique. "No, young children cannot take hormones or change their sex." PolitiFact, March 5, 2021, https://www.politifact.com/factchecks/2021/mar/05/viral-image/no-young-children-cannot-take-hormones-or-change-t/.

300   Nelson, Louis. "Orlando shooter's father attends Clinton rally." Politico, August 9, 2016, https://www.politico.com/story/2016/08/orlando-shooter-father-clinton-226819.

According to her, Mateen registered as a Democrat in 2006, so it's possible that his political views have changed since then.[301]

A bit odd that he never changed his affiliation if that were the case.

FACT-CHECKER READS MINDS TO EXCUSE HILLARY CLINTON ON BENGHAZI

In an "explainer"-style article, PolitiFact's Lauren Carroll argued that there was no way Hillary Clinton would have lied to Patricia Smith about the 2012 Benghazi terrorist attack that killed her son Sean Smith and three other Americans.[302]

At the 2016 RNC, Smith said in a speech that Clinton told her a "video" was the spark for the 2012 terrorist attack, even though she knew that wasn't true. "When I saw Hillary Clinton at Sean's coffin ceremony, just days later, she looked me squarely in the eye and told me a video was responsible. Since then, I have repeatedly asked Hillary Clinton to explain to me the real reason why my son is dead. I'm still waiting," she recalled.

Susan Rice infamously popularized the bogus talking point that an anti-Muslim video is what led to the Benghazi attack. Smith previously said on CNN years earlier, on October 10, 2012, that Rice "talked to me personally, and she said this is the way it was. It was because of this film that came out."[303]

Smith said a year later at a House hearing that Clinton and President Obama also individually told her the attack stemmed from the video. Of Clinton specifically, Smith said on Megyn Kelly's Fox show in 2015, "She lies. Very simple. She is not telling the truth."[304]

But according to Carroll, simply because there's the possibility that Hillary didn't know she was being untruthful, it's therefore untrue to say that she lied. "If she did say something about the video, would it have been an intentional lie? It's very possible that this is one of the many conflicting pieces of intelligence that the administration was working

---

301   LaCapria, Kim. "Orlando Shooter Was a Democrat?" Snopes, May 30, 2016, https://www.snopes.com/fact-check/orlando-shooter-was-democrat/.

302   Adair, Bill, and Lauren Carroll. "Checking Patricia Smith's claims about Clinton and Benghazi." PolitiFact, July 18, 2016, https://www.politifact.com/article/2016/jul/19/checking-patricia-smiths-claims-about-clinton-and-/.

303   Ibid.

304   Ibid.

with at the time," Carroll reasoned. She also tries to cast doubt on Smith's account because "some, but not all, family members who have spoken to the media said Clinton mentioned a video or protests in their meeting."

While it's possible for one to unintentionally spread misinformation, Hillary did indeed do it intentionally here.

Documents released by the House Select Committee on Benghazi five months after Carroll's article was published revealed that the State Department's employees were met with "shock and disbelief" to see Rice pushing the bogus "video" theory on talk shows in the aftermath of the attacks.[305]

Gregory Hicks, the deputy chief of mission in Tripoli, Libya, said that Rice's "video" comments contradicted Libyan officials who correctly pointed to terrorists being behind the attack. "I have been a professional diplomat for 22 years. I have never been as embarrassed in my life, in my career, as on that day. There have been other times when I've been embarrassed, but that's the most embarrassing moment of my career," Hicks said. [306]

Meanwhile, the senior Libya desk officer for the State Department's Bureau of Near Eastern Affairs said in an email to colleagues, "I think Rice was off the reservation on this one." The deputy director for the bureau's Office of Press and Public Diplomacy wrote back, "Off the reservation on five networks!"[307]

Snopes also came to Hillary Clinton's defense when she falsely said during a campaign event on MSNBC in 2016 that "we didn't lose a single person in Libya," which ignores the four killed in the Benghazi attack.

Kim LaCapria rated those accurately quoting Hillary as "Mostly False," claiming that the remark was taken out of context. LaCapria notes that the next line out of Hillary was, "We didn't have a problem in supporting our European and Arab allies [during the 2011 intervention in Libya]…in working with NATO…and now we've gotta support the Libyan people." And she concludes from this that Hillary was only talking about the Libya invasion.[308]

305 Engel, Pamela. "BENGHAZI REPORT: State Department employees reacted in shock to Susan Rice's first TV appearances." Insider, June 28, 2016, https://www.businessinsider.com/state-department-susan-rice-benghazi-2016-6.
306 Ibid.
307 Ibid.
308 LaCapria, Kim. "Hillary Clinton: 'We Didn't Lose a Single Person' in Libya." Snopes, March 16, 2016, https://www.snopes.com/fact-check/hillary-clinton-benghazi-msnbc/.

However, Hillary also defended her support for the invasion of Libya in part due to the two democratic elections that have taken place since, in 2012 and 2014 (which was after the Benghazi attack).

CNN'S FALSE FACT-CHECK ON JAMES COMEY

CNN had to "clarify" a fact-check that played defense for former FBI director James Comey.

During Donald Trump's post-impeachment acquittal speech (Ukraine edition), he incorrectly recalled that Comey first admitted to leaking information when questioned by Chuck Grassley during a committee meeting. Comey had admitted to leaking sensitive information (and was referred for criminal prosecution for leaking and document theft), just not under the circumstances Trump recalled.

CNN's Daniel Dale jumped on the claim with an article headlined, "Fact check: President Trump falsely claims former FBI Director James Comey admitted to leaking," where Dale tells us that "Trump's claim was the opposite of the truth. Comey denied being a leaker in that meeting of the Senate Judiciary Committee in May 2017."[309]

But the next month, in June 2017 testimony before the Senate Select Committee, Comey admitted coordinating a leak by giving memos with recorded conversations with Trump to Columbia law professor Daniel Richman. Comey said:

> I woke up in the middle of the night on Monday night, because it didn't dawn on me originally, that there might be corroboration for our conversations, might be a tape, my judgement was that I needed to get that out into the public square and so I asked a friend of mine to share the content of the memo with a reporter. I didn't do it myself for a variety of reasons, but asked him to, because I thought that it might prompt the appointment of a Special Counsel. I asked a close friend of mine to do that.[310]

---

309 Wagner, Meg, et al. "President Trump speaks after impeachment acquittal." CNN Politics, February 6, 2020, https://www.cnn.com/politics/live-news/trump-impeachment-acquitted-02-06-20/h_3a06947bb7db93271f9b20ba53540d8b.

310 Pavlich, Katie. "Comey Admits to Leaking: I Had a Friend Give My Memos To a Reporter." Townhall, June 8, 2017, https://townhall.com/tipsheet/katiepavlich/2017/06/08/comey-admits-to-leaking-i-had-a-friend-give-my-memos-to-a-reporter-n2338328.

After Dale became aware of the June 2017 comments, instead of admitting that Comey had admitted to leaking, he decided to debunk Trump on a technicality, and updated his article's headline to "Fact check: Trump falsely claims Comey admitted to leaking to Grassley." An editor's note referencing the headline change was added to the story, but there was no mention that Comey did admit to leaking under other circumstances.

CNN ADDS WORDS TO QUOTE SO THEY CAN RATE IT FALSE

When Senator Rick Scott said that Biden's $1 trillion American Rescue Act contributed towards inflation, CNN's fact-checker Daniel Dale claimed this was untrue, because "to blame rising gas prices and food prices exclusively on government spending is false." Dale inserted the word "exclusively" so that he could reach the conclusion he wanted.[311]

ROBERT MUELLER'S "DEMOCRAT TEAM" ACTUALLY "ONLY" 77 PERCENT DEMOCRAT

During the 2017–2019 special counsel era of the Spygate saga, FactCheck. org criticized Trump for stating that Robert Mueller's team is "a group of investigators that are all Democrats" when "only" thirteen of the seventeen are registered as Democrats and zero as Republicans. One hundred percent of the team members whose affiliation we know are Democrats, as are 77 percent of all members, yet FactCheck.org still rated this claim as an "embellishment."[312]

In a similar vein, when Trump said that Mueller team investigators went to Hillary Clinton's 2016 election night party, FactCheck.org offered the rebuttal that only one person from Mueller's team attended. "So that's one, but not 'some,' as the president says."[313]

---

311 Howell, Mike. "Fact Check: Fact-Checkers Falsely Claim They Are Fact-Checkers." The Heritage Foundation, January 7, 2022, https://www.heritage.org/progressivism/commentary/fact-check-fact-checkers-falsely-claim-they-are-fact-checkers.

312 Kiely, Eugene, et al. "FactChecking Trump's Tweetstorm." FactCheck.org, March 20, 2018, https://www.factcheck.org/2018/03/factchecking-trumps-tweetstorm/.

313 Farley, Robert. "Trump's Misleading Attack on Mueller Team." FactCheck.org, May 4, 2018, https://www.factcheck.org/2018/05/trumps-misleading-attack-on-mueller-team/.

MARTHA'S VINEYARD, SHORT-LIVED SANCTUARY

In response to Governor Ron DeSantis sending illegal aliens (who are technically classified as asylum seekers) to Martha's Vineyard over the summer of 2020, and the epically hypocritical response that followed from the island's liberal residents who couldn't get rid of them fast enough, PolitiFact's Madison Czopek attempted to provide spin for the embarrassed residents of the island.

In search of a claim to try to debunk, Czopek decided on a random social media post mocking the island's virtue signaling residents for "deporting 50 illegals after only 24 hours." Czopek then rated this claim false on the basis that the illegals couldn't be "deported" because the word "deported" means removal from the country as a whole, not from a particular area.[314]

Of course, anyone using the term "deported" in this context is well aware of this, and is using the word as a synonym for "removed." While Czopek is clearly grasping at straws here in her quest to prove any right-leaning claim about Martha's Vineyard hypocrisy wrong, she at least didn't embarrass herself by trying to argue that the post wasn't true because the illegals were actually deported after nearly forty-eight hours, not "just" twenty-four.

Meanwhile, also at PolitiFact, fact-checker Gabrielle Settles decided to try to pick apart the claim that Martha's Vineyard "was a sanctuary city until the buses arrived" with dubious reasoning.

Like Czopek, Settles begins with semantics by telling us what we already know, that Martha's Vineyard is an island and not itself a city.[315] This basically amounts to complaining that people aren't being more specific and calling it a "sanctuary island," even though the policies of that "sanctuary" would be identical.

Nearly making a point of substance, Settles points out that of the six towns on the island, only three did vote to adopt sanctuary policies (which was in 2017). This would be relevant if the illegals arrived on one of the three towns that didn't adopt sanctuary (island) policies, but

---

314   Czopek, Madison. "Claim that Martha's Vineyard 'deported' migrants is wrong." PolitiFact, September 21, 2022, https://www.politifact.com/factchecks/2022/sep/21/instagram-posts/claim-marthas-vineyard-deported-migrants-wrong/.

315   Settles, Gabrielle. "At least three Martha's Vineyard towns adopted sanctuary policies in 2017." PolitiFact, September 27, 2022, https://www.politifact.com/factchecks/2022/sep/27/peggy-hubbard/least-three-marthas-vineyard-towns-adopted-sanctua/.

they stayed in Edgartown, which was one of the three to vote to become a sanctuary (though apparently not for longer than forty-eight hours).

FACT-CHECKER CALLS INTO QUESTION THE EXISTENCE OF ANTIFA ITSELF

As part of a fact-check aimed at helping memory hole nationwide riots in 2020, a *Newsweek* fact-checker attempted to cast doubt on whether antifa is even a group that really exists.

The poorly argued fact-check came in response to an appearance from Senator Ted Cruz on ABC's *The View*, when the panel got into a fiery debate over who the "real election deniers" are.

As Whoopi Goldberg began to bring up January 6th, Cruz fired back, "Did I miss an entire year of Antifa riots where cities across this country were burning...?" to which she dopily replied, "I don't know what an Antifa riot is."

To justify rating Cruz's claim false, *Newsweek*'s Tom Norton argues that the majority of riots in 2020 occurred between late May to early June immediately before admitting that some of them did in fact continue for "nearly" a year in Portland, an antifa stronghold.[316]

To wiggle out of admitting that fiery antifa riots did in fact go on for longer than a year while rating Cruz's claim that they did false, Norton then comically adds that *not all* the Portland riots were characterized by arson. Here Norton inverts an infamous CNN chyron, arguing that the riots were violent but mostly non-fiery.

As if this wasn't embarrassing enough, Norton also tries to argue that antifa actually-sort-of-technically doesn't exist, as there's no formal organization called "antifa." Was he expecting a violent militant left-wing group to register a 501(c)(3)?

---

316   Norton, Tom. "Fact Check: Ted Cruz's Claim That 'Antifa' Burnt U.S. Cities for a Year." *Newsweek*, October 26, 2022, https://www.newsweek.com/fact-check-ted-cruzs-claim-that-antifa-burnt-us-cities-year-1754884.

The Ruling

False.

The "Antifa riots" Cruz refers to are almost certainly the protests, which followed George Floyd's death. Most of these occurred between late May to early June 2020. Although many buildings were damaged or destroyed by fire during protests, this did not carry on throughout the year.

While protests did continue in Portland, Oregon for nearly a year, according to media reports, these were not all characterized by arson. Most other cities quietened down after June 2020.

Labeling the protests as "Antifa riots" is misleading too as there is no organization or group known as such.

FACT CHECK BY Newsweek's Fact Check team

False: The claim is demonstrably false. Primary source evidence proves the claim to be false.
Read more about our ratings.

99.992 PERCENT TRUE CLAIM FROM GOV. RON DESANTIS RATED FALSE

Amid Hurricane Ian slamming Florida, PolitiFact's Yacob Reyes rated it "Mostly False" when Governor Ron DeSantis said that Lee County was not inside the hurricane's forecast cone.[317]

The justification for the "False" rating was that one largely uninhabited barrier island with fewer than two dozen residencies named Cayo Costa,[318] which is inside Lee County, falls inside the storm's path. If we were to assume an average three people per residence on Cayo Costa, the

317   Reyes, Yacob. "Most of Florida's Lee County wasn't in the cone three days before hurricane, but parts of it were." PolitiFact, October 4, 2022, https://www.politifact.com/factchecks/2022/oct/04/ron-desantis/most-floridas-lee-county-wasnt-cone-three-days-hur/.

318   Lanum, Nikolas. "Conservative frustration with fact checkers grows after several dubious PolitiFact articles in one week." Fox News, October 8, 2022, https://www.foxnews.com/media/conservative-frustration-fact-checkers-grows-dubious-politifact-articles-one-week

island's population would account for roughly 0.008 percent of the population of Lee County (760,822) as of the 2020 Census.[319]

But even that would be an overestimate, as Governor DeSantis' press secretary also pointed out that the island was completely uninhabited at the time.[320]

The population of Cayo Costa is not mentioned at any time by Reyes.

FACT-CHECKERS VS. JOKES

Fact-checking satirical websites like the Babylon Bee isn't below them, and neither is fact-checking jokes without even bothering to acknowledge them as such.

In one of the funniest moments of television during the 2020 Democrat presidential primaries, MSNBC's Brian Williams was joined by the *New York Times'* Mara Gay, who aimed to quantify just how much money the over $500 million Michael Bloomberg wasted on his presidential campaign really was.

"Somebody tweeted recently that actually with the money he spent he could have given every American a million dollars," Gay said. "When I read it tonight on social media, it kind of all became clear," Williams replied. As they spoke, a tweet from Mekita Rivas appeared on the screen that read, "Bloomberg spent $500 million on ads. The U.S. population is 327 million. He could have given each American $1 million and still have money left over."

And the math checks out—if you take six zeroes off the 327 million in the denominator. Of course, the actual math comes out to about $1.53 per citizen. (Of note, PolitiFact themselves covered this debacle, correctly rating Gay's claim "Pants on Fire.")[321]

The incident became emblematic of how plausible the absurd is to the leftist pundit class when it confirms what they want to be true. To claim that one man spending a fraction of his wealth could've been

---

319 "QuickFacts: Lee County, Florida." United States Census Bureau, https://www.census.gov/quickfacts/leecountyflorida.

320 Pushaw, Christina. October 4, 2022, https://twitter.com/ ChristinaPushaw/status/1577473373277339648.

321 McCarthy, Bill. "Bad math at MSNBC: Bloomberg's ad spending wasn't enough to give every American $1 million." PolitiFact, March 6, 2020, https://www.politifact.com/factchecks/2020/mar/06/msnbc/bad-math-msnbc-bloombergs-ad-spending-wasnt-enough/.

enough to make every American a millionaire should've aroused some suspicion, even among those not mathematically inclined. But nowhere in the chain of command started by Mekita Rivas, herself a contributing editor for politics at *Cosmopolitan Magazine* who has also written for the *New York Times*, Gay, Williams, and his graphics team, did this seem implausible.

Mass mockery ensued, which Gay inevitably blamed on racism,[322] and the mathematical blunder itself became something of an internet meme.

But not everyone gets the joke.

It wasn't until 2022 that one would go viral and make it on PolitiFact's radar.

After Elon Musk announced that he'd be pursuing a purchase of Twitter for $44 billion, no shortage of liberals took this as an opportunity to extol their virtue over how they'd spend a hypothetical $44 billion they'll never possess. Many of them blasted Musk for not spending the money on world hunger, even though $44 billion is less than what the U.S. spends on food stamps every year, and thus clearly would not be enough to fix the problem on a global scale.

A Twitter user named Gabe (@gbuchdahl), who claims to be a student at Yale University, decided to poke fun at those virtue-signaling their generosity with other people's money by bringing back the old joke, posting, "With 40 billion dollars, Elon Musk could have given each of the 330M people living in America a million dollars and still had $7B left over. Why aren't more people talking about this?"

The tweet got over 150,000 "likes," with the comments section showing a healthy mix of people getting the joke and others explaining basic division to Gabe.

PolitiFact's Jeff Cercone found himself in the latter category.

"No, Elon Musk couldn't give every American $1M with money he spent on Twitter," he wrote fact-checking the joke tweet, which was correctly (and also pointlessly) rated "False."[323] Kind enough to save us the mental bandwidth required to punch two numbers into a calculator, Cercone tells us that "using the figures in the post, and a calculator, split-

---

322   Wulfsohn, Joseph. "New York Times' Mara Gay mocked for attacking 'racist Twitter mob' following MSNBC math fiasco." Fox News, March 11, 2020, https://www.foxnews.com/media/new-york-times-mara-gay-msnbc-math-fiasco.

323   Cercone, Jeff. "No, Elon Musk couldn't give every American $1M with money he spent on Twitter." PolitiFact, April 28, 2022, https://www.politifact.com/factchecks/2022/apr/28/facebook-posts/no-elon-musk-couldnt-give-every-american-1m-money-/.

ting $40 billion among 330 million Americans would mean each person would get $121.21."

After the "fact-check," Gabe added to his Twitter bio: "math guy that had a viral tweet about bad math." He also posted a link to the aforementioned PolitiFact article about the Mara Gay math incident two years prior to mock them for not realizing what he was joking about.

Cercone then missed the joke a second time, adding to his article in an update: "The author seems to be handling the error in good humor. In his Twitter biography, he calls himself a 'math guy that had a viral tweet about bad math.' And after being called out on his error, he pinned the tweet to the top of his feed and also shared a previous fact check PolitiFact did of a similar claim from MSNBC about former presidential candidate Michael Bloomberg's expenditures on campaign ads."

Woosh.

Making matters even more surreal, Cercone wasn't the only one to not get the joke. *USA Today's* Bayliss Wagner spent five hundred words correcting the arithmetic, only to then admit that the post is a joke, which she had explained to her by "Greg" when she reached out for comment.[324]

Snopes, too, ran a fact-check of the tweet and didn't realize they were fact-checking a joke while having the joke practically spelled out to them, writing: "This isn't the first time that bad math has been employed to criticize people with vast amounts of wealth. In fact, the above-displayed tweet was followed up with a message about a similar incident in March 2020 when MSNBC anchor Brian Williams, while reading a viral tweet, said that former New York City Mayor Mike Bloomberg could have given every American $1 million instead of spending $500 million on ads." They also made note that PolitiFact debunked Gay's claim after she made it back in 2020.[325]

They're so close, aren't they?

In another case, PolitiFact's Tom Kertscher took on FreedomWorks' tongue-in-cheek social media post that "the Democrats want you American taxpayers to shell out $3 billion for 'non-racist' trees."

FreedomWorks was making reference to and mocking a $3 billion "tree equity" program. Kertscher nearly comes close to realizing that he's

---

324 Wagner, Bayliss. "Fact Check: Musk's Twitter offer would be enough to give every American $120." *USA Today*, April 28, 2022, https://www.usatoday.com/story/news/factcheck/2022/04/28/fact-check-musks-twitter-offer-not-enough-give-all-americans-1-m/9561162002/.

325 McCarthy, "Bad math at MSNBC."

effectively fact-checking a joke, writing, "The phrase 'non-racist' trees' appears to be a mocking reference to a climate-change policy that proponents of the Democrats' plans call tree equity. But the phrase mangles the definition of that concept."[326]

Kertscher then went on to explain how the program works and rated FreedomWorks' claim "Mostly False" without ever realizing the hilarity of people unironically using the phrase "tree equity."

---

326 Kertscher, Tom. "'Tree Equity' part of $3.5T bill targets low-income areas that have fewer trees." PolitiFact, September 29, 2021, https://www.politifact.com/factchecks/2021/sep/29/freedomworks/tree-equity-part-35t-bill-targets-low-income-areas/.

BAD ECONOMICS

As someone with an economics background, I can confidently say that every fact-checker opining on economics would themselves fail an economics course, which isn't all too surprising considering there isn't a single economist among the fact-checkers featured in this chapter.

Since the major fact-checkers have their fact-checkers examine a diverse array of topics rather than a field they're specialized in, they rely primarily on experts. Setting aside the already documented problem of fact-checkers fielding responses from experts that favor their pre-determined conclusion, even in a world where they were evenly soliciting opinions from both sides of a debate, this would be a problem because they're unqualified to dissect the quality of arguments they're delivering a verdict on.

While economists don't agree on much, the fact-checkers aren't in line with the rare consensus opinions on a number of economic issues when that consensus supports a right-of-center perspective.

The minimum wage is one such issue where there's limited disagreement that, all variables held equal, increasing the cost of labor will decrease its supply (though there is a debate among economists about when the benefits can offset the job losses, depending on the size of the hike).

So rather than admit that consequence, the fact-checkers instead downplay it. In one PolitiFact article, fact-checker Chris Nichols debunked Kevin McCarthy's claim that raising the national minimum wage to $15 an hour would cost 3.7 million jobs, which was rated "False" because the report McCarthy cited found that as many as 2.7 million jobs could be lost. Even when as many as 2.7 million jobs could be lost as a consequence, Nichols was able to find an exaggerated claim of its negative impact to make it look smaller by comparison.[327]

---

327   Nichols, Chris. "GOP House Leader Kevin McCarthy Distorts Job Loss Estimates For $15 Minimum Wage Hike." PolitiFact, February 11, 2021, https://www.politifact.com/factchecks/2021/feb/11/kevin-mccarthy/gop-house-leader-kevin-mccarthy-distorts-job-loss-/.

Other minimum wage–related fact-checks on PolitiFact have documented how the minimum wage isn't keeping up with inflation[328] and how it tends to be increased under Democrats, which is presented as a positive.[329]

Another issue is rent control, which economists overwhelmingly oppose because it has the unintended consequence of freezing the construction of new housing. As has been the case throughout the history of rent control laws, landlords aren't incentivized to build more housing when they can't turn a profit. Yet when presenting both sides of the debate on a California rent control measure, PolitiFact's Chris Nichols presents the consensus opinion as one that economists "generally agree with" but that "other experts" disagree with.[330] A poll of top economists from the University of Chicago asked if they believed that local ordinances limiting rent increases in New York and San Francisco have had a positive impact over the past three decades—which 1 percent agreed with, and 4 percent were undecided. The other 95 percent either disagreed or strongly disagreed.[331] Yet the opinion held by 95 percent of economists was presented as "general agreement."

Even concepts as basic as adjusting for inflation are a source of confusion for the fact-checker.[332]

PolitiFact Wisconsin's Madeline Heim rated the claim that inflation-adjusted wages hadn't increased in the three decades leading up to 2020 "Mostly True," justifying the ruling with the nonsensical explanation that:

---

328   Heim, Madeline. "Yes, it's been decades since the minimum wage kept up with inflation, and years since it increased." PolitiFact, June 19, 2021, https://www.politifact.com/factchecks/2021/jun/19/mandela-barnes/yes-its-been-decades-minimum-wage-kept-inflation-a/.

329   Putterman, Samantha. "Yes, Democrats held majority almost every time Congress approved a minimum wage increase." PolitiFact, February 14, 2019, https://www.politifact.com/factchecks/2019/feb/14/facebook-posts/yes-democrats-held-majority-almost-every-time-cong/.

330   Nichols, Chris. "Fact-checking claims about California's rent control measure Prop 10." PolitiFact, October 11, 2018, https://www.politifact.com/article/2018/oct/11/fact-checking-claims-about-californias-rent-contro/.

331   "Rent Control." IGM Forum, February 7, 2012, https://www.igmchicago.org/surveys/rent-control/.

332   White, Bryan W. "PolitiFact Wisconsin: Real wages increasing but not keeping up with inflation." PolitiFact Bias, March 5, 2020, https://www.politifactbias.com/2020/03/politifact-wisconsin-real-wages.html.

A quick comparison shows that *wages today are slightly higher than what they were then, once inflation is factored in* [emphasis mine]. But the cost of everyday goods like rent, groceries and cars have outpaced that median wage growth.[333]

Her comment nonsensically translates to "inflation adjusted wages are rising but they're not keeping up with inflation." Inflation is an average, so the prices of common items increasing above the official rate of inflation are offset by the prices of items rising at rates slower than it or decreasing. Heim doesn't even fully comprehend the words she's using, yet simply by virtue of her employment at PolitiFact, gets to be the "final say" on whether or not it's true that wages are keeping up with inflation.

Nor can PolitiFact even agree with themselves on if wages are going up or not. In 2019, fact-checker Louis Jacobson rated Kamala Harris' claim that "the cost of living is going up, but paychecks aren't keeping up"[334] as false. If only Harris had waited until she was VP to make that comment, her claim would've been true.[335]

FACT-CHECKER OPINES ON NATIONAL DEBT WITHOUT UNDERSTANDING HOW TO MEASURE THE NATIONAL DEBT

PolitiFact's Louis Jacobson showcased an embarrassing level of economic illiteracy in his analysis of Joe Scarborough's claim in September 2018 that "President Trump's Republican Party will create more debt in one year than was generated in the first 200 years of America's existence," a "Pants on Fire" statement that he rated "Mostly True."[336]

Jacobson begins with some context:

333 White, Bryan W. "PolitiFact Wisconsin vs. PolitiFact." Zebra Fact Check, March 16, 2020, https://www.zebrafactcheck.com/politifact-wisconsin-vs-politifact/.

334 Jacobson, Louis. "Are paychecks failing to keep up with inflation?" PolitiFact, January 30, 2019, https://www.politifact.com/factchecks/2019/jan/30/kamala-harris/are-paychecks-failing-keep-inflation/.

335 Furman, Jason. "Even in a Hot Economy, Wages Aren't Keeping Up With Inflation." *Wall Street Journal*, April 12, 2022, https://www.wsj.com/articles/even-in-a-hot-economy-wages-arent-keeping-up-with-inflation-unemployment-job-growth-federal-reserve-11649779113.

336 White, Bryan. "PolitiFact flubs GDP comparison between added debt and cumulative debt." PolitiFact Bias, September 12, 2018, https://www.politifactbias.com/2018/09/politifact-flubs-gdp-comparison-between.html.

The first question to answer is, when do you start counting to calculate debt for "the first 200 years of America's existence"?

Probably the most obvious way to do it is to look at the cumulative debt between 1776, the date of the Declaration of Independence, and 1976, the national bicentennial year.

At the end of 1976, the public debt was $477.4 billion, and the gross federal debt was just under $629 billion.

So how does that compare to Trump's record?

The amount of public debt added in 2017 -- a year when Trump was president for all but 20 days and when the Republicans were in control of Congress -- was $497.8 billion, while the amount of gross federal debt added was $666.3 billion.[337]

Right off the bat, Jacobson errs by comparing the national debt in nominal terms. The public debt of $477.4 billion in 1976 is equal to $2.1 trillion when adjusted for inflation in 2018 dollars, and the gross federal debt of $629 billion is roughly $3 trillion.[338]

While he didn't adjust those figures for inflation, Jacobson does quote an economist in his article who informs him (correctly) that a better way to look at debt over periods of time is by measuring it against the nation's gross domestic product (GDP). This gives context to the size of the debt by measuring it relative to the size of the U.S. economy.

He then misunderstands how to use this sort of measurement, incorrectly concluding that when looking at public debt relative to the economy, Scarborough is correct in his comparison because "public debt as a percentage of GDP in 2017 was far higher (almost 77 percent) than it was in 1976 (about 27 percent)."

But Scarborough *did not say that the national debt was higher* in 2018 than it was in 1976. He *said that the cumulative debt added* during the first two hundred years of the republic (ending in 1976) was less than the

---

337 Jacobson, Louis. "Will Trump, GOP create more debt in one year than in first 200 years of U.S.?" PolitiFact, September 12, 2018, https://www.politifact.com/factchecks/2018/sep/12/joe-scarborough/will-trump-gop-create-more-debt-one-year-first-200/.

338 "CPI Inflation Calculator." U.S. Bureau of Labor Statistics, https://www.bls.gov/data/inflation_calculator.htm.

debt added in the single year of 2018. For Scarborough's statement to be true, it would mean that debt as a share of GDP would've had to increase by over 27 percentage points in a single year.

Jacobson's article also contained a chart of historical public debt (debt the government owes to non-federal entities) that further contradicts his case. As he describes the chart, it shows public debt as a percent of GDP decreasing from 76.7 percent to 76.5 percent from 2016 to 2017 but being projected to increase to 78.8 percent in 2018. So according to his own math, ninety times as much debt relative to GDP would've had to be added for his statement to be true.

Public debt as a percentage of gross domestic product, 1940-2023

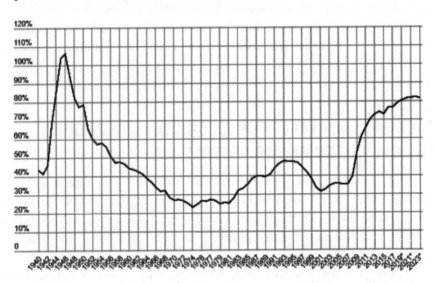

THE TRUTH, THE HALF-TRUTH, AND NOTHING BUT THE TRUTH

PolitiFact's W. Gardner Selby rated only "Half True" Ted Cruz's August 2012 statement that the U.S. national debt is greater than the size of the entire U.S. economy.[339]

Selby acknowledges that as of writing, U.S. GDP was $15.6 trillion, and the national debt was $15.9 trillion (while I'm no math expert, I can confirm that 15.9 trillion is greater than 15.6 trillion).

Selby then goes on to argue that this doesn't really count because, of the $15.9 trillion in debt, $11.2 trillion is publicly held debt (owed to non-federal entities), and $4.8 trillion is intragovernmental debt (debt that one part of the federal government owes to another part of the government). Of the intragovernmental debt, Selby states, "Such money will have to be repaid, it's presumed, but the demand is less pressing right now and it doesn't affect credit markets."

So Cruz correctly stated that the national debt exceeds the size of the U.S. economy, but that gets reduced to a "Half True" statement because Selby thinks that whether or not debt counts as debt is contingent on how pressing it is that you pay it back relative to your other debt.

FACT-CHECKER FALLS FOR A COMMON MYTH ABOUT ILLEGAL ALIENS PAYING FEDERAL TAXES

During the third and final presidential debate, when taking digs at Trump's immigration agenda, Hillary Clinton said that half of the illegal immigrants in the U.S. pay federal income tax, which PolitiFact's Lauren Carroll claimed to validate, pointing to estimates from the Urban-Brookings Tax Policy Center.[340]

While it is the case that IRS, Social Security, and CBO data show that half of illegal immigrants file federal tax returns, virtually none of them pay net federal taxes. The IRS uses the Individual Taxpayer Identification Number (ITIN) in lieu of a Social Security number for certain illegal aliens and legal residents. Obtaining an ITIN allows illegal

---

339 Selby, W. Gardner. "Ted Cruz, addressing delegates, says national debt exceeds the U.S. gross domestic product." PolitiFact, August 28, 2012, https://www.politifact.com/factchecks/2012/aug/29/ted-cruz/ted-cruz-addressing-delegates-says-national-debt-e/.

340 Carroll, Lauren. "Clinton: Undocumented workers pay more than Trump in federal income taxes." PolitiFact, October 27, 2016, https://www.politifact.com/factchecks/2016/oct/27/hillary-clinton/clinton-undocumented-workers-pay-more-trump-federa/.

aliens to be able to claim the Child Tax Credit of up to $1,000 per child per year—and 72 percent of them end up paying no federal income tax and claiming the child credit. In contrast, only 14 percent of people who file tax returns with a Social Security number both pay no income tax and receive that payment.[341]

MULTIPLE FACT-CHECKERS STRUGGLE TO TELL THE EUROPEAN UNION AND GERMANY APART

PolitiFact's Louis Jacobson rated as false Trump's true statement that the European Union exports millions of cars to the U.S. through a creative reinterpretation of his statement.

Trump stated in a 2018 speech, "The European Union…they send us Mercedes, they send us—by the millions—the BMWs—cars by the millions."[342]

And in 2018 alone, the EU exported 1,155,488 cars to the U.S., worth about €37.3 billion.[343]

So how does Trump's statement get a false rating? Because of Jacobson's questionable reading comprehension. According to him, Trump "singled out German cars" by talking about Mercedes and BMWs, and those two firms don't export millions of cars to the U.S. Those brands being prefaced by "the European Union" was of no relevance to Jacobson.[344]

This would be the equivalent of me saying, "Hershey makes hundreds of types of candies—Reese's, Twizzlers, Kit Kats—more than you can count," and Jacobson rating it false because that's only three brands. There is no ambiguity in Trump's statement that he was talking about total EU exports.

PolitiFact partnered with the television network Newsy to create video fact-checks, and they too tackled Trump's easily understood comment and misinterpreted it in the same way.

341 Agresti, James D. "Illegal Immigrants and Federal Income Taxes." Just Facts, November 7, 2016, https://www.justfactsdaily.com/illegal-immigrants-and-federal-income-taxes/.

342 Jacobson, Louis. "Donald Trump wrong that Mercedes, BMW import cars to U.S. by the millions." PolitiFact, July 2, 2018, https://www.politifact.com/factchecks/2018/jul/02/donald-trump/donald-trump-wrong-mercedes-bmw-import-cars-us-mil/.

343 "EU-US Automobile Trade: Facts and Figures." European Automobile Manufacturers Association, March 2019, https://www.acea.auto/files/EU-US_automobile_trade-facts_figures.pdf.

344 White, Bryan W. "PolitiFact: "European Union"=Germany." PolitiFact Bias, July 6, 2018, https://www.politifactbias.com/2018/07/politifact-european-uniongermany.html.

Like Jacobson, Newsy's James Packard is under the bizarre impression that the European Union exports are a synonym for German exports, claiming that "according to the Center for Automotive Research, BMW and Daimler—which makes Mercedes-Benz—sold 729,000 cars in the U.S. last year."

"That's not millions. That's not even 1 million," Packard continues, assuring us that he can perform basic arithmetic.

Packard did at least respond to feedback from critics and noted in an article accompanying the video that if Trump was talking about the whole EU (which he was), then there are just under 1.2 million annual car exports (he was quoting figures from 2016), and that's not millions *plural*.[345] While this is obvious nitpicking on his side, it can be nitpicked in response that Trump didn't specify that he was talking about a single year.

Oddly, they missed an actual factual error in Trump's speech while they were focused on "debunking" a fact. At one point in the speech, Trump incorrectly stated that our trade deficit with the Union as a whole was $151 billion the year prior when it was actually $101 billion. There was a false claim in Trump's speech they could've quite easily fact-checked, yet they missed that, and the best they could manage was fact-checking a sentence they didn't even understand.

ASSESSING THE PUTIN PRICE HIKE

In the early stages of denial of the historic inflation about to take place on his watch, President Joe Biden falsely predicted that the inflation that was starting to flare up would merely be "transitory." After Russia invaded Ukraine, Biden added the so-called "Putin price hike" talking point to his list of excuses.

"Make no mistake: The current spike in gas prices is largely the fault of Vladimir Putin," stated Biden in a speech on March 14, 2022, to the National League of Cities.

PolitiFact's Louis Jacobson came to Biden's defense to give him the fact-checker seal of approval that his excuses were valid.

"The most recent spike in gas prices has stemmed largely from Putin's invasion of Ukraine. However, gas prices were rising long before

---

345 Packard, James. "Trump Says These Cars Are Imported 'By The Millions' — They Aren't." Newsy, July 5, 2018, https://www.newsy.com/stories/bmw-mercedes-imports-lower-than-trump-says/.

the Russian troop buildup around Ukraine became front-page news, primarily from growing demand due to the economic recovery from the pandemic," Jacobson wrote, justifying his "Mostly True" rating.[346]

Below is a chart of the national average gas price ending the date Jacobson's article was published.

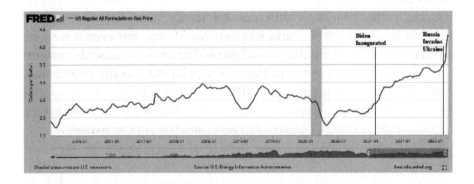

Prices increased from $2.39 the week Biden was elected to $3.53 the week Russia invaded Ukraine (an increase of $1.14), and then they jumped 78 cents to $4.31 the week Jacobson's article defended Biden blaming the rise on Putin.

Jacobson even acknowledges this, noting what Biden's framing leaves out is that the gas price rise following Putin's military buildup accounted for a fraction of the overall rise in gasoline prices, but rates the claim "Mostly True" because Biden was blaming the "current spike in gas prices," which Jacobson interprets as being in recent weeks. But the trend has already been going up, and this was just an acceleration of an existing trend. Biden is focusing on one increase to divert attention from the prior increase.

Just a month later, Biden would go from blaming rising gas prices to blaming all inflation on the Kremlin.

During an April 2022 event in Greensboro, North Carolina, Biden said in response to inflation as measured by the consumer price index clocking in at 8.5 percent in March on a year-over-year basis,[347] "Putin's

---

346   Jacobson, Louis. "How much blame does Putin deserve for high gasoline prices?" PolitiFact, March 16, 2022, https://www.politifact.com/factchecks/2022/mar/16/joe-biden/joe-biden-blame-putin-high-gasoline-prices/.

347   (Meaning inflation was up 8.5 percent when comparing inflation in March 2022 to March 2021.)

invasion of Ukraine has driven up gas prices and food prices all over the world. Ukraine and Russia are the one and two largest wheat producers in the world. We're three. They're shut down. We saw that in yesterday's inflation data. What people don't know is that 70% of the increase in inflation was the consequence of Putin's Price Hike because of the impact on oil prices, 70%."[348]

Biden was at least specific enough to say that 70 percent of the increase he's blaming on Putin was only for March. But even if we were to take him at his word, that would prove that only a minuscule percentage of total inflation is due to Putin, as can be seen on the chart below, with inflation data ending April 2022.

12-month percentage change, Consumer Price Index, selected categories, not seasonally adjusted

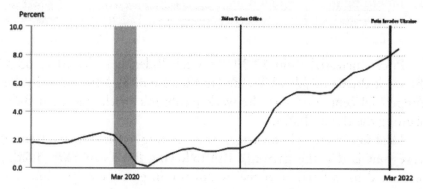

Hover over chart to view data.
Note: Shaded area represents recession, as determined by the National Bureau of Economic Research.
Source: U.S. Bureau of Labor Statistics.

As pictured in the chart above, inflation went from averaging under 2 percent a month on a year-over-year (YOY) basis under Donald Trump to 8.5 percent YOY in March, and Biden is blaming 70 percent of the jump from February to March 2022 on Putin. On a non-annualized basis, inflation was 0.8 percent in February and 1.2 percent in March—meaning Putin would be responsible for inflation of only 0.28 percent of the March increase by Biden's math.

Perhaps Biden was hoping people would be misled into thinking most of all the recent inflation was due to Putin from his comments.

348   "President Biden Delivers Remarks on Building a Better America 4/14/22 Transcript." Rev, April 17, 2022, https://www.rev.com/blog/transcripts/ president-biden-delivers-remarks-on-building-a-better-america-4-14-22-transcript.

With few exceptions, the media's alleged fact-checkers were happy to either ignore this comment from Biden or handle it with kid gloves when examining its merits.

The *Washington Post*'s Glenn Kessler looked into Biden's claim and didn't award it any "Pinocchios" (points on the *WaPo*'s ratings scale) despite saying he was tempted to award it two Pinocchios, which is reserved for claims that have "significant omissions and/or exaggerations." "Many people might believe the president was referring to the headline annual number in the inflation report — 8.5 percent… We certainly did when we first heard this line," Kessler admitted, adding that he believes Biden's claim is still defensible since it's specific to March. "Biden's math is defensible…but at the same time, ordinary people might certainly have assumed he was referring to the 12-month inflation rate, not the one-month figure."[349] No kidding.

In the end, it's left to the reader to decipher Biden's comments, with Kessler concluding, "But he did refer to the invasion that began 50 days ago. So we will leave this unrated and let readers decide for themselves." And that's exactly what Biden was hoping people would do—decide for themselves incorrectly.

If only there were someone to check the facts.

TAXES ARE TAX SAVINGS ACCORDING TO FACT-CHECKER LOGIC

Nancy Pelosi said at a January 2018 press conference about the Children's Health Insurance Program (CHIP) that it would save the American taxpayer money, claiming:

> The reauthorization "should have been done in September, first of all," Pelosi said in her Jan. 18, 2018. "Second of all, we wanted 10 years…which, by the way, saves $6 billion."

> Republicans, she added, rejected a 10-year reauthorization. "Doing it for six years saves $1 billion. That's good," she said. "Doing it 10 years, saving $6 billion is better. In fact, it's best."[350]

---

349 Kessler, Glenn. "Biden's claim that 70% of inflation jump is due to 'Putin's price hike.'" *Washington Post*, April 15, 2022, https://www.washingtonpost.com/politics/2022/04/15/bidens-claim-70-inflation-jump-was-due-putins-price-hike/.

350 Jacobson, Louis. "Nancy Pelosi correct that renewing kids' health program saves money." PolitiFact, January 24, 2018, https://web.archive.org/web/20180131020916/http://www.politifact.com/truth-o-meter/statements/2018/jan/24/nancy-pelosi/nancy-pelosi-correct-renewing-kids-health-program-/.

PolitiFact's Louis Jacobson rated the claim true "because the reauthorization of CHIP would essentially take the place of more expensive programs, doing so would essentially net savings for the government."

Jacobson's key piece of evidence is a letter from CBO director Keith Hall, who explained that: "Extending funding for CHIP for 10 years yields net savings to the federal government because the federal costs of the alternatives to providing coverage through CHIP (primarily Medicaid, subsidized coverage in the marketplaces, and employment-based insurance) are larger than the costs of providing coverage through CHIP during that period."

The letter was accompanied by a chart showing that the CHIP funding legislation would increase spending by $6.9 billion and increase tax revenues by $12.9 billion,[351] the difference being the $6 billion in savings that Pelosi claims.

In other words, what is being presented as "savings" is really just increased taxes.[352]

This is simply economic newspeak. If we're going to start framing tax increases as "savings," they'd be the only "savings" in the world that cost you more money.

SPENDING CUTS VS. HYPOTHETICAL SPENDING CUTS

PolitiFact's Madeline Heim rated Biden's statement that Senator Ron Johnson "wants to put Social Security and Medicare on the chopping block every single year" as "Mostly True," despite him never explicitly calling for that.[353]

Heim bases her verdict on comments Johnson made in a radio interview in August 2022 that he believes all federal spending should be discretionary and reviewed by Congress every year. The federal government will spend just over $6 trillion in 2022 year, and most of it is in the

---

351   There is no explanation given explaining where the increased tax revenues are coming from, but it is likely due to CHIP beneficiaries dropping employment-based coverage, which would result in them receiving less of their income in nontaxable health benefits and wages.

352   White, Bryan W. "Does CHIP renewal save $6 billion over 10 years?" Zebra Fact Check, February 5, 2018, https://www.zebrafactcheck.com/chip-renewal-save-6-billion-10-years/.

353   Heim, Madeline. "Biden mostly on track that Ron Johnson wants annual approval of Social Security and Medicare." PolitiFact, September 26, 2022, https://www.politifact.com/factchecks/2022/sep/26/joe-biden/biden-mostly-track-ron-johnson-wants-annual-approv/.

category of "mandatory spending," while only about $1.7 trillion (28 percent) is discretionary spending, and can be modified.[354]

During the radio interview, Johnson explained that he believed converting all spending into discretionary spending would allow fiscally challenged programs to be fixed. "If you qualify for the entitlement you just get it, no matter what the cost. And our problem in this country is that more than 70% of our federal budget, of our federal spending, is all mandatory spending. It's on automatic pilot. It never…you just don't do proper oversight. You don't get in there and fix the programs going bankrupt," he told host Joe Giganti.

Heim acknowledges that Johnson never called for cutting Social Security and Medicare, but said that because making them eligible for being cut is a consequence of being converted into discretionary spending, the claim is thus "Mostly True." A hypothetical consequence of a policy is thus treated as its intended goal.

A POINTLESS FACT-CHECK ABOUT TEXAS GOV. ABBOTT AND PROPERTY TAXES

Ahead of losing another governor's race, Beto O'Rourke claimed that under Texas governor Greg Abbott, "property taxes have gone up $20 billion," a claim PolitiFact's Nusaiba Mizan rated as "Mostly True."[355]

As Mizan notes, property tax receipts increased by $20 billion from $52 billion in 2015 (when Abbott took office) to $74 billion by 2021, a 43 percent increase.

The only reason Mizan gives this claim a "Mostly True" rating instead of a "True" rating is that the governor has no role in setting property taxes—local municipalities do—and that rising home values could be responsible for part of the increase in property taxes. In other words, only O'Rourke's implication that Abbott is responsible for the increase is being rated false here. Yet without that implication, what's the point in O'Rourke making the statement?

354   Amadeo, Kimberly. "U.S. Federal Budget Breakdown." The Balance, June 24, 2022,
      https://www.thebalancemoney.com/u-s-federal-budget-breakdown-3305789.

355   Mizan, Nusaiba. "O'Rourke right about property tax going up under
      Abbott, but governor's role is indirect." PolitiFact, May 19, 2022,
      https://www.politifact.com/factchecks/2022/may/19/beto-orourke/
      orourke-right-about-estimated-property-tax-revenue/.

While property tax revenues are on the rise on an absolute basis (as you'd expect in a state that is drawing millions from the rest of the country and had its homeownership rate reach an all-time high of 70 percent by the end of 2020),[356] they declined slightly on a percentage basis over the time period in question.

- In 2015, Texas had an average property tax rate of 1.9 percent on homeowners.[357]

- In 2020 (the most recent year the Tax Foundation has data for), Texas had an average property tax rate of 1.66 percent.[358]

Rising home prices (and thus assessed property values) are the driving factor behind rising property tax receipts.

Texas is among the states adding the most population due to internal migration, which is increasing home prices, and in turn leading to an increased tax base. The 2020 Census revealed that while nearly half of all U.S. counties lost population since 2010, of the five counties that gained three hundred thousand or more people, two were in Texas.[359] While not the fastest growing on a percentage basis, Texas was the number one state for population added between 2010 and 2020, growing by four million people. Over the specific time period relevant to this analysis (2015–2021), Texas' population grew 7.5 percent (or by two million people).[360]

Home prices in Texas increased 43 percent from 2015 to 2021, the exact amount of the percent increase in property tax receipts, and the state has an overall residential appraised ratio of 98 percent of market

356 Falcon, Julia. "Texas homeownership rate reaches an all-time high." HousingWire, November 18, 2020, https://www.housingwire.com/articles/texas-homeownership-rate-reaches-an-all-time-high/.

357 Walczak, Jared. "How High Are Property Taxes in Your State?" Tax Foundation, August 13, 2015, https://taxfoundation.org/how-high-are-property-taxes-your-state/.

358 "Facts & Figures: How Does Your State Compare? 2022." Tax Foundation, March 2022, https://taxfoundation.org/wp-content/uploads/2022/03/Facts-Figures-2022-How-Does-Your-State-Compare.pdf.

359 Mackun, Paul, et al. "Around Four-Fifths of All U.S. Metro Areas Grew Between 2010 and 2020." U.S. Census Bureau, August 12, 2021, https://www.census.gov/library/stories/2021/08/more-than-half-of-united-states-counties-were-smaller-in-2020-than-in-2010.html.

360 "Resident Population in Texas." St. Louis Federal Reserve, https://fred.stlouisfed.org/series/TXPOP.

value.[361] In just one year, appraisals increased 15–30 percent in Harris County, 20 percent in Tarrant County, 24 percent in Dallas County, 25 percent in Bexar County, and 53 percent in Travis County.[362]

Bizarrely, not only does PolitiFact's Mizan acknowledge that the governor doesn't set property tax rates, but she also acknowledges that Abbott has promoted property tax relief while still rating O'Rourke's claim as "Mostly True."

Mizan admits:

> …in 2019, the [Republican-controlled Texas] Legislature required cities, counties and most special districts to seek voter approval to set a property tax that raises revenues more than 3.5%. For junior colleges and hospital special districts, the threshold for voter approval is 8%. For school districts, it is 2.5%.
>
> …
>
> Texas Republicans have campaigned on property tax relief too. Abbott added property tax relief to the Legislature's third special session agenda in 2021 that resulted in a now-approved amendment to the Texas Constitution. Abbott similarly publicized his support for property tax relief as a priority in a May 2 tweet ahead of May 7 elections.[363]

Abbott's campaign responded to O'Rourke's ad by saying Abbott reduced property taxes by $18 billion since taking office and that O'Rourke increased property taxes as an El Paso City Council member.

Texas voters approved Proposition 2 in 2022, which raises the homestead exemption for school district property taxes from $25,000 to $40,000. They also approved Proposition 1, which corrected a 2019

361 Haney, Josh. "The (Long, Long) History of the Texas Property Tax." Texas Comptroller, October 2015, https://comptroller.texas.gov/economy/fiscal-notes/2015/october/proptax.php.

362 Wilder, Forrest. "What the Bleep Is Going On With Texas Property Taxes?" *exas Monthly*, August 2022, https://www.texasmonthly.com/news-politics/high-property-tax-home-appraisals/.

363 Mizan, "O'Rourke right about property tax going up under Abbott, but governor's role is indirect."

oversight in tax relief that did not apply to homeowners who
or sixty-five or older because their school tax burden is capp

By PolitiFact's own admission, it's estimated that wit
propositions, total property taxes would've been $69.7 billio
(vs. the $67.2 billion it actually was), $74.5 billion in 2020
billion), and $79 billion in 2021 (vs. $73 billion), for $12.5
total savings.

FACT-CHECKERS VS. OUR OWN EYES AND EARS

For the fact-checker, "Who are ya gonna believe? Me or your own eyes?" is their catchphrase.

The process of finding bad fact-checks for this book was at least made slightly easier by a handful of supposed fact-checks that immediately stood out in the theme of trying to dispute what I knew I had seen with my own eyes or heard with my own ears.

As soon as Joe Biden makes a new gaffe, the fact-checkers mobilize as if there's a race against time to produce a plausible explanation for the embarrassing clip the American public has just seen.

In one particularly odd case, video from an April 2022 speech in North Carolina went viral showing a confused Biden shaking hands with the air, then awkwardly wandering behind his podium before he's finally directed to walk off the stage.

And in an attempt to convince people that they didn't actually just watch what they did, PolitiFact tweeted out, "You might have seen a clip of President Joe Biden 'shaking hands' with thin air. It never happened. Here's the truth, as well as how misinformers manufacture and embellish embarrassing presidential moments." They then come up with an excuse, that "videos show that Biden was actually pointing at the audience behind him with his whole hand. He acknowledges the right side, then the left, and begins to walk forward."[364]

PolitiFact added that the video is just the latest in a series of videos that supposedly misleadingly portray Biden as senile by showing how he behaves. And thanks to their "fact-check," the circulation of the embarrassing gaffe got suppressed on Facebook and Twitter, preventing potentially millions from seeing it.

---

364   PolitiFact. April 20, 2022, https://twitter.com/politifact/
      status/1516838083051855879?lang=en.

Lead Stories also tried to rewrite reality surrounding the video, claiming, "While some footage seems to show the president inexplicably trying to offer a handshake to someone who isn't there, in a wider view of the event posted on YouTube, Biden's gesture appears to be more of a greeting or acknowledgement than an attempted handshake, and does not seem so out of place."[365]

None of this was true.

Indeed, they're so unconfident in their "fact-checking" abilities that they have to hedge their own language by using terms like "appears to be" and "does not seem so" because even they know they're full of it.

While it's often the case that deceptively edited or out-of-context information goes viral and becomes the de facto truth (such as the Trump "very fine people" myth that PolitiFact helped spread), that wasn't the case for the prior example or any of the others in this chapter.

POLITIFACT SAYS MAXINE WATERS DIDN'T INCITE VIOLENCE, WATERS SAYS SHE DID

PolitiFact's Tom Kertscher was evaluating whether or not it was true that Maxine Waters said Trump supporters are "not welcome here" and that "we must welcome everyone who crosses our borders."

"No, California Rep. Maxine Waters didn't say Trump supporters 'not welcome here'" was Kertscher's verdict, while rating the claim "Mostly False."[366]

There are two quotes from Waters here, but the relevant one is the one saying that Trump supporters "are not welcome."

While Kertscher's fact-check was published in 2021, it's about comments that Waters made in June 2018, which are as follows:

> **Waters:** Let's make sure we show up wherever we have to show up. And if you see anybody from that Cabinet in a

---

365 Thompson, Sarah. "Fact Check: Biden's Gesture Was NOT Directed To Empty Space -- There Was Audience Seating There." Lead Stories, April 19, 2022, https://leadstories.com/hoax-alert/2022/04/fact-check-bidens-gesture-was-not-directed-to-empty-space-there-was-audience-seating-there.html.

366 Kertscher, Tom. "No, Calif. Rep. Maxine Waters didn't say Trump supporters 'not welcome here." PolitiFact, January 25, 2021, https://www.politifact.com/factchecks/2021/jan/25/facebook-posts/no-calif-rep-maxine-waters-didnt-say-trump-support/.

restaurant, in a department store, at a gasoline station, you get out and you create a crowd. And you push back on them. And you tell them they're not welcome anymore, anywhere. We've got to get the children connected to their parents.

We don't know what damage has been done to these children. All that we know is they're in cages. They're in prisons. They're in jails. I don't care what they call it, that's where they are and Mr. President, we will see you every day, every hour of the day, everywhere that we are to let you know you cannot get away with this.

She then went on MSNBC to double down, telling the host: "The people are going to turn on them. They're going to protest. They're going to absolutely harass them until they decide that they're going to tell the president, 'No, I can't hang with you.'"[367]

Kertscher's explanation for why the quote doesn't count as Waters saying that Trump supporters aren't welcome is laughable. In his words, "…while Waters did make statements suggesting Trump Cabinet members should be singled out in public, she did not direct her comments at Trump supporters broadly."[368]

While Waters' June 2018 comments were what Kertscher focused on, Waters herself would admit to regularly threatening "[Trump's] constituents and supporters" all that time in response to criticism of those comments.

As The Hill reported in September 2018, in a speech where Waters would otherwise claim to be against inciting violence, she:

…mockingly said in a speech last weekend that she threatens Trump supporters all the time, defending her comments in June that said people should confront members of President Trump's administration.

Waters said she was not threatening Trump supporters or constituents when she called on people to confront Trump

---

367 Hains, Tim. "Maxine Waters Warns Trump Cabinet: 'The People Are Going To Turn' On You." RealClearPolitics, June 24, 2018, https://www.realclearpolitics.com/video/2018/06/24/maxine_waters_the_people_are_going_to_turn_on_trump_enablers.html.

368 Kertscher, "No, Calif. Rep. Maxine Waters didn't say Trump supporters 'not welcome here.'"

Cabinet members and supporters in June—and said Trump was wrong to accuse her of doing so at the time.

"I did not threaten [Trump] constituents and supporters. *I do that all the time, but I didn't do that that time*," [emphasis mine] Waters said to laughter from a crowd in Los Angeles.[369]

Yet that quote didn't make the "fact-check."

If Trump called for violence against Democrat members of Congress, do you think we'd be reading PolitiFact "fact-checks" assuring us that he at least didn't incite it against Democrat voters, just members of Congress?

FACT-CHECKERS INTRODUCE DOUBT OVER ALEXANDRIA OCASIO-CORTEZ CLEARLY SAYING WE SHOULDN'T ALLOW BILLIONAIRES TO EXIST

Snopes fact-checked a Turning Point USA meme that quoted Representative Alexandria Ocasio-Cortez as saying, "A society that allows billionaires to exist…is wrong." The statement came from an interview with writer Ta-Nehisi Coates.

Snopes said this is false because what AOC said is that it was wrong for billionaires to exist side-by-side with chronic poverty and deprivation. Poverty has always existed long before billionaires, and unless AOC thinks it's going to disappear soon, this "context" doesn't seem to do much to deny the motion that AOC doesn't think there should be billionaires.

AOC's disdain for billionaires and her statement that she doesn't think they should exist right now is also made clear in one of the parts of her conversation "providing context" included in their own article.

> **Coates:** Do you think it is moral for individuals to, for instance—do we live in a moral world that allows for billionaires? Is that a moral outcome—
>
> **Ocasio-Cortez:** No—
>
> **Coates:** —in and of itself?

369   Keller, Megan. "Maxine Waters mocks: I threaten Trump supporters 'all the time.'" The Hill, September 10, 2018, https://thehill.com/homenews/house/405877-maxine-waters-i-threaten-trump-supporters-all-the-time/.

Ocasio-Cortez: —it's not. It's not. And I think it's important to say that—I don't think that necessarily means that all billionaires are immoral. It is not to say that someone like Bill Gates, for example, or Warren Buffett, are immoral people. I do not believe that. I'm not saying that, but I do think a system that allows billionaires to exist when there are parts of Alabama where people are still getting ringworm because they don't have access to public health, is wrong.

Or put simpler:

- AOC says that billionaires shouldn't exist in a world with poverty.

- We live in a world with poverty.

Therefore, she doesn't think billionaires should exist.

FACT-CHECKERS DENY WHAT DEMOCRAT PRESIDENTIAL CANDIDATES SAID ON TV IN FRONT OF TENS OF MILLIONS OF PEOPLE

On the second night of the Democrat presidential debates hosted by CNN in September 2019, Savannah Guthrie asked the candidates to "raise your hand if your government plan would provide coverage for undocumented immigrants."

Every single candidate raised their hand, which included Marianne Williamson, John Hickenlooper, Andrew Yang, Pete Buttigieg, Joe Biden, Bernie Sanders, Kamala Harris, Kirsten Gillibrand, Michael Bennet, and Eric Swalwell.

This practically handed the GOP a layup and inevitably found its way into a thirty-second Trump ad that centered on Guthrie's comments and the response. "They are all the same," the ad narrated over footage of the Democrats raising their hands. "These Democrats support giving illegal immigrants free health care at our expense." The ad continues, stating that Democrats want to "spend taxpayer dollars covering illegal aliens."

But according to PolitiFact's Miriam Valverde, just because Democrats want to give illegal aliens health care, that doesn't mean it's "free" (i.e. taxpayer-funded). Valverde writes:

Is it true that Democrats at a June debate said they support free health care—at the expense of taxpayers—for immigrants illegally in the United States?

The ad is misleading. Candidates were asked whether their health care plans would cover immigrants here illegally. They were not, however, directly asked if that coverage would be free.[370]

Valverde wants us to believe there's ambiguity over whether health care will be "free" or not among a stage full of Democrats, nearly all of whom support some form of a Medicare for All "universal health care" program that would make the federal government the primary spender in the U.S. health-care market.

Two candidates, in particular, elaborated on their stances, Pete Buttigieg and Joe Biden, neither of whom make any reference to illegals paying any out-of-pocket costs.

> **Buttigieg:** Our country is healthier when everybody is healthier. And remember, we're talking about something people are getting a—given a chance to buy into. In the same way that there are undocumented immigrants in my community who pay, they pay sales taxes, they pay property taxes directly or indirectly. This is not about a handout. This is an insurance program. And we do ourselves no favor by having 11 million undocumented people in our country be unable to access health care.

Valverde interprets Buttigieg's comment about illegals deserving government health care because they pay taxes as Buttigieg saying that people would "buy" the coverage, and thus it's "not about a handout."

Meanwhile, Biden said that no one, regardless of immigration status, can go uncovered.

> **Biden:** You cannot let—as the mayor [Buttigieg] said, you cannot let people who are sick, no matter where they come

---

370 Valverde, Miriam. "Fact-checking Trump ad on Democrats, health care for immigrants illegally in the country." PolitiFact, August 1, 2019, https://www.politifact.com/factchecks/2019/aug/01/donald-trump/fact-checking-trump-ad-democrats-health-care-immig/.

from, no matter what their status, go uncovered. You can't do that. It's just going to be taken care of, period. You have to. It's the humane thing to do. But here's the deal. The deal is that he's right about three things. Number one, they in fact contribute to the well-being of the country, but they also— for example, they've increased the lifespan of Social Security because they're—they have a job. They're paying the Social Security tax. That's what they're doing. It's increased the lifespan. They would do the same thing in terms of reducing the overall cost of health care by them being able to be treated and not wait until they're in extremis.

Somehow, Valverde concludes from those comments that "some candidates on stage that night support universal health-care coverage, through Medicare for All. But there isn't agreement among all candidates on the provisions of that type of coverage. A version of Medicare for All would offer coverage to all individuals by replacing premiums, co-pays and deductibles. One way the government would pay for Medicare for All would be through payroll taxes; so immigrants in the country illegally who do pay income taxes would contribute that way."

It's ironic because it's usually conservatives responding to liberals talking about "free" health care who point out that "it's not free; it's tax-payer-funded." Now we have conservatives accusing Democrats of wanting to give free health care to illegal aliens, and the fact-checker is arguing that it is not really free because it is taxpayer-funded.

This wasn't the only time the candidates had explained their health-care plans and if they'd cover illegals:[371]

- Joe Biden said during the first 2020 Democrat debate: "You cannot let people who are sick, no matter where they come from, no matter what their status, go uncovered."

- Pete Buttigieg said to the *Washington Post*: Undocumented immigrants should be able to buy coverage through the public option,

371 "Do you believe all undocumented immigrants should be covered under a government-run health plan?" *Washington Post*, March 16, 2021, https://web.archive.org/web/20210414212706/https:/web.archive.org/web/20190819095053/https://www.washingtonpost.com/graphics/politics/policy-2020/medicare-for-all/undocumented-immigrant-health-care/.

- Marianne Williamson said to the *Washington Post*: "Yes."

- Bernie Sanders to the *Washington Post*: "My plan would cover all U.S. residents."

- Elizabeth Warren, Kamala Harris, and Kirsten Gillibrand: Co-sponsored Sanders' Medicare for All bill, which would give free health care to illegals.

Or phrased more simply, there would be illegal aliens receiving U.S. health care at the taxpayer's expense—like Trump's ad said.

BIDEN CALLS FOR GETTING RID OF FOSSIL FUELS, FACT-CHECKERS SAY HE NEVER SAID THAT

During a rally in New Hampshire in February 2020, Biden told the crowd, "*We are going to get rid of fossil fuels.*" A number of protesters who seemed to be environmentalists started to heckle, which prompted Biden to add, "That's okay, these guys are okay, they want to do the same thing that I want to do, they want to phase out fossil fuels and we're going to phase out fossil fuels."

Biden also said there would be no more coal plants on his watch. Elsewhere on the campaign trail, Biden had called for putting fossil fuel executives in prison.[372]

During a live fact-check of the Mike Pence vs. Kamala Harris debate, when Pence said, "Joe Biden and Kamala Harris want to abolish fossil fuels and ban fracking," PolitiFact chimed in: "Pence's claim is False. Biden has not called for banning fracking outright. He wants to block the federal government from issuing new permits for drilling on public land. And, *Biden has never said that he wants to abolish fossil fuels.*"[373]

Except for the time he did months prior, on video.

---

372 Kartch, John. "Joe Biden: "We Are Going to Get Rid of Fossil Fuels." Americans for Tax Reform, February 8, 2020, https://www.atr.org/joe-biden-we-are-going-get-rid-fossil-fuels/.

373 PolitiFact. October 8, 2020, https://twitter.com/PolitiFact/status/1314213079001886722.

BIDEN SAYS N-WORD ON VIDEO, BUT IT DOESN'T COUNT

In 2020, Snopes and PolitiFact rated it "False" that Joe Biden has used the n-word as a senator, which there is video of him using.

The quote in question was from a 1985 Senate hearing considering Ronald Reagan's nomination of William Bradford Reynolds to serve as associate AG of the U.S. Biden said, "The court concluded, quote: 'The governor's opposition to the Nunez plan was predicated in significant part on his delineation of a majority Black district centered in Orleans Parish.' And in confidential portions of your staff memo, they brought to your attention the allegation that an important legislator, in defeating the Nunez plan in the basement, said, quote: 'We already have a (n——) mayor; we don't need another (n——) big-shot.'"

Snopes, with the headline "Did Biden Use Racial Slurs in the Senate?" rated the claim "False"[374] because Biden was quoting somebody else using the word when he used the word, as did PolitiFact.[375]

"Missing context" would be an appropriate rating to assign the claim here, but something that happened can't be "False."

VP HARRIS AND THE CASE OF EQUITY-BASED AID

After Vice President Kamala Harris voiced that she believes the federal government should politicize disaster relief to prioritize "communities of color" (i.e. nonwhite people), the fact-checkers mobilized to cast doubt that Harris really did just say the quiet part out loud.

VP Harris' comments were made during a fireside chat in early October 2022 with Priyanka Chopra Jonas, where Harris said: "We have to address this [natural disasters] in a way that is about giving resources based on equity, understanding that we fight for equality, but we also need to fight for equity…sometimes we have to take into account those disparities."

Harris admitted that prioritizing disaster relief is a policy she would like to see advanced, which some incorrectly interpreted as Harris admit-

374 Mikkelson, David. "Did Biden Use Racial Slurs in the Senate?" Snopes, October 22, 2020, https://web.archive.org/web/20220209013635/ https://www.snopes.com/fact-check/biden-n-word-senate/.

375 O'Rourke, Ciara. "Biden was quoting a memo during a Senate hearing." PolitiFact, July 22, 2020, https://web.archive.org/web/20211109002052/https://www.politifact.com/ factchecks/2020/jul/22/viral-image/biden-was-quoting-memo-during-senate-hearing/.

ting that disaster aid for Hurricane Ian, which had just ripped through Florida, would be prioritized in such a way.

The context for the exchange is as follows:[376]

> **Priyanka Chopra Jonas:** So just talking about a point that I am very concerned about, and I'm sure so is this room: You and the administration obviously are working around the clock right now to support relief efforts in Florida and to prepare citizens as Hurricane Ian now is closing in on South Carolina.
>
> …
>
> So can you talk just a little bit about the relief efforts, obviously, of Hurricane Ian and what the administration has been doing to address the climate crisis in the states?
>
> But — and just a little follow up, because this is important to me: We consider the global implications of emissions, right? The poorest countries are affected the most.

Leading VP Harris to reply:

> **VP Harris:** So, first of all, again, thanks to the leadership in this room, which were part of the propelling force in the 2020 election so that we could actually be in office — because one of the requests — dare I say, "demands" — of this group was, "Do something about the climate crisis." And so, we were able to be elected. Thank you, everyone here.
>
> And then have the $370 billion in the Inflation Reduction Act dedicated to address the climate crisis — not only because it is a crisis, as it evident — as evidenced, as you have mentioned by Ian, by the wildfires happening in California, the floods, the hurricanes, but also because of America's leadership and what it should be globally on this issue. And so that has happened, and it will propel a lot of good work.

376 "Remarks by Vice President Harris During Fireside Chat with Priyanka Chopra Jonas." The White House, September 30, 2022, https://www.whitehouse.gov/briefing-room/speeches-remarks/2022/09/30/remarks-by-vice-president-harris-during-fireside-chat-with-priyanka-chopra-jonas/.

The crisis is real, and the clock is ticking. And the urgency with which we must act is without any question.

And the way that we think of it and the way I think of it is both in terms of the human toll and — I know we are all thinking about the families in Florida, in Puerto Rico with Fiona — and what we need to do to help them in terms of an immediate response and aid, but also what we need to do to help restore communities and build communities back up in a way that they can be resilient — not to mention, adapt — to these extreme weather conditions, which are part of the future.

On the point that you made about disparities: You know, when I was — back when I was District Attorney of San Francisco — I was elected in 2003 — I started one of the first environmental justice units of any DA's office in the country focused on this issue. *And in particular on the disparities, as you have described rightly, which is that it is our lowest income communities and our communities of color that are most impacted by these extreme conditions and impacted by issues that are not of their own making* [emphasis mine].

Chopra then inquired if "women" also were included in this category, and Harris agreed that they were. Harris then added what would be the most widely clipped and quoted part of the exchange: "And so, we have to address this in a way that is about giving resources based on equity, understanding that we fight for equality, but we also need to fight for equity; understanding that not everyone starts out at the same place. And if we want people to be in an equal place, sometimes we have to take into account those disparities and do that work."

Her comments set off a firestorm, leading to FEMA director Deanne Criswell being forced to clarify in a CBS News interview that relief wouldn't be prioritized in such a way. Florida governor Ron DeSantis spokeswoman Christina Pushaw also called Harris' statements "false" and said they were "causing undue panic and must be clarified."[377]

---

377   Phillips, Jack. "FEMA Chief Responds to Kamala Harris Claim About Prioritizing 'Communities of Color.'" *Epoch Times*, October 2, 2022, https://www.theepochtimes.com/fema-chief-responds-to-kamala-harris-claim-about-prioritizing-communities-of-color_4769877.html.

Whether or not Harris was implying that aid would be prioritized by race for Hurricane Ian is up for interpretation, as she may have been talking about future natural disasters that she questionably blames on "climate change." Either way, Harris either wants to see disaster relief based on so-called "equity," or lied that she's already doing so because she sees it as such a noble cause.

PolitiFact's Jeff Cercone decided to try to downplay the racist insanity of VP Harris' comments by creating confusion about what she's alleged to have said in the first place. [378] Instead of focusing on the unquestionably true statement that VP Harris favors prioritizing aid by race, Cercone instead decides to attack the more ambiguous claim that VP Harris' comments imply that such a policy was already happening.

To do this, Cercone penned a fact-check based around a single comment from Senator Rick Scott during an interview with CBS host Margaret Brennan, who he told, "I think what we got to do is we got to bring everybody together. I'd also say that what Vice President Harris said yesterday or the day before yesterday, that, you know if you have a different skin color, you're going to get relief faster, that's not helpful either."

While it's fine to fact-check a false interpretation of a claim, Cercone uses this as an opportunity to obscure the true interpretation of a claim— that Harris favors race-based aid.

Among Cercone's arguments is that "Harris did not say any particular race would be prioritized in relief efforts"—which I suppose is "technically" true in that she only admitted by process of elimination which particular race *wouldn't* be prioritized.

The concept of so-called "environmental justice" on the left is hardly anything new, and the EPA's website under the Biden admin has an entire section on it.[379] It would be more out of character if VP Harris wasn't spouting the kind of rhetoric she's "accused" of—and the great irony of those denying that VP Harris said we should prioritize race in relief aid is that if such a policy were to take effect, they'd be the same people immediately defending it.

Cercone also claims that "there is nothing on websites for FEMA or the federal Disaster Assistance Improvement Program about race or

378 Cercone, Jeff. "No, Kamala Harris didn't say Hurricane Ian relief would be based on skin color." PolitiFact, October 3, 2022, https://www.politifact.com/factchecks/2022/oct/03/rick-scott/no-kamala-harris-didnt-say-hurricane-ian-relief-wo/.

379 "Environmental Justice." United States Environmental Protection Agency, https://www.epa.gov/environmentaljustice.

equity, just information about where Floridians affected by Hurricane Ian can find information about how to receive federal aid." Yet a cursory Google search for "Disaster Assistance Improvement Program equity" will turn up an article from FEMA's website with the header "FEMA Makes Changes to Individual Assistance Policies to Advance Equity for Disaster Survivors" as the second search result.[380]

It's also the case that FEMA issued a 2022–2026 strategic plan that openly states its goal is to "instill equity as a foundation of emergency management, lead the whole of community in climate resilience, and promote and sustain a ready FEMA and prepared nation."[381]

In another section of their website explaining the plan, titled "Objective 1.3 - Achieve Equitable Outcomes for Those We Serve," FEMA uses "underserved communities" as a euphemism for "communities of color," stating that "underserved communities experience differences in how prepared they are to respond to disasters, how well their homes have been adapted to mitigate against local hazards, and how quickly their communities are able to resume social and economic life after a major event. FEMA must direct its resources to eliminate disparities in these outcomes. FEMA assistance is not designed to solve societal inequities. However, by intentionally directing resources to communities most in need, FEMA will be able to counteract systemic disaster inequities."[382]

Among those quoted in PolitiFact's article is White House deputy press secretary Andrew Bates, who lied to them in an email that "the vice president was addressing a different subject: long-term climate resilience investments passed with strong bipartisan support." After PolitiFact's article went live, Bates then tweeted out the article citing him saying that Harris' comments were taken out of context as proof that Harris' comments were taken out of context.[383]

---

380 "FEMA Makes Changes to Individual Assistance Policies to Advance Equity for Disaster Survivors." FEMA, September 2, 2021, https://www.fema.gov/press-release/20210902/fema-makes-changes-individual-assistance-policies-advance-equity-disaster.

381 "Equity." FEMA, last updated October 1, 2022, https://www.fema.gov/emergency-managers/national-preparedness/equity.

382 "Objective 1.3 - Achieve Equitable Outcomes for Those We Serve." FEMA, last updated January 10, 2022, https://www.fema.gov/about/strategic-plan/goal-1/objective-1-3.

383 Bates, Andrew. October 4, 2022, https://twitter.com/AndrewJBates46/status/1577386718692450304.

The Associated Press fact-checker,[384] Reuters fact-checker,[385] and FactCheck.org[386] all joined the party too, furthering suspicions that the "fact-checkers" coordinate which absurd narratives they want to declare factual. Like PolitiFact, they all fact-checked a tangential false claim (that Hurricane Ian aid should be based on race) to cover up the true claim (that Harris wishes this were the case).

384 Goldin, Melissa. "Harris comments on addressing climate inequity misrepresented." Associated Press, October 4, 2022, https://apnews.com/article/fact-check-kamala-harris-hurricane-climate-change-516043387200.

385 "Fact Check-Clip of Kamala Harris on hurricane relief and equity taken out of context online." Reuters, October 4, 2022.

386 Kiely, Eugene. "What Vice President Harris Said — And Didn't Say — About Hurricane Relief." FactCheck.org, October 3, 2022, https://www.factcheck.org/2022/10/what-vice-president-harris-said-and-didnt-say-about-hurricane-relief/.

PREBUNKING GONE AWRY

Sometimes the fact-checker will double as a prophet, attempting to spin the narrative on things that haven't even happened yet. Not only will they fact-check you when you make an argument—they'll fact-check your predictions too.

This, too, reveals that narrative comes before fact. After all, if someone predicts that something will happen, what good does trying to preemptively fact-check if that prediction is correct or not do, as opposed to simply waiting to see how the prediction panned out and then refuting it accordingly?

The answer, of course, is none—unless the true goal is to shield liberal narratives from any and all criticism. Ironically, in this very process, the fact-checkers have ended up embarrassing themselves the most.

The most epic case of one of these attempts at preemptive fact-checking blowing up in their faces was PolitiFact's aforementioned continued denial that Barack Obama's health-care plan would lead to people losing their health-care plans, which they went as far as calling the "Lie of the Year," only to later have to reverse course and rate Obama's promise the "Lie of the Year."

That was well over a decade ago, and now the Poynter Institute actively promotes what they call "prebunking"—which they define as preemptively refuting false narratives, misinformation, or manipulation techniques.[387]

Whether or not prebunking is acceptable depends on the day of the week. Often PolitiFact will fact-check a prediction—and other times, decide something can't be fact-checked because it's a prediction.

In one case, PolitiFact's Clara Hendrickson defended Joe Biden and Democrat senator Gary Peters against an ad that highlighted their posi-

---

387 Smalley, Seth. "Prebunking is effective at fighting misinfo, study finds." The Poynter Institute, September 1, 2022, https://www.poynter.org/educators-students/writelane/reporting/2022/what-is-prebunking-fact-checking/.

tions on transgender issues and warned the public that they "support legislation that would destroy girls' sports" (referring to the Equality Act).

Hendrickson, however, said the allegations in the ad couldn't be fact-checked because "their specific criticism is that allowing transgender girls and women to compete on the basis of their gender identity would create an uneven playing field for student athlete and ultimately end girls' and women's sports. That's a prediction we can't fact-check."[388]

But they never had a problem fact-checking any of the predictions in this chapter—and as you'll see from their track record, they really ought not to have.

FACT-CHECKER TRIES TO GET AWAY WITH IGNORING NEW DETAILS DAMNING TO HILLARY CLINTON

During the 2016 presidential campaign cycle, PolitiFact's Lauren Carroll rated Hillary Clinton's false statement that she "never received nor sent any material that was marked classified" through her private email server as "Half True."[389]

That fact-check went live on July 3—a mere two days before James Comey issued a statement refuting Clinton's claims, citing 110 emails in fifty-two email chains that contained classified information that was classified at the time they were sent or received. There were also two thousand additional emails that were later "up-classified" to make them confidential.[390] Carroll then incorporated Comey's comments into her article but didn't change the rating because she says PolitiFact "bases [their] rulings on when a statement was made and the information available at the time."

---

388   Hendrickson, Clara. "Ad watch: Conservative PAC claims Gary Peters would 'destroy girls' sports." PolitiFact, September 15, 2020, https://www.politifact.com /article/2020/sep/15/ad-watch-peters-supports-ending-discrimination-bas/.

389   Carroll, Lauren. "Fact-checking Clinton's claim she 'never received nor sent any material that was marked classified." PolitiFact, July 3, 2016, https://web.archive.org/ web/20160704003217/http://www.politifact.com/truth-o-meter/statements/2016/ jul/03/hillary-clinton/fact-checking-clintons-claim-she-never-received-no/.

390   FBI National Press Office, "Statement by FBI Director James B. Comey on the Investigation of Secretary Hillary Clinton's Use of a Personal E-Mail System." FBI, July 5, 2016, https://www.fbi.gov/news/press-releases/press- releases/statement-by-fbi-director-james-b-comey-on-the-investigation- of-secretary-hillary-clinton2019s-use-of-a-personal-e-mail-system.

The fact-checkers may not respond to facts, but they do respond to public mockery when it's loud enough, and the next day, Carroll published a new article reversing course and giving Hillary's claim a false rating.[391]

JANUARY 6 SPIN: FACT-CHECKERS DENY ROLE OF INFILTRATORS AND INFORMANTS

Desperate to dispel any narrative that there could've been outside influence during the mostly peaceful protests on January 6, 2021, PolitiFact's Bill McCarthy was deployed to address the case of John Sullivan, a left-wing anti-Trump activist who was captured on video giving orders at the Capitol building.

"Let's go! Get up here!" Sullivan's phone recorded himself saying as protesters began scaling the walls of the Capitol. Sullivan yelled through a microphone outside the Capitol building, "Get in that shit! Let's go! Let's go! Move! Move! Move! Move! Storm that shit! This s—t is ours! This is our f—king house!"

He pointed at a door and said, "Why don't we go in there?" after which someone hit the door. He yelled as he entered the Capitol, "Let's burn this shit down," "We gotta get this shit burned," "It's our house mother---ers."[392]

Sullivan is also the person who filmed the killing of Ashli Babbitt at the hands of Lieutenant Michael Byrd, who had been disciplined years prior for leaving a weapon unattended in the Capitol bathroom.[393] Sullivan was among the first people to be named as potential infiltrators on January 6.

The exact claim McCarthy chose to fact-check was a Facebook post that "says left-wing activist John Sullivan 'incited (the) insurgence of

---

391 Carroll, Lauren. "FBI findings tear holes in Hillary Clinton's email defense." PolitiFact, July 6, 2016, https://www.politifact.com/factchecks/2016/jul/06/hillary-clinton/fbi-findings-tear-holes-hillary-clintons-email-def/.

392 Lynn, Anna, and James D. Agresti. "PolitiFact Warps Reality About Left-Wing Activist Inciting Capitol Riot." Just Facts Daily, February 1, 2021, https://www.justfactsdaily.com/politifact-warps-reality-about-left-wing-activist-inciting-capitol-riot.

393 Tully-McManus, Katherine. "Capitol Police weapon left unattended in Capitol bathroom, again." Roll Call, February 27, 2019, https://rollcall.com/2019/02/27/capitol-police-weapon-left-unattended-in-capitol-bathroom-again/.

(the) U.S. Capitol,'" which he rates "Mostly False." The Facebook post also said that Sullivan led a group called Insurgence USA.[394]

In a fact-check just two days later, on January 8, McCarthy claimed, "There's no evidence that Sullivan 'incited (the) insurgence' alone amid a crowd of thousands. Video he uploaded online shows his perspective as he filmed." McCarthy doesn't even represent the random Facebook page he's fact-checking correctly, as it does not accuse Sullivan of single-handedly inciting the "insurgence" at the Capitol.

McCarthy also denies that Sullivan was inciting violence and cites NPR/CNN photojournalist Jade Sacker, who was inside the Capitol building on January 6 (but was not there on behalf of either publication), and backed up Sullivan's account that he was just there to document what was happening.

Amazingly, video footage later would reveal that Sacker was complicit in Sullivan's plan. Sullivan's camera captured the following conversation between the two:

Sacker: I'll give you your hug now. We did it!

Sullivan: [Laughter]

Sacker: You were right, we did it.

Sullivan: Dude, I was trying to tell you. I couldn't say much.

Sacker: You were right [laughter].

Sullivan: You just have to watch my chat.

Sacker: Oh my God!

Sullivan: Is this not gonna be the best film you've ever made in your life?

Sacker: Yeah [unintelligible].

Sullivan: Nah, you gotta give me a real kiss for that shit.

Sacker: That's it.

Sullivan: Hell, yeah!

Sacker: Hell, yeah?

Sullivan: Hell, yeah!

---

394 Kertscher, Tom. "Photographer with man arrested in Capitol siege was not working for CNN or NPR." PolitiFact, January 18, 2021, https://www.politifact.com/factchecks/2021/jan/18/facebook-posts/photographer-man-arrested-capitol-siege-was-not-wo/.

...

>**Sacker:** Wait, you weren't recording, were you?
>
>**Sullivan:** I'll delete that shit after. But I didn't record you or me. We're just voices.

Sullivan later sold some of his January 6 footage to CNN and NBC for $350,000 each.[395]

Six days after McCarthy's fact-check was published, Sullivan was slapped with a slew of charges, including "one count of knowingly entering or remaining in any restricted building or grounds without lawful authority, one count of violent entry and disorderly conduct on Capitol grounds, and one count of interfering with law enforcement engaged in the lawful performance of their official duties incident to and during the commission of civil disorder."[396]

After this, McCarthy added an update to his article and kept the "Mostly False" rating based on the never-claimed premise that Sullivan single-handedly led a mob.

Elsewhere, PolitiFact's Tom Kertscher rated "False" an ad from Republican Mauro Garza, who asked in a campaign ad about January 6, "Were FBI agents used as political agitators?" He spends only a single paragraph mentioning people who have been identified as potential FBI informants, such as Ray Epps and Rally Runner. Kertscher's "rebuttal" to the allegations against the duo is that they both deny the accusations against them, which is all the proof he needs.[397]

WISCONSIN HEALTH DEPARTMENT THROWS FACT-CHECKER UNDER THE BUS

In one amusing case of fact-checking gone awry, the free-market think tank MacIver Institute published a report in September 2020 on flaws in

395 Feuerherd, Ben. "Anti-Trump Capitol rioter sold footage for $35K to NBC and CNN: court papers." *New York Post*, February 17, 2021, https://nypost.com/2021/02/17/accused-capitol-rioter-john-sullivan-sold-footage-for-35k-to-nbc-cnn/.

396 U.S. Attorney's Office, District of Columbia. "Utah Man Charged in Federal Court Following Events at the United States Capitol." Department of Justice, January 14, 2021, https://www.justice.gov/usao-dc/pr/utah-man-charged-federal-court-following-events-united-states-capitol.

397 Kertscher, Tom. "GOP Texas House candidate repeats false claim that FBI agents instigated Jan. 6 attack on US Capitol." PolitiFact, February 7, 2022, https://www.politifact.com/factchecks/2022/feb/07/mauro-garza/gop-texas-house-candidate-repeats-false-claim-fbi-/.

how Wisconsin's Department of Health Services (WDHS) was calculating its daily COVID-19 positive test rate, which the fact-checkers then criticized before the WDHS[398] themselves incorporated the MacIver Institute's suggestions.

It was being calculated as the number of positive cases divided by the number of people tested for the *first time*, which the MacIver Institute explained was an "incredible admission" because:

> If the goal is to calculate the daily positive test rate, then WDHS is using the wrong numerator and denominator. What they're actually calculating is the daily percentage of new COVID-19 cases among those who have never been tested before—a fairly meaningless statistic. It is not the positive test rate.

> On that same day, Sep. 15th, WDHS recorded the rate as 11%. That was calculated by comparing 1,352 new cases to 12,266 new people tested. However, there were almost 20,000 tests collected that day. If WDHS compared that day's number of positive tests to the total number of test results, the rate would have been much lower—possibly as low as 6.7%. They've been making this same mistake since the spring.

> This systematic error means WDHS is tossing hundreds of thousands of negative test results when calculating the positive test rate. The real rate could be half of what WDHS claims.[399]

The difference in the positivity rate between the WDHS's method and what the MacIver Institute was suggesting can be viewed in the chart below:

---

398 MacIver uses the abbreviation "DHS," but I've changed it to WDHS here to avoid confusion with the federal agency bearing that acronym.

399 MacIverNews. "Banned By Facebook – DO NOT READ! Bad Math Driving Wisconsin's Exploding Positive Test Rate." MacIver Institute, October 22, 2020, https://www.maciverinstitute.com/2020/10/bad-math-driving-wisconsins-exploding-positive-test-rate/.

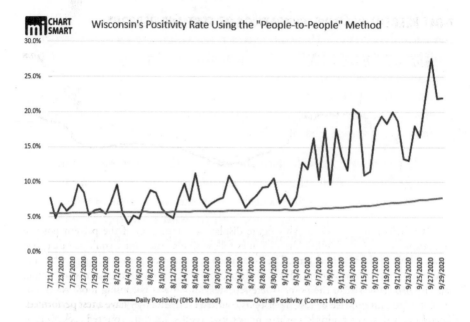

They recommended the WDHS begin calculating its daily positivity rate using each day's number of positive test results divided by the total number of test results.

In response, PolitiFact's Eric Litke rated the criticism "Pants on Fire," claiming that the MacIver Institute is "wrong on multiple fronts because they're asserting manipulated math is behind the increase in test positivity, but it's actually because the number of people testing positive has risen based on human behavior." He adds that there's no "bad math" here and that "the state WDHS uses a methodology (tallying people tested rather than raw tests) that is widely used by health agencies around the country," as if it being widely used doesn't make it any less misleading.[400]

Adding some hilarity to the situation, a single day after that PolitiFact article went live, the WDHS adopted the MacIver Institute's suggestions on how to better calculate the positive test rate.[401] The positivity rate fell by almost half under the new measurement:

---

400   Litke, Eric. "Analysis bashing DHS COVID-19 calculations is built on errors, omissions." PolitiFact, September 29, 2020, https://www.politifact.com/factchecks/2020/sep/29/maciver-institute/analysis-bashing-dhs-covid-19-calculations-built-e/.

401   MacIverNews, "DHS Caves to MacIver, Throws Politifact Under the Bus." MacIver Institute, September 30, 2020, https://www.maciverinstitute.com/2020/09/dhs-caves-to-maciver-throws-politifact-under-the-bus/.

7-DAY PERCENT POSITIVE, COMPARISON OF TEST AND PERSON*

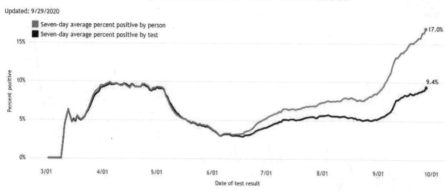

Updated: 9/29/2020

*Understanding the Data: This figure displays a comparison of the percent positive by both person and test. While the two lines follow similar trajectory, you'll see that they began to split off around mid-June. The 7-day percent positive by person is higher, while the percent positive by test is lower. This is likely because at this point in the pandemic, testing capacity had increased to the point where repeated testing was becoming more common-place. For percent positive by test, a person is counted each time they have a test performed. Therefore, if they get multiple positive or negative results, they are counted each time as they are tested. This makes the 7-day percent positive by test appear lower as there are many repeat tests included in the denominator of the calculation.

By contrast, 7-day percent positive by person only includes each person once across the duration of the pandemic. Therefore, the denominator of percent positive by per-son is smaller as it only includes each person once, no matter how many times they have been tested.

Litke added the following note at the end of his fact-check: "Note: WDHS updated their COVID-19 dashboard Sept. 30, the day after this story published, to include test positivity in terms of both tests and peo-ple. That does not affect the rating for this item since the per-person method remains on the WDHS website and remains an acceptable and even preferred approach."

THE CASE OF THE POLITIFACT LEGAL BRAINTRUST VS. THE TEXAS SUPREME COURT

PolitiFact completely ignored one of their fact-checks being struck down by the Texas Supreme Court.[402]

---

402   Strack, Haley. "The Texas Supreme Court Just Debunked PolitiFact's 'Fact Check' Of
       Ted Cruz." The Federalist, August 11, 2021, https://thefederalist.com/2021/08/11/
       the-texas-supreme-court-just-debunked-politifacts-fact-check-of-ted-cruz/.

In July 2021, nearly sixty Texas State House Democrats attempted to block a voter integrity bill by leaving the state to prevent a quorum. The stunt gridlocked the State Capitol for thirty-eight days until Democrats dropped their holdout.

Senator Ted Cruz took a no-B.S. approach when the stunt was still ongoing and called for their arrest because "there is clear legal authority to handcuff and put in leg irons legislators that are trying to stop the legislature from being able to do business."

But not so fast, said PolitiFact's Brandon Mulder, who isn't a lawyer but decided to fact-check the former solicitor general of Texas, rating what Senator Cruz said as false.

Mulder wrongly explained in his ruling: "The Texas House Rules states that absent lawmakers can 'be sent for and arrested, wherever they may be found.' But, because absent lawmakers aren't charged with a crime, it's unclear how the use of the word 'arrest' should be interpreted in this context. This is because no Texas court has reviewed how this provision is to be enforced. Thus, there is no legal clarity."[403]

This was obliterated by the Texas Supreme Court (whose members do have law degrees!) less than a month later when they allowed for the arrest of Democrats who don't show up to the legislature. That led to arrest warrants immediately being issued for fifty-two Democrats and to the end of their political stunt.[404]

Mulder never updated his article to acknowledge this.

FACT-CHECKERS FUEL THE MEDIA'S BOGUS LAFAYETTE SQUARE NARRATIVE

President Donald Trump's photo op at St. John's Church on June 1, 2020, amid the violent George Floyd riots that resulted in dozens of deaths and billions in property damage (including to the church), was the source of one fact-checker-approved bogus media narrative that collapsed a year later.

Fox News senior editor David Rutz summarized the media hysteria:

---

403   Mulder, Brandon. "Is there 'clear legal authority to handcuff' truant Texas Democrats?" PolitiFact, July 16, 2021, https://www.politifact.com/factchecks/2021/jul/16/ted-cruz/laws-surrounding-arrests-texas-democrats-are-far-c/.

404   McFall, Caitlin. "Texas Supreme Court allows for arrest of Democrats who don't show up to legislature." Fox News, August 10, 2021, https://www.foxnews.com/politics/texas-supreme-court-allows-for-arrest-of-democrats-who-dont-show-up-to-legislature.

At the time, there were numerous examples of media figures pushing the story that Trump demanded protesters to be cleared. CNN correspondent Jim Acosta asserted at a briefing that the White House had "gassed and pummeled protesters" so Trump could have a photo-op. MSNBC anchor Joy Reid said it happened so Trump could have his picture taken with a Bible. And CNN's Anderson Cooper said it "obviously" happened for Trump's photo-op.

The New York Times reported, "Protesters Dispersed With Tear Gas So Trump Could Pose At Church." ABC News, MSNBC, NPR, the Washington Post, and other outlets also reported the story at the time. The Post produced a 12-minute video about how police "cleared the way for the president to cross Lafayette Square."[405]

Acting U.S. Park Police Chief Gregory Monahan would testify later that month that Trump's photo op was not the motivation for clearing Lafayette Square, telling Congress "we did not clear the park for a photo op. There was 100%, zero, no correlation between our operation and the President's visit to the church."[406]

But that didn't seem to matter to the narrative-makers in the media—or the fact-checkers.

Seven months after Chief Monahan's testimony, CNN "fact-checker" Daniel Dale was still railing against those going counter to the narrative. When Trump attorney Michael van der Veen said that the clearing of Lafayette Square happened to "establish an appropriate security perimeter" from a "riotous mob," Dale fired back, "No. They cleared peaceful protesters out of the way for a Trump photo-op."[407]

And if Chief Monahan's earlier comments weren't enough to refute Dale, an inspector general report a year later would vindicate exactly what he said.

---

405 Rutz, David. "Collapsed Lafayette Square narrative is yet another 'fact-checked' story gone bad." Fox News, June 11, 2021, https://www.foxnews.com/media/collapsed-lafayette-square-fact-checked-story.

406 Schultz, Marisa. "Park Police chief denies clearing Lafayette Square for Trump photo-op." Fox News, July 28, 2020, https://www.foxnews.com/politics/u-s-park-police-defends-clearing-lafayette-park-for-president-trump-photo-opp.

407 Dale, Daniel. February 13, 2021, https://twitter.com/ddale8/status/1360682884747698176.

In June 2021, a review from the Interior Department's Office of the Inspector General found that the Park Police (USPP) had cleared Lafayette Square to erect fencing, and the Park Police incident commander was unaware that Trump would be visiting.[408]

To quote the report directly:

> Protests began in and around Lafayette Park on May 29, 2020. On May 30, the USPP and U.S. Secret Service established a unified command to coordinate the law enforcement response to the protests. From May 30 to 31, at least 49 USPP officers were injured while policing the protests, and Federal and private property was vandalized. On the morning of June 1, the Secret Service procured antiscale fencing to establish a more secure perimeter around Lafayette Park that was to be delivered and installed that same day. The USPP, in coordination with the Secret Service, determined that it was necessary to clear protesters from the area in and around the park to enable the contractor's employees to safely install the fence. The USPP planned to implement the operation as soon as the fencing materials and sufficient law enforcement officers arrived at the park. Six other law enforcement agencies assisted the USPP and the Secret Service in the operation to clear and secure areas near the park. The operation began at 6:23 p.m. and was completed by 6:50 p.m. Shortly thereafter, at 7:01 p.m., President Trump walked from the White House through Lafayette Park to St. John's Church. At 7:30 p.m., the contractor began assembling and installing the antiscale fence and completed the work by approximately 12:30 a.m. on June 2.
>
> …
>
> The evidence we obtained did not support a finding that the USPP cleared the park to allow the President to survey the damage and walk to St. John's Church.

---

408   Office of Inspector General. "Review of U.S. Park Police Actions at Lafayette Park." Department of Interior, June 8, 2021, https://www.doioig.gov/reports/review/review-us-park-police-actions-lafayette-park.

Among the nuggets in the report was revealing that the Park Police "did not know about the President's" visit to the area until hours after they began developing their operational take, and that tear gas wasn't used to clear the protesters by Park Police, but it was used by the D.C. Police Department. Ironically, the mayor of D.C. had blamed Trump for ordering the use of tear gas.[409]

Dale, who once tweeted asking his followers to "please verify things before turning them into viral tweets,"[410] has never corrected the record and still seems to think that the truth of the matter is up for debate. He wrote in a December 2021 article, six months after the IG report:

> There has been particularly intense public and congressional interest in what prompted the use of force against peaceful racial justice protesters in Lafayette Square shortly before Trump held up a Bible for the cameras outside St. John's Church, where a fire had been set in the basement the night before.[411]

It was indeed the subject of intense congressional interest, but they did get to the bottom of it.

Only the fact-checkers haven't figured it out.

PREEMPTIVE *WAPO* FACT-CHECK ON TERRORISTS RECEIVING STIMULUS CHECKS DEBUNKED BY EVENTUAL REALITY

The *Washington Post*'s Glenn Kessler's fact-check regarding the Boston Bomber and other murderers receiving stimulus checks aged like milk.

In a March 6 tweet, Senator Tom Cotton wrote, "Dylann Roof murdered nine people. He's on federal death row. He'll be getting a $1,400 stimulus check as part of the Democrats' 'COVID relief' bill."[412] He

409 Hemingway, Mollie. "Flashback: DC Mayor Honored At DNC For Riot Response. New Reports Reveal She, Not Trump, Teargassed Protesters." The Federalist, June 14, 2021, https://thefederalist.com/2021/06/14/flashback-dc-mayor-honored-at-dnc-for-riot-response-new-reports-reveal-she-not-trump-teargassed-protesters/.

410 Dale, Daniel. June 2, 2021, https://twitter.com/ddale8/status/1400223920444383236.

411 Dale, Daniel. "Fact check: Several news outlets inaccurately reported key detail of Meadows story about Trump and protesters." CNN, December 14, 2021, https://www.cnn.com/2021/12/13/politics/fact-check-meadows-trump-church-photo-op/index.html.

412 Cotton, Tom. March 6, 2021, https://twitter.com/tomcottonar/status/1368282575576440834.

added days later that Dzhokhar Tsarnaev would also get benefits.[413] Senator John Barrasso had also voiced concerns that this was a possibility.

Roof is on death row for murdering nine African Americans at Emanuel African Methodist Episcopal Church in a racially motivated massacre in 2015, while Tsarnaev, who is also on death row, is one of the 2013 Boston Marathon bombers.

"But for all the hype, there's less to these claims than one might imagine," began Kessler's article in which he dismisses the senators' concerns as "just theater." The bulk of his fact-check doesn't even fully dispute that murderers could receive payments but that it could be inconvenient for them to do so. For instance, Kessler argues:

> Dylann Roof has been in prison since 2016 and presumably would earn little or no income. But he or any other prisoner could file a form with the IRS that they had no income but were eligible for a payment, prisoner advocates said. But it has been difficult for many people in jail to receive payments. The IRS started to send people prepaid debit cards, which cannot be used in jail and often are seized by prison authorities.

> The difficulty of getting payments to prisoners also underscores how difficult it would be for the Treasury Department to determine whether people receiving payments met one of the conditions set in the Social Security law.[414]

In the end, Kessler gave Cotton and Barrasso "two Pinocchios" for their claims and praised Barrasso for "not resort[ing] to Cotton's scaremongering, more carefully saying that prisoners *might* receive a stimulus check [emphasis mine]."

But there was no "scaremongering" here.

Kessler's supposed fact-check was published on March 9, 2021—and it was revealed that Tsarnaev did indeed receive a stimulus check in early January 2022.

---

413   Cotton, Tom. March 8, 2021, https://twitter.com/TomCottonAR/status/ 1368933167630069761.

414   Kessler, Glenn. "Murderers, undocumented immigrants: Hyped-up claims about who's getting stimulus checks." *Washington Post*, March 9, 2021, https://www.washingtonpost.com/politics/2021/03/09/murderers-undocumented-immigrants-hyped-claims-about-whos-getting-stimulus-checks/.

After that news broke, Kessler added an update to the article to explain away his incompetence, instead putting the blame on Cotton for not phrasing his allegation to his liking:

> Cotton primarily received the Two-Pinocchio rating because his comments lacked context. He suggested this problem was the result of something Democrats did, when he had previously voted for legislation with the same language that allowed for checks to be issued to prisoners. He also made it clear that he intended to weaponize this debate for campaign ads.
>
> Still, Cotton's predictive powers should be acknowledged. He said the Boston bomber would get a stimulus check—and Tsarnaev did. Now, if the government is successful, this money will go to victims. So Tsarnaev still will not keep it. But in retrospect, the use of the phrase "scaremongering" was inappropriate. Cotton had raised a legitimate issue of concern, even if he framed it in a political way. The term "hyped up" in the headline went too far as well.
>
> Thus, we will reduce the rating on this claim to One Pinocchio—our version of "mostly true." His statement still lacks some context but he was certainly correct that Tsarnaev would receive a stimulus check.[415]

In other words, Cotton was right all along, but it upset Kessler that the facts could be used to rally the Republican base.

Later in September, the IRS revealed that over 1.1 million incarcerated people got stimulus checks, totaling over $1.3 billion. 163,000 were serving life sentences. 156,000 were sent to prisoners at the federal level, and 982,000 to prisoners at the state level.[416]

---

415   Kessler, "Murderers, undocumented immigrants."

416   King, Ryan. "Prison inmates received more than $1 billion in COVID-19 stimulus checks, IRS admits." *Washington Examiner*, September 2, 2022, https://www.washingtonexaminer.com/policy/economy/prison-inmates-received-1-billion-covid-stimulus-checks.

FACT-CHECKERS TRY TO COVER UP THE BIDEN ADMINISTRATION CRACK PIPE GIVEAWAY

In February 2022, the Washington Free Beacon broke a story that seemed to indicate Hunter Biden is calling the shots in the White House.

According to their reporting, a $30 million grant program that was set to begin in May would give money to nonprofits and local governments to help make drug use safer for addicts. Their reporting also stated that "applicants for the grants are prioritized if they treat a majority of 'underserved communities,' including African Americans and 'LGBTQ+ persons,' as established under President Joe Biden's executive order on 'advancing racial equity.'"[417]

Part of the plan includes providing crack pipes to addicts, which the HHS claimed will "reduce the risk of infection when smoking substances with glass pipes, which can lead to infections through cuts and sores." San Francisco, a city that has 50 percent more drug addicts than high school students, has implemented a similar program in the past.[418]

Impressively, one so-called fact-checker managed to fact-check this supposedly "misrepresented" story while admitting that it was true.

Mostly False
About this rating ⤢

What's True
In 2022, a U.S. Department of Health and Human Services substance abuse harm reduction grant did require recipients to provide safer smoking kits to existing drug users. In distributing grants, priority would be given to applicants serving historically underserved communities. However...

What's False
This was just one of around 20 components of the grant program and far from its most prominent or important one, despite being the primary focus of outraged news reports. The purpose of the program was to reduce harm and the risk of infection among drug users, not to advance racial equity, although that was a secondary consideration.

---

417   Hauf, Patrick. "Biden Admin To Fund Crack Pipe Distribution To Advance 'Racial Equity.'" Washington Free Beacon, February 7, 2022, https://freebeacon.com/biden-administration/biden-admin-to-fund-crack-pipe-distribution-to-advance-racial-equity/.

418   Ohanian, Lee. "San Francisco's "Progressive" Drug Policies Kill Hundreds Annually." Hoover Institution, January 12, 2021, https://www.hoover.org/research/san-franciscos-progressive-drug-policies-kill-hundreds-annually.

According to the brainiacs at Snopes:

> [The crack pipe distribution] was just one of around 20 components of the grant program and far from its most prominent or important one, despite being the primary focus of outraged news reports. The purpose of the program was to reduce harm and the risk of infection among drug users, not to advance racial equity, although that was a secondary consideration.[419]

So, according to Snopes' logic, it's not true that the Biden administration has a program to distribute crack pipes to addicts because the Biden administration has a plan to distribute crack pipes to addicts in combination with other policies in a similar theme.

Lead Stories joined in, offering a similarly weak fact-check that mostly centers around quoting an HHS official calling this a "harm reduction" program. Lead Stories also quotes the HHS as denying that any part of the "reduction program" funds will be used towards crack pipes, but the Beacon had already confirmed that they will.

USA Today's fact-checker published an article headlined, "What's inside a safe smoking kit to stop opioid overdose? No, it's not a crack pipe."[420] FactCheck.org headlined theirs, "Biden Initiative Funds Drug Overdose Prevention, Not 'Crack Pipes.'"[421]

Then—press secretary Jen Psaki also attempted to cast doubt on the Beacon story during a presser on February 9, lying to the American public that "They were never a part of the kit. It was inaccurate reporting."

As if those excuses weren't flimsy enough, the fact-checkers' cases further collapsed in May, when the program began and the Free Beacon proved the kits would include free crack pipes by obtaining the kits… which had free crack pipes.[422]

---

419   MacGuill, Dan. "Did Biden Admin 'Fund Crack Pipes' To 'Advance Racial Equity'?" Snopes, February 9, 2022, https://www.snopes.com/fact-check/biden-crack-pipes-racial-equity/.

420   Shen, Michelle. "What's inside a safe smoking kit to stop opioid overdose? No, it's not a crack pipe." *USA Today*, February 11, 2022, https://www.usatoday.com/story/news/politics/2022/02/10/biden-smoking-kits-pipes-addiction/6724719001/.

421   Jones, Brea. "Biden Initiative Funds Drug Overdose Prevention, Not 'Crack Pipes.'" FactCheck.org, March 3, 2022, https://www.factcheck.org/2022/02/biden-initiative-funds-drug-overdose-prevention-not-crack-pipes/.

422   Hauf, Patrick. "Yes, Safe Smoking Kits Include Free Crack Pipes. We Know Because We Got Them." Washington Free Beacon, May 12, 2022, https://freebeacon.com/biden-administration/yes-safe-smoking-kits-include-free-crack-pipes-we-know-because-we-got-them/.

The Beacon visited five harm-reduction organizations and called over two dozen more, and every single one visited included crack pipes in their kits.[423]

It was later reported by the Beacon in August 2022 that two Maine organizations set to receive funding from the Biden administration's grant program actively distribute crack pipes to addicts.

A Free Beacon reporter picked up a crack pipe and meth pipe (not for personal use) at one of the groups, "The Church of Safe Injection," which was set to receive $1.2 million from the Biden administration. A second group, Maine Access Points, provided the Beacon reporter with a bag of crack pipes, foil, and a smoking kit that provided, among other things, instructions on how to smoke crack.[424]

Only Snopes updated their verdict in light of the new information, which they cowardly only changed from "Mostly False" to "Outdated," and blamed them being wrong on not being privy to certain information at the time.

USA Today never updated their story, while FactCheck.org acknowledged this new information yet remained in denial and justified their lack of revision because the HHS sent them a statement claiming that no federal funding is used directly to purchase pipes.

Around this time, Texas GOP representative Troy Nehls joked that in Joe Biden's America, our kids are more likely to have a crack pipe than a mask-free education. The joke soared over the head of PolitiFact's Tom Kertscher, who devoted an eight-hundred-word article to checking the math on a comment never meant to be taken literally. The joke police rated Nehls' obvious joke "Pants on Fire," a rating reserved for the most egregious lies.[425]

---

423   Ibid.

424   Hauf, Patrick. "These Harm-Reduction Facilities Are Slated for Biden Administration Grants. They're Also Distributing Crack Pipes." Washington Free Beacon, August 3, 2022, https://freebeacon.com/biden-administration/these-harm-reduction-facilities-are-slated-for-biden-administration-grants-theyre-also-distributing-crack-pipes/.

425   Kertscher, Tom. "Claim that kids more likely to have access to crack pipes than mask-free education is Pants on Fire!" PolitiFact, February 10, 2022, https://www.politifact.com/factchecks/2022/feb/10/troy-nehls/claim-kids-more-likely-have-access-crack-pipes-mas/.

FACT-CHECKERS VS. FACT-CHECKERS

Can the fact-checkers even agree with each other?

There are countless cases in this book where multiple fact-checking organizations have seemingly collectively tossed logic by the way-side to unite and debunk a claim with identical tortured logic no two people could conjure up independently. This theme of fact-checks generally applies to viral videos that are damning to the Biden administration, and is common in the "Fact-Checkers vs. Our Own Eyes and Ears" chapter. So damning is what the viewer has seen, that the fact-checkers have no choice but to coordinate their counter-narrative in a desperate attempt to make it believable.

But what about when two fact-checkers happen to fact-check the same claim by coincidence? If they were just checking facts, you'd expect them to be in agreement with one another always—yet that's hardly the case.

In 2017, Chloe Lim, then a PhD student at Stanford University, obtained 1,178 fact-checks from PolitiFact and 325 from the *Washington Post*'s fact-checker. Of those statements evaluated, there were seventy-seven overlap statements from PolitiFact and the *Washington Post*.

Of the seventy-seven overlap statements, the fact-checkers completely agreed on forty-nine of them, or roughly 64 percent of the time. Among the twenty-eight cases where they disagreed, most of the disagreements were minor, but in nearly one in ten cases, the fact-checkers either mostly or entirely disagreed with one another.

That the fact-checkers are reaching a different conclusion nearly one out of ten times when they examine the same claim doesn't bode well for the reliability of the rest of their work. Even a 1 percent margin of error wouldn't be acceptable for organizations that now have become social media's de facto arbiters of truth.

In one such example, *Washington Post*'s fact-checker gave Hillary Clinton's claim during a Democrat primary debate that she had never run a negative ad about Bernie Sanders "1 Pinocchio" (the equivalent of "Mostly True" on PolitiFact's scale), while PolitiFact rated Clinton's statement as "False."

Lim notes that the type of statements that fact-checkers are most consistent in their evaluations of tend to be outright falsehoods or obvious truths, but the agreement rate is much lower "in the more ambiguous scoring range." Lim found that "in many cases, discrepancy in ratings often stemmed from differences in fact-checkers' subjective judgment of the significance of inaccuracies in a statement, rather than their disagreement on whether the statement itself was true or not."

As Lim notes, it's often the case that claims rated "Half True" or "Mostly False" are subtle claims that politicians use to deliberately deceive—such as presenting a true fact with missing context to mislead, making straw man arguments, or cherry-picking—and this is not only where the public would be best served by fact-checkers but also where they perform the worst because it requires their subjective judgment (and they're terrible at their jobs).

Lim points to two examples of this:

> Both fact-checkers evaluated Jeb Bush's claim that "Florida led the nation in job creation." The two fact-checkers provided identical sets of rationales for why Bush's claim may be misleading: (a) Bush relied on raw job totals; (b) the year 1999 was omitted; (c) much of Florida's job gains were due to an increase in low-paying jobs. [*Washington Post*] Fact Checker decided that Bush deserved "4 Pinocchios" while PolitiFact concluded that these exact same fallacies were not nearly as egregious, rating the claim "Half True."

> Another source of discrepancies in ratings is differences in the number of counter-examples or evidence each fact-checker uses in support of, or against, the statement in question. For instance, [*WaPo*] gave "3 Pinocchios" (roughly equivalent to "Mostly False") to Rick Perry's claim that "In the last seven years of [his] tenure, Texas created 1.5 million new jobs," while PolitiFact rated the claim "Mostly True." Upon carefully analyzing the fact-checkers' explanation, it seems that [*WaPo*] gave a higher dishonesty rating because [*WaPo*] found an additional fault in Perry's statement. In addition to offering the same set of evidence presented by PolitiFact

(i.e., cherry-picked data sources), [*WaPo*] also pointed out that he had aggregated unemployment numbers in an incorrect manner.[426]

In addition to overlapping statements, Lim also evaluated statements she categorized as "murky." For example, if one fact-checker was evaluating the claim that "we have the highest murder rate in this country in 45 years" while another was examining the statement that "we have an increase in murder within our cities, the biggest in 45 years," this would be put in the "murky" category, as the claims are similar but different (the first focused on the murder rate, while the latter was about the size of an increase in murder).

Among murky statements, the fact-checkers tended to agree on immigration, security, and campaign issues, while they disagreed (at a rate rendering them unreliable) on social policy, health care, Hillary Clinton, and the economy at rates "much lower" than what is acceptable for scientific coding.

FACT-CHECKERS NOT EXACTLY SURE HOW TO SPIN HILLARY CLINTON ADMITTING HER PRO-OPEN BORDERS AGENDA

The fact-checkers couldn't decide on an angle for spinning a comment supporting "open borders" from Hillary Clinton.

During one of the 2016 presidential debates, moderator Chris Wallace asked Hillary about a statement she made in a 2013 speech to a Brazilian bank that was revealed in a leaked email, where she said her "dream is a hemispheric common market with open trade and open borders."

Hillary responded, "Well, if you want one to read the rest of the sentence, I was talking about energy."

For context, the full quote from the speech is as follows:

> My dream is a hemispheric common market, with open trade and open borders. I think we have to have a concerted plan to increase trade already under the current circumstances. There is so much more we can do, there is a lot of low-hanging fruit, but businesses on both sides have to make it a priority, and it's not for governments to do but governments can either

---

426   Lim, Chloe. "Checking How Fact-Checkers Check." *Research & Politics,* vol. 5, no. 3, 2018, 205316801878684. doi:10.1177/2053168018786848.

make it easy or make it hard and we have to resist protection-ism, other kinds of barriers to market access, and to trade, and I would like to see this get much more attention.[427]

So, not much about energy there.

Hillary is clearly lying here, and the fact-checkers know it. But they couldn't keep the script constant when trying to play defense for her regardless.

NPR reporter Danielle Kurtzleben wasn't sure what to make of it, writing that "fact-checks have debated what exactly this means. While Clinton's campaign says it's about energy, reasonable people have dis-agreed." She did attempt to defend Hillary by pointing out that "how-ever one interprets this, it is also true that Clinton has not called for 'open borders' as a policy during this campaign." Of course, it's a poli-tician's private statements that are more likely to reflect what they actu-ally believe than their poll-tested public comments, so her lack of public comments has no relevance to if she actually does support open borders.

PolitiFact's Amy Sherman rated as "Mostly False" the claim that Hillary Clinton "wants to have open borders." She quoted experts who believe Hillary was just talking about trade and some who think she was talking about trade and immigration. The full quote that debunks the notion that it has anything to do with energy is never included. Instead, Sherman hedges herself and claims she "can't fully evaluate her remarks to a bank because we don't have the full speech."[428]

FactCheck.org somehow concluded that "as that quote shows, Clinton's comment about open borders was related to trade, not immi-gration"[429]—an interpretation not even Clinton herself agrees with.

Similarly, when Trump said on the debate stage that Hillary wanted open borders, ABC rated the claim "yes and no," claiming that "Clinton

---

427   Wolfgang, Ben. "Hillary Clinton dreams of 'open borders': leaked speech excerpts." *Washington Times,* October 8, 2016, https://www.washingtontimes.com/news/2016/oct/8/hillary-clinton-dreams-open-borders-leaked-speech-/.

428   Sherman, Amy. "Donald Trump says Hillary Clinton wants to have open borders." PolitiFact, October 19, 2016, https://www.politifact.com/factchecks/2016/oct/19/donald-trump/donald-trump-says-hillary-clinton-wants-have-open-/.

429   Gore, D'Angelo, et al. "Trump Twists Facts on WikiLeaks." FactCheck.org, October 12, 2016, https://www.factcheck.org/2016/10/trump-twists-facts-on-wikileaks/.

says she was talking about energy, not immigration, and her immigration plan does not call for open borders or amnesty."[430]

Hillary's running mate Tim Kaine opted for the denial strategy. When asked by CNN's Jake Tapper, "Is that her dream? Is that what she wants? Open borders? An open market?" Kaine responded, "Yes, Jake, I'm glad you asked it that way, because I don't think we can dignify documents dumped by WikiLeaks and just assume that they're all accurate and true. Anybody who hacks in to get documents is completely capable of manipulating them."[431]

GLENN KESSLER FACT-CHECKS HIMSELF

WaPo's Kessler had to fact-check himself after he prematurely tweeted out a fact-check of Donald Trump that flubbed the facts.

Trump had tweeted on April 7, 2020, during the early days of the COVID-19 pandemic, questioning whether the IG had ever commissioned a report "on the failed H1N1 Swine Flu debacle where 17,000 people died?" under Obama.

Kessler replied, tweeting out, "Guess what, the HHS IG did do a lengthy examination of the government's response to the swine flu in 2009. Let's tweet out a few key findings…." He then shared findings from a report on the Obama administration's handling of the swine flu.

After the initial tweet was retweeted over six thousand times, Kessler realized that he got it wrong, as the HHS IG did not commission the report he was citing.

Kessler (responsibly, to his credit) deleted the thread and issued a correction: "Rule #1: never try to do an instant fact check on Twitter. I tweeted from a government report, incorrectly saying it was an IG report, when in fact it was not," Kessler wrote in his correction. "Dumb mistake,

430 "Presidential Debate Fact-Check: What Donald Trump and Hillary Clinton Are Claiming." ABC News, October 19, 2016, https://abcnews.go.com/Politics/presidential-debate-fact-check-donald-trump-hillary-clinton/story?id=42906344.

431 Jilani, Zaid. "Tim Kaine plays dumb about Wikileaks revelations from Hillary Clinton's paid speeches." The Intercept, October 9, 2016, https://theintercept.com/liveblogs/seconddebate/tim-kaine-plays-dumb-about-wikileaks-revelations-from-hillary-clintons-paid-speeches/.

and I am glad it was brought to my attention. I have deleted the tweet, shown below, mea culpa."[432]

In another case of Kessler-on-Kessler violence, he gave himself "Three Pinocchios" in 2014 for repeating the line that Obamacare's Medicaid expansion covered 3.9 million Americans. Kessler explained: "The Fact Checker noted some fuzziness about the figure, but used terminology such as this: 'The law included a significant expansion of Medicaid, which in just two months has added as many as 3.9 million people to its rolls.' We didn't quite say there was a connection to the Affordable Care Act, but readers certainly might have gotten that impression." As it turned out, only 1.9 million of those 3.9 million new signups were people who even lived in states that accepted the Medicaid expansion.[433]

Kessler repeated the misleading "3.9 million" claim in a fact-check of a Daily Caller article that reported Obamacare debuted with more canceled plans than enrollments. Kessler wrote in giving that claim "Four Pinocchios": "On its face, this claim by the Daily Caller is wrong because the law included a significant expansion of Medicaid, which in just two months has added as many as 3.9 million people to its rolls."

A FACT-CHECKER DOUBLE STANDARD: WHEN TO ADJUST FOR THE COST OF LIVING

In doing any comparison in wages across states, one must adjust for the varying costs of living in each state to have a truly apples-to-apples comparison.

In 2020, what $100 would be able to purchase in the average state would only be able to purchase $86 worth of items in New York but $113 in Oklahoma.[434] Any comparison between living standards in both states would need to account for this, and PolitiFact agrees—selectively.

---

432   Hasson, Peter. "Washington Post Fact-Checker Corrects Himself After Botching Facts in Viral Twitter Thread." The Daily Caller, April 16, 2020, https://dailycaller.com/2020/04/16/washington-post-fact-check-glenn-kessler-coronavirus-inspector-general-h1n1/.

433   Hurtubise, Sarah. "WaPo's Fact Checker Admits Failure in Obamacare Defense." The Daily Caller, January 20, 2014, https://dailycaller.com/2014/01/20/wapos-fact-checker-admits-hes-got-the-wrong-obamacare-facts/.

434   Watson, Garrett. "What Is the Real Value of $100 in Your State?" Tax Foundation, August 5, 2020, https://taxfoundation.org/price-parity-purchasing-power-100-state-2020/.

In March 2018, PolitiFact's Jon Greenberg examined a claim from leftist watchdog Good Jobs First that Oklahoma teachers "are the poorest paid teachers in the U.S., in a state that gives nearly $500 million in tax handouts to energy companies."

The claim was rated "Mostly True," with the main evidence for the ruling being a National Education Association survey of public schools that ranked Oklahoma third from the bottom in average teacher pay, which Greenberg acknowledges is "very low," but not the lowest.[435]

However, he didn't adjust for the cost of living, which drastically affects their ranking vs. the rest of the nation. One estimate from 2015 to 2016 found Oklahoma's teacher salaries going from forty-eighth lowest in the nation to thirtieth with a cost-of-living adjustment. Expensive states like California go from having the third highest-paid teachers in the nation to the twenty-fifth when you make the same adjustment.[436]

After being criticized for his juvenile economic analysis, Greenberg published a follow-up article in April acknowledging the existence of three studies putting the cost-of-living-adjusted Oklahoma teacher salaries as between the thirtieth and thirty-fifth highest in the nation before largely dismissing them because "labor and education economists say it's not that simple."[437]

His article now concludes with a section headed "The temptation of cost-of-living adjustments," as if it's one of the seven deadly sins to try to adjust data to accurately present it.

Oddly, adjusting for the cost of living was the norm previously on PolitiFact, with prior articles fact-checking claims about California having the nation's highest poverty rate correctly adjusting for inflation when analyzing the claim, and in another article evaluating what a middle-class income is in a place as expensive as Manhattan.[438]

---

435   Greenberg, Jon. "Are Oklahoma teachers the lowest paid? Nearly."
      PolitiFact, March 7, 2018, https://www.politifact.com/factchecks/2018/
      mar/07/good-jobs-first/are-oklahoma-teachers-lowest-paid-nearly/.

436   Butler, Baylee, and Byron Schlomach. "Teacher Pay: Facts to Consider." The 1889
      Institute, March 2017, http://nebula.wsimg.com/eceb7479d649258032e15a8a803dd8c9
      ?AccessKeyId=CB55D82B5028ABD8BF94&disposition=0&alloworigin=1.

437   Greenberg, Jon. "Oklahoma teacher pay dispute: Does cost of living make
      a difference?" PolitiFact, April 4, 2018, https://www.politifact.com/article/
      2018/apr/04/oklahoma-teacher-pay-dispute-cost-of-living-calcul/.

438   England, Trent. "PolitiFact's Double Standard Makes Oklahoma Teachers Look Poorer
      Than They Really Are." The Federalist, April 11, 2018, https://thefederalist.com/2018/
      04/11/politifacts-double-standard-makes-oklahoma-teachers-look-poorer-really/.

A SERIES OF BAD ABORTION FACT-CHECKS

So clueless is the modern fact-checker that they'll occasionally refute their own point within an article without realizing it.

PolitiFact's Sara Swann attempted to fact-check the claim from pro-life Lila Rose that "Colorado Governor Jared Polis has just signed into law a bill legalizing abortions through all nine months, up until the moment of birth."[439]

Swann offered the false clarification that "Colorado's new law guarantees an individual's right to contraceptives and an abortion. It does not allow abortions 'up until the moment of birth.'"

In the article, Swann states that the bill in question, the Reproductive Health Equity Act, codifies into the state's statute the right to an abortion and that a government entity may not "deny, restrict, interfere with or discriminate against an individual's fundamental right to use or refuse contraception or to continue a pregnancy and give birth or to have an abortion." The purpose of the law was to have something in place protecting abortion as a hedge against *Roe v. Wade* being overturned, which happened just less than three months after it was signed (as was expected due to the ruling being leaked).

Swann states that the law is simply upholding an existing right to an abortion in the state before she douses her argument in gasoline and lights it on fire, adding that "Colorado's law protects the right to have an abortion and *does not make distinctions or regulations around a time or stage during pregnancy* [emphasis mine]."

That's quite the contrast from the first sentence of Swann's article, which states: "No, this Colorado law does not allow abortions 'up until the moment of birth.'"

But alas, despite accidentally acknowledging that Rose's claim is true, she rates it "False."

According to the pro-choice think tank Guttmacher Institute, the restrictions on abortion in Colorado only include the following:

- Abortion is not covered in insurance policies for public employees.

439   Swann, Sara. "No, this Colorado law does not allow abortions 'up until the moment of birth.'" PolitiFact, April 7, 2022, https://www.politifact.com/factchecks/2022/apr/07/facebook-posts/no-colorado-law-does-not-allow-abortions-until-mom/.

- The parent of a minor must be notified before an abortion is provided.

- Public funding is available for abortion only in cases of life endangerment, rape, or incest.[440]

Swann also included irrelevant information in her article to distract the reader from what she was actually fact-checking, such as pointing out that the overwhelming majority of abortions occur before thirteen weeks, and fewer than 1 percent occur after twenty-one weeks.

It's common for those who favor late-term abortion to, rather than try the impossible and defend its practice explicitly, opt to instead defend it as something so rare as to almost not exist regardless.

This sort of deflection forms the entire basis for her rating Rose's claim false, with Swann concluding:

> Colorado's new law codifies existing protections around an individual's right to use or refuse contraceptives, continue with a pregnancy and give birth, or to have an abortion.
>
> Abortions that occur later in a pregnancy — at 21 weeks gestation or later — are rare.
>
> We rate this claim False.[441]

There are far more deaths from late-term abortions each year than there are from mass shootings, but no one would rate it "false" that mass shootings occur in America because they're rare, and account for fewer than 1 percent of deaths.

The only false claim from Lila Rose is her characterizing the law as creating a *new* policy allowing for abortion up to birth, but the "shock" of the claim she's fact-checking, that Colorado allows for abortion up until birth, is true, and Swann admits that.

During Trump's State of the Union address in 2019, Trump said, "Lawmakers in New York cheered with delight upon the passage of leg-

---

440 "State Facts About Abortion: Colorado." Guttmacher Institute, June 2022, https://www.guttmacher.org/fact-sheet/state-facts-about-abortion-colorado.
441 Swann, "No, This Colorado Law Does Not Allow Abortions 'Up Until the Moment of Birth.'"

islation that would allow a baby to be ripped from the mother's womb moments from birth."[442]

The *Post*'s fact-checker says the bill wouldn't permit the type of abortions Trump says because:

> …that a health-care practitioner "may perform an abortion when, according to the practitioner's reasonable and good faith professional judgment based on the facts of the patient's case: the patient is within twenty-four weeks from the commencement of pregnancy, or there is an absence of fetal viability, or the abortion is necessary to protect the patient's life or health."

The language of the law is consistent with Trump's characterization, however, as the law's final provision permits abortions at any stage "if necessary to protect" women's "health." SCOTUS rulings in *Doe v. Bolton* and the now-overturned *Roe v. Wade* defined "health" as including "physical, emotional, psychological, familial" factors, including the "stigma of unwed motherhood," the work of "child care," and "the distress, for all concerned, associated with the unwanted child."

Or, in other words, for any reason.

This same type of fact-checker denialism over late-term abortion was also present when Trump criticized Hillary Clinton's stance on it during the 2016 presidential debates.

So indefensible are Hillary's views on abortion that the fact-checkers would not fully acknowledge them in their attempts to obfuscate.

Trump had stated in the third and final presidential debate prior to Hillary's loss in the 2016 election: "Well, I think it's terrible. If you go with what Hillary is saying, in the ninth month, you can take the baby and rip the baby out of the womb of the mother just prior to the birth of the baby." When Hillary was pressed on late-term abortions, she merely said that there "could" be restrictions on them, but didn't express any support for any.[443]

---

442   Agresti, James. "Wash Post Repeatedly Botches Fact Check of Trump's State of the Union Address." Just Facts Daily, February 8, 2019, https://www.justfactsdaily.com/wash-post-repeatedly-botches-fact-check-of-trumps-state-of-the-union-address.

443   Payne, Daniel. "No Fact-Checkers Can Cover for Hillary Clinton's Ghastly Abortion Views." The Federalist, October 21, 2016, https://thefederalist.com/2016/10/21/no-fact-checkers-can-cover-hillary-clintons-ghastly-abortion-views/.

The *WaPo's* Glenn Kessler decided to attack an adjacent claim from Trump made during the same debate, that "in the ninth month you can take the baby and rip the baby right out of the womb, just prior to the birth of the baby" so he wouldn't have to address Hillary's support of that.

Kessler faux-debunks Trump's claim by pointing out that late-term abortion is, fortunately, rare[444]—but Trump wasn't saying that they weren't rare. He was saying that late-term abortions happen, which they do.

The *Los Angeles Times'* fact-check was almost identical, quoting the same statistics from Guttmacher and telling us that Trump offered a "graphic description of late-term abortion," but "such procedures are extremely rare."[445]

Politico's fact-checker writes that Trump "misses the mark" in an article that also says, "Technically Trump is right that in a handful of states, abortions may be performed late in pregnancy. But late-term abortions are exceedingly rare."[446]

PolitiFact attempted to sanitize Hillary's abortion views, issuing a fact-check in response to Ted Cruz, who said a month prior that she "supports unlimited abortion on demand up until the moment of birth, including partial-birth abortion, with taxpayer funding." Fact-checker W. Gardner Selby rates the claim "False" in an article where they admit that Clinton supports repealing the Hyde Amendment, which prohibits taxpayer funding of abortion except in cases of rape, incest, or to save the life of the mother. [447]

Selby acknowledges that Hillary voted against the Partial-Birth Abortion Ban Act of 2003, which was signed into law under George W. Bush and upheld by the SCOTUS in 2007. Since this sole fact destroys Selby's entire case, she glosses over it and then points to more recent

---

444   Kessler, Glenn. "Fact Check: Trump's claim on abortions up until the moment of birth." *Washington Post*, October 19, 2016, https://www.washingtonpost.com/politics/2016/ live-updates/general-election/real-time-fact-checking-and-analysis-of-the-final-2016-presidential-debate/fact-check-trumps-claim-on-abortions-up-until-the-moment-of-birth/.

445   Mason, Melanie. "Donald Trump offers graphic description of later-term abortion, but such procedures are extremely rare." *Los Angeles Times,* October 19, 2016, https:// www.latimes.com/nation/politics/trailguide/la-na-trailguide-third-presidential-donald-trump-offers-graphic-description-1476931077-htmlstory.html.

446   Pradhan, Rachana. "Trump misses the mark on 'partial-birth' abortion laws." Politico, October 19, 2016, https://www.politico.com/blogs/2016-presidential-debate-fact-check/2016/10/trump-misses-the-mark-on-partial-birth-abortion-laws-230029.

447   Selby, W. Gardner. "False: Ted Cruz claim that Hillary Clinton backs 'unlimited abortion' to moment of birth." PolitiFact, October 9, 2016, https://www.politifact.com /factchecks/2016/oct/09/ted-cruz/false-ted-cruz-claim-hillary-clinton-backs-unlimit/.

quotes from Clinton on the campaign trail where she's tried to moderate her position (because she knows it's unpopular).

Hillary's defense when asked about her 2003 vote (which Selby never mentions) is revealing. When she was asked about it by Chris Wallace in the third presidential debate, the exchange went as follows:

> **Wallace:** I'm going to give you a chance to respond. But I wanted to ask you secretary Clinton, I want to explore how far you think the right to abortion goes. You have been quoted as saying that the fetus has no constitutional rights. You also voted against a ban on late term partial birth abortions. Why?
>
> **Clinton:** Because Roe v. Wade very clearly sets out that there can be regulations on abortion so long as the life and the health of the mother are taken into account. And when I voted as a senator, I did not think that that was the case.[448]

It's common for liberals to cite a lack of exceptions for things such as rape, incest, or the life of the mother in opposing specific abortion laws—but when have they ever been on board with abortion restrictions that do incorporate those exceptions? Never.

While not relevant to Selby's fact-check, it's worth pointing out that Hillary's characterization of how late-term abortion works is inaccurate. As David Harsanyi pointed out:

> Both medical literature and late-term abortion providers show the majority of late-term procedures are not performed for "maternal health complications or lethal fetal anomalies discovered late in pregnancy." Even the propagandists at the Planned Parenthood spun-off Guttmacher Institute found—in the only study on the attitudes of women who get late-term abortions—that in "many ways, women who had later abortions were similar to those who obtained first-trimester procedures."[449]

But don't ever expect to learn that from a fact-checker.

---

448   "Full transcript: Third 2016 presidential debate." Politico, October 20, 2016, https://www.politico.com/story/2016/10/full-transcript-third-2016-presidential-debate-230063.

449   Harsanyi, David. "Wrong, PolitiFact: Hillary Supports Tax-Funded Abortion on Demand." The Federalist, October 12, 2016, https://thefederalist.com/2016/10/12/wrong-politifact-hillary-supports-tax-funded-abortion-demand/.

BIDEN ASSAULTS THE FACTS ON THE ASSAULT WEAPONS BAN

One case of PolitiFact's blatant policy advocacy disguised as a fact-check came when they claimed to substantiate a claim from Biden arguing in favor of the 1994 assault weapons ban that was based on bad data.

Biden stated on May 24, 2022: "When we passed the assault weapons ban, mass shootings went down. When the law expired, mass shootings tripled."

The Federal Assault Weapons Ban (AWB) was signed into law by Bill Clinton in September 1994 and prohibited the purchase of semiautomatic weapons classified as "assault weapons" and large-capacity magazines. It expired in 2004. It was an assault weapons "ban" in that it prohibited sales of "assault weapons" after the bill was passed, but everyone who already owned one was grandfathered in and did not have to relinquish their firearms.

PolitiFact's Jon Greenberg rated Biden's claim as "Mostly True," which he says is supported by "several studies," but he only cites one in his article (that's behind a $60 paywall) to make his case.[450]

The study is a 2019 study from the New York School of Medicine that found mass shooting deaths involving assault weapons fell "slightly" in the decade of the AWB and rose dramatically after it ended. Greenberg does acknowledge that the decline during the ban is too small to draw any conclusions from (but apparently not too small to assign a "Mostly True" rating from).

JustFacts' James Agresti, who bit the bullet and shelled out $60 for the study, immediately noted some glaring flaws in it, the first being that it had a chart of mass shooting deaths that showed zero deaths in 1994, 1995, 1996, 1997, 2001, 2002, and 2004—all ban years, and all years where there were people killed in mass shootings.[451]

Agresti charted mass shooting deaths relative to population, and the chart shows a weak and unclear pattern—but it is clear that there's no tripling in deaths post–ban expiration.

---

450   Greenberg, Jon. "Joe Biden said mass shootings tripled when the assault weapon ban ended. They did." PolitiFact, May 25, 2022, https://www.politifact.com/factchecks/2022/may/25/joe-biden/joe-biden-said-mass-shootings-tripled-when-assault/.

451   Agresti, James. "There's No Objective Evidence the Federal 'Assault Weapons' Ban Saved Lives." Just Facts Daily, June 15, 2022, https://www.justfactsdaily.com/no-objective-evidence-the-federal-assault-weapons-ban-saved-lives.

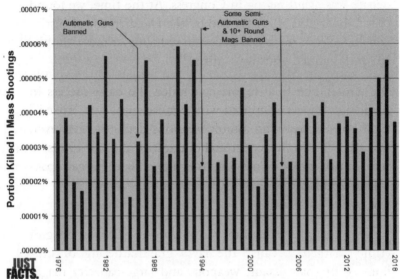

Portion of U.S. Population Killed in Mass Shootings

Columbia University's Dr. Louis Klarevas also picked apart the study, noting that "the authors misidentified the involvement of assault weapons in roughly half of the incidents [mass shootings]…when erroneous cases are recalibrated the number of incidents involving assault weapons drops 62%…and the number of fatalities resulting from such shootings drops 46%…. This brings the percentage of mass shootings involving assault weapons in the [study's] data set from 77% to 30%, which is consistent with other studies that have found that assault weapons are used in 25% to 36% of active shootings."[452]

The fact-checkers also don't agree on this issue.

FactCheck.org evaluated a nearly identical claim from Biden months prior in March and rated it "Unclear," noting a sea of contradictory research, the most significant being that the government's own research couldn't find support for the assault weapons ban:

452 Klarevas, Louis. "Letter to the Editor Re: DiMaggio, C. Et Al. 'Changes in U.S. Mass Shooting Deaths Associated with the 1994-2004 Federal Assault Weapons Ban: Analysis of Open-Source Data. J Trauma Acute Care. 2019;86(1):11-19.'" *The Journal of Trauma and Acute Care Surgery*, vol. 86, no. 5, 2019, pp. 926–28. doi:10.1097/TA.0000000000002220.

We wrote about this issue eight years ago, when the gun debate was again raging in Congress. At the time, we found that a three-part study funded by the Department of Justice concluded that the ban's success in reducing crimes committed with banned guns was "mixed."

We wrote: The final report concluded the ban's success in reducing crimes committed with banned guns was "mixed." Gun crimes involving assault weapons declined. However, that decline was "offset throughout at least the late 1990s by steady or rising use of other guns equipped with [large-capacity magazines]."

Ultimately, the research concluded that it was "premature to make definitive assessments of the ban's impact on gun crime," largely because the law's grandfathering of millions of pre-ban assault weapons and large-capacity magazines "ensured that the effects of the law would occur only gradually" and were "still unfolding" when the ban expired in 2004. [453]

The *WaPo*'s Kessler gave a more mixed analysis. He argued that the evidence was lacking that the AWB reduced the frequency of mass shootings but that there is "some evidence" that the restrictions on large-capacity magazines "may have" reduced death tolls when they did occur.[454]

---

453 Farley, Robert. "FactChecking Biden's Claim that Assault Weapons Ban Worked." FactCheck.org, March 26, 2021, https://www.factcheck.org/2021/03/factchecking-bidens-claim-that-assault-weapons-ban-worked/.

454 Kessler, Glenn. "What research shows on the effectiveness of gun-control laws." *Washington Post*, May 27, 2022, https://www.washingtonpost.com/politics/2022/05/27/what-research-shows-effectiveness-gun-control-laws/.

BATTING FOR THE BIDEN ADMINISTRATION

In addition to censoring the spread of information embarrassing to the leftist agenda, the fact-checkers also force writers who rely on social media to spread their work to frame their coverage in a way that hedges against fact-checks and provides qualifiers for Biden's behavior when they aren't needed.

Some other writers I speak with regularly have made a game out of predicting just how the fact-checkers will try to deny reality.

When it was brought to light that millions of barrels of oil were drained from the strategic oil reserve and sold to a Chinese firm linked to Hunter Biden,[455] a friend half-jokingly predicted that the fact-checkers would rate that as false because "Biden didn't sell oil to China, he sent millions of barrels that just happened to have oil in them."

The Biden administration's propagandists have largely gone ignored by the fact-checkers.

Four months into the job as press secretary, Karine Jean-Pierre hadn't been fact-checked once by FactCheck.org, Reuters, the AP, *Washington Post*, or CNN. Only PolitiFact fact-checked anything she said, rating two of her claims "False," while Snopes fact-checked a claim about a past comment by her.[456]

The two statements from Jean-Pierre that PolitiFact did fact-check were her false statements that twenty million people were on unemployment when Biden took office, and that overturning *Roe v. Wade* was unconstitutional.

---

455   Moore, Mark. "House Republicans want answers about oil sale to Hunter Biden-linked China company." *New York Post*, July 20, 2022, https://nypost.com/2022/07/20/house-republicans-want-answers-about-oil-sale-to-hunter-biden-linked-china-co/.

456   Lanum, Nikolas. "Nearly every major fact-checker has completely ignored Karine Jean-Pierre since taking over for Psaki." Fox News, September 13, 2022, https://www.foxnews.com/media/nearly-every-major-fact-checker-completely-ignored-karine-jean-pierre-since-taking-over-psaki.

The false statements they and everyone else missed included:

- Jean-Pierre claiming that nobody is "just walking in" across the southern border.[457]

- Jean-Pierre claiming there was zero percent inflation in July 2022.[458]

- Jean-Pierre's denial that she publicly stated the 2016 election was stolen.[459]

- Jean-Pierre blaming inflation on Vladimir Putin, or claiming that it would be transitory.[460]

- Jean-Pierre denying that Biden's stimulus bill fueled rising inflation.[461]

- Jean-Pierre falsely claiming that Biden had condemned the attempted assassination of Supreme Court justice Brett Kavanaugh.[462]

- Jean-Pierre's denial about critical race theory being taught in schools.[463]

Just to name a few.

---

457 Heckman, Elizabeth. "Karine Jean-Pierre is lying about the border and knows media won't cover what's really happening." Fox News, August 30, 2022, https://www.foxnews.com/media/brandon-judd-karine-jean-pierre-lying-border-knows-media-cover-really-happening.

458 Zilber, Ariel. "Karine Jean-Pierre roasted over 'Orwellian' tweet touting '0% inflation.'" *New York Post*, August 11, 2022, https://nypost.com/2022/08/11/karine-jean-pierre-roasted-over-orwellian-tweet-touting-0-inflation/.

459 Elkind, Elizabeth. "'That's a ridiculous comparison': Karine Jean-Pierre snaps back at Fox News' Peter Doocy for grilling her on why she said Trump 'stole' the 2016 election—after Biden's MAGA Republican speeches." *Daily Mail*, September 6, 2022, https://www.dailymail.co.uk/news/article-11186309/Karine-Jean-Pierre-Biden-press-secretary-peter-doocy-trump.html.

460 Griswold, Kylee. "Even With The Media Tossing Her Softballs, Biden Press Secretary Karine Jean-Pierre Can't Get The Bat Off Her Shoulder." The Federalist, June 15, 2022, https://thefederalist.com/2022/06/15/even-with-the-media-tossing-her-softballs-biden-press-secretary-karine-jean-pierre-cant-get-the-bat-off-her-shoulder/.

461 Ibid.

462 Ibid.

463 Poff, Jeremiah. "White House says GOP is lying about critical race theory in schools, evidence shows otherwise." *Washington Examiner*, November 5, 2021, https://www.washingtonexaminer.com/restoring-america/community-family/white-house-says-gop-is-lying-about-critical-race-theory-in-schools-evidence-shows-otherwise.

In addition to unconvincingly explaining away Biden's gaffes and other blunders, the fact-checkers play the role of narrative solidifier—even to the point of joining the administration in redefining words. While I tried to keep the lengthiest fact-checks of fact-checks in the final chapter of this book, this chapter opens with a lengthy critique of the Biden administration's attempt to redefine the definition of a "recession" ahead of poor economic news confirming the nation was in one in the first half of 2022. This was a particularly egregious assault on reality, and yet the media, and the fact-checkers, happily went along with the administration-spawned lie, all pretending that the new rules written the week prior had always been the case.

Just as journalism is supposed to hold the powerful to account yet largely serves as a propaganda arm of the Democratic Party, the fact-checkers, which were born out of the journalism industry, do the same. Rather than search for independent information to confirm or disprove the administration's narrative, they'll rely on what the White House says as proof enough. As you'll read, there are even cases where the White House will falsify a transcript to cover up a Biden gaffe—only for the fact-checkers to cite the falsified transcript as proof the gaffe didn't happen.

As is the case for most of the fact-checks you've read thus far, the reasoning is often baffling enough that the articles don't make any sense unless the conclusion was written first and the "reasoning" that had no choice to support it came next.

REDEFINING RECESSION

In anticipation of the quarterly GDP figures being released in July 2022, the Biden administration launched a mini-campaign to obfuscate what exactly a recession even is.

Conventionally, when there are two consecutive negative quarters of economic growth, the economy is in a "technical recession." This definition is widely used outside the U.S. as well, with the U.K.'s central bank,[464] France's national statistics bureau,[465] Germany's central bank,[466]

---

464 "Why does economic growth matter?" Bank of England, May 19, 2020, https://www.bankofengland.co.uk/knowledgebank/why-does-economic-growth-matter.

465 "Definition - Recession." L'Institut national de la statistique et des études économiques, August 5, 2022, https://www.insee.fr/en/metadonnees/definition/c2129.

466 "Glossary." Deutsche Bundesbank, August 5, 2022, https://www.bundesbank.de/dynamic/action/en/homepage/glossary/729724/glossary?firstLetter=R&contentId=653260.

and Canada's Federal Balanced Budget Act defining it as such,[467] and Australia's parliament using it as an official definition of a recession.[468]

The same is true within the financial industry. Both the Series 7 exam,[469] which is required for the solicitation, purchase and/or sale of securities products, and the Series 65 exam, which qualifies individuals to professionally provide finance advice to clients, define recession as "a contraction of the national economy that lasts more than two quarters (six months)."[470]

Since there was negative growth in the first quarter of 2022, the White House knew that another quarter of negative growth in the second quarter would immediately set off headlines that the U.S. economy had fallen into recession. As explained numerous times already, if the administration could get the fact-checkers on their side in effectively redefining the definition of the word everyone had used until a week prior, when the economy does fall into a technical recession, no publication can report that "the U.S. economy just fell into a recession" without being "fact-checked."

While the National Bureau of Economic Research (NBER) is the body that gives the official recession declaration, it doesn't meet regularly and sometimes waits months until a recession is over to declare that the U.S. economy had been in one. Thus, even if the NBER were to eventually declare a recession, the Biden administration would still be able to play spin doctor for long enough until the economy was no longer in one.

Notable members of the Biden administration, including Treasury Secretary Janet Yellen[471] and Press Secretary Karine Jean-Pierre,[472] began publicly denying the traditional definition of "recession," as did others

---

467   Federal Balanced Budget Act (S.C. 2015, C. 36, S. 41). June 6, 2015, https://laws-lois.justice.gc.ca/eng/acts/F-5.8/page-1.html.

468   Bloomberg. "Yellen says signs of U.S. recession aren't in sight 'when you're creating almost 400,000 jobs a month.'" Fortune, July 24, 2022, https://fortune.com/2022/07/24/yellen-says-signs-of-u-s-recession-arent-in-sight-when-youre-creating-almost-400000-jobs-a-month/.

469   "Series 7: Recession." Solomon Exam Prep, https://solomonexamprep.com/content-gl/541/34/recession.

470   "Series 65: Recession." Solomon Exam Prep, https://solomonexamprep.com/content-gl/541/1/recession.

471   Ibid.

472   Hains, Tim. "White House Spokesperson: 'I'm Not Going to Define' What A Recession Is." RealClearPolitics, July 26, 2022, https://www.realclearpolitics.com/video/2022/07/26/white_house_spokesperson_im_not_going_to_define_what_a_recession_is.html.

in the administration in anticipation of the second-quarter GDP growth figures release.

A post on the official White House blog read, "While some maintain that two consecutive quarters of falling real GDP constitute a recession, that is neither the official definition nor the way economists evaluate the state of the business cycle."[473]

Curiously, in the past, members of the Biden administration had no trouble defining a recession as "two consecutive negative quarters."

- In March 2008, National Economic Council director Brian Deese said, "Of course economists have a technical definition of recession, which is two consecutive quarters of negative growth."[474] After two consecutive negative quarters under Biden, Deese said, "As Secretary Yellen said...two negative quarters of GDP growth is not the technical definition of recession."[475]

- Biden's economic adviser Jared Bernstein said in September 2019 that a recession is "defined as two consecutive quarters of declining growth."[476] After that happened under Biden, he denied that the economy was in recession and argued that data on job growth, consumer spending, and industrial production was "simply inconsistent with a recessionary call."[477]

473 The White House. "How Do Economists Determine Whether the Economy Is in a Recession?" July 21, 2022, https://www.whitehouse.gov/cea/written-materials/2022/07/21/how-do-economists-determine-whether-the-economy-is-in-a-recession/.

474 "Clinton Campaign Advisers Hold a News Teleconference." April 1, 2008, https://prod-static.gop.com/media/documents/CLINTON_CAMPAIGN_ADVISERS_HOLD_A_NEWS_TELECONFERENCE_1_1658927995.PDF#page=10.

475 Hains, Tim. "WH: "Two Negative Quarters of GDP Growth Is Not The Technical Definition of A Recession." RealClearPolitics, July 26, 2022, https://www.realclearpolitics.com/video/2022/07/26/wh_two_negative_quarters_of_gdp_growth_is_not_the_technical_definition_of_a_recession.html.

476 Bernstein, Jared. "The Self-Inflicted Recession: The Next Downturn Will Be Political—and Tough to Escape." *Foreign Affairs Magazine*, September 10, 2019, https://www.foreignaffairs.com/articles/2019-09-10/self-inflicted-recession.

477 Nelson, Amy. "White House economist insists data is 'inconsistent' with recession despite second quarter of negative GDP." Fox News, July 28, 2022, https://www.foxnews.com/media/white-house-economist-insists-data-inconsistent-recession-despite-second-quarter-negative-gdp.

— Biden's economic adviser Heather Boushey said in May 2019 that a "rule of thumb" definition of a recession is "two quarters of negative growth in GDP."[478] After Biden's economy met the rule of thumb definition, Boushey said that the negative GDP report "does not necessarily indicate that we are in a recession right now" because of consumer spending data.[479]

Nor was there much question among other top Democrats.

In July 2008, House Speaker Nancy Pelosi said while arguing for another stimulus package, "And so while they may have saved the second quarter from a technical definition of recession, the fact is, we are now into the third quarter and we need to have another stimulus package."[480]

In December 2000, Bill Clinton said during a White House press event held with then-president-elect George W. Bush, "A recession is two quarters in a row of negative growth."[481]

The media fell in line amazingly quickly, with Politico taking the cake for the most Orwellian reporting on the eve of the second quarter GDP figures release, writing: "Tomorrow we get the first, possibly inaccurate and certain to be revised reading of U.S. economic performance in the second quarter of this deeply weird economic year—one metric to measure if we're in a recession."[482]

In a similar fashion, Politico's chief economics correspondent Ben Smith defended the Biden administration's spin, writing that the White House "is pretty obviously right" and that "getting people to understand that and the nuances of our strange, vexing, economic moment is really

478   Boushey, Heather, et al. "The Damage Done by Recessions and How to Respond." *Recession Ready: Fiscal Policies to Stabilize the American Economy,* edited by H. Boushey, et al., 2019, pp. 11–47.

479   Chamlee, Virginia. "President Biden's Economic Adviser Addresses Americans' Burning Questions About Possible Recession." *People,* July 28, 2022, https://people.com/politics/president-biden-economic-adviser-addresses-questions-about-possible-recession/.

480   Margolis, Matt. "Pelosi in 2008: Two Quarters of Negative Growth Is 'Technical Definition of Recession.'" PJ Media, July 29, 2022, https://pjmedia.com/news-and-politics/matt-margolis/2022/07/29/pelosi-in-2008-two-quarters-of-negative-growth-is-technical-definition-of-recession-n1616841.

481   Singer, Paul. "Clinton welcomes Bush, will discuss North Korea." UPI, December 29, 2000, https://www.upi.com/Archives/2000/12/19/Clinton-welcomes-Bush-will-discuss-North-Korea/4196977202000/.

482   Politico. July 28, 2022, https://twitter.com/politico/status/1552444242735370246.

hard."[483] Like everyone else, when Trump was in office, in March 2020, Smith wrote that first-quarter growth was downgraded to -2.1 percent and that "the second quarter will be down by double digits. All of this just means we are in a recession right now."[484]

Smith's tune changed the most transparently of all those listed, as it was just mere weeks before the Biden administration started redefining recession that he was worried that the economy was about to slide into a recession. "While we might not be in one [a recession] yet (though it's possible we are), I'm sorry to report that the conditions are ripe for a slide in gross domestic product that lasts at least two quarters, the technical definition of a recession." The article was titled "Actually, a recession is inevitable."[485] How quickly things change.

The Associated Press' Christopher Rugaber made a similar argument, acknowledging that the "two quarters" definition is the "common definition" for a recession but "isn't the one that counts." This is all semantics and effectively is just fact-checking anyone specifically accusing the White House of changing the "official" definition of recession instead of the "most commonly used" definition.[486]

That definition seemed to be the "one that counts" for the AP when they reported just months prior, in January 2021, that Mexico's economy fell into "a technical recession at the end of last year with two consecutive quarters of contraction."[487]

Reuters wrote in a tweet, "Going by the 'two quarters' rule, U.S. GDP data from the first two quarters of 2022 may show that the economy is in recession," before hedging with "but there has never been a recession declared without a loss of employment, and thousands of jobs are being added monthly."[488]

---

483   White, Ben. July 27, 2022, https://twitter.com/
       morningmoneyben/status/1552275594200637441.

484   White, Ben. March 27, 2020, https://twitter.com/
       morningmoneyben/status/1243539703711875074.

485   White, Ben. "Actually, a recession is inevitable." Politico, June
       22, 2022, https://www.politico.com/newsletters/politico-nightly/
       2022/06/22/actually-a-recession-is-inevitable-00041577.

486   Rugaber, Christopher. "EXPLAINER: How Do We Know When a Recession Has
       Begun?" Associated Press, July 28, 2022, https://apnews.com/article/inflation-covid-
       health-gross-domestic-product-economy-89cbfc145ad34a91679ffa43e617c896.

487   Ibid

488   Reuters. July 9, 2022, https://twitter.com/Reuters/status/1545940869823418369.

In prior articles, Reuters commonly used the "two quarters" definition. One article from 2021 discussed Australian government spending to counteract a recession "defined as two successive quarters of negative output figures."[489] Back in the '08 financial crisis, Reuters reported that "two successive quarters of economic contraction are regarded as a recession."[490]

And the fact-checkers had their back.

Newsweek "fact-checker" Tom Norton rated it "False" that the White House redefined the word "recession," where he points out that the NBER also uses other variables in determining if the U.S. is in recession besides negative GDP growth, such as real personal income, employment, consumer spending, and industrial production and that there are no "fixed rules or thresholds" for those variables.[491]

PolitiFact's Louis Jacobson wrote an "explainer"-style article on what a recession is to defend the White House spin, where he wrote that defining a recession was a "confusing topic," and that the "two-quarter rule is an informal metric."[492] In 2015, Jacobson wrote that Donald Trump was wrong to suggest that a negative quarter of GDP growth under Obama suggested the U.S. economy was in recession because "the general rule of thumb is that it takes two quarters of negative growth to signal a recession."[493] Things weren't so confusing then.

Among the fact-checkers, there was no ambiguity whatsoever as to what a recession was prior to the Biden administration redefining it.

In 2015, the *Washington Post*'s Kessler fact-checked the same Donald Trump quote that Jacobson did, which he determined to be false because

489   Cole, Wayne. "Australia government spending binge may help dodge recession." Reuters, August 30, 2021, https://www.reuters.com/world/asia-pacific/australia-government-spending-climbs-q2-adds-gdp-2021-08-31/.

490   Falloon, Matt, and Desai Sumeet. "Recession fears grow on factory output data." Reuters, July 7, 2008, https://www.reuters.com/article/uk-britain-manufacturing/recession-fears-grow-on-factory-output-data-idUKL0771552520080707.

491   Norton, Tom. "Fact Check: Did the White House 'Change Definition of Recession'?" *Newsweek*, July 25, 2022, https://www.newsweek.com/fact-check-did-white-house-change-definition-recession-1727641.

492   Jacobson, Louis. "What exactly is a recession? Sorting out a confusing topic." PolitiFact, July 26, 2022, https://www.politifact.com/article/2022/jul/26/what-exactly-recession-sorting-out-confusing/.

493   Jacobson, Louis. "Donald Trump gets claim about U.S. GDP doubly wrong." PolitiFact, June 16, 2015, https://www.politifact.com/factchecks/2015/jun/16/donald-trump/donald-trump-says-us-gdp-never-negative-ter/.

"after all, two negative quarters in a row is a standard indicator for an economic recession."[494]

CNN's fact-checker Daniel Dale, who was also fact-checking a similar Trump claim about the Obama economy, said, "There was no recession in the late Obama term. The economy was growing though growth had slowed in 2016, to 1.7%, there were no quarters of negative growth in 2016. You need two straight for a recession."[495]

In a *USA Today* fact-check in 2020, fact-checker Doug Stanglin acknowledged, "A recession is generally defined as two consecutive quarters of declining GDP."[496]

As the administration's newspeak foreshadowed, the economy did further contract in the second quarter of 2022, marking a technical recession in the first half of the year.

Only once in history, back in 1947, was there a case where there were two consecutive quarters of negative growth and a recession wasn't declared by the NBER. In that particular case, the NBER was likely accounting for the fact that the decline in GDP had been a result of the demobilization from WWII in 1946–1947, not a decline in private-sector activity.[497] In every single other case where there were two consecutive quarters of negative growth, a recession was declared.

The only other exceptions to the "two consecutive negative quarters" rule were in 2001,[498] when the NBER declared a recession in a year where there was negative economic growth in the first and third quarter

494 Kessler, Glenn, and Michelle Ye Hee Lee. "Fact checking Donald Trump's presidential announcement speech." *Washington Post,* June 17, 2015, https://web.archive.org/web/20220423103904/https://www.washingtonpost.com/news/fact-checker/wp/2015/06/17/fact-checking-donald-trumps-presidential-announcement-speech/.

495 Meyer, Ken. "CNN's Daniel Dale Fact Checks RNC Convention's Second Night: 'Laughable' to Claim Trump Brought Peace to Middle East." Mediaite, August 26, 2020, https://www.mediaite.com/tv/cnns-daniel-dale-fact-checks-rnc-conventions-second-night-laughable-to-claim-trump-brought-peace-to-middle-east/.

496 Stanglin, Doug. "Fact Check: Do Republican presidents oversee recessions and Dems oversee recoveries?" *USA Today,* May 31, 2020, https://www.usatoday.com/story/news/factcheck/2020/05/28/fact-check-do-gop-presidents-oversee-recessions-dems-recoveries/5235957002/.

497 Barro, Robert J. "Yes, the US Economy Is Likely in Recession." Project Syndicate, August 1, 2022, https://www.project-syndicate.org/commentary/two-consecutive-quarters-negative-us-growth-predict-recession-since-1948-by-robert-j-barro-2022-07.

498 Chinn, Menzie. "The "Non-Technical Recession" Recession of 2001." Econbrowser, July 2, 2022, https://econbrowser.com/archives/2022/07/the-non-technical-recession-recession-of-2001.

of the year, and the 2020 recession, which lasted only two months.[499] Or in other words, a case where a recession was called when there were two quarters of negative growth, but nonconsecutive, and one where there was a recession called when there were less than two quarters of decline (due to the severity of the decline).

The NBER's Business Cycle Dating Committee's general definition of recession is even less strict than the "two quarters" definition, defining one as "a significant decline in economic activity that is spread across the economy and lasts more than a few months."

The NBER aside, federal statutes, the Congressional Budget Office, and other governing bodies use the "two negative consecutive quarters" definition. As economic historian Phil Magness noted, the Gramm-Rudman-Hollings Act of 1985, which put spending constraints on the federal budget, defines a recession as "real economic growth...less than zero with respect to each of any two consecutive quarters within such period."[500]

Magness himself would later be censored by Facebook for saying the economy was in recession after the second quarter GDP print, as were many who said it was,[501] with Facebook directing people on his post to a PolitiFact article by Louis Jacobson titled "No, the White House didn't change the definition of 'recession.'"[502] Jacobson's article makes similar arguments to his aforementioned "explainer"-style article that's contradicted by his own past writing.

The Biden administration is hardly the first in history to warp language to its advantage, and they're not even the first to do it in this manner.

When Alfred Kahn, the economist in charge of fighting inflation under Jimmy Carter, said that failing to contain inflation would lead to recession, he was instructed to never use the word "recession" again.[503]

499   Cox, Jeff. "It's official: The Covid recession lasted just two months, the shortest in U.S. history." CNBC, July 19, 2021, https://www.cnbc.com/2021/07/19/its-official-the-covid-recession-lasted-just-two-months-the-shortest-in-us-history.html.

500   Miltimore, Jon. "The Biden Administration Says US Not in a Recession, but Federal Statutes Say Otherwise. Who is Right?" Foundation for Economic Education, July 28, 2022, https://fee.org/articles/the-biden-administration-says-us-not-in-a-recession-but-federal-statutes-say-otherwise-who-is-right/.

501   Soave, Robby. "Facebook, Instagram Posts Flagged as False for Noting Biden's Recession Wordplay." *Reason Magazine*, July 29, 2022, https://reason.com/2022/07/29/recession-facebook-fact-check-biden-politifact/

502   Jacobson, Louis. "No, the White House didn't change the definition of 'recession.'" PolitiFact, July 27, 2022, https://www.politifact.com/factchecks/2022/jul/27/instagram-posts/no-white-house-didnt-change-definition-recession/.

503   Miltimore, "The Biden Administration Says US Not in a Recession."

Before Carter, Nixon became the first to try to redefine recession after it entered a downturn in November 1973 that it wouldn't emerge from until the spring of 1975. As the economy approached two quarters of negative growth, Nixon declared during his January 1974 State of the Union that there "will be no recession."

To hedge against the headlines in the face of a looming second quarter of decline, Nixon, like Biden, sent his treasury secretary (George P. Shultz) to redefine the word. Shultz dismissed recession fears to the *New York Times* and slammed the "simple-minded" two-quarters definition of a recession.[504] The NBER would later determine that the economy had been in recession from November 1973 to March 1975.[505]

The only difference was that the media didn't uncritically repeat the Nixon administration's redefinition of the word, and there was no army of fact-checkers ready to gaslight anyone contradicting them.

GEORGE WHO?

In a pointless fact-check, *WaPo*'s Meg Kelly accused Republicans of sharing a misleading video showing Biden getting confused and saying he was running for president against George W. Bush in 2020.[506]

Biden said in the speech, "Four more years of George, uh, George, uh, he, uh, are going to find ourselves in a position where if, uh, Trump gets elected, uh, we are going to be, uh, in a different world."

Kelly defends Biden by arguing that he actually could've been referring to George Lopez, who had originally asked him the question—and also is not Donald Trump.

---

504   Magness, Phillip W. "Biden Borrows the Nixon Playbook on Recessions." American Institute for Economic Research, August 1, 2022, https://www. aier.org/article/biden-borrows-the-nixon-playbook-on-recessions/.

505   "Business Cycle Expansions and Contractions." NBER, https://web. archive.org/web/20070705190514/http://www.nber.org/cycles.html.

506   Kelly, Meg. "No, Biden did not confuse George W. Bush and Donald Trump." *Washington Post*, October 26, 2020, https://www.washingtonpost.com/politics/ 2020/10/26/no-biden-did-not-confuse-george-w-bush-donald-trump/.

"HE WHO CONTROLS THE TELEPROMPTER CONTROLS THE PRESIDENCY"

During an amusing Ron Burgundyesque gaffe, Joe Biden read directly off his teleprompter its instructions "end of quote. Repeat the line." This was just less than two weeks after Biden was photographed holding notes reminding/instructing him to take his seat after greeting participants at an event in the Roosevelt Room.[507]

Biden said:

> One of the most extraordinary parts of the decision, in my view, is the majority writes, and I quote, "Women..."—it's a quote now, from the majority—"Women are not without electoral or political power. It is noteworthy that the percentage of women who registered to vote and cast a ballot is consistently higher than the percentage of the men who do so."
>
> End of quote. Repeat the line: "Women are not without electoral..." and/or political—"or"—let me be precise; not "and/or"—"...or political power."

White House assistant press secretary Emilie Simons provided the official talking point to explain away the incident, which the fact-checkers would mindlessly embrace, that Biden actually had said, "Let me repeat that line."[508] The official White House transcript then altered Biden's quote to read, "End of quote. Let me repeat the line."[509]

The fact-checkers then uncritically cited the doctored official White House transcript to prove that Biden didn't actually say what he said.

FactCheck.org's Brea Jones cited the White House transcript and falsely claimed that clips being shared on social media of Biden's gaffe

507   Dasgupta, Sravasti. "Biden cheat sheet shows instruction for him to 'take YOUR seat.'" *Yahoo Sports,* June 24, 2022, https://sports.yahoo.com/biden-cheat-sheet-shows-instruction-074352962.html.

508   Washington Free Beacon Staff. "Biden Aide Gaslights Americans on President's Teleprompter Flub." Washington Free Beacon, July 8, 2022, https://freebeacon.com/biden-administration/biden-aide-gaslights-americans-on-presidents-teleprompter-flub/.

509   "Remarks by President Biden on Protecting Access to Reproductive Health Care Services." The White House, July 8, 2022, https://www.whitehouse.gov/briefing-room/speeches-remarks/2022/07/08/remarks-by-president-biden-on-protecting-access-to-reproductive-health-care-services/.

were a "a shortened clip" of his remarks, [510] and the Poynter Institute's Louis Jacobson and Andy Nguyen quoted Simons' bogus defense in trying to spin Biden's gaffe.[511]

FACT-CHECKERS ATTEMPT TO MAKE SENSE OF BIDEN SAYING HE HAS CANCER

It's never a good sign when a president says that they have cancer and the public's immediate reaction is that they're mistaken and it's just their dementia speaking, but such was the case with Biden in July 2022.

During a speech near his childhood home in Delaware, Biden spoke about global warming and the emissions from oil refineries near his home. "That's why I and so damn many other people I grew up with have cancer and why for the longest time Delaware had the highest cancer rate in the nation," Biden said.

After video of his casual cancer diagnosis reveal began going viral online, White House spokesman Andrew Bates shared a tweet from *Washington Post* fact-checker Glenn Kessler to provide some supposed clarification. "Check out Biden's medical report. Before he became president, he'd had non-melanoma skin cancers removed," Kessler wrote.[512]

While this is true, it's hardly applicable to Biden's comments. Biden said, "I have cancer," in the present tense and said that he had cancer due to emissions from oil companies, not the sun.

Biden obviously just misspoke, as he does regularly. How hard is it for them to just admit that?

READ MY LIPS, NO NEW TAXES FOR INCOMES BELOW $400,000

On the 2020 campaign trail, Joe Biden said that he would only be raising taxes "for anybody making over $400,000," and there would be "no new taxes" for anyone earning less than that. In every utterance of this state-

510   Jones, Brea. "Social Media Posts Misleadingly Edit and Misrepresent Biden Remarks from Teleprompter." FactCheck.org, July 14, 2022, https://www.factcheck.org/2022/07/social-media-posts-misleadingly-edit-and-misrepresent-biden-remarks-from-teleprompter/.

511   Jacobson, Louis, and Andy Nguyen. "Did President Biden read directions to 'repeat the line' from a teleprompter?" The Poynter Institute, July 12, 2022, https://www.poynter.org/fact-checking/2022/joe-biden-read-teleprompter-repeat-line/.

512   Kessler, Glenn. July 20, 2022, https://twitter.com/GlennKesslerWP/status/1549833485552058370.

ment made throughout the campaign Biden clearly was speaking about individual income, not household income, and this is further supported by his 2020 campaign website that promises "Joe Biden will not raise taxes on *anyone* making less than $400,000. Period."[513]

The fact-checkers analyzed Biden's tax plans as presented to them and determined that Biden was telling the truth that none of them would raise taxes on individuals earning less than $400,000. The *WaPo*'s Glenn Kessler's analysis stated that Biden's tax plan as outlined up until that point wouldn't directly raise taxes on those earning below $400,000, but could if companies passed the costs of a corporate income tax onto consumers.[514]

USA Today fact-checkers McKenzie Sadeghi and Chelsey Cox wrote an article claiming to debunk the claim that the Biden tax plan would raise taxes on families earning $75,000, which they rated false based on Biden's "no new taxes below $400k" promise.[515]

By just Biden's second full month into the presidency, that number became subject to change, with Press Secretary Jen Psaki "clarifying" for the first time on March 17, 2021, that the $400,000 threshold applies to household income, not individual income. Thus, someone making $200,000 could see their taxes rise if their spouse earns the same.[516] Just hours earlier that day, during an interview on *Good Morning America*, Biden said, in contradiction, "Anybody making more than $400,000 will see a small to a significant tax increase. You make less than $400,000, you won't see one single penny in additional federal tax."[517] The Wall Street

---

513 "A Tale of Two Tax Policies: Trump Rewards Wealth, Biden Rewards Work." Democratic National Committee, https://joebiden.com/two-tax-policies/#.

514 Kessler, Glenn. "Joe Biden's claim that he won't raise taxes on people making less than $400,000." *Washington Post,* August 31, 2020, https://web.archive.org/web/20210330043137/https://www.washingtonpost.com/politics/2020/08/31/joe-bidens-claim-that-he-wont-raise-taxes-people-making-less-than-400000/.

515 Sadeghi, McKenzie, and Chelsey Cox. "Fact check: Biden tax plan would raise rates for those who make more than $400K, corporations." *USA Today,* August 30, 2020, https://www.usatoday.com/story/news/factcheck/2020/08/30/fact-check-biden-tax-plan-raises-rates-those-who-make-over-400-k/3418926001/.

516 Nelson, Steven. "Biden tax hike could hit people earning $200K, White House clarifies." *New York Post,* March 17, 2021, https://nypost.com/2021/03/17/biden-tax-hike-could-hit-people-earning-200k-white-house-says/.

517 Cook, Nancy, and Jennifer Jacobs. "Biden vows to raise taxes on anyone earning over $400,000." *Los Angeles Times,* March 17, 2021, https://web.archive.org/web/20210317133342/https://www.latimes.com/politics/story/2021-03-17/biden-vows-to-raise-taxes-on-anyone-earning-more-than-400-000.

Journal Editorial Board blasted Biden's "bait and switch" on taxes in an op-ed following Psaki's comments.[518]

It was a radical reversal from Psaki too, who just two days prior boldly stated that "the president remains committed to his pledge from the campaign that nobody making under $400,000 a year will have their taxes increased."[519]

Later, in July 2022, a spending deal was reached by Senators Chuck Schumer and Joe Manchin, which the nonpartisan Joint Committee on Taxation said would increase taxes in aggregate by $16.7 billion on earners making below $200,000 in 2023, and another $14.1 billion on taxpayers making between $200,000 and $500,000. Press Secretary Karine Jean-Pierre denied the Joint Committee's findings when questioned on them during a press briefing, calling their analysis "incomplete," but not once tried to lower the "400k" threshold to "200k" like Psaki once did.[520]

Biden also claimed that "this bill will not raise taxes on anyone making less than $400,000 a year," during a speech promoting it.[521] And thus, the $400,000 threshold had become the norm again—and at a time when taxes would directly be raised on those earning below that.

FACT-CHECKER REDEFINES MEANING OF "ENERGY INDEPENDENT" TO DEFEND BIDEN BECAUSE U.S. BECAME ENERGY INDEPENDENT UNDER TRUMP

When in doubt, the fact-checker can simply redefine words to mean whatever they want.

The Media Research Center had twenty-seven of their posts on Facebook and Instagram censored because French fact-checker Agence

518 The Editorial Board. "Down the Biden Tax Threshold." *Wall Street Journal*, March 21, 2021, https://web.archive.org/web/20210726011036mp_/https://www.wsj.com/articles/down-the-biden-tax-threshold-11616360766.

519 "Press Conference: Jen Psaki Holds a Press Briefing at the White House - March 15, 2021." Factbase, https://web.archive.org/web/20211004012332mp_/https://factba.se/biden/transcript/joe-biden-press-conference-briefing-jen-psaki-march-15-2021.

520 Alic, Haris. "White House denies Manchin spending bill will raise taxes on Americans making less than $400k." Fox Business, August 1, 2022, https://www.foxbusiness.com/politics/white-house-denies-manchin-spending-bill-will-raise-taxes-americans-making-less-than-400k.

521 Catenacci, Thomas. "Most Americans will feel tax pain from Dem inflation bill despite Biden's past promises: analysis." Fox Business, August 1, 2022, https://www.foxbusiness.com/politics/most-americans-feel-tax-pain-dem-inflation-bill-despite-bidens-past-promises.

France-Presse (AFP) found them to be "missing context." The posts in question were promoting a mini-documentary called "Killing Keystone," and had captions holding Joe Biden accountable for the U.S. losing the energy independent status it gained under Donald Trump's presidency. These captions are what the AFP took issue with.

Both AFP fact-checks were written by Rob Lever, who tries to refute reality by redefining the definition of energy independence, writing: "The US became a 'net annual petroleum exporter' in 2020, according to official government data, which some commentators touted as energy independence. But supply is not a one-sided metric; data from the US Energy Information Administration (EIA) shows that *American exports that year amounted to about 8.51 million barrels per day (bpd), while imports were still about 7.86 million bpd* [emphasis mine]."[522]

Energy independence, at least for how everyone except Lever defines it, is when a country has more energy exports than imports. It is not, as he believes, when there are no energy imports.

And there is no debate over this whatsoever. As the Media Research Center's Joseph Vazquez notes:

> There was widespread agreement in the media on this point.
>
> ABC 4 News wrote on March 7, 2022: "Last year was neck and neck but technically the U.S. was energy independent since it exported more than it imported." Forbes published a piece March 8, 2022, headlined: "Surprise! The U.S. Is Still Energy Independent." Axios published a story Feb. 19, 2022, headlined: "The U.S. is now energy independent." [523]

Furthermore, the Facebook-approved fact-checkers can't reach a conclusion on U.S. energy independence. Vazquez added that:

> Fellow Facebook fact-checker Lead Stories contradicted AFP, writing in a May 2021 fact-check: "In 2019, when Donald Trump was president, the U.S. did achieve energy independence, something that had not happened since 1957."

522   Lever, Rob. "Posts mislead on US energy independence." AFP Fact Check, March 29, 2022, https://factcheck.afp.com/doc.afp.com.326T98W.

523   Vazquez, Joseph. "REPORT: Facebook Fact-Checker Redefines 'Energy Independence' to Silence Biden Critics." NewsBusters, May 24, 2022, https://www.newsbusters.org/blogs/business/joseph-vazquez/2022/05/24/report-facebook-fact-checker-redefines-energy-independence.

Apparently these aligned fact-checkers didn't have their story straight.[524]

In addition to Lead Stories, even other traditionally god-awful fact-checkers such as PolitiFact and CNN's Daniel Dale agreed that the U.S. reached energy independence under Trump when it happened.[525]

ONE NATION, UNDER DIMWITTED FACT-CHECKERS

During the 2020 Democratic National Convention (DNC), video of a moderator during the Muslim Delegates Assembly omitting the "under God" from the Pledge of Allegiance went viral.

A. J. Durrani, a superdelegate for 2016–2020, led the pledge: "I pledge allegiance to the flag of the United States of America, and to the republic for which it stands, one nation, indivisible, with liberty and justice for all."

This wasn't great optics for the DNC, leading the fact-checkers to mobilize and try to "debunk" this incident by weakly arguing that while the pledge wasn't read at some events, it was at least read at other events.

In rating the claim that the DNC omitted the phrase "under God" from the pledge "Mostly False," they admit that the phrase was omitted from at least two recitations of the pledge, but that "the DNC did not issue any guidelines forbidding the use of the phrase," and that the pledge was used at the start of each of the three nights at the 2020 DNC.

PolitiFact's Daniel Funke rated it "Mostly False" that the DNC omitted "one nation under God" from the pledge, because while some caucuses omitted the "under God," the line wasn't excluded from the convention's primetime spots.[526]

That the "under God" was included in the pledge on some occasions doesn't disprove that it wasn't in other cases. How this leads to a "False" or "Mostly False" rating instead of at least a "Half True" can only be explained by bias.

In a similar vein, PolitiFact rated Trump's correct observation about the DNC's 2020 national convention "Half True," that there was "not

---

524 Ibid.
525 Ibid.
526 Funke, Daniel. "The DNC did not omit 'one nation under God' from the Pledge of Allegiance." PolitiFact, August 21, 2020, https://www.politifact.com/factchecks/2020/aug/21/peggy-hubbard/dnc-did-not-omit-one-nation-under-god-pledge-alleg/.

one American flag on the massive stage at the Democratic National Convention until people started complaining—then a small one. Pathetic."

PolitiFact's Aaron Sharockman acknowledges that there were no physical flags on the stage on day one, but because there was a video board with a virtual American flag displayed on screen on the stage, he uses that as justification for rating a "True" claim "Half True."[527]

Somehow that wasn't even the worst of it. When Snopes looked into the matter, they used pictures of flags on stage the second day of the convention to claim they were present on stage for the first day.[528]

FACT-CHECKERS ASSURE AMERICAN PUBLIC THERE'S TOTALLY NOTHING TO WORRY ABOUT OVER AT THE IRS

I wasn't aware that the IRS had a positive reputation to anyone—but the fact-checkers seem to believe they have one worth protecting.

In late 2021, the Biden administration briefly floated a proposal to collect information on bank accounts with over $600 in transactions per year, which would be nearly all of them.

The *Washington Post*'s Salvador Rizzo defended the proposal and based his defense on government talking points, such as a Treasury fact sheet that claimed only bank accounts with unusual activity risked IRS attention.[529]

The Biden administration ended up backing down on this proposal in October 2021, but renewed efforts to bolster the size and scope of the IRS didn't take long for the administration to implement, and for the fact-checkers to downplay the reality of what was happening.

In August, Joe Biden signed a reconciliation bill that would include nearly $80 billion to fund the IRS, which the administration claimed would be to target high income earners. One was left to wonder why the

---

527 Sharockman, Aaron. "Red, white and where? What happened to the American flag at the DNC?" PolitiFact, July 27, 2016, https://www.politifact.com/factchecks/2016/jul/27/donald-trump/dnc-flag-missing-controversy/.

528 Hasson, Peter. "Snopes Caught LYING About Lack of American Flags at Democratic Convention." The Daily Caller, July 28, 2016, https://dailycaller.com/2016/07/28/snopes-caught-lying-about-lack-of-american-flags-at-democratic-convention/.

529 Rizzo, Salvador. "No, Biden isn't proposing that the IRS spy on bank records." *Washington Post*, October 20, 2021, https://www.washingtonpost.com/politics/2021/10/20/no-biden-isnt-proposing-that-irs-spy-bank-records/.

IRS isn't doing that already, as they audit the poor five times higher than everyone else.[530] For the sake of efficiency, even a strained IRS would want to prioritize targeting wealthy tax cheats than poorer ones, as the taxation recovered per person for a wealthy person will always be an order of magnitude larger than what it will be from a poor person.

The $80 billion will be used to boost the IRS's workforce by about eighty-seven thousand new employees. At this time, the IRS was putting up job listings seeking applicants for their enforcement division who were "willing to use deadly force"—which they quickly deleted after it got negative media coverage.[531]

In response to these facts, the fact-checkers decided to set up and then set alight straw man arguments instead of addressing the facts at hand.

PolitiFact's Jon Greenberg tried to sanitize the IRS hiring spree by debunking tangential claims that all eighty-seven thousand employees would be working specifically in enforcement and not other parts of the agency such as IT.[532]

Reuters debunked the claim that all eighty-seven thousand new hires would be armed agents,[533] while Lead Stories headlined their article, "Fact Check: IRS Is NOT Trying to Arm All Its Agents."[534] The Lead Stories fact-check was in response to a social media post that never actually claimed the IRS was trying to arm all its agents, because they couldn't actually find anyone notable making the argument they were fact-checking.

As for fears that the IRS will increase audits on the middle class, the *Washington Post*'s Glenn Kessler says that's not true because the govern-

---

530   "IRS Audits Poorest Families at Five Times the Rate for Everyone Else."
      Syracuse University, March 8, 2022, https://trac.syr.edu/tracirs/latest/679/.

531   Glebova, Diana. "IRS Deletes Job Posting Seeking Applicants Willing to 'Use
      Deadly Force.'" National Review, August 10, 2022, https://www.nationalreview.
      com/news/irs-deletes-job-posting-seeking-applicants-willing-to-use-deadly-force/.

532   Greenberg, Jon. "Kevin McCarthy's mostly false claim about an army of 87,000 IRS
      agents." PolitiFact, August 11, 2022, https://www.politifact.com/factchecks/2022/
      aug/11/kevin-mccarthy/kevin-mccarthys-mostly-false-claim-about-army-8700.

533   Reuters Fact Check. "Fact Check-The IRS is not hiring thousands of armed agents,
      job ads show opening for specialized unit." Reuters, August 17, 2022, https://www.
      reuters.com/article/factcheck-irs-armed/fact-check-the-irs-is-not-hiring-thousands-
      of-armed-agents-job-ads-show-opening-for-specialized-unit-idUSL1N2ZT296.

534   Dillard, Christina. "Fact Check: IRS Is NOT Trying To Arm All Its
      Agents." Lead Stories, August 12, 2022, https://leadstories.com/hoax-
      alert/2022/08/fact-check-irs-is-not-trying-to-arm-all-its-agents.html.

ment says they're intended for the rich (and he just believes them),[535] and the aforementioned PolitiFact article makes the same argument. Less than two weeks later, the Congressional Budget Office admitted that it would be increasing audits on the middle class.[536]

The arming of the IRS was something the fact-checkers bizarrely tried to downplay as totally normal on the basis that it's been happening already.

In June 2022, Florida Representative Matt Gaetz informed millions of Americans for the first time during an appearance on Jesse Watters' show that the IRS has been loading up on guns and ammo for quite some time now—and that it's continued during the pro-gun-control Biden administration.[537]

"Call me old-fashioned, but I thought the heaviest artillery an IRS agent would need would be a calculator. I imagine the IRS in green eye-shades and cubicles — not busting doors down and emptying Glock clips on our fellow Americans. Certainly it's troubling that in 2022 alone, the IRS has spent around $725,000 on ammunition," he told Fox News' Jesse Watters.

"And there was a report that showed over a 10-year period, the IRS actually stockpiled $11 million worth of ammunition," he added.

Tucker Carlson later covered the story in August after Gaetz introduced a bill to disarm the IRS and noted in his coverage that the IRS had spent $20 million on guns and ammo between 2006 and 2019.[538]

PolitiFact's Jeff Cercone decided to cover the revelation in a fact-check titled "No, Biden is not arming up the IRS with guns and ammunition"—and it's immediately evident that the article doesn't live up to its headline.

Cercone confirms the figures that Gaetz cited and then arbitrarily decides that there's nothing suspect going on here because the IRS has been doing this for a while; "The division's spending on ammunition this year is on par with previous years and less than what was spent a decade

535 Kessler, Glenn. August 18, 2022, https://twitter.com/
GlennKesslerWP/status/1560276946147102720.
536 Rigolizzo, John. "CBO: IRS Will Increase Audits On Middle Class, But
Only A 'Small Fraction' Of New Tax Revenues." The Daily Wire, August
27, 2022, https://www.dailywire.com/news/cbo-irs-will-increase-audits-
on-middle-class-but-only-a-small-fraction-of-new-tax-revenues.
537 *Jesse Watters Primetime*, Fox News, June 21, 2022.
538 *Tucker Carlson Tonight*, Fox News, August 4, 2022.

ago" writes Cercone, irrelevantly. Gaetz and Carlson both acknowledged that this spending wasn't unique to the Biden administration.

The headline of Cercone's fact-check, denying that Biden is arming the IRS, is quite literally contradicted by its first sentence, which says the IRS is buying guns and ammo. Cercone's fact-check is of something never claimed, that this is something unique to the Biden administration.

As argued earlier, among the most common strategies of the faux fact-checker to rate a true claim false is to nitpick anything else the person uttering it may have said that can be fact-checked in lieu of the claim of substance. So, in this case, because fact-checking the data points that Gaetz cited would produce a "True" verdict, Cercone decided to make the specific claim he's rating false Gaetz's opinion statement that "Joe Biden is raising taxes, disarming Americans, so of course they are arming up the IRS like they are preparing to take Fallujah," which he made during the appearance on Tucker.

Cercone rates that statement false because "there is no evidence this continued tradition of spending by the IRS has any connection to Biden's positions on taxes and gun restrictions"—but that's not the story. The story is that the IRS is stockpiling guns and ammo.

This further demonstrates how in politicized fact-checking, framing is everything. In addition to the mental gymnastics that Cercone had to subject himself to in order to get the "False" rating he wanted to give

Gaetz, this is further evidenced by the fact that the fact-checkers couldn't even agree with each other on this one.

Local news is notably less partisan than national news, so it's no surprise that when Texas local NewsWest 9's "Verify" fact-checking segment tackled Gaetz's statement that the IRS purchased $700,000 in ammunition between March and June of 2022, they rated it "True" (because it is) while acknowledging that this isn't new for the IRS (because Gaetz never said or implied that it was).[539]

USA TODAY AND THE CASE OF THE GUN REGISTRY

In response to an explosive Washington Free Beacon report revealing the Bureau of Alcohol, Tobacco, Firearms and Explosives (ATF) admitted to Congress that it maintains nearly a billion gun and gun owners' records, a *USA Today* fact-checker jumped in to opine on a subject he doesn't understand.

The Beacon report, authored by Adam Kredo, revealed that that Biden administration was in possession of almost one billion records detailing the firearm purchases of American citizens—920,664,765 to be exact. When a licensed gun store goes out of business, their private transaction records become ATF property, hence how they obtained them. Naturally, the existence of these records fuels concerns that they could be eventually used for gun confiscation purposes.[540]

But according to *USA Today*'s Daniel Funke, there's nothing to see here.[541]

Since there was nothing untrue in Kredo's reporting, Funke decided to wait for someone to misrepresent it, and then fact-check them instead. Funke specifically chose to target the "Gun Owners of America" Facebook page for the fact-check, which shared the Beacon article with their own editorializing: "BREAKING: ATF gun registry includes almost 1 BILLION firearm records. Make no mistake—this is Biden's next step towards gun confiscation," which he says is "missing context."

---

539 NewsWest 9. "Yes, the IRS did buy nearly $700K in ammunition in 2022 | Verify." YouTube, July 21, 2022, https://www.youtube.com/watch?v=zeE1CCgarsg.

540 Kredo, Adam. "Biden Admin Has Records on Nearly One Billion Gun Sales." Washington Free Beacon, January 31, 2022, https://freebeacon.com /guns/biden-admin-has-records-on-nearly-one-billion-gun-sales/.

541 Funke, Daniel. "Fact Check: Claim that ATF has 'gun registry' with 1 billion records is missing context." *USA Today*, February 9, 2022, https://www.usatoday.com/story/news/ factcheck/2022/02/09/fact-check-claim-atf-has-gun-registry-missing-context/9304431002/.

Kredo warned that these records *could* be used as a gun registry, not that there was one. Despite the fact that Funke is fact-checking a social media post incorrectly representing Kredo's reporting, his fact-check was still in turn used to justify censorship of the Beacon article on Facebook. Only in the world of political fact-checking can someone misrepresenting your point get you yourself censored.

Funke is mainly just fact-checking a caption here, and while attempting to add some "clarity" about the database, he makes a number of factual errors of his own, as Gun Owners of America's Aidan Johnston laid out extensively: [542]

- Funke says that ATF's out-of-business records aren't a "searchable database." These records are collected and maintained digitally and physically at the ATF's Out-of-Business Records Center. They're then used by the National Tracing Center for Record Search Requests to trace guns used in crimes. Furthermore, "USA Today's own sources disprove its own claim that there is no 'searchable database.' April Langwell, chief of the ATF's public affairs division, refers to 'searching for records' and UCLA Professor Adam Winkler states 'there is a database.'"

- Funke says it's "missing context" that the ATF has hundreds of thousands of records. The only missing context here is that they have way more. To quote the ATF itself: "In total, ATF manages 920,664,765 OBR as of November 2021. This includes digital and an estimated number of hard copy records that are awaiting image conversion. It is currently estimated that 865,787,086 of those records are in digitalized format."

- One of the alleged experts quoted in the piece by Funke states that the ATF's out-of-business database "includes names of the purchasers of guns used in crime." The database contains more than just that however; it also includes information about hundreds of millions of guns never used in crimes, and tens of millions of gun owners who have never committed crimes.

---

542 Guns and Gear. "Facebook Censors ATF's Gun Registry with Error-Laden USA Today 'Fact Check.'" The Daily Caller, February 14, 2022, https://dailycaller.com/2022/02/14/facebook-censors-atfs-gun-registry-with-error-laden-usa-today-fact-check/.

- Funke quotes a 2016 NRA fact sheet stating that here is no federal gun registry to refute a report from 2022 providing new information. The NRA would later comment on the Beacon's report that the ATF's vast out-of-business database is "understandably concerning" and warned that they would aid gun confiscation.

- Lastly, Funke says on four occasions that the ATF's out-of-business records can only be accessed during a criminal investigation. But the ATF's website provides a process by which "private citizen needing to obtain the serial number of a stolen firearm purchased from an FFL which has since discontinued business."

This isn't the first time the fact-checkers have screwed up badly in going after Johnston's organization:

> Leading up to the 2020 election, Gun Owners of America similarly was censored by Facebook, working with the French government, to cover up our reporting of the fact that Kamala Harris opposes the individual right to keep and bear arms. Facebook went so far as to label as "fake news" a link to the Harris *amicus* brief which she filed in opposition to that individual right in the landmark Second Amendment *D.C. v. Heller* case.

Clearly, there's a fact-checker bias against guns too.

CASH FOR ILLEGALS: WHEN $450,000 ISN'T $450,000

In October 2021, the *Wall Street Journal* broke the bombshell story that the Biden administration was in talks to offer illegal alien families separated during the Trump administration around $450,000 each.[543]

The *WSJ* said that 940 claims had been filed by families separated at the border they crossed illegally.

---

543 Hackman, Michelle, et al. "U.S. in Talks to Pay Hundreds of Millions to Families Separated at Border." *Wall Street Journal,* October 28, 2021, https://www.wsj.com/articles/biden-administration-in-talks-to-pay-hundreds-of-millions-to-immigrant-families-separated-at-border-11635447591.

When asked about the report days later, Joe Biden called it "garbage" and said that the payments were "not gonna happen."[544]

He was immediately contradicted by the ACLU's executive director Anthony D. Romero, who suggested (quite charitably) that Biden was "out of the loop." "President Biden may not have been fully briefed about the actions of his very own Justice Department as it carefully deliberated and considered the crimes committed against thousands of families separated from their children as an intentional governmental policy. But if he follows through on what he said, the president is abandoning a core campaign promise to do justice for the thousands of separated families," Romero said.[545]

The next day, then White House principal deputy press secretary Karine Jean-Pierre implausibly said that Biden's reaction was to "the dollar figure," not the plan itself, and that he was "perfectly comfortable" with the Justice Department trying to settle those cases.[546]

In contrast to Biden's position, his DOJ would later decide that the families were not entitled to compensation, and pulled out of settlement talks on December 16.

In a January brief related to one lawsuit, the DOJ argued, "At issue in this case is whether adults who entered the country without authorization can challenge the federal government's enforcement of federal immigration laws. They cannot."[547]

The whole ordeal was a PR trainwreck for the Biden administration, so inevitably the fact-checkers were looking for some angle to get involved.

That came after Republican GOP Senate primary candidate Jim Lamon ran a campaign that shows an image resembling a check with

---

544 Morris, Kyle. "Biden labels report government to pay separated immigrants $450,000 'garbage.'" Fox News, November 3, 2021, https://www.foxnews.com/politics/biden-calls-report-to-pay-separated-immigrants-450k-garbage.

545 "ACLU Comment on Biden Statement on Settlements for Family Separation." American Civil Liberties Union, November 3, 2021, https://www.aclu.org/press-releases/aclu-comment-biden-statement-settlements-family-separation.

546 "Press Briefing by Principal Deputy Press Secretary Karine Jean-Pierre." The White House, November 4, 2021, https://www.whitehouse.gov/briefing-room/press-briefings/2021/11/04/press-briefing-by-principal-deputy-press-secretary-karine-jean-pierre-3/.

547 Miller, Andrew. "Biden DOJ says families separated at border don't deserve compensation, despite his call for it." Fox News, January 12, 2022, https://www.foxnews.com/politics/biden-doj-says-families-separated-border-dont-deserve-compensation-despite-his-support.

the Biden-Harris 2020 logo on it, which is written out to "Illegal Immigrants" for $450,000. "Do you support giving illegal immigrants $450,000 checks?" the ad asks.

In response, PolitiFact's Tom Kertscher wrote that it's false to suggest that the Biden administration wants to do this because "the claim is inaccurate and several weeks out of date."[548] From there, Kertscher argues that while it was in fact reported that the Biden administration was going to cut $450,000 checks to illegals, that didn't end up happening, so we should apparently just ignore that this sort of insanity was floated in the first place.

BIDEN AND THE HANDGUN BAN

In 2020, PolitiFact's Samantha Putterman wrote an article in response to the NRA's claim that "Joe Biden wants to ban 9mm pistols," rating their claim "False" while herself falsely claiming that Biden was only talking about banning high-capacity magazines.

The NRA's source for Biden's stance was a *Seattle Times* story that reported, "While saying he supports the Second Amendment, Biden called the absolutist arguments of some gun-rights supporters 'bizarre.' Noting people can't own machine guns or bazookas, Biden said, 'Why should we allow people to have military-style weapons including pistols with 9-mm bullets and can hold 10 or more rounds?'"

The comment is certainly up for interpretation, and Putterman just goes off the word of Biden campaign propagandist Andrew Bates, who said that the NRA was lying about Biden's views.

Amusingly, when the House Republicans wrote in a tweet in 2021 that "President Biden says he wanted to ban handguns," PolitiFact's Jon Greenberg rated the claim false, with the justification that it's not all handguns Biden wants to ban, but *only* 9mm pistols that he wants to ban.

The House Republicans Twitter shared a video of Biden giving the following response to a question on gun control during a 2021 town hall: "*The idea you need a weapon that can have the ability to fire 20, 30, 40, 50, 120 shots from that weapon, whether it's a 9-millimeter pistol or*

548 Kertscher, Tom. "GOP Ariz. Senate hopeful Lamon falsely claims that Biden wants to give 'illegal immigrants' $450,000." PolitiFact, January 26, 2022, https://www.politifact.com/factchecks/2022/jan/26/jim-lamon/gop-ariz-senate-hopeful-lamon-falsely-claims-biden/.

whether it's a rifle, is ridiculous. I'm continuing to push to eliminate the sale of those things."

Greenberg concludes his article:

> House Republicans said Biden wants to ban handguns. That is incorrect.
>
> Biden was talking about banning assault weapons and magazines that carry 20 to 120 rounds of ammunition. Those policies would not affect the most popular handgun models. Even if some smaller set of pistols came under such a ban, that would not translate to a ban on handguns across the board.[549]

In reality, banning the sale of 9mm firearms would amount to criminalizing 57 percent of all handgun sales in America.[550]

Further contradicting Putterman, in May 2022 in response to the elementary school massacre in Uvalde, Texas, Biden made another comment on 9mm bullets that seemed to hint at supporting a ban on 9mm pistols as a whole. "A 22-caliber bullet will lodge in the lung, and we can probably get it out, may be able to…save the life. A 9mm bullet blows the lung out of the body,'" Biden said. "So the idea that these high-caliber weapons is of—there's simply no rational basis for it in terms of self-protection, hunting…and remember, the Constitution, the Second Amendment was never absolute."[551]

"NO BIGGIE" TO LEAVE TALIBAN BILLIONS OF DOLLARS' WORTH OF WEAPONS, DECIDES FACT-CHECKER

One theme of fact-checking seeks to protect Democrats by fact-checking an extreme version of a claim against them so the truth doesn't seem as bad in comparison.

---

549 Greenberg, Jon. "No, Joe Biden doesn't want to ban handguns." PolitiFact, July 22, 2021, https://www.politifact.com/factchecks/2021/jul/22/national-house-republicans/no-joe-biden-doesnt-want-ban-handguns/.

550 Moldae, Jade. "Charting 9mm's Dominance in 2010s." Shooting Industry, https://shootingindustry.com/industry-news/charting-9mms-dominance-in-2010s/.

551 Rahman, Khaleda. "Joe Biden Says 9mm Bullet 'Blows the Lung Out of the Body.'" *Newsweek,* May 31, 2022, https://www.newsweek.com/joe-biden-says-9mm-bullet-blows-lung-out-body-1711551.

For example, if crime were to have skyrocketed 50 percent under a Democrat's watch, a fact-checker could find someone exaggerating the truth and claiming a 200 percent increase, in which case the reality being revealed as a 50 percent increase then seems small by comparison, and also generates a "False" rating.

Such a technique was deployed to defend Biden's absolutely insane decision to leave behind billions of dollars' worth of weapons in Afghanistan that the Taliban then took.

The *Washington Post*'s Glenn Kessler decided to tackle Donald Trump's claim that the Taliban seized $83 billion in U.S. weapons following the Biden administration's botched withdrawal from Afghanistan.

Kessler headlined his article, "No, the Taliban did not seize $83 billion of U.S. weapons," though the truth wasn't much better.

Kessler explains that the $83 billion figure was an estimate of all spending on the Afghan Security Forces Fund since the U.S. invasion in 2001, and that only 29 percent of the funds were spent on equipment, so the true total is probably $24 billion or less.[552]

Perhaps $24 billion looks small relative to $83 billion, but that's the only context in which it's small. For reference, $24 billion is larger than the annual military budgets of all but twelve countries, and the Taliban's annual income is estimated at between $300 million and $1.5 billion a year.[553]

PolitiFact gave a similar analysis, with Tom Kertscher arguing that the amount of weapons Biden left to a terrorist organization may be as low as "less than $10 billion," citing only one person.[554] It's as if he asked for an estimate, got one that he realized would be the lowest he'd be able to quote, and then stopped working there.

---

552 Kessler, Glenn. "No, the Taliban did not seize $85 billion of U.S. weapons." *Washington Post,* August 31, 2021, https://www.washingtonpost.com/politics/2021/08/31/no-taliban-did-not-seize-83-billion-us-weapons/.

553 Mehra, Tanya, et al. "Weapons in Afghanistan: The Taliban's Spoils of War." International Centre for Counter-Terrorism, February 2022, https://icct.nl/app/uploads/2022/02/The-Spoils-of-War-final.pdf.

554 Kertscher, Tom. "No proof Biden left Taliban $80B in weapons, or that he wants Americans' pistols." PolitiFact, August 20, 2021, https://www.politifact.com/factchecks/2021/aug/20/viral-image/no-proof-biden-left-taliban-80b-weapons-or-he-want/.

COVID-19-ERA FACT-CHECKING

After getting its first leg up in the aftermath of the 2016 presidential election, the 2020 COVID-19 pandemic represented the second major boost of power for the fact-checkers as they became widely adopted by Facebook, Twitter, and others to try to censor and discredit anything that went counter to the dominant narrative on lockdowns, the efficacy of masks, the harms of school closures, and later information pertaining to the COVID-19 vaccine.

Science itself is built entirely on debating conflicting evidence, yet here the fact-checker gives one side of the debate a monopoly on the truth without even being scientists themselves.

In 2022, it was revealed that the CDC coordinated with Big Tech to censor anything that went counter-narrative on COVID-19, which would be justified by fact-checking offending posts.

Internal communications obtained by America First Legal found that for at least six months starting in December 2020, the CDC communicated with Twitter, Facebook, and Google to censor what they called "vaccine misinformation." Sometimes the CDC would flag specific posts themselves that they wanted removed. [555]

One email from a Twitter employee to a CDC staffer says that they were "looking forward to setting up regular chats" between the two. Another email revealed that a CDC official appeared at a "Trusted Media Summit" held by Google in 2020 that was billed as being "for journalists, fact-checkers, educators, researchers and others who work in the area of fact-checking, verification, media literacy, and otherwise fighting misinformation." In the same email chain, a Google employee offered to

---

555   Simonson, Joseph. "How the CDC Coordinated With Big Tech to Censor Americans." Washington Free Beacon, July 27, 2022, https://freebeacon.com/biden-administration/how-the-cdc-coordinated-with-big-tech-to-censor-americans/.

introduce that CDC staffer to someone at Google "working on programs to counter immunization misinfo."[556]

And much of the time, as is the case with everything else, they were wrong.

Former *New York Times* reporter Alex Berenson emerged as the most prominent contrarian during the COVID-19 pandemic, broadcasting from his Twitter account information that contradicted the prevailing narrative on the risk of the virus, mask mandates, the impacts of lockdowns and school closures, the efficacy of the vaccines, and more.

A thorn in the side of the establishment, Berenson was eventually permanently suspended from Twitter for "repeat violations of [their] COVID-19 misinformation rules."

The tweet that triggered the ban was one arguing that the COVID-19 vaccine would be better categorized as a "therapeutic" instead of a vaccine because unlike every other vaccine out there, the COVID-19 vaccine doesn't stop infection or transmission. "It doesn't stop infection. Or transmission. Don't think of it as a vaccine. Think of it—at best—as a therapeutic with a limited window of efficacy and terrible side effect profile that must be dosed IN ADVANCE OF ILLNESS. And we want to mandate it? Insanity," Berenson tweeted.

Berenson wasn't even saying that the vaccine is ineffective in that particular tweet—he was saying that it doesn't meet the definition of a vaccine. Mind you, this was in August 2021 when even CNN was reporting that the fully vaccinated can catch COVID-19 and transmit the virus.[557]

Berenson sued over the ban, leading to his account being unsuspended in July 2022. A Twitter spokesman said after the settlement that "the parties have come to a mutually acceptable resolution. Twitter has reinstated Mr. Berenson. Upon further review, Twitter acknowledges Mr. Berenson's Tweets should not have led to his suspension at that time."[558]

As an added victory, the lawsuit revealed internal Twitter communications that exposed the extent of the White House's coordination with the platform to censor their opposition.

---

556   Ibid.

557   Holcombe, Madeline, and Christina Maxouris. "Fully vaccinated people who get a Covid-19 breakthrough infection can transmit the virus, CDC chief says." CNN, August 6, 2021, https://www.cnn.com/2021/08/05/health/us-coronavirus-thursday/index.html.

558   Wulfsohn, Joseph A. "Twitter reinstates Alex Berenson after 'permanently' suspending his account in 2021 over COVID tweets." Fox News, July 6, 2022, https://www.foxnews.com/media/twitter-reinstates-alex-berenson-account-covid-tweets.

A Twitter employee recalled in the company's internal Slack chat a White House meeting four months before Berenson was banned where they faced "one really tough question about why Alex Berenson hasn't been kicked off the platform" from the administration. Another employee in the chat recalled how during that meeting Biden's COVID Response Team senior adviser Andrew Slavitt complained specifically about Berenson, who he called an "epicenter of disinfo."[559]

The leaked chat showed that the employees discussing this meeting disagreed with the administration, with one of them saying that he took a deep dive into Berenson's account and couldn't find anything to justify kicking him off the platform.

Berenson was first suspended months later on the same day that Biden accused social media companies of "killing" people for "encouraging vaccine hesitancy" by not censoring enough alleged misinformation, and then permanently in August 2021.

Four days before Berenson was banned, former FDA commissioner and current Pfizer board member Dr. Scott Gottlieb sent an email complaining about Berenson's reporting to a contact of his at Twitter. "This is what's promoted on Twitter. This is why Tony [Dr. Fauci] needs a security detail," he wrote, linking to reporting from Berenson. He kept monitoring Berenson after the ban and continued emailing his contact at Twitter when Berenson would post through different accounts.[560]

That the hyper-focus on "COVID-19 disinformation" wasn't out of actual concern about disinformation can be seen in how these concerns were only ever applied to information that threatened the power of the state, and rarely anything in the category of "COVID-19 hysteria."

Governments used COVID-19 to justify an unprecedented level of control over the lives of its citizens, and as they did that, the fact-checkers were there to rewrite reality in their favor.

---

559 Berenson, Alex. "The White House privately demanded Twitter ban me months before the company did so." Unreported Truths, August 12, 2022, https://alexberenson.substack.com/p/the-white-house-privately-demanded.

560 Berenson, Alex. "Pfizer board member Scott Gottlieb secretly pressed Twitter to censor me days before Twitter suspended my account last year." Unreported Truths, October 13, 2022, https://alexberenson.substack.com/p/pfizer-board-member-scott-gottlieb.

THE GREAT MASK DEBATE

It didn't take long after the onset of the COVID-19 pandemic for it to become conventional wisdom that masks would slow the spread of the virus. As is always the case, this quickly became "settled science," and going counter-narrative on masks got one branded as a "science denier" and such questioning was banned from major social media platforms such as Facebook[561] and Twitter.[562]

One of the many cliches of the COVID-19 era was that we should "follow the science"—yet that's impossible when one party in the scientific debate is silenced.

In April 2022, a European study concluded masks were not effective in preventing the transmission of COVID-19 when it was most needed, and even showed a positive correlation between mask usage and COVID-19 deaths. The study began getting picked up in American media after National Pulse reporter Natalie Winters covered its findings.

The peer-reviewed study, "Correlation Between Mask Compliance and COVID-19 Outcomes in Europe," was published in the *Cureus Journal of Medical Science* by Beny Spira, an associate professor at the University of São Paulo.

Winters explained in her summary of the study:

> "Countries with high levels of mask compliance did not perform better than those with low mask usage," found a new study, whose data and analysis instead discovered a "moderate positive correlation between mask usage and deaths."

> "Data from 35 European countries on morbidity, mortality, and mask usage during a six-month period were analyzed and crossed," continued the study, which encompassed a total of 602 million people.

> "The findings presented in this short communication suggest that countries with high levels of mask compliance did not

---

561   Crist, Carolyn. "Facebook Removes Anti-Maskers for Misinformation." WebMD, July 22, 2020, https://www.webmd.com/lung/news/20200721/facebook-removes-anti-maskers-for-misinformation.

562   "COVID-19 Misleading Information Policy." Twitter, https://web.archive.org/web/20220103012302/https://help.twitter.com/en/rules-and-policies/medical-misinformation-policy.

perform better than those with low mask usage in the six-month period that encompassed the second European wave of COVID-19," Spira summarized.

"The lack of negative correlations between mask usage and COVID-19 cases and deaths suggest that the widespread use of masks at a time when an effective intervention was most needed, i.e., during the strong 2020-2021 autumn-winter peak, was not able to reduce COVID-19 transmission [emphasis mine]."[563]

In responding to Winters' article on this explosive study, PolitiFact's Gabrielle Settles decided to narrowly fact-check the claim that "there's a 'positive correlation' between higher mask usage and COVID-19 deaths," which she rated false. Settles frames the fact-check as follows: "the study stopped short of saying the masks caused deaths, as the post suggests."[564]

But it wasn't Winters suggesting this, it was the study itself.

Settles then turned to criticizing the study's main conclusion that masks were effectively useless by quoting one epidemiologist who said that the study's logic was flawed because "masking protocols were put into place because of the high risk of the virus at the time," but no numbers were given as to how this may change the study's results. And this logic itself is flawed. It could be the case that higher masking was associated with more COVID-19 cases because more masking followed a spike in COVID-19 cases—but this doesn't explain why there were fewer deaths in the places that didn't mask up as much during their spikes.

Settles then pointed to a pro-mask mandate CDC study from 2020 to argue that masks do work in the United States (as if they'd conclude anything else). No reason is given for why we're supposed to trust this study over the latest data, which is of an entire continent instead of a single country.

Settles lastly justifies her "False" ruling mainly on the basis that "public health officials recommend masking as one way to help reduce transmission." The logic here is circular: public health officials recommend

---

563 Winters, Natalie. "Study Finds 'Positive Correlation' Between Higher Mask Usage and COVID-19 Deaths." The National Pulse, May 16, 2022, https://thenationalpulse.com /2022/05/16/study-finds-correlation-between-mask-compliance-and-covid-deaths/.

564 Settles, Gabrielle. "No evidence that masks caused COVID-19 deaths." PolitiFact, May 27, 2022, https://www.politifact.com/factchecks/2022/ may/27/facebook-posts/no-evidence-masks-caused-covid-19-deaths/.

masking, so any studies saying masking is pointless are false because public health officials recommend masking. The prevailing narrative always takes priority over the evidence challenging it.

PolitiFact has a curious relationship with correlation and causation. When Joe Biden said that mass shootings went down after the assault weapons ban, and then went up after it expired (plenty of studies dispute whether or not this is a causal relationship), PolitiFact rated the claim "Mostly True" because they argued the correlation was there (even though it wasn't) and didn't have any concerns about causation then.[565]

FACT-CHECKERS DECIDE COVID IS UNDER CONTROL THE EXACT MOMENT BIDEN SAYS IT IS

After Joe Biden declared the COVID-19 pandemic over in a *60 Minutes* interview, his handlers scrambled to explain that his comments didn't mean what everyone would understand them to mean.[566]

Speaking to *60 Minutes* on September 18, 2022, Biden told host Scott Pelley, "The pandemic is over. We still have a problem with COVID. We're still doing a lot of work on it...but the pandemic is over. If you notice, no one's wearing masks. Everybody seems to be in pretty good shape. And so I think it's changing."[567]

No one else in the administration got the memo that Biden was going to declare the pandemic over in that interview, which was unexpectedly prompted by Pelley's question.

For most of America, the pandemic had been over long before Biden declared it as such, but his comments did catch his administration, one that has been thrilled with the powers the pandemic afforded them, off guard.

Department of Health and Human Services spokeswoman Sarah Lovenheim took to Twitter after Biden's comments to clarify that "The

565 Greenberg, Jon. "Joe Biden said mass shootings tripled when the assault weapon ban ended. They did." PolitiFact, May 25, 2022, https://www.politifact.com/factchecks/2022/may/25/joe-biden/joe-biden-said-mass-shootings-tripled-when-assault/.

566 Cercone, Jeff, and Louis Jacobson. "Is COVID-19 'under control' in the U.S.? Experts say yes." PolitiFact, September 22, 2022, https://www.politifact.com/truth-o-meter/promises/biden-promise-tracker/promise/1517/get-covid-19-under-control.

567 *60 Minutes*, CBS, aired September 18, 2022.

COVID Public Health Emergency remains in effect & HHS will provide a 60-day notice to states before any possible termination or expiration."[568]

When White House press secretary Karine Jean-Pierre was asked about Biden's statement during an appearance on MSNBC's *Morning Joe*, she avoided directly answering the question of whether or not it was the administration's position that the pandemic was over, and pivoted to defending the administration's handling of the pandemic as a whole instead.[569]

And then there was the obvious question of when exactly it was decided that the pandemic ended if Biden was just telling us now. Had he thought this for months and just kept it a secret? As was the case with everything during the pandemic, it was a game of Calvinball, with the rules made up as they went along.

Making matters even more bizarre, the declaration came just weeks after Biden invoked COVID emergency powers to forgive some student loan debt. Even after Biden's comments, no one acted as if they carried any weight. That same week, Nancy Pelosi extended proxy voting in the house, citing the pandemic,[570] and Senate Republicans announced that they'd be forcing a vote on ending the COVID-19 national emergency declaration that wasn't lifted after Biden's comments.

Fulfilling their duties as regime-approved fact-checkers, PolitiFact came to Biden's defense, though that required them to reinterpret his comment that the pandemic is "over" as saying that it's "under control"—and then proceeded to quote a bunch of people who agreed that it was indeed under control. Most on the right made the same assessment long before that, and the timing is almost comical. What are the odds that on their own PolitiFact would've come to this same conclusion if a Republican had instead been the one to declare the pandemic over? It's as if Biden's comments were a green light to the media that it was okay to tone down the COVID hysteria a dial.

568 Lovenheim, Sarah. September 19, 2022, https://twitter.com/HHS_Spox/status/1571928648256552960.

569 Antle III, W. James. "Biden navigates COVID-19 contradictions as voters move on." *Washington Examiner*, September 29, 2022, https://www.washingtonexaminer.com/news/white-house/biden-navigates-covid-19-contradictions-as-voters-move-on.

570 Phippen, Thomas. "Pelosi extends proxy voting in the House until November due to coronavirus pandemic which Biden said 'is over.'" Fox News, September 23, 2022, https://www.foxnews.com/politics/pelosi-extends-proxy-voting-house-until-november-coronavirus-pandemic-biden-said-over.

SCIENCE FEEDBACK STRIKES AGAIN

John Stossel isn't the only person to tangle with Science Feedback. One article exposing a trove of evidence that masking children to protect the spread of COVID-19 is ineffective was unjustifiably censored by them.

The main passage that unjustifiably got *City Journal* writer John Tierney in trouble with the fact-checkers is as follows:

> Researchers from the University of Witten/Herdecke in Germany have catalogued other problems. They established an online registry for parents to report on the side effects of mask-wearing. Among the nearly 18,000 parents who chose to respond (not a random sample, obviously), more than half reported that the masks were giving their children headaches and making it difficult for them to concentrate. More than one-third cited other side effects: increased reluctance to go to school, unhappiness, malaise, impaired learning, drowsiness, and fatigue. After considering those reports as well as testimony from other researchers, a court in Weimar, Germany, recently ruled in favor of a parent arguing that her children's basic rights were being violated by the mandates for masks and social distancing at her children's two schools. The court ordered the schools to end the mandates, declaring that they damaged the "mental, physical and spiritual well-being" of students while failing to offer "any discernible benefit for the children themselves or for third parties."[571]

The study passed peer review at the medical journal *Monthly Pediatrics*—but not at Science Feedback, who slapped anyone sharing the article on Facebook with a warning: "Partly False Information. Checked by independent fact-checkers."

Most of Science Feedback's criticisms of the study were already included as disclaimers by Tierney himself. Science Feedback critiques the study for not being a random sample, but Tierney already acknowledged that in presenting the study. They called the study "unsupported"

---

571   Tierney, John. "Much to Forgive." *City Journal*, April 20, 2021, https://www.city-journal.org/masking-children-unnecessary-and-harmful.

because it "cannot demonstrate a causal relationship between mask-wearing and these effects in children."[572]

Science Feedback also stated that "masks are safe for children over the age of two to wear" because the American Academy of Pediatrics says so. The Academy also openly admits they have a gun control agenda, supports biological males competing in girls' sports, and supports gender transitions for children (among other leftist causes).[573]

And as Tierney points out, this German study is consistent with the existing literature:

> The mask problems reported by the German parents had been observed in dozens of previous experiments and observational studies, as another team of German researchers recently noted in a peer-reviewed article in the Journal of Environmental Research and Public Health.
>
> After reviewing 65 scientific papers—original studies, literature reviews, and meta-analyses—the researchers concluded there was statistically significant evidence of what they termed "Mask-Induced Exhaustion Syndrome." This syndrome includes various physiological changes and subjective complaints: decrease in blood oxygen saturation; increase in blood carbon dioxide; increase in heart and respiratory rates; difficulty breathing; dizziness; headache; drowsiness; and decreased ability to concentrate and think. These risks were so well-known, the researchers noted, that many countries have occupational safety regulations limiting usage of masks. Germany, for instance, requires workers to take a half-hour break after wearing a cloth mask for two hours.[574]

When they appealed to Science Feedback with this information, they were unsuccessful.

572 Teoh, Flora. "German study did not find wearing face masks harms children; study wasn't designed to accurately test these effects." Science Feedback, January 6, 2021, https://sciencefeedback.co/claimreview/german-study-did-not-find-wearing-face-masks-harms-children-study-wasnt-designed-to-accurately-test-these-effects/.

573 Wheeler, Liz. "The American Academy of Pediatrics is polluted by leftist ideology." YouTube, March 27, 2022, https://www.youtube.com/watch?v=re1-QjdbohQ&ab_channel=LizWheeler.

574 Tierney, John. "This Article Is 'Partly False.'" City Journal, May 17, 2021, https://www.city-journal.org/facebook-and-its-fact-checkers-spread-misinformation.

Also of note, when Donald Trump was predicting a COVID-19 vaccine was imminent in September 2020, Science Feedback labeled the prediction "inaccurate."[575] The vaccine rollout then began in December 14, making Science Feedback's prediction about a prediction inaccurate. Despite the rollout, the fact-check rating the claim inaccurate was never updated.

POLITIFACT, GEORGE WASHINGTON VACCINE, AND HERD IMMUNITY

On July 30, 2021, PolitiFact's Ciara O'Rourke rated it "Mostly True" that General George Washington "mandated smallpox vaccines for the Continental Army" despite the fact that vaccines didn't yet exist:

> The smallpox vaccine didn't exist when Washington was commander in chief of the Continental Army, but the point remains: he ordered the inoculation of troops against smallpox by the means that was then available, variolation.[576]

This came amid a national debate over vaccine mandates that was ignited by the COVID-19 vaccine, which threatened to put millions out of work, including a sizeable part of the U.S. armed forces.

While O'Rourke is trying to argue here that vaccine mandates have a long history in the U.S. armed forces, variolation means intentionally infecting people with smallpox in an attempt to cause a less severe illness. PolitiFact is treating naturally acquired immunity as a vaccine here—six months after they criticized Trump for saying that contracting COVID-19 is a "very powerful vaccine in itself."[577]

---

575   Carballo-Carbajal, Iria. "COVID-19 vaccines aren't expected to be available for the public in several weeks, contrary to viral claim on social media." Health Feedback, October 4, 2020, https://healthfeedback.org/claimreview/covid-19-vaccines-are-not-expected-to-be-available-for-the-public-before-several-months-contrary-to-viral-claim-on-social-media/.

576   O'Rourke, Ciara. "Yes, George Washington ordered troops to be inoculated against smallpox during the Revolutionary War." PolitiFact, July 30, 2021, https://www.politifact.com/factchecks/2021/jul/30/viral-image/yes-george-washington-ordered-troops-be-inoculated/.

577   White, Bryan. "PolitiFact has it both ways on 'vaccination.'" PolitiFact Bias, August 5, 2021, https://www.politifactbias.com/2021/08/politifact-has-it-both-ways-on.html.

DONALD TRUMP AND THE CASE OF THE "ALMOST IMMUNE"

When Donald Trump said that children are "almost immune from this disease [COVID]," PolitiFact's Amy Sherman rated the claim false, but it all comes down to how you interpret Trump's comment.

In the first sentence of her article, we're told, "Children represent about 7.3% of COVID-19 cases in the U.S and less than 0.1% of deaths, according to the CDC."

If accounting for 0.1 percent of deaths from a virus that has less than a 0.5 percent death rate at the time across the board doesn't count as "almost" being immune, I don't know what does.

Instead, Sherman decides to spend thousands of words explaining that she thinks Trump is wrong because kids can still *catch* the virus, even though she acknowledges that "kids rarely get severe cases."

In summary, her entire fact-check is based on semantics about how to define the word "immune."

POLITIFACT ATTEMPTS TO DEBUNK TRUMP WITH NUMBERS THAT PROVE HIM RIGHT

In July 2020, still in the early days of the COVID-19 pandemic, PolitiFact's Jon Greenberg rated false President Donald Trump's claim that 99 percent of COVID-19 cases are "totally harmless."

"We have tested over 40 million people. By so doing, we show cases, 99% of which are totally harmless. Results that no other country will show, because no other country has testing that we have — not in terms of the numbers or in terms of the quality," Trump said.

The subjectiveness of the phrase "totally harmless" (especially from someone as hyperbolic as Trump) aside, by Greenberg's own admission his fact-check is far too premature to actually be conclusive, leading to the obvious question of why he bothered writing it then.

Greenberg starts by citing a massively inflated COVID-19 death rate of 4.5 percent based on the number of identified cases (at the time the CDC reported 2.8 million cases and 130,000 deaths). Greenberg did at least include the caveat that "researchers don't know the number of people infected — only the confirmed cases. The infection tally would be larger than the number of identified cases."[578]

---

578 Greenberg, Jon. "Donald Trump's false claim that 99% of COVID-19 cases are harmless." PolitiFact, July 6, 2020, https://www.politifact.com/factchecks/2020/jul/06/donald-trump/donald-trumps-false-claim-99-covid-19-cases-are-ha/.

Greenberg also pointed to hospitalizations as another example of harm, quoting numbers from the COVID Tracking Project: "The rate has been falling since early June, when it was 8%. But it still sits at 4%, or four times higher than Trump's 1% figure." These figures are similarly inflated from asymptomatic cases going undetected.

Amazingly, Greenberg then provides some estimates of total infections that prove Trump right without realizing it, writing:

> By one CDC estimate, the total could be 10 to 12 times higher than the number of identified cases. If deaths and hospitalizations remained the same, the threat of death and harm would fall dramatically.

Greenberg then argues that total deaths could also be undercounted, however:

> The problem is, Thea said, we lack reliable numbers to fill in any of those boxes. He expects the estimated number of infections to grow, but so will the estimated number of deaths.

> "We're undercounting those deaths by 20% to 40%, conservatively," [Boston University Professor Donald] Thea said. "There is a year-to-year-stability in death rates. We've seen an enormous amount of excess deaths, and the large majority of the excess mortality is due to the infection itself."

But even if deaths attributable to COVID-19 are 20 percent to 40 percent higher than reported, with the denominator increased tenfold, the percent of those that catch COVID-19 that either die or are hospitalized only exceeds 1 percent in a worst case scenario.

THE DEMOCRATS' GREAT VACCINE FLIP-FLOP

One of the great narrative shifts of all time from the Democrats occurred from late 2020 to early 2021 on the topic of the COVID-19 vaccine(s), which in just months went from being a garbage product that then-president Donald Trump had tried to rush ahead of a presidential election to something the government needed to mandate with the threat of unemployment and social ostracization.

The examples are endless, but to name just a few from Congress in September 2020:[579]

- Representative Ilhan Omar (D-MN): "We can't trust the President and take his word, and take a vaccine that might cause harm to us."

- Senator Sheldon Whitehouse (D-RI) said the FDA and CDC "have gotten screwed up by President Trump" and that "unfortunately, they aren't the gold standard any longer, so you need to take a slightly closer look" at a vaccine.

- Senator Patty Murray (D-WA): "We cannot take for granted this process [of developing a vaccine] will be free of political influence."

- Senator Tina Smith (D-MN) suggested that if a vaccine was announced before election day, it would be because of political pressure.

Thirteen senators signed a letter that month calling on the FDA to commit to full transparency on the COVID-19 vaccine review process "amidst mounting political pressure from the President to approve a vaccine before Election Day." The signatories included Dianne Feinstein (D-CA), Kirsten Gillibrand (D-NY), Richard Blumenthal (D-CT.), Tina Smith (D-MN), Jeffrey A. Merkley (D-OR), Angus S. King, Jr. (I-ME), Jack Reed (D-RI), Christopher S. Murphy (D-CT.), Mazie K. Hirono (D-HI.), Tammy Baldwin (D-WI), Bernard Sanders (D-VT), Michael F. Bennet (D-CO.), and Sherrod Brown (D-OH).[580]

Meanwhile, former Love Gov. Andrew Cuomo said in October 2020, "I believe all across the country you're going to need someone other than this FDA and this CDC saying it's safe," and said that he wasn't confident in the FDA's approval process. He also said that he wasn't going to

---

579 "Democrats Repeatedly Undermined the Vaccine." Republican National Committee, August 4, 2021, https://gop.com/research/democrats-repeatedly-undermined-the-vaccine/.

580 "Warren, Hassan, Colleagues to FDA: Maintain Public Trust in COVID-19 Vaccine Decisions by Making Reviews Transparent." September 15, 2020, https://www.warren.senate.gov/newsroom/press-releases/warren-hassan-colleagues-to-fda-maintain-public-trust-in-covid-19-vaccine-decisions-by-making-reviews-transparent.

trust the federal government's opinion on if the vaccine is safe, and said he wouldn't recommend it to New Yorkers based on their opinion.[581]

Over on the West Coast, Washington governor Jay Inslee said, "I believe we will need to have access to the vaccine results so we can make our independent assessment to make sure that Donald Trump's fingerprints are not on it."[582]

Similar remarks could be found among the liberal pundit class. MSNBC's Joy Reid tweeted to her followers, "I mean, will anyone… anyone at all…ever fully trust the CDC again? And who on God's earth would trust a vaccine approved by the FDA?? How do we get a vaccine distributed after this broken, Trumpist nonsense has infected everything? Even if Biden wins?"[583] By January 2022, she'd be excoriating the SCOTUS for striking down OSHA's COVID-19 vaccine mandate, claiming that the court was more interested in "DeSantis-style right-wing politics than they are in favor of saving lives."[584]

Hysterical liberal commentator Amy Siskind chimed in: "Trump is taking a page from Putin's playbook, and trying to bully the FDA into making a COVID-19 vaccine available before Stage 3 of testing is complete. HE WILL KILL US ALL!" Just one day short of a year later, after accepting the Gospel of Pfizer, she tweeted, "Let it rain vaccine mandates."[585]

MSNBC's Wajahat Ali tweeted in December 2020, "COVID approves the 'Trump Vaccine.' Good luck, MAGA." Nine months later, he'd write of the same vaccine "People would rather die than take a vaccine that works. We live in remarkable times."[586]

A full list of the politicians and pundits who flip-flopped on this without explanation would exceed the length of this book, but the point

581 Geraghty, Jim. "Andrew Cuomo: Americans Can't Trust the FDA and CDC on a Vaccine." National Review, October 19, 2020, https://www.nationalreview.com /corner/andrew-cuomo-americans-cant-trust-the-fda-and-cdc-on-a-vaccine/.

582 Inslee, Jay. September 22, 2020, https://twitter.com/govinslee/status/ 1308596575422132229.

583 Joy-Ann (Pro-Democracy) Reid. September 18, 2020, https://twitter.com/joyannreid/status/ 1306762734076342273.

584 Adams, Biba. "Joy Reid calls out SCOTUS for vaccine mandate ruling." Yahoo! Life, January 14, 2022, https://www.yahoo.com/lifestyle/joy-reid-calls-scotus-vaccine-180511849.html.

585 Defiant L's. September 9, 2021, https://twitter.com/defiantls/status/ 1436132047626686466.

586 Defiant L's. September 16, 2021, https://twitter.com/defiantls/status/ 1438691925666766849.

is that the narrative shift from "Trump vaccine will kill us all" to "110% safe vaccine that you must take unless you want people to die" was uniform and had no obvious catalyst other than a change in administration.

Every single one of these people quoted above did a 180 on their initial position, as did two other notable individuals who wield considerable political power.

In August 2020, Joe Biden said that "if and when the vaccine comes, it's not likely to go through all the tests…and trials that are needed to be done."[587] The next month he questioned the safety of the vaccine, saying, "Who's going to take the shot? Are you going to be the first one to say sign me up?"[588] A week later, he added that the American people shouldn't have any confidence in the vaccine unless it meets his campaign's criteria.[589]

Then–Biden press secretary Symone Sanders wouldn't answer if Biden would take the vaccine if it was approved before Election Day. Kamala Harris also refused to say if she'd take the vaccine before Election Day, because "I think that's going to be an issue for all of us." She also suggested the vaccine might not be effective.

Eventual White House chief of staff Ron Klain bolstered that rhetoric, asking, "When you read how Team Trump played politics with testing it makes you wonder how they will handle vaccines?"[590]

Amazingly, there was no social media censorship to be seen when this rhetoric was being spread by the left—though conservatives who expressed any concerns about the vaccines' effectiveness and whether or not it should be mandated were later punished for their doubts.

And even more amazingly, in the alternate reality of the fact-checkers, none of this happened!

---

587   Yahoo News. "Newsmaker plenary with former Vice President Joe Biden." YouTube, August 6, 2020, https://www.youtube.com/watch?v=iCpyx2T-lDA&ab_channel=YahooNews.

588   "Q-and-A with former vice president Joe Biden." *WKMG News 6 & ClickOrlando,* September 3, 2020, https://www.clickorlando.com/news/local/2020/09/03/q-and-a-with-former-vice-president-joe-biden/.

589   "American's Health Depends on Confidence in the Safety of a Coronavirus." Rev, https://www.rev.com/transcript-editor/shared/LJNe2BdE2dd34l4mYzcBW8ERIFR qwdZmsO5gH0uyniTh9olrL1s4S7DRkFER6Q0wqqgrm1985iw-JdYskQrFFqAw B9Q?loadFrom=PastedDeeplink&ts=504.52.

590   Klain, Ronald. July 31, 2020, https://twitter.com/ronaldklain/status/1289237994625409030.

Did Joe Biden and Kamala Harris distrust the COVID-19 vaccines? No—that's "False" according to PolitiFact's dimmest fact-checker Tom Kertscher.[591] "Video clips appear to show Joe Biden and Kamala Harris raising doubts about COVID-19 vaccines, but they were raising concerns about the rollout by then-President Donald Trump, not the vaccines themselves," Kertscher falsely claims.

Humorously, that premise is refuted by Harris herself, who he quotes in his own article. When asked if she would take the vaccine, Harris said: "Well, I think that's going to be an issue for all of us. I will say that I would not trust Donald Trump. And it would have to be a credible source of information that talks about the efficacy and the reliability of whatever he's talking about. I will not take his word for it. He wants us to inject bleach. I — no, I will not take his word."

There's another part of the same quote he excluded, where Harris is asked if public health experts and scientists will get the last word on the efficacy of a vaccine, answering, "If past is prologue that they will not, they'll be muzzled, they'll be suppressed, they will be sidelined. Because [Trump is] looking at an election coming up in less than 60 days and he's grasping to get whatever he can to pretend he has been a leader on this issue when he is not."

Harris voiced skepticism of taking the vaccine, and Kertscher managed to present that as her having a problem with logistics.

The fact-checkers could also be covering for themselves here because their consensus in early 2020 was that Trump's vaccine timeline of "before the end of the year" was impossible. To quote a sampling of the bogus wisdom from our fact-checker overlords:

- "Fact check: Coronavirus vaccine could come this year, Trump says. Experts say he needs a 'miracle' to be right." – NBC News, May 2020[592]

- "Trump gets a fact check on coronavirus vaccines — from his own officials" – Politico, March 2020[593]

591 Kertscher, Tom. "Biden, Harris distrusted Trump with COVID-19 vaccines, not the vaccines themselves." PolitiFact, July 23, 2021, https://www.politifact.com/fact checks/2021/jul/23/tiktok-posts/biden-harris-doubted-trump-covid-19-vaccines-not-v/

592 Timm, Jane C. "Fact check: Coronavirus vaccine could come this year, Trump says. Experts say he needs a 'miracle' to be right." NBC News, May 15, 2020, https://www.nbcnews.com/politics/donald-trump/fact-check-coronavirus-vaccine-could-come-year-trump-says-experts-n1207411.

593 Allen, Arthur, and Meridith McGraw. "Trump gets a fact check on coronavirus vaccines — from his own officials." Politico, March 5, 2020, https://www.politico.com/news/2020/03/05/coronavirus-trump-vaccine-rhetoric-121796.

- "Fact-checking Trump's accelerated timeline for a coronavirus vaccine" – The *Washington Post*, March 2020

- "Trump promises coronavirus vaccine by end of the year, but his own experts temper expectations" – ABC, May 2020

- "Widespread Covid-19 vaccination is not expected before mid-2021." – Science Feedback

Yet the fact-checkers never addressed those claims—before or after the vaccine was delivered on schedule.

ANOTHER VACCINE FLIP-FLOP

After White House coronavirus response coordinator Dr. Deborah Birx made a number of statements admitting that the "experts" oversold the benefits of the COVID-19 vaccine in that it would prevent infection, PolitiFact's Yacob Reyes wrote a lengthy article rating it "False" that Birx ever flip-flopped on the issue of the vaccine's efficacy herself in an article whose conclusion is contradicted by its own sources.[594]

Birx admitted that the experts overpromised on the COVID-19 vaccine a number of times in mid-2022. During a Fox News appearance on July 22, she told Neil Cavuto that "I knew these vaccines were not going to protect against infection. And I think we overplayed the vaccines, and it made people then worry that it's not going to protect against severe disease and hospitalization. It will."[595]

The next day, Birx testified before Congress. While facing questioning from Representative Jim Jordan, Birx admitted that "we knew early on, in January of 2021, in late December 2020, that reinfection is occurring after natural infection. Once you see that—and I want to make it clear to you all, and to anyone that is listening—this is not measles, mumps, and rubella—those vaccines produce long term immunity, and can create herd immunity."

---

594 Reyes, Yacob. "No, Dr. Deborah Birx didn't change her 'tune' on COVID vaccines." PolitiFact, July 29, 2022, https://www.politifact.com/factchecks/2022/jul/29/facebook-posts/no-deborah-birx-didnt-change-her-tune-covid-vaccin/.

595 Fox News Staff. "Dr. Deborah Birx says she 'knew' COVID vaccines would not 'protect against infection.'" Fox News, July 22, 2022, https://www.foxnews.com/media/dr-deborah-birx-knew-covid-vaccines-not-protect-against-infection.

Jordan asked twice, "When the government told us that the vacci-nated couldn't transmit it, was that a lie, or was that a guess?"—prompting an "I don't know," and "I think it was hope that the vaccines would work in that way." No denial was made of the government's false narrative.[596]

This is in direct contradiction to Birx's past public statements, but not if you accept Reyes' framing, who is forced to construct and burn down a straw man to pretend Birx didn't flip-flop. While Birx publicly flip-flopped on the vaccine stopping the spread of the virus (while privately knowing the truth the whole time), Reyes says he could find "no record of Birx saying the vaccine could provide complete protection against infection." The words "complete protection" are used as weasel words to justify a false rating in a fact-check overlooking Birx promoting the vaccine as effective enough to stop infection by reaching herd immunity.

While accusing people of taking Dr. Birx's comments out of context, Reyes takes a comment from Birx from December 6, 2020, out of con-text, quoting her as saying during an NBC interview, "I want to be very frank to the American people: The vaccine is critical, but it's not going to save us from this current surge."

Reyes presents this as Birx saying that the vaccine "could not curtail an uptick in COVID-19 cases"—but the reason Birx said this is because the vaccine wasn't available at the time and wouldn't begin to rollout in significant volume for months, hence why she said the vaccine wouldn't save us from a "current surge" in that context. Reyes cuts off the rest of Birx's quote, where she said, "We won't have a vaccine for even the most vulnerable Americans. I'm thrilled with the vaccines, but we won't have them for the most vulnerable Americans until February." Her comment was about availability and logistics, not efficacy.[597]

Reyes also pointed to an interview Birx did with Live 5 News on December 27, 2020, writing that "Birx said in a televised interview that much was still unknown about the level of protection the vaccines pro-vide. She distinguished between what was known about the vaccine's

596   "Dr. Birx Says She Knew of Natural COVID-19 Reinfections as Early as December 2020." C-SPAN, June 23, 2022, https://www.c-span.org/video/?c5021092/dr-birx-knew-natural-covid-19-reinfections-early-december-2020.

597   Hammond, Jeremy R. "Fact Check: Yes, Dr. Birx did change her tune on COVID-19 vaccines." Jeremyhammond.com, August 15, 2022, https://www.jeremyrhammond.com/2022/08/15/fact-check-yes-dr-birx-did-change-her-tune-on-covid-19-vaccines/.

ability to prevent infection and what was known about its ability to prevent disease."[598]

This, too, is out of context—and neglects to mention that earlier in the interview Birx said that the vaccines would bring about herd immunity, which, as Jeremy Hammond puts it succinctly, "is literally defined as a situation in which most people exposed to the virus do not become infected and therefore do not spread the virus to others." It was only later in the interview, when questioned, that Birx said the vaccinated "may" still spread the virus, which wasn't an authoritative declaration that they would.

Reyes only acknowledges one quote from Birx contrary to his case, when she stated on December 16, 2020, to ABC News, "This is one of the most highly effective vaccines we have in our infectious disease arsenal," only to then ignore the significance of her pitching the vaccine as among the "most highly effective" because it's his opinion that the vaccine can still be "highly effective" even if it doesn't totally stop the spread of the virus.

The day prior, on December 15, Birx said that if 70–80 percent of the population got vaccinated, then the U.S. would "truly achieve herd immunity"—which can only happen by significantly slowing the spread. Reyes makes no mention of this.

The only in-context quote Reyes could find to make his case is when Birx said, "We have to make it very clear to the American people that your protection against infection wanes"—but this was in May 2022, just two months before she made headlines for flip-flopping and after it became impossible to deny that breakthrough infections were commonly occurring.

It's also worth noting here that while what's being examined is whether or not Birx herself overplayed the vaccine—her comments prove that the White House and so-called experts did. That's the reason her admission got such a reaction.

After all, Joe Biden told a CNN town hall in July 2021 (one year before catching COVID-19 himself) that "you're not going to get COVID if you have these vaccinations,"[599] and CDC chief Rochelle Walensky promised in March 2021 that "vaccinated people do not carry

---

598   Ibid.
599   CNN Presidential Town Hall With Joe Biden, July 21, 2021.

the virus."[600] Meanwhile, Dr. Fauci told CBS in May 2021 that "when you get vaccinated, you not only protect your own health and that of the family but also you contribute to the community health by preventing the spread of the virus throughout the community."[601] Pfizer CEO Albert Bourla tweeted that a Phase 3 trial with their vaccine from South Africa found it "100% effective in preventing COVID19 cases in South Africa. 100%!"[602]

And according to Dr. Birx, they all knew better. How could they not have?

COMPARING COVID-19 DEATHS: TRUMP VS. BIDEN

Joe Biden's campaign promise to "shut down" COVID-19 as president became his "read my lips, no new taxes" moment (or at least would've if the media held him accountable for anything).

When Trump was running the show, Biden called on him to resign over his handling of the pandemic. During one of the presidential debates, Biden said, "220,000 Americans dead. If you hear nothing else I say tonight, hear this…Anyone who's responsible for that many deaths should not remain as president of the United States."

Yet Biden himself presided over 220,000 COVID-19 deaths during within just the first eight months of his presidency.[603] As Biden closed out 2021, total COVID-19 deaths topped eight hundred thousand, officially marking more on his watch than on Trump's, and that's with a vaccine and better COVID-19 treatments available than existed the year prior.

With over one thousand COVID-19 deaths per day at the time, and a clear trajectory, some right-wing pundits in the early weeks of December began to prematurely (by only a few weeks) declare that there had been "more COVID deaths under Biden than Trump."

600   Haroun, Azmi, and Hillary Brueck. "CDC director says data 'suggests that vaccinated people do not carry the virus.'" Business Insider, March 30, 2021, https://www.businessinsider.com/cdc-director-data-vaccinated-people-do-not-carry-covid-19-2021-3.

601   "Transcript: Dr. Anthony Fauci on 'Face the Nation,' May 16, 2021." CBS News, May 16, 2021, https://www.cbsnews.com/news/transcript-dr-anthony-fauci-face-the-nation-05-16-2021/.

602   Bourla, Albert. April 1, 2021, https://twitter.com/AlbertBourla/status/1377618480527257606.

603   On August 29, 2021, as per the CDC's data. https://covid.cdc.gov/covid-data-tracker/#trends_totaldeaths_select_00.

And, similar to the fact-check of Gingrich's claim about food stamp usage under Obama, the fact-checkers appear to have fact-checked a claim about to become true to then later ignore when it does become true.

Newsweek's Yevgeny Kuklychev[604] rated the claim that there were more COVID-19 deaths under Biden false just ten to twenty-three days (depending on the data source) before it become true.[605]

He begins the fact-check, which was published on December 21, 2021, with the following figures:

> According to the latest data from the Centers for Disease Control and Prevention (CDC), dated December 19, 2021, 803,593 people have died due to COVID since the beginning of the pandemic.

> OurWorldInData's figure for December 19 is slightly higher, putting the total at 806,439 deaths. Of those, 351,754 deaths occurred in 2020, meaning that indeed there are more deaths—nearly 455,000—in 2021.

> However, as he acknowledges, we need to define an end point for the Trump presidency and start point for when Biden takes responsibility, which would be January 20, 2021:

> On that day the cumulative U.S. COVID death count stood at 424,401, according to CDC data, meaning that fewer people have died under Biden—379,192 in total (up to December 19).

> Finally, according to OurWorldInData, which relies on Johns Hopkins University figures, cumulative deaths stood at 412,892 as of January 20, still significantly more than the 393,547 recorded under Biden through to December 19.

And yet using those metrics, it would become the case that COVID-19 deaths under Biden exceeded Trump's just days after this so-called

---

604   Sorry to whoever has to pronounce this for the audiobook.

605   Kuklychev, Yevgeny. "Fact Check: Have More Americans Died From COVID Under Joe Biden Than Donald Trump?" *Newsweek*, December 21, 2021, https://www.newsweek.com/fact-check-have-more-americans-died-covid-under-joe-biden-donald-trump-1661528.

fact-check—which was easy to predict because the virus was killing a thousand-plus people a day at this time.

Based on the CDC's data, Trump left office on January 20, 2021, with 424,388 COVID-19 deaths under his watch. By January 14, 2022, there were 851,697, more than double Trump's tally.[606] Going off OurWorldInData, Trump left office on January 20, 2021, with 412,434 COVID-19 deaths under his watch. By December 31, 2021, there were 825,929, more than double the Trump tally.[607] Note that the data both organizations collect is constantly updated, hence, why my starting figures are slightly different.

The *Washington Post* was more creative in misleading the public with their fact-check. They decided to start the clock for Trump on March 11, 2020, even though the first reported COVID-19 death in the U.S. occurred nearly two months prior. Since they were only counting ten months of the Trump presidency, they used that to justify only counting the first ten months under Biden presidency to count fewer deaths on his watch.[608]

FACT-CHECKER SAYS TRUMP RIGHT ABOUT FAUCI'S FLIP-FLOPS BUT ALSO SOMEHOW WRONG

On such case where a statement was analyzed as "true but not true" came during a presidential debate with Joe Biden when Trump said that Fauci changed his mind about wearing masks. "Dr. [Anthony] Fauci said the opposite, he very strongly said masks aren't good and then he changed his mind, he said masks are good," Trump said in the September 2020 debate.

Trump was referencing what Fauci said back in on March 8, 2020: "There's no reason to be walking around with a mask. When you are in the middle of an outbreak, wearing a mask might make people feel a

---

606 "Trends in Number of COVID-19 Cases and Deaths in the US Reported to CDC, by State/Territory." COVID Data Tracker, Centers for Disease Control and Prevention, https://web.archive.org/web/20220822081305/https://covid.cdc.gov/covid-data-tracker/.

607 "Cumulative confirmed COVID-19 deaths." Our World in Data, https://ourworldindata.org/explorers/coronavirus-data-explorer?zoomToSelection= true&time=2020-03-01..latest&facet=none&pickerSort=asc&pickerMetric= location&Metric=Confirmed+deaths&Interval=Cumulative&Relative+to+ Population=false&Color+by+test+positivity=false&country=~USA.

608 Blake, Aaron. "How Biden and Trump actually compare on coronavirus deaths." *Washington Post*, November 30, 2021, https://www.washingtonpost.com/politics/ 2021/11/30/biden-trump-compare-covid-deaths/.

little bit better and it might even block a droplet, but it is not providing the perfect protection that people think that it is. And, often, there are unintended consequences--people keep fiddling with the mask and they keep touching their face."[609]

While this wasn't known at the time, Fauci was singing the same tune in private too. A month prior, Sylvia Burwell, who was HHS secretary for three years under Obama, wrote to Fauci seeking advice on wearing masks while traveling. On February 5, 2020, Fauci wrote back, "Masks are really for infected people to prevent them from spreading infection to people who are not infected rather than protecting uninfected people from acquiring infection. The typical mask you buy in the drug store is not really effective in keeping out virus, which is small enough to pass through material. It might, however, provide some slight benefit in keep out gross droplets if someone coughs or sneezes on you."[610]

Nevertheless, the CNN fact-checker decided that this doesn't count as a real flip-flop. "Fauci, the Director of the National Institute of Allergy and Infectious Diseases, did change his mind about masks," the CNN fact-checker tells us, "but the need to wear one is not an ongoing debate, as Trump implied."[611]

They then go on to quote Fauci as saying in the spring he was unaware that so many people carrying the virus were asymptomatic early on as justification for his flip-flop. Fauci's reason for changing his tune on masks, and the current array of (contradictory) evidence on their efficacy, is irrelevant to the truth of if Fauci flip-flopped on masks.

Which he did.

Speaking of lies, the CNN fact-checker never mentioned the other reason Fauci himself gave for changing his tune on masks in June 2020—that he knew there were already shortages of masks and didn't want to encourage the public to purchase more, as there wouldn't be enough for health-care workers.

---

609   Farmer, Brit McCandless. "March 2020: Dr. Anthony Fauci talks with Dr John LaPook about COVID-19." CBS News, March 8, 2020, https://www.cbsnews.com/news/preventing-coronavirus-facemask-60-minutes-2020-03-08/.

610   Roche, Darragh. "Fauci Said Masks 'Not Really Effective in Keeping Out Virus,' Email Reveals." *Newsweek*, June 2, 2021, https://www.newsweek.com/fauci-said-masks-not-really-effective-keeping-out-virus-email-reveals-1596703.

611   "Did Fauci Change His Mind on the Effectiveness of Masks?" CNN, https://edition.cnn.com/factsfirst/politics/factcheck_c791ae08-1e5b-4458-a3a8-6c8449e1bc9f.

So either Fauci doesn't believe that masks work and is advocating for them now while knowing that, or he believes that masks do work and lied to the American people to dissuade them from buying something he thought would protect them from COVID-19.[612] Neither scenario paints a good picture of his moral character.

It is true that in science, unlike politics, people are forced to change their tune because the evidence changed, and they're not flip-flopping like a politician in response to a poll. But time and time again, "changing science" has been used to justify what are flip-flops. There's never any explanation of how exactly "the science" changed—just that it did.

TESTING OR NO TESTING?

Pfizer's president of international markets Janine Small admitted to European Parliament in October 2022 that they had not tested the COVID-19 vaccine's impact on transmission of the virus before it entered the market in December 2020.

As mostly right-leaning websites picked up the bombshell, the Associated Press fact-checker described the framing as "misleading" because "Pfizer never claimed to have studied the issue before the vaccine's market release."[613]

That there was testing done on the vaccine to confirm that it would stop transmission of COVID-19 was more than just implied when Pfizer sold the product as having the exact benefit. Only a fact-checker could think that "they lied and oversold the benefits of their product" is a rebuttal to someone saying Pfizer never tested if their vaccine stopped transmission of COVID-19.

612   Jankowicz, Mia. "Fauci said US government held off promoting masks because it knew shortages were so bad that even doctors couldn't get enough." Insider, June 15, 2020, https://www.businessinsider.com/fauci-mask-advice-was-because-doctors-shortages-from-the-start-2020-6.

613   Goldin, Melissa, and Angelo Fichera. "Posts mislead on Pfizer COVID vaccine's impact on transmission." Associated Press, October 13, 2022, https://apnews.com/article/fact-check-pfizer-transmission-european-parliament-950413863226.

DID DENMARK BAN THE COVID-19 VACCINE FOR CHILDREN?

Is it true that Denmark banned the COVID-19 vaccine for children? Fact-checkers say no, but Denmark says almost.

The Associated Press (AP) fact-checker looked into claims that Denmark had banned the vaccine for children, and questionably concluded that the nation was merely not recommending the vaccine for the under-eighteen age group, not banning it.

The AP claims that "The Danish Health Authority will no longer recommend the COVID-19 vaccine for those under the age of 18, but it hasn't placed an overall ban on the shots for that age group. Children and youths who are at risk of developing a severe case of COVID-19 can still receive the vaccine in Denmark if recommended by a doctor."

The exception for those at risk of developing a severe case is the AP's entire basis for rating it "false" that Denmark banned COVID-19 vaccines for children. Likely because it implodes their entire argument, the AP doesn't ever admit that the vaccine is effectively banned for everyone else under the age of eighteen.

The AP misleadingly describes Denmark's new policy as: "Starting Sept. 1, youths will no longer get the second dose although those who are at risk of developing serious illness can still get the vaccine after a medical assessment."

The wording "will no longer get" is in stark contrast to the language from the Danish Health Authority's directly, which was: "From 1 July 2022, *it was no longer possible* for children and adolescents aged under 18 to get the first injection and, from 1 September 2022, *it was no longer* possible for them to get the second injection [emphasis mine]."[614]

The AP's phrasing throughout their entire supposed fact-check leaves enough ambiguity that one could get the impression that Denmark simply discouraged the COVID-19 vaccine for those under age eighteen—as opposed to a virtual ban on it with exceptions.

---

614   "Vaccination against covid-19." Danish Health Authority, https://www.sst.dk/en/english/corona-eng/vaccination-against-covid-19.

Vaccination of children against covid-19

Children and adolescents rarely become severely ill from the Omicron variant of covid-19.

From 1 July 2022, it was no longer possible for children and adolescents aged under 18 to get the first injection and, from 1 September 2022, it was no longer possible for them to get the second injection.

A very limited number of children at particularly higher risk of becoming severely ill will still be offered vaccination based on an individual assessment by a doctor.

The effective ban comes even as the Danish Health Authority predicted that "many people will be infected with covid-19 during autumn and winter." While they never explicitly state that children are so low risk that the risks of the vaccine outweigh the potential benefits, that is the most obvious implication of their policy change. The Danish Health Authority does maintain a pro-vaccine stance for those age fifty and over, citing their elevated risk from the virus.

Why are people aged under 50 not to be re-vaccinated? —

The purpose of the vaccination programme is to prevent severe illness, hospitalisation and death. Therefore, people at the highest risk of becoming severely ill will be offered booster vaccination. The purpose of vaccination is not to prevent infection with covid-19, and people aged under 50 are therefore currently not being offered booster vaccination.

People aged under 50 are generally not at particularly higher risk of becoming severely ill from covid-19. In addition, younger people aged under 50 are well protected against becoming severely ill from covid-19, as a very large number of them have already been vaccinated and have previously been infected with covid-19, and there is consequently good immunity among this part of the population.

It is important that the population also remembers the guidance on how to prevent the spread of infection, including staying at home in case of illness, frequent aeration or ventilation, social distancing, good coughing etiquette, hand hygiene and cleaning.

Further demonstrating their incompetence as fact-checkers, the AP claims that "The Danish Health Authority still recommends that people who are completely unvaccinated still receive primary vaccination." Yet once you click through to their source, you find that the Danish Health Authority never actually says this; they said that vulnerable people "with severely impaired immune systems" have been able to receive a booster if their doctor deemed that they would benefit.[615] The word "unvaccinated" doesn't even appear once on that Danish Health Authority webpage the AP linked to.

Reuters' fact-checker chimed in too with a similar fact-check to the AP's, also arguing that this wasn't really a *ban* on the vaccine for children because there are exceptions.[616] While that's technically true, I suspect this sort of logic would never be applied to other issues. If, for example, a Republican were to say that a ban on all abortions isn't really an abortion ban because of exceptions for rape or incest, the probability a fact-checker like the AP or Reuters would agree is roughly zero.

---

615 "Booster vaccination before start-up of autumn vaccination programme." Danish Health Authority, https://web.archive.org/web/20220920092041/https://www.sst.dk/en/English/Corona-eng/Vaccination-against-covid-19/Vaccination-fall-and-winter-2022-2023.

616 Reuters Fact Check. "Fact Check-Headline that claims Denmark has banned COVID-19 vaccines for children is misleading." Reuters, August 16, 2022, https://www.reuters.com/article/factcheck-coronavirus-denmark/fact-check-headline-that-claims-denmark-has-banned-covid-19-vaccines-for-children-is-misleading-idUSL1N2ZS0J8.

ADVENTURES IN MENTAL GYMNASTICS

If the fact-checkers can be credited for anything, it's their creativity. Much like a child who wants to change the rules of a game after losing, the fact-checkers will go to epic lengths to avoid admitting they're wrong that would be humiliating for any honest individual.

The often-humorous writer Jim Treacher likens the strategy of the fact-checkers to a comment from Dan Rather's friends in the *New York Times* during the 2004 Killian documents controversy, in which the journalist presented inauthentic documents later proven to be forgeries about George W. Bush's service in the Texas Air National Guard months before the election.

Rather was fired over the bogus reporting but not before his friends at the *Times* backed him up with a truly incredible headline: "Memos on Bush Are Fake but Accurate, Typist Says."

As Treacher puts it, "That's the standard when the target is Republican. Just because something isn't true, that doesn't mean it can't be useful."[617]

That was nearly two decades ago, and all that's changed is that now the people who are supposed to be acting as watchdogs are presenting the same kind of illogic in the liberal media's defense.

As you'll realize by the end of this chapter; if the fact-checkers competed at the Olympics, they'd handily take the gold for mental gymnastics.

IT'S NOT HAPPENING, BUT IT'S GOOD THAT IT IS

That Democrats' affinity for illegal aliens has to do more with the fact that a large majority would vote Democrat if they were granted amnesty is so blatantly obvious only a fact-checker could deny it.

---

617   Treacher, Jim. "'Fake but Accurate' Has a New Friend, Courtesy of WaPo: 'Nonsense Fact.'" The Daily Caller, March 13, 2015, https://dailycaller.com/2015/03/13/fake-but-accurate-has-a-new-friend-courtesy-of-wapo-nonsense-fact/.

Former Senate candidate Blake Masters pointed out the obvious in a tweet where he stated that "Democrats want open borders so they can bring in and amnesty tens of millions of illegal aliens — that's their electoral strategy."

It took two PolitiFact "fact-checkers" to tackle this statement, which they rated false, Jon Greenberg and Amy Sherman. They break out their fact-check into three headings:

– They argue that the border isn't *literally* open, as if anyone using the term "open borders" means that. At the minimum it is a synonym for "weak border enforcement."

– They argue it would take years to turn illegals into voters, though it's unclear why they think this is worth including. The truth that Democrats want to turn illegals into voters isn't contingent on how long it will take, and this argument reads as a reluctant admission.

– They argue that there's no guarantee that illegals will vote for Democrats. They point to political diversity within the Hispanic community—but Hispanics who came to America legally have drastically more critical views of liberal policies such as illegal immigration than those who come to the country illegally.

That Democrats want more legal immigration in hopes that it will help them isn't even an open secret. It's just out in the open.

A 2013 report from the Center for American Progress, when John Podesta was still chairman of the board, titled "Immigration Is Changing the Political Landscape in Key States" argued:

As we move into the congressional debate on immigration reform, we should remember that the political shifts that have opened a space for reform—grounded in demographic changes—were not a phenomenon that debuted in 2012. These changes began in the mid-1990s, when anti-immigrant politics in California helped turn the state reliably blue.

And as our nation moves toward a point where by 2043 we will have no clear racial or ethnic majority, 11 other states such as Arizona, Texas, North Carolina, and even Georgia are also reaching demographic tipping points. Whether or not these states turn blue in the future has a lot to do with how politicians in both parties act and what they talk about on the subject of immigration reform.[618]

CNN's Michael Smerconish said, in an interview with a demographer who was discussing when whites would be a minority in the U.S.: "Long term, the GOP's got a problem. That's the bottom line. That's how I apply your demographic information to the current political dynamic."

The *Washington Post*'s Greg Sargent in 2012 said the election was "all about demographics," and praised how "Obama's team made the right bet on the true nature of the American electorate. Rather than reverting to the older, whiter, more male version Republicans had hoped for, it continues to be defined by what Ron Brownstein has called the 'coalition of the ascendant.'" Nearly a decade later, Sargent slammed Republican Rep. Elise Stefanik for saying that Democrats want to grant amnesty to eleven million illegals to "overthrow our current electorate and create a permanent liberal majority in Washington."[619]

In 2008, the *Los Angeles Times* predicted that Democrats would gain in historically conservative areas due to the white population shrinking. "That new formula was evident in state exit polls and county-level election results showing that Democrats scored gains from a voting base that is growing progressively less white than the population that helped forge Republican advantages in past elections," the article said. "In state after state, from GOP strongholds like North Carolina, Indiana and Colorado, minorities made up a larger share of the vote than in the past, and in each case they helped turn states from red to blue."[620]

Then–Democratic San Antonio mayor Julian Castro said that demographic changes would turn his state blue on CBS's *Face the Nation* in 2013: "In a couple of presidential cycles, you'll be on election night. You'll be announcing that we're calling the 38 electoral votes of Texas

618 Wolgin, Philip, and Ann Garcia. "Immigration Is Changing the Political Landscape in Key States." Center for American Progress, April 8, 2013, https://www.americanprogress.org/article/immigration-is-changing-the-political-landscape-in-key-states/.

619 Lowry, Rich. "The Replacement-Theory Hypocrites." National Review, May 17, 2022, https://www.nationalreview.com/corner/the-replacement-theory-hypocrites/.

620 Wallsten, Peter. "Texas in Democrats' Sights." *Los Angeles Times,* November 9, 2008, https://www.latimes.com/archives/la-xpm-2008-nov-09-na-assess9-story.html.

for the Democratic nominee for president. It's changing. It's going to become a purple state, and then a blue state, because of the demographics, because of the population growth of folks from outside of Texas."

With the backing of the fact-checkers, conservatives who have taken note of these statements have been smeared as supporting a "great replacement" theory.

For example, Tucker Carlson has stated on his Fox show that "as with illegal immigration, the long-term agenda of refugee resettlement is to bring in future Democratic voters, obviously," and that "the whole point of their immigration policy is to ensure political control. Replace the population. Get a different outcome," among many other similar comments. PolitiFact's Bill McCarthy framed this as Tucker invoking a "racist and antisemitic 'great replacement theory'" that has been cited by mass shooters.[621]

McCarthy is conflating two "great replacement" theories here; one that tends to be associated with the far-right that postulates that the goal of immigration is to lower the white population (which Tucker is not endorsing), and another that immigration will produce an electorate more likely to vote Democrat, which Democrats openly admit. Yet, when someone simply quotes back to Democrats their motives, they're smeared as racist, and the "fact-checkers" sign off on it.

FACT-CHECKER STRUGGLES TO INTERPRET EASILY UNDERSTOOD BIDEN COMMENT

PolitiFact's Tom Kertscher struggled to explain what Joe Biden could've possibly meant when he said he wants to shut down oil drilling. While most people would interpret this comment as Biden wanting to shut down oil drilling, Kertscher believes there may be more to the matter than meets the eye.

The exact quote from Biden on CNN in question was: "Number one, no more subsidies for fossil fuel industry. No more drilling on federal lands. No more drilling, including offshore. No ability for the oil industry to continue to drill, period, ends, number one."

---

621   McCarthy, Bill. "Tucker Carlson feigned ignorance over 'great replacement theory,' despite talking about it often." PolitiFact, May 19, 2022, https://www.politifact.com/article/2022/may/19/tucker-carlson-feigned-ignorance-over-great-replac/.

Biden said he wants no more oil drilling, no new fracking, and wants to ban new oil and gas permitting on public lands and waters, yet Kertscher rates "Mostly False" the characterization that Biden wants to "completely shut down drilling for oil and natural gas on day one of his administration."

To help twist the meaning of Biden's easily understood comment, Kertscher gets philosophical when it comes to what the phrase "shut down" means, writing:

> A Facebook post says Biden "just announced on CNN he will completely shut down drilling for oil and natural gas on day one of his administration." In a CNN debate, Biden said "no more drilling" for oil. Taken literally, that could be interpreted to mean he supports ending oil drilling. But he did not use the words "shut down" and his stated position has been to ban new oil drilling on federal lands and water, not end ongoing work.[622]

Even if Biden were speaking solely of new drilling on federal lands, those lands account for roughly a quarter of U.S. oil production.[623] At least a "Half True" rating would've been appropriate in the case.

POLITIFACT TRIES AND FAILS TO FACT-CHECK FACT THAT CALIFORNIA HAS SIX EXTRA REPRESENTATIVES IN CONGRESS DUE TO ILLEGALS

PolitiFact's Tom Kertscher took issue with an article I wrote arguing that California has six more representatives in the U.S. House because illegal aliens are counted as part of population in the Census.[624]

---

622   Kertscher, Tom. "In debate, Joe Biden said no more oil drilling and no new fracking, didn't say shutdowns." PolitiFact, March 20, 2020, https://www.politifact.com/factchecks/2020/mar/20/facebook-posts/debate-joe-biden-said-no-more-oil-drilling-and-no-/.

623   Smith, Lee. "Drilling Down on Federal Leasing Facts." American Petroleum Institute, March 24, 2022, https://www.api.org/news-policy-and-issues/blog/2022/03/24/drilling-down-on-federal-leasing-facts.

624   Palumbo, Matt. "Report: California Has Six Extra Representatives Because Illegals Are Counted in Census." Bongino, July 23, 2020, https://bongino.com/report-california-has-six-extra-representatives-because-illegals-are-counted-in-census.

This fact-check, which found my claim "Mostly False," showcases Kertscher's usual sloppiness. The source for my claim was a report from FAIR (the Federation for American Immigration Reform), but Kertscher mistakenly wrote that a Facebook page called "Unbiased America" (which had done a post reporting on the study too) was the source of the claim. [625]

After not being able to do as much as correctly identify the source of my claim, the bulk of Kertscher's case against me is his own inability to prove what I wrote. From that point on, he just quotes a few people who disagree with me and then labels the claim false, concluding:

> We found no evidence to back a claim that California has six more House seats than it would have if people in the country illegally were excluded from the apportionment. [626]

This isn't because the evidence does not exist, but merely because Kertscher isn't competent enough as a fact-checker to find it. Even the "experts" he quotes offer no justification for why they disagree.

Kertscher quotes demographer Dudley Poston Jr., an emeritus professor of sociology at Texas A&M University, as saying my claim "is off base," with no explanation of why. He and other experts Kertscher talked to told him that California likely has "two to four" more seats than they would if illegal aliens weren't counted as population in the census. There is no explanation provided of how they came to this number, or how my claim is "Mostly False" when four seats instead of six would be "Mostly True."

Does he really think that "actually California only has four extra representatives due to illegals, not six!" is a satisfying rebuttal to anyone who doesn't want illegals counted in terms of determining representation (which is almost everyone)? [627]

Had Kertscher been competent, he could've at least attempted to make it look like he put some effort into the fact-check, perhaps by walking the reader through the process by which representatives are appor-

---

625 Kertscher, Tom. "Fact-checking a claim about immigrants and california's 'extra' House seats." PolitiFact, August 6, 2020, https://www.politifact.com/factchecks/2020/aug/06/facebook-posts/calif-has-extra-us-house-seats-because-illegals-no/.

626 Ibid.

627 Palumbo, Matt. "Poll: 70% Don't Want Illegals Counted in Assigning Congressional Seats." Associated Press, August 6, 2020, https://bongino.com/poll-70-dont-want-illegals-counted-in-assigning-congressional-seats.

tioned, and then providing estimates of the illegal alien population in California. But he doesn't care about the truth—he cares about suppressing it.

So little effort did Kertscher put into his fact-check, that he didn't even bother to interact with the data underpinning the claim from its source, the aforementioned FAIR study. Illegal aliens make up roughly 17 percent of California's population (compared to a national average of 3.3 percent),[628] and the six extra representatives California has due to illegals being counted as population represent roughly 11 percent of California's representatives. If there's anything in the math, it's more likely to be due to FAIR underestimating representation due to illegals, not them overstating it.

FACT-CHECKERS HELP STACEY ABRAMS COVER UP HER ROLE IN THREATENING AN MLB BOYCOTT

In another case of Democrat PR disguised as fact-checks, PolitiFact's Louis Jacobson tried to rewrite history to create a narrative that Stacey Abrams didn't support the MLB All-Star Game boycott she caused in protesting so-called "voter suppression legislation." Those concerns ended up being unfounded and followed record voter turnout in the state in subsequent elections,[629] but at the time were the source of mass hysteria.

The entirety of Jacobson's fact-check has to do with Abrams' public comments, but politicians often change those based on public opinion. Abrams did noticeably change her rhetoric about the virtues of boycotts when it became clear just how unpopular the All-Star boycott would be, but she did play a role in causing it.

Business reporter Charles Gasparino, who covered the MLB fiasco, confirmed that MLB commissioner Rob Manfred's decision to pull the game out of Atlanta came after speaking with Stacey Abrams, which, Gasparino noted, "is odd since she has now said she's against the boycott." He tweeted out, breaking the story:

---

628 "U.S. unauthorized immigrant population estimates by state, 2016." Pew Research Center, February 5, 2019, https://www.pewresearch.org /hispanic/interactives/u-s-unauthorized-immigrants-by-state/.

629 Stiles, Andrew, and Thaleigha Rampersad. "WATCH: Stacey Abrams Struggles To Explain Why Black Turnout Is Soaring Under 'Jim Crow 2.0.'" Washington Free Beacon, May 24, 2022, https://freebeacon.com/democrats/stacey-abrams-jim-crow-suppression/.

MLB sources say owners were blindsided at least by the timing of Rob Manfred's decision to pull the All-Star game from Atlanta. Also said his decision came after speaking with Stacey Abrams, which is odd since she has now said she's against the boycott.[630]

Gasparino reported soon after:

Abrams told a senior league official that she wanted him [Robert Manfred] to denounce the Georgia voting rights law, according to people with direct knowledge of the matter. People associated with Sharpton's civil rights organization, and Lebron James's voting right group, "More than a Vote" also pressured league officials, according to people with direct knowledge of the matter.

After these conversations, Manfred believed the All Star game would be turned into a political event and players would boycott the game, these people say. *Baseball sources say that Abrams' current stance, that she is disappointed about the Georgia boycott, is suspect because she was among the most prominent political operatives to pressure the league to denounce the new law* [emphasis mine]. James has publicly supported the Georgia boycott.

People close to Manfred believe Abrams' group and Sharpton also wanted the league to support other issues, including voter drives and H.R. 1, the For the People Act — sweeping election reform that recently passed the House.

"They wanted us to do more than just a pre-game ceremony...Baseball would have to be in the market for doing stuff involving voting rights," a senior MLB executive with direct knowledge of the matter tells Fox News.[631]

---

630 Gasparino, Charles. April 7, 2021, https://twitter.com/CGasparino/status/1379845340795392002.
631 Gasparino, Charlie, and Morgan Phillips. "MLB commissioner decided to move All-Star Game after pressure from Stacey Abrams on voting issues: sources." Fox News, April 9, 2021, https://www.foxnews.com/politics/stacey-abrams-urged-mlb-commissioner-move-all-star-game.

Jacobson doesn't even acknowledge any of the active lobbying on Abrams' part.

The largest part of his fact-check is spent downplaying a now-infamous *USA Today* op-ed where Abrams argued that the advancement of civil rights has relied on economic boycotts but comes just short of literally telling people to boycott in an op-ed romanticizing them.[632]

Despite hedging herself slightly by not explicitly calling for boycotts, Abrams later watered down her tone, had stealth revisions made to the article, and changed statements to make the article sound anti-boycott. Of note, *these revisions were after the MLB moved the All-Star game out of Atlanta.*[633] If anyone thought that the article could be interpreted as pro-boycott despite attempts at crafting it in a way to give plausible deniability, it was Abrams herself.

The original article began with the sentence: "Boycotts work. The focused power of No, trained on corporate actors used to being told Yes, can yield transformative results." That line was changed to: "Boycotts work—when the target risks losing something highly valued and the pain becomes unbearable."

Jacobson includes the following quote from the original op-ed to argue Abrams wasn't calling for boycotts in an article extolling them: "One lesson of boycotts is that the pain of deprivation must be shared to be sustainable. Otherwise, those least resilient bear the brunt of these actions; and in the aftermath, they struggle to access the victory. And boycotts are complicated affairs that require a long-term commitment to action. I have no doubt that voters of color, particularly Black voters, are willing to endure the hardships of boycotts. *But I don't think that's necessary — yet* [emphasis mine]…I ask you to bring your business to Georgia and, if you're already here, stay and fight. Stay and vote."

Jacobson does acknowledge that *USA Today* "quietly updated the op-ed a few days later," which he doesn't find at all suspicious. The stan-

---

632   Abrams, Stacey. "3 ways for corporations to show they get what's at stake on voting rights." *USA Today*, March 31, 2021, https://web.archive.org/web/20210331210632if_/https://www.usatoday.com/story/opinion/2021/03/31/voter-suppression-will-corporations-redeem-themselves-column/4820354001/.

633   Justice, Tristan. "USA Today Retroactively Edits Stacey Abrams's Op-Ed To Downplay Her Call For Georgia Boycotts." The Federalist, April 27, 2021, https://thefederalist.com/2021/04/27/usa-today-retroactively-edits-stacey-abramss-op-ed-to-downplay-her-call-for-georgia-boycotts/.

dard is for articles to include an editor's note of revisions—that this was done without that should raise some red flags.

USA Today's parent company Gannett later apologized for this journalistic malpractice, which Jacobson makes no mention of, and then wrongly says that the updated version makes "essentially the same arguments against a boycott as the initial version did."[634]

Jacobson makes no mention of the paragraph immediately preceding the one he quoted, which was heavily edited to change its meaning, which reads:[635]

> The impassioned response to the racist, classist bill that is now the law of Georgia is to boycott in order to achieve change. Events hosted by major league baseball, world class soccer, college sports and dozens of Hollywood films hang in the balance. At the same time, activists urge Georgians to swear off of hometown products to express our outrage. Until we hear clear, unequivocal statements that show Georgia-based companies get what's at stake, I can't argue with an individual's choice to opt for their competition.

Abrams stealth-edited that passage, keeping the first sentence the same but changing what followed to: "Events that can bring millions of dollars to struggling families hang in the balance. Major League Baseball pulled both its All-Star Game and its draft from Georgia, which could cost our state nearly $100 million in lost revenue." It's clear that the purpose of the stealth edits was to make it look like Abrams was against what had just happened, when in reality she helped cause that.

CNN's fact-checker Daniel Dale deceptively presented Abrams deceptively editing her articles as her "adding nuance" to her "anti-boycott" position and made no mention that the changes were done without informing the reader.[636]

---

634 Adams, Becket. "Gannett apologizes for stealth-editing Stacey Abrams's op-ed." *Washington Examiner*, April 27, 2021, https://www.washingtonexaminer.com/opinion/gannet-apologizes-for-stealth-editing-stacey-abramss-op-ed.

635 Abrams, "3 ways for corporations to show they get what's at stake on voting rights."

636 Dale, Daniel. "Fact check: Tom Cotton suggested Stacey Abrams endorsed a boycott of Georgia. She opposed it." CNN, April 23, 2021, https://www.cnn.com/2021/04/23/politics/fact-check-tom-cotton-stacey-abrams-boycott-georgia-baseball-all-star/index.html.

THE OBAMA APOLOGY TOUR

On numerous occasions throughout the 2012 presidential election cycle, PolitiFact fact-checked the claim that President Barack Obama went on an "apology tour" to world leaders, which then–presidential candidate Mitt Romney commonly used as a talking point.

One of these many fact-checks was authored by Editor in Chief Angie Drobnic Holan, who, in a lengthy article, quoted numerous experts and consulted the dictionary on what the word "apology" means before concluding, "Yes, there is criticism [of America] in some of his speeches, but it's typically leavened by praise for the United States and its ideals, and often he mentions other countries and how they have erred as well. There's not a full-throated, sincere apology in the bunch. And so we rate Romney's statement False."[637]

One of the experts, Nile Gardiner, told Holan that Obama was "definitely apologizing, and it's not good," which she just ignores. Of course, when one has to bring in multiple experts to define what the word "apologize" means, it's because she's fishing for a specific definition that will fit her fact-check's predetermined conclusion. I'm going to go out on a limb and assume that Holan knew what apologies are before writing about them in 2012.

Going off *Webster's* definition, an apology is "an admission of error or discourtesy accompanied by an expression of regret," and going off Obama's public statements, there are numerous that fit that definition:[638]

- Obama on April 3, 2009, in Strasbourg, France: "In America, there's a failure to appreciate Europe's leading role in the world. Instead of celebrating your dynamic union and seeking to partner with you to meet common challenges, there have been times where America has shown arrogance and been dismissive, even derisive."

- Obama on April 6, 2009, in Ankara, Turkey, to the Turkish Parliament: "Another issue that confronts all democracies as

637 Holan, Angie Drobnic. "Obama's Remarks Never a True 'Apology.'" PolitiFact, March 15, 2010, https://www.politifact.com/factchecks/2010/mar/15/mitt-romney/obama-remarks-never-true-apology/.

638 Washington Free Beacon Staff. "Five Times Obama Has Apologized for America." Washington Free Beacon, August 31, 2012, https://freebeacon.com/politics/five-times-obama-has-apologized-for-america/.

they move to the future is how we deal with the past. The United States is still working through some of our own darker periods in our history."

- Obama on April 17, 2009, in Port of Spain, Trinidad and Tobago, at the Summit of the Americas: "While the United States has done much to promote peace and prosperity in the hemisphere, we have at times been disengaged, and at times we sought to dictate our terms."

- Obama on April 20, 2009, in Langley, Virginia, at the CIA headquarters: "Don't be discouraged that we have to acknowledge potentially we've made some mistakes. That's how we learn."

- Obama on May 21, 2009, at the National Archives in Washington, D.C.: "Unfortunately, faced with an uncertain threat, our government made a series of hasty decisions.... I also believe that all too often our government made decisions based on fear rather than foresight; that all too often our government trimmed facts and evidence to fit ideological predispositions. Instead of strategically applying our power and our principles, too often we set those principles aside as luxuries that we could no longer afford. And during this season of fear, too many of us — Democrats and Republicans, politicians, journalists, and citizens — fell silent. In other words, we went off course."

These statements clearly fit the dictionary definition for "apology"—though I do understand if Holan needs to bring in thousands more experts to individually define all the words quoted above before acknowledging this.

FACTUAL, BUT NOT A BIG DEAL

Even when you're right, you can be right, but it doesn't matter.

In a writeup on "the so-called 'facts' that keep getting repeated" ahead of a Republican primary debate in 2011, *WaPo*'s Glenn Kessler examined the "frequent claim…that the Congressional Budget Office, the nonpartisan scorekeeper of Washington, documented how the health-care law will 'kill' jobs. Sometimes, a number is attached to this claim — 800,000."[639]

While this "800,000" statistic is initially presented as if it's being pulled out of someone's behind, Kesler then immediately acknowledges, "The CBO in August 2010 estimated that over the next decade the new health-care law would reduce the number of overall workers in the United States by one-half of 1 percent, which translates into 800,000 people."

Kessler says that some of these eight hundred thousand people losing work aren't doing so because their job was "killed," but rather there are some people who only work for health insurance and would no longer need to work because "the health-care law guarantees they would have access to health care." He adds, "As an example, think of someone who is 63, a couple of years before retirement, who is still in a job only because he or she is waiting to get on Medicare at age 65."

But Obamacare mainly expanded Medicaid, not Medicare. And I suppose he didn't want to write, "For instance, picture someone who stopped working once they got more handouts." Perhaps that's why he doesn't quote from the CBO report he references, which states:

> The net reduction in the supply of labor is largely attributable to the substantial expansion of Medicaid and the provision of subsidies that will reduce the cost of insurance obtained through the insurance exchanges. Those changes in law will effectively increase individuals' financial resources, which will encourage some people to work fewer hours or to withdraw from the labor market. In addition, the phaseout of the subsidies as income rises will effectively increase marginal tax rates, which will also discourage work. [640]

But above all else, according to Kessler, eight hundred thousand jobs just aren't a big deal because "the United States is a big country," and the

---

639   Kessler, Glenn. "GOP debate preview: the so-called 'facts' that keep getting repeated." *Washington Post*, September 22, 2011, https://www.washingtonpost.com/blogs/fact-checker/post/gop-debate-preview-the-so-called-facts-that-keep-getting-repeated/2011/09/21/gIQAHAVSmK_blog.html#pagebreak.

640   "CBO's Analysis of the Major Health Care Legislation Enacted in March 2010." Congressional Budget Office, March 30, 2011, https://web.archive.org/web/20110510063129/https://www.cbo.gov/ftpdocs/121xx/doc12119/03-30-HealthCareLegislation.pdf.

0.5 percent (or 1 in 200 jobs) it would reduce are "basically a rounding error."

Years later, after Obamacare was signed into law, the CBO in 2014 estimated that it would reduce the size of the U.S. workforce by 2.3 million workers.[641]

WaPo's Kessler tried to portray the glass as half full and said the decline in workers "initially would lead to higher wages as employers competed to hire people."[642]

But the same CBO report says that Obamacare will cause "reductions in wages or other compensation" and that those wage reductions are among the reasons people will leave the workforce:

> Beginning in 2015, employers of 50 or more full-time equivalent workers that do not offer health insurance (or that offer health insurance that does not meet certain criteria) will generally pay a penalty. That penalty will initially reduce employers' demand for labor and thereby tend to lower employment. Over time, CBO expects, the penalty will be borne primarily by workers in the form of reduced wages or other compensation, at which point the penalty will have little effect on labor demand but will reduce labor supply and will lower employment slightly through that channel.[643]

So that isn't it.

TRUE CLAIM ABOUT PROPOSAL CREATING VOTER ID LOOPHOLE RATED MOSTLY FALSE

In response to a comment from musician Ted Nugent, who posted to his Facebook page that Michigan's Proposal 2 would "permanently put in the Constitution that you never have to show an ID to vote ever again," PolitiFact's Madison Czopek rated it "Mostly False" while admitting that he's right.

---

641   Congressional Budget Office, *The Budget and Economic Outlook:
      2014 to 2024*, Congress of the United States, 2014, 127.
642   Kessler, Glenn. "No, CBO did not say Obamacare will kill 2 million jobs." *Washington
      Post*, February 4, 2014, http://www.washingtonpost.com/blogs/fact-checker/
      wp/2014/02/04/no-cbo-did-not-say-obamacare-will-kill-2-million-jobs/.
643   Congressional Budget Office, *The Budget and Economic Outlook*, 124.

Czopek writes that the proposal wouldn't end the state's photo ID requirement because voters would still be asked to show photo ID before they receive a ballot. Czopek then admits that as a result of the proposal people who don't have a photo ID would be able to vote if they sign an affidavit swearing to their identity. This loophole that effectively neutralizes photo ID requirements was obviously what Nugent was highlighting, yet Czopek rates his claim false because it merely nullifies it instead of directly repealing it.[644]

STACEY ABRAMS TRIES TO COVER UP CONNECTIONS TO DEFUND THE POLICE MOVEMENT WITH THE HELP OF FACT-CHECKERS

FactCheck.org's Eugene Kiely and Sean Christensen came to the defense of Stacey Abrams' record on the police after she began publicly calling for increased police funding in June 2022, leading to many noticing a very public flip-flop on the issue. This came as many cities that mindlessly hopped on the "defund the police" bandwagon in 2020 were reversing course because of the predictable disaster that followed.[645]

They decided to fact-check a claim from a pro–Georgia governor Brian Kemp ad, which narrated that Abrams "said 'yes' to defunding the police," and showed a clip of CNN's Alisyn Camerota interviewing Abrams from June 2020, where she asked, "So yes, to some defunding?" and Abrams responds, "We have to reallocate some resources, so yes."

To provide more context than the ad, Abrams' full comment was: "We have to reallocate resources, so yes. If there's a moment where the resources are so tight that we have to choose between whether we murder Black people or serve Black people, then absolutely our choice must be service. But I actually think it's creating a false choice and a false narrative that's playing into the hands of Donald Trump and the Republicans and sometimes into a media narrative that seeks to make overly simplistic decisions."

644   Czopek, Madson. "Michigan's Proposal 2 doesn't end the state's voter ID requirement." PolitiFact, September 30, 2022, https://web.archive.org/web/20221009050150/https://www.politifact.com/factchecks/2022/sep/29/ted-nugent/michigans-proposal-2-doesnt-end-states-voter-id-re/.

645   Kiely, Eugene, and Sean Christensen. "Stacey Abrams on Violent Crime, Defunding the Police." FactCheck.org, June 29, 2022, https://www.factcheck.org/2022/06/stacey-abrams-on-violent-crime-defunding-the-police/.

For the "full context" for Abrams' comments in her CNN interview, FactCheck.org quotes a response that Abrams gave previously in response to a question about them during an interview with Fox News' Martha MacCallum:

> **MacCallum:** So, what's your reaction to that? And do you believe that you've changed your tune on defunding the police?
>
> **Abrams:** No, because if you listen to the whole clip, which Brian Kemp conveniently leaves out, I said, if the choice is between the murder of Black people and serving Black people, then certainly. But I don't think that's where we are and I don't think that's where we have to be.
>
> My intent is to balance public safety and justice. Because doing otherwise has never worked. We cannot punish our way into public safety. But we also have to recognize that there are deep challenges in how law enforcement engages our communities. And that is why I'm pushing both for public safety measures, accountability measures and criminal justice reform measures.

And with that, FactCheck.org decides that Abrams never supported "defund the police."

But what did we actually learn here? That Abrams supports reallocating police resources if they're so tight that "we have to choose between whether we murder Black people or serve Black people, then absolutely our choice must be service"? No attempt is even made to translate into plain English what exactly that means.

Abrams spoke with slightly more clear language the day before her CNN interview during an appearance on ABC's *New Day*, where she said the defund movement provides a false choice, and that "the reality is we need two things." She added "we'll use different language to describe it, but, fundamentally, we must have reformation and transformation."[646]

As was the case with the MLB boycott, Abrams wants to play both sides here, appealing to the ideological vision of "defund the police" while

---

646   O'Reilly, Andrew. "Stacey Abrams says 'Defund the Police' movement creates 'a false choice idea.'" Fox News, June 14, 2020, https://www.foxnews.com/politics/stacey-abrams-says-defund-the-police-movement-creates-a-false-choice-idea.

being cognizant of how unpopular actual police defunding is. Abrams finds herself in a position where police defunding is extremely unpopular overall, yet popular among her base. This was evidenced in a June 2020 interview with the State Department's Karen Donfried when Abrams was asked, "So do you support defunding the police?" to which Abrams replied, "I support the vision that is underlying that cry," giving the most middle-of-the-road answer possible.

This is one of many cases where a politician's public statements are betrayed by their private actions.

While trying to distance herself from its views, Abrams joined the Marguerite Casey Foundation in May 2021 and received at least $52,500 in income from them according to her financial disclosures. The foundation has publicly supported the "defund the police" movement and, in 2020, awarded $250,000 to the pro-defunding Movement for Black Lives. They also gave $200,000 that year to the Black Organizing Project, which is part of a thirteen-group committee pushing to defund the Oakland police. The group has also funded pro-prison abolition "scholars." On the board of the foundation is outspoken "defunding" activist Rashad Robinson, who joined the board at the same time as Abrams.[647]

Over one hundred Georgia sheriffs have condemned Abrams for her connection to the group.[648]

Years prior in 2016, the George Soros–backed Georgia Justice & Safety PAC paid Abrams' firm Sage Works LLC $15,000 for "consulting services." The "Georgia Justice & Safety PAC" is part of Soros' effort to weaken law and order in America by supporting so-called progressive prosecutors.[649]

---

647 Schoffstall, Joe. "Stacey Abrams group increased anti-police funding shortly after she joined its board, and with her support." Fox News, June 6, 2022, https://www.foxnews.com/politics/stacey-abrams-group-increased-anti-police-funding-joined-board-support.

648 Keene, Houston, and Joe Schoffstall. "Over 100 Georgia sheriffs condemn Stacey Abrams over 'defund the police' foundation ties." Yahoo, January 1, 2022, https://web.archive.org/web/20220630032005/https://news.yahoo.com/over-100-georgia-sheriffs-condemn-194057205.html.

649 Schoffstall, Joe. "Stacey Abrams' firm received thousands to consult George Soros district attorney efforts, filings reveal." Fox News, August 30, 2022, https://www.foxnews.com/politics/stacey-abrams-firm-received-thousands-consult-george-soros-district-attorney-efforts.

MAN WHO TRIED TO OVERTURN PRIOR ELECTION TAKES BOLD STANCE AGAINST OVERTURNING ELECTIONS

As the "House Select Committee on the January 6 Attack" began airing public hearings on primetime, some couldn't help noticing the irony in a committee accusing Donald Trump of trying to overturn the results of a presidential election being headed by Bennie Thompson, who has himself tried to reverse the results of a presidential election.

PolitiFact somehow managed to be the most honest here and reviewed a specific claim from the House Republican Conference that "Bennie Thompson objected to the 2004 Presidential election," which Louis Jacobson rated as "Mostly True." There's some editorializing in the "Mostly" part of the objectively "True" statement, where Jacobson provides the "context" that "the 2005 objection was known by everyone at the time to be a procedural dead end, since the losing Democratic candidate, Sen. John Kerry, had conceded the election and had stated his opposition to the objection effort."[650] So in other words, the claim is true, but Jacobson won't rate it as such because he thinks trying to overturn an election counts less because Kerry opposed it and because it had little of chance of succeeding (which could also be said of Trump's efforts).

Abby Llorico, writing a fact-check for local network WUSA9, took the denial approach, headlining her article, "No, leaders of the Jan. 6 committee didn't try to overturn previous elections." This article was about Bennie Thompson and addressed allegations that panel member Jamie Raskin (who tried to challenge the count for Florida during the Electoral College vote certification in 2017)[651] tried to overturn past elections. In her case, she confirms the allegations but then decides that they just don't count. "While they opposed the electoral certification of certain states, that is a relatively common process that would not have

---

650   Jacobson, Louis. "Fact-checking whether Jan. 6 committee chairman Bennie Thompson objected to the 2004 election." PolitiFact, June 10, 2022, https://www.politifact.com/factchecks/2022/jun/10/house-republicans/fact-checking-whether-bennie-thompson-objected-200/.

651   Hains, Tim. "FLASHBACK: Lead Impeachment Manager Jamie Raskin Attempted to Object to Electoral Vote Certification for Trump in 2017." RealClearPolitics, January 13, 2021, https://www.realclearpolitics.com/video/2021/01/13/flashback_lead_impeachment_manager_jamie_raskin_attempted_to_object_to_electoral_vote_certification_for_trump_in_2017.html.

been enough to overturn an election."[652] Nor were Trump's many lawsuits enough to overturn an election.

Thompson also refused to attend Trump's 2016 inauguration, questioning the legitimacy of the election as part of his reason. He said in a statement that "the Russian hack was, at its core, an attempt to delegitimize our democracy," and a spokesman for Thompson made a similar comment in a statement, that "Congressman Thompson continues to have concerns about the role that Russia had in our country's democratic process."[653]

Challenging the electoral certification of certain states is indeed nothing new—Democrats objected to more states in 2016 than Republicans did in 2020. While these "fact-checks" are specific to Thompson and Raskin because they're on the Jan. 6 committee, they weren't the only ones.

On January 6, 2017, Jim McGovern objected to Alabama's votes, Pramila Jayapal objected to Georgia's, Raul Grijalva objected to North Carolina's, Sheila Jackson Lee objected to North Carolina, South Carolina, Wisconsin, and Mississippi, Barbara Lee objected to the announcement of Michigan's votes (citing mythical Russian interference), while Maxine Waters objected to Wyoming.

By contrast, January 6, 2021, saw four objectors: Mo Brooks who objected to Nevada's votes, Marjorie Taylor Greene who objected to Michigan's, Louie Gohmert, who objected to Wisconsin's votes, and Jody Hice, who objected to Georgia's votes.[654]

FACT-CHECKERS BACK GENDER MADNESS

Amidst the transgender hysteria permeating many of America's institutions, PolitiFact's Yacob Reyes tried to downplay the extent to which

652   Llorico, Abby. "No, leaders of the Jan. 6 committee didn't try to overturn previous elections." WUSA, June 9, 2022, https://web.archive.org/web/20220609125413/https://www.wusa9.com/article/news/verify/no-leaders-of-the-january-6-committee-didnt-try-to-overturn-previous-elections/65-3a9538fe-64c7-4bbc-8c24-c5796e377790.

653   Berry, Deborah Barfield. "Rep. Bennie Thompson won't attend Trump's inauguration." *USA Today*, January 17, 2017, https://www.usatoday.com/story/news/2017/01/17/thompson-not-atten-trumps-inauguration/96655990/

654   Greene, Shayna. "Fact Check: Did Democrats Object to More States for 2016 Than Republicans for 2020?" *Newsweek*, January 13, 2021, https://www.newsweek.com/fact-check-did-democrats-object-more-states-2016-republicans-2020-1561407.

gender transition surgeries or related procedures are being performed in children.[655]

In a fact-check replying to a comment from Florida governor Ron DeSantis, who said at a press conference that "they are literally chopping off the private parts of young kids," Reyes relies on a definition of children as those under age ten (based off the Florida Department of Health's definition) and says he found no examples of "young kids" receiving transition-related surgery.

This rebuttal effectively amounts to stating that many young people making permanent life altering decisions may not be old enough to drive a car, but at least they're not technically kids. It's also a definition that contradicts what DeSantis was clearly talking about. The full quote from DeSantis, which Reyes provides in his own article, is that "they want to castrate these young boys, that's wrong. We stood up and said, from the health and children's well-being perspective, you don't disfigure 10, 12, 13-year-old kids based on gender dysphoria."

Reyes adds at the end of his fact-check that "there are no examples we could find, or the governor's office provided, of transition-related surgeries for people under the age of 14." That came fourteen paragraphs after he wrote that "the procedure is mostly offered to teenagers 15 and older, The New York Times reported. However, we found one report of a 14-year-old who obtained the procedure, and there isn't a consensus on a specific age requirement among medical guidelines."

Among the "experts" Reyes relies on for his article is Jack Turban, a psychiatrist who specializes in "LGBTQ health" and research on transgender youth and has received funding for his research from the American Academy of Child & Adolescent Psychiatry, which is financially supported by pharma giants Arbor and Pfizer, which both produce off-label puberty blockers.[656]

Another "expert" is C. P. Hoffman from the National Center for Transgender Equality, who uses "they/she" pronouns.

---

655   Reyes, Yacob. "Transition-related surgery limited to teens, not 'young kids.' Even then, it's rare." PolitiFact, August 10, 2022, https://www.politifact.com/factchecks/2022/aug/10/ron-desantis/transition-related-surgery-limited-to-teens-not-young/.

656   Downey, Caroline. "'Advocate Rather Than a Scientist': The Compromised Research of Child Gender-Transition Doctor Jack Turban." National Review, August 16, 2022, https://www.nationalreview.com/news/advocate-rather-than-a-scientist-the-compromised-research-of-child-gender-transition-doctor-jack-turban/.

Two days later, Reyes tackled a video posted by the Twitter account Libs of TikTok, which shares videos from liberals espousing absurd views on social justice topics. The video in question was from Boston Children's Hospital, which features a short video from a doctor explaining so-called "gender affirming hysterectomies." Libs of TikTok captioned the post on August 11, "Boston Children's Hospital is now offering 'gender-affirming hysterectomies' for young girls." The video was part of a series of videos. In others, a doctor explains that toddlers can know they're transgender.

In another video, Elizabeth Boskey, a self-described "queer research-er," says that "many surgical centers require you to be 18. At Boston Children's Hospital for top surgeries (double mastectomies), we'll see people as young as 15 if they've been affirmed in their gender for a long period of time." Boston Children's Hospital deleted the video from Boskey (and all others on the topic of youth transgender care) from their YouTube channel to cover their tracks after Libs of TikTok began sharing them.[657]

But not so fast, says Reyes, who says in response that one must be eighteen or older and have a letter from a doctor to qualify for the procedure, quoting the children's hospital's website.[658] Reyes also points out that the doctor in the video didn't herself say that the children's hospital was providing them.

What Reyes doesn't mention is that Boston Children's Hospital updated their website amid the pushback from Libs of TikTok sharing their video, and the specific line, "We only perform gender-affirming hysterectomies on patients who are age 18 or older," was added after public criticism.[659] Another tab on the hospital's website says, "We only perform gender-affirming hysterectomies on patients who are age 18 or older,"[660]

657   Boston Children's Hospital. "Surgical Transition: Who Is Eligible?" YouTube, https://web.archive.org/web/20220810092134/https://www.youtube.com/watch?v=qTXVd2Mcmx8.

658   Reyes, Yacob. "No, Boston Children's Hospital doesn't provide hysterectomies for children." PolitiFact, August 12, 2022, https://www.politifact.com/factchecks/2022/aug/12/tweets/no-boston-childrens-hospital-doesnt-provide-hyster/.

659   "Our approach to transgender reproductive health." Boston Children's Hospital, http://web.archive.org/web/20220812191705/https://www.childrenshospital.org/programs/transgender-reproductive-health-service.

660   "Our approach to gender surgery." Boston Children's Hospital, https://www.childrenshospital.org/programs/center-gender-surgery-program.

and similarly, that specific line didn't appear on the website until after backlash, as archived versions of the page show.[661]

Those quotes were from the part of the hospital's website specific to their Center for Gender Surgery (CfGS).

And what is the CfGS? According to one study published in the National Library of Medicine in March 2022:

> The Center for Gender Surgery (CfGS) at Boston Children's Hospital (BCH) was the first pediatric center in the United States to offer gender-affirming chest surgeries for individuals over 15 years old and genital surgeries for those over 17 years of age. In the four years since its inception, CfGS has completed over 300 gender-affirming surgeries.[662]

The study in question identified "204 gender affirmation surgical cases, 177 chests/top surgeries, and 27 genital/bottom surgeries" between the ages of 15 and 35 and was "approved by the institutional review board of Boston Children's Hospital." The median age was eighteen, and 32 percent were minors.[663]

In 2018, Dr. Oren Ganor, the co-director for the Center for Gender Surgery, was interviewed by a local news outlet called WBUR. In the article, its author reports that while international guidelines suggest waiting until a patient is eighteen, "Children's, Ganor said in an email, is 'slightly flexible' when it comes to the age of transgender girls seeking genital surgery 'because of the difficulty young women can experience accessing gendered spaces—like dorms and bathrooms—if they still have male genitalia.'"[664]

And all of this is obscuring all the other life-altering "treatments" the hospital offers to children. The Children Hospital's Gender Multispecialty Service welcomes children as young as three and offers services

---

661 "Center for Gender Surgery." Boston Children's Hospital., http://web. archive.org/web/20220727060330/https://www.childrenshospital. org/programs/center-gender-surgery-program.

662 Aquino, Nelson, et al. "A Single Center Case Series of Gender-Affirming Surgeries and the Evolution of a Specialty Anesthesia Team." J Clin Med, March 31, 2022, https://www.ncbi.nlm.nih.gov/pmc/articles/PMC9000168.

663 Ibid, 3.

664 Bebinger, Martha. "Boston Children's Hospital Constructs Penis For Transgender Man — A First In Mass." WBUR, August 17, 2018, https://www.wbur.org/news/ 2018/08/17/hogle-penis-trans-surgery.

that includes prescribing puberty blockers, testosterone, estrogen, and plastic surgery.

FACT-CHECKERS SANITIZE MARGARET SANGER'S EUGENICS ADVOCACY

In a *New York Times* op-ed in April 2021, Planned Parenthood president Alexis McGill Johnson finally admitted what conservatives have been saying for decades: their founder Margaret Sanger is a racist.

In the op-ed, Johnson distances the organization from its founder, writing, "…Up until now, Planned Parenthood has failed to own the impact of our founder's actions. We have defended Sanger as a protector of bodily autonomy and self-determination, while excusing her association with white supremacist groups and eugenics as an unfortunate "product of her time." Johnson mentions Sanger speaking at a KKK rally in New Jersey, Sanger's endorsement of the SCOTUS's 1927 decision in *Buck v. Bell* allowing states to sterilize "unfit" people without their consent, and more.

Johnson continues: "Sanger remains an influential part of our history and will not be erased, but as we tell the history of Planned Parenthood's founding, we must fully take responsibility for the harm that Sanger caused to generations of people with disabilities and Black, Latino, Asian-American, and Indigenous people…. We will no longer make excuses or apologize for Margaret Sanger's actions. But we can't simply call her racist, scrub her from our history, and move on. We must examine how we have perpetuated her harms over the last century — as an organization, an institution, and as individuals."[665]

In response to the admission, the Babylon Bee's founder Seth Dillon couldn't help but point out all the times the fact-checkers previously rushed to Sanger's defense to deny her racism.[666]

In one of them, an NPR fact-check, they responded to Ben Carson stating that Sanger started Planned Parenthood to control the black

---

665 "Alexis McGill Johnson, President of Planned Parenthood: We're Done Making Excuses for Our Founder – Margaret Sanger!" Apicciano, April 19, 2021, https://apicciano.commons.gc.cuny.edu/2021/04/19/alexis-mcgill-johnson-president-of-planned-parenthood-were-done-making-excuses-for-our-founder-margaret-sanger/.

666 Olohan, Mary Margaret. "Babylon Bee CEO Revels In How Fact Checkers Carried Water For Planned Parenthood Founder." The Daily Caller, April 20, 2021, https://dailycaller.com/2021/04/20/seth-dillon-babylon-bee-planned-parenthood-margaret-sanger/.

population. NPR argued in response that while Sanger did believe in eugenics, it was "not in the way Carson implied." While Sanger's attitude towards "African-Americans can certainly be viewed as paternalistic, there is no evidence she subscribed to the more racist ideas of the time or that she coerced black women into using birth control," they wrote.

Elsewhere, Snopes' Kim LaCapria ran a fact-check on a photo of Margaret Sanger at a KKK rally, which she claims was "miscaptioned." The image in the article of Sanger speaking to KKK members was indeed fake, but LaCapria is also quick to downplay the actual speech she did give to the Klan.

"Although the image was a fabrication, it did include a grain of (distorted) truth in its assertion that Sanger once addressed female KKK members in Silver Lake, New Jersey." The "distorted" truth is that we're supposed to believe the spin that Sanger only spoke to the Klan merely because she was willing to speak to anyone. Again, in the modern age of guilt by association, the likes of LaCapria would never see this as an excuse for any conservative who spoke before a radical group.

The *Washington Post*'s Kessler called Sanger a "racial pioneer" in response to the charges from Cain and claimed that "there is no evidence that Sanger ever sought to kill black babies, either through the Negro Project or any other endeavor."

PolitiFact examined the claim that Sanger was a "white supremacist, spoke at KKK events, and [was] supported by Democrats," and rated it "Mostly False" because Sanger had only spoken at a singular Klan event, and that it's "subjective" whether or not she was a white supremacist.[667]

HUFFINGTON POST REDEFINES "GASLIGHTING" TO GASLIGHT

Even rags like the Huffington Post have entered the fact-checking game to some extent—and struck out after attempting to take a swing at so-called "Master Gaslighter" Ted Cruz, who correctly pointed out in April 2021 that Republicans never tried to pack the Supreme Court when they controlled the government.

---

667   Parkins, Katie, and Allie Pecorin. "Margaret Sanger, alleged white supremacist?" PolitiFact, October 5, 2017, https://www.politifact.com/factchecks/2017/oct/05/andrew-koenig/margaret-sanger-alleged-white-supremacist/.

Cruz said:

> You didn't see Republicans, when we had control of the
> Senate, try to rig the game. Just a few years ago, Republicans
> were in the same position. 2017, all of us were here, we had a
> Republican President, a Republican Senate, and a Republican
> House. We didn't do this. We could have… You didn't see us
> try to pack the court. There was nothing that would have
> prevented Republicans from doing what they're doing other
> than respect for the rule of law, other than respect for basic
> decency, other than recognizing that democracy matters.
> And packing the court and tearing down the institutions that
> protect our rights is fundamentally wrong.

How is this Cruz's "biggest lie yet"? Because, according to HuffPo,
while Republicans may have never tried expanding the Supreme Court,
"at least 174 district court judges and 54 appeals court judges" were
appointed under Trump.[668]

In other words, to debunk Cruz requires both redefining what
court packing means (adding seats to the Supreme Court) and not even
addressing the same court Cruz was talking about.

HuffPo then further conflates "nominating and confirming judges"
with "court packing," stating, "Senate Republicans also confirmed three
Supreme Court Justices."

And they sure did—while keeping the number of seats on the
court at nine.

LOCAL FACT-CHECKER VALIDATES STORY, RATES IT FALSE ANYWAY

Ryan Laughlin, a local reporter in New Mexico, attempted to fact-
check an attack ad from a group supporting the Republican challenger
to Governor Michelle Lujan Grisham which accused the governor of
releasing hundreds of prisoners early from jail early to fight COVID,
highlighting one prisoner who then went on to kill his ex-girlfriend after
his release.[669]

---

668   HuffPost. April 23, 2021, https://twitter.com/HuffPost/status/1385650929228152834.
669   Laughlin, Ryan. "Fact Check: Ad claims murder case is tied to governor's
       pandemic policy." KOB4, October 13, 2022, https://www.kob.com/new-mexico/
       fact-check-ad-claims-murder-case-is-tied-to-governors-pandemic-policy/.

In his fact-check, Laughlin explains that prisoner Christopher Beltran was released early as a result of an executive order allowing prisoners with less than thirty days left to serve out early as a result of COVID, but he was back within jail in a week for violating his probation. He was then let out early a second time, and he killed his ex-girlfriend shortly after. Laughlin also notes that Beltran threatened to kill his ex-girlfriend while making phone calls on a recorded line from prison.

You'd think that a setup like this would produce an obvious "True" rating, but not according to Laughlin, who says, "While the Governor of New Mexico did release this criminal from prison early and he did kill his ex-girlfriend right after he got out, it did not happen the way the ad portrays."[670]

So what was so misleading about the ad? Because Beltran says the second time the Grisham administration let him out of jail early it wasn't due to a pandemic era policy. "His [Beltran's] parole was supposed to expire in November 2021," narrates Laughlin, who then adds, "however, when Beltran was released in June of 2021, Department of Correction documents show that it wasn't due to the public health order, but because he did his time."

Laughlin doesn't elaborate at all to explain how it was that Beltran got out of jail five months earlier than expected, and then decides that so long as the reason isn't the pandemic order, it's in no way the fault of the governor and/or her administration. And the exact reason for his early release is up for debate, but there's no question he was released early.

A spokeswoman for the New Mexico Department of Corrections maintains that Beltran got credit for five months of good time, but according to Dianna Luce, the DA for the 5th Judicial District in New Mexico, that's impossible. She said in a statement that "The Lujan Grisham administration clearly miscalculated when it came to awarding Beltran good time in order to release him early. Under New Mexico law, offenders who violate parole through absconding and are sent back to prison are only eligible for 4 days of good time credit for every 30 days served. Moreover, offenders who make threats on prison phone calls and are held in segregation — as was the case with Beltran — are not eligible for any good time."[671]

---

670   Laughlin, Ryan. October 14, 2022, https://twitter.com/RyanLaughlinKOB/status/1580929493828411393.

671   Chacón, Daniel J. "Man accused in killing becomes key figure in governor's race." Yahoo! News, October 15, 2022, https://www.yahoo.com/news/man-accused-killing-becomes-key-150700872.html.

Or in summary, a criminal was let out of jail early thanks to the governor and then went on to kill his girlfriend—just like the ad said, but with a few extra steps along the way.

FACT-CHECKER SEES BALD EAGLE, IMMEDIATELY THINKS OF NAZIS

USA Today decided to look into whether or not Trump campaign shirts contained secret Nazi imagery.[672]

What was the imagery? The bald eagle.

In a truly incredible tweet, *USA Today* shared their article with the following caption: "The claim: Trump campaign shirts feature imperial eagle, a Nazi symbol. Our ruling: True."[673]

So desperate is *USA Today* to make this sort of reductio ad Hitlerum that they forget the bald eagle is the national symbol of the United States, which Donald Trump was campaigning for reelection for president in.

---

672   Peebles, Will. "Fact check: Trump campaign accused of T-shirt design with similarity to Nazi eagle." *USA Today*, July 11, 2020, https://www.usatoday.com/story/news/factcheck/2020/07/11/fact-check-trump-2020-campaign-shirt-design-similar-nazi-eagle/5414393002/.

673   USA Today. July 12, 2020, https://twitter.com/usatoday/status/1282259909032189952.

They later added two clarifying tweets: "Clarification: The claim that Trump 2020 has put out a T-shirt with a symbol similar to a Nazi eagle and is being criticized for it is true. Worth noting, the eagle is a longtime U.S. symbol, too."

No kidding.

And then they almost accepted accountability and slightly changed their rating to pretend there's some ambiguity: "Update: The rating on this article has been changed to inconclusive. It was updated to reflect further reporting and analysis."

Hopefully they can get to the bottom of this soon.

LIBERAL HYPOCRISY REFRAMED AS RIGHT-WING RACISM

Amid a media and political environment that was blaming Republicans for COVID-19 vaccine hesitancy, Texas lieutenant governor Dan Patrick pointed out that the same argument could be made for a demographic that votes Democrat at a higher rate than any other, yet liberals would never weaponize rhetoric against them.

While it is true that a larger share of Democrats than Republicans were vaccinated against COVID-19, Republicans were vaccinated at a higher rate than African Americans, a demographic which votes 90+ percent Democrat in presidential elections. In cities such as Washington, D.C., vax mandates to attend public school had to be delayed due to the terrible optics of its enforcement, which would've resulted in 40 percent of the city's black students being forced out of school.

This is only relevant to point out in that it highlights an inconsistency in the left's rhetoric. While Republicans were "scientific illiterates," who were in for a "dark winter" (as Joe Biden put it) for their vaccine hesitancy, they were the only demographic Democrats were willing to single out for slander.

Or as Lt. Gov. Patrick phrased it in an interview in August 2021: "Democrats like to blame Republicans [for low vaccination rates]. Well, the biggest group in most states are African Americans who have not been vaccinated. The last time I checked, over 90% of them vote for Democrats."

In response, PolitiFact's Brandon Mulder opted to invent a claim and frame his fact-check in the most asinine way conceivable, beginning it with the line, "No, the COVID surge can't be pinned on the black population,"[674] and rating the claim nobody made "False."

And like that, a statement pointing out an inconsistency in the left's blame game rhetoric is reframed as Lt. Gov. Patrick being racist for pointing out the hypocrisy.

Mulder sourced the video of Lt. Gov. Patrick's comments from Aaron Rupar, a serial propagandist known for posting sensationalized videos with misleading captions and deceptive edits.[675] Rupar captioned this one, "Texas Lt. Gov. Dan Patrick blames unvaccinated Black people for Covid spread in his state," and Mulder uncritically accepted that bogus framing.

"Republican Lt. Gov. Dan Patrick, asked last week to defend the Texas response to surging coronavirus cases, blamed Democrats for the present COVID-19 wave, specifically African Americans, who he said are reliable Democratic voters," Mulder writes of Lt. Gov. Patrick, who never blamed Democrats or African Americans for the present COVID-19 wave.

Mulder continued, "Regardless of whether or not he was referring to vaccination rates, he did not seek to change his main point, that Black populations are playing a major role in fueling the present COVID-19 surge. But there's no evidence to support that"—and there's also no evidence to support that Patrick was implying "Black populations" were driving the present COVID-19 surge. The entirety of his fact-check has Mulder creating his own villain to fight.

By the end of the "fact-check," Mulder invents another new claim, that this is all part of "an attempt to blame vaccine hesitancy on Democrats." How he came to that conclusion remains a mystery, though he does come incredibly close to the truth by the end of his fact-check, writing:

> His on-air statement is wrong. Black people aren't the largest group of unvaccinated people in any state. *But his revised statement, that vaccination rates among the Black population lag behind that of other racial groups, is correct.* [emphasis mine]

674   Mulder, Brandon. "No, COVID surge can't be pinned on the Black population." PolitiFact, August 26, 2021, https://www.politifact.com/factchecks/2021/aug/26/dan-patrick/no-you-cant-tie-present-covid-surge-black-populati/.

675   "Vox 'journalist' Aaron Rupar is a master of the 'self own.'" *Post Millennial,* February 13, 2021, https://thepostmillennial.com/journalist-aaron-rupar-is-a-master-of-the-self-own.

He then adds the following to justify bending reality and rating the claim false: "Nonetheless, Patrick's underlying claim — that Black communities are driving the current surge — is not supported by evidence. We rate this claim False."

If that's what Lt. Gov. Patrick said, it would be false.

But it wasn't.

FACT-CHECKING BIDEN'S MENTAL HEALTH

Representative and former White House physician Ronny Jackson has made a number of public comments questioning Joe Biden's mental fitness and called for him to resign.

In response to the headlines that's generated, PolitiFact's Monique Curet debunked a claim that no one made after digging to the bottom of the barrel for any possible angle to minimize Jackson's concerns.

Of all possible places to respond to reporting on Jackson, Curet found a meme on a Facebook page called "David 93FZF" that fewer than two hundred people reacted to. The page itself doesn't even have one thousand followers. "NOT FIT TO LEAD! WHITE HOUSE PHYSICIAN DEMANDS Biden's IMMEDIATE RESIGNATION FOLLOWING HIS 'OBVIOUS' COGNITIVE DECLINE!" read the post.

According to Curet, the post, which doesn't state if it's referring to a current or former White House physician, "mischaracterizes who has called for Biden's resignation." That's impossible because it doesn't actually name anyone.

The only purpose of this pointless "fact-check," which acknowledges Representative Jackson's criticisms, seems to be providing a counternarrative to headlines about Biden's mental fitness. Curet writes that the "current White House physician gave President Joe Biden a full medical evaluation in November and said he is fit to carry out his duties." She doesn't mention that this "full medical evaluation" did not include a cognitive test.[676]

Curet also saw fit to mention past scandals of Jackson that have nothing to do with the fact-check at hand, which included drinking alcohol on a presidential trip, in an attempt to smear him.

---

676 Klawans, Justin. "Joe Biden, Unlike Trump, Didn't Take Cognitive Test in Annual Exam, Sanjay Gupta Says." *Newsweek*, November 19, 2021, https://www.newsweek.com/joe-biden-unlike-trump-didnt-take-cognitive-test-annual-exam-sanjay-gupta-says-1651558.

Further making a blatant attempt to discredit Jackson, Curet frames any concern over Biden's senility as a conspiracy theory:

> Jackson and other Republican lawmakers have demanded that Biden take a cognitive assessment. Their efforts are part of a years-long campaign by Trump and his allies to paint 79-year-old Biden as weak and senile.

This is a hit piece disguised as a fact-check. Curet had to dig through the depths of Facebook to find any sort of post that had any sort of ambiguity as to which White House physician was concerned about Biden's mental health to justify writing an article.

And even then, the post does not claim that the current White House physician called for Biden's resignation—yet that's what the "False" rating for Curet's fact-check is for. A claim nobody made.

MISQUOTING JUSTICE THOMAS

Not only did most fact-checkers completely ignore an easily debunked but widely spread report about Clarence Thomas, but at least one of them spread the lie.

Justice Thomas had written, in a dissenting opinion for a case denying a religious liberty challenge to New York's COVID-19 vaccine mandate for health-care workers that some "[pro-lifers] object on religious grounds to all available COVID-19 vaccines because they were developed using cell lines derived from aborted children."

This is not his opinion—*Science Magazine* has noted that the COVID-19 vaccines were "manufactured using cells derived from human fetuses electively aborted decades ago." And as the *Washington Examiner*'s Timothy P. Carney summarizes: "Pfizer and Moderna, while developing the vaccines, tested them on a line of cells that was derived from the kidney of an aborted Dutch baby. Johnson & Johnson used a cell line derived from a different aborted baby not in the testing, but in the manufacture of the vaccine. The cells derived from the baby aren't in the vaccine, but the cells act as something of a catalyst for a crucial ingredient (the adenovirus) in the J&J vaccine."[677]

---

677 Carney, Timothy P. "*Politico, Axios,* and NBC News peddle a weird smear of Clarence Thomas." *Washington Examiner*, July 1, 2022, https://www.washingtonexaminer.com /opinion/politico-axios-and-nbc-news-peddle-a-weird-smear-of-clarence-thomas.

Most relevant to the subsequent reporting on Justice Thomas' comments, note how he wasn't expressing a personal opinion. Justice Thomas was quoting the concerns of others, and he never says the vaccines contain the cells of aborted fetuses. He said they were derived from aborted fetuses. Contrast that with how NBC News, Axios, and Politico reported on the dissent.

- "In a sharply worded dissent, Justice Clarence Thomas expressed support Thursday for a debunked claim that all Covid vaccines are made with cells from 'aborted children,'" wrote NBC's Adam Edelman and Aria Bendix. "It is not true that Covid vaccines are manufactured using fetal cell lines, nor do they contain any aborted cells."[678]

- "Supreme Court Justice Clarence Thomas suggested Thursday in a dissenting opinion that coronavirus vaccines were developed using cells from 'aborted children,'" reported Axios. "Reality check: No coronavirus vaccine in the U.S. contains the cells of aborted fetuses."[679]

- Politico headlined its article, "Clarence Thomas suggests Covid vaccines are developed using cells of 'aborted children,'" but, "None of the Covid-19 vaccines in the United States contain the cells of aborted fetuses."[680]

Impressively, all managed to respond to an allegation "from" Justice Thomas that he didn't himself actually make, and they couldn't even summarize that argument correctly in responding to it.

Amid all this, not one of the media fact-checkers stepped in to clarify the record. In fact, at least one of them, the *Washington Post's* Glenn Kessler, was more than happy to circulate the bogus story.

---

678 Edelman, Adam, and Aria Bendix. "Justice Thomas cites claim that Covid vaccines are made with cells from 'aborted children.'" NBC News, June 30, 2022, https://www.nbcnews.com/politics/supreme-court/justice-thomas-cites-debunked-claim-covid-vaccines-are-made-cells-abor-rcna36156.

679 Gonzalez, Oriana. "Clarence Thomas Says COVID Vaccines Are Created with Cells from 'Aborted Children.'" Axios, June 30, 2022, https://www.axios.com/2022/06/30/clarence-thomas-aborted-children-vaccine-covid?.

680 Hooper, Kelly. "Clarence Thomas cites claim that Covid vaccines are 'developed using cell lines derived from aborted children.'" Politico, June 30, 2022, https://www.politico.com/news/2022/06/30/clarence-thomas-covid-vaccines-dissent-00043483.

↻ **Glenn Kessler Retweeted**

POLITICO ✔ @politico · 18h   ···
Clarence Thomas claimed in a dissenting
opinion that Covid vaccines are derived from
the cells of "aborted children."

No Covid vaccines in the U.S. contain the
cells of aborted fetuses.

The fake story was also retweeted by short-lived Disinformation Governance Board head Nina Jankowicz, who was sharing a post from Cindy Otis, a self-proclaimed "disinformation expert." She seems to be taking her job title a bit too literally.

↻ Nina Jankowicz  Retweeted

Cindy Otis   ···
@CindyOtis_

When misinformation makes it into a SCOTUS judge's dissent.
twitter.com/politico/statu...

> This Tweet was deleted by the Tweet author. Learn more

2:39 PM · Jun 30, 2022 · Twitter Web App

Politico eventually added a correction to the article stating that "an earlier version of this report misattributed the claim that Covid-19 vaccines were 'developed using cell lines derived from aborted children' to Thomas. The headline and article have been updated to directly state that Thomas was referencing petitioners' claims." But there's no explanation for why that was so hard for them to figure out in the first place.

You'd think it's something a fact-checker would catch.

SNOPES SEMANTICS OVER TRUMP'S TAXES

Snopes' Bethania Palma rated "True" the claim that Donald Trump said that "not paying taxes 'makes [him] smart,'" even though he never said that.

"Donald Trump proclaimed during the first presidential debate of 2016 that not paying federal taxes made him 'smart,' then denied having said it" was Palma's verdict.[681]

Trump supposedly stating that not paying taxes makes him smart comes from the following exchange:

> **Clinton:** For 40 years, everyone running for president has released their tax returns. You can go and see nearly, I think, 39, 40 years of our tax returns, but everyone has done it. We know the IRS has made clear there is no prohibition on releasing [returns] when you're under audit.
>
> So you've got to ask yourself, why won't [Trump] release his tax returns? And I think there may be a couple of reasons. First, maybe he's not as rich as he says he is. Second, maybe he's not as charitable as he claims to be. Third, we don't know all of his business dealings, but we have been told through investigative reporting that he owes about $650 million to Wall Street and foreign banks.
>
> Or maybe he doesn't want the American people, all of you watching tonight, to know that he's paid nothing in federal taxes, because the only years that anybody's ever seen were a couple of years when he had to turn them over to state authorities when he was trying to get a casino license, and they showed he didn't pay any federal income tax.
>
> **Trump:** That makes me smart.

Palma also says Trump contradicted himself after the debate, quoting an exchange he had with CNN's Dana Bash.

---

681 Palma, Bethania. "Did Donald Trump Say Not Paying Taxes 'Makes Me Smart'?" Snopes, September 28, 2016, https://www.snopes.com/fact-check/trump-taxes-smart/.

Dana Bash: My question for you is, first of all, it sounds like you admitted that you hadn't paid federal taxes and that, that was smart. Is that what you meant to say?

Trump: No, I didn't say that at all. I mean if they say I didn't, I mean it doesn't matter. I will say this, I hate the way our government spends our taxes because they are wasting our money. They don't know what they're doing. They're running it so poorly. Whether it's spent in Iraq or wherever they're spending it, they are wasting our money. So I do hate the way our government spends our money.

Here Trump is clarifying that he wasn't saying he didn't pay any taxes. He was saying that even if he didn't, there would be nothing wrong with that. Palma instead frames it in her favor, writing, "Trump disclaimed that he said his paying no federal income taxes made him smart, quickly pivoting off the subject onto a complain about government spending."

To believe otherwise, Palma writes, would "require a good deal of semantic contorting."

She would know.

LONG-FORM FACT-CHECKS OF FACT-CHECKERS

Anumber of fact-checks of fact-checkers ended up taking the form of essays and became far too long to include in prior chapters that generally rebutted bad fact-checks in under a thousand words, so I saved the most in-depth for last.

The fact-checks of fact-checkers in this chapter are, in my opinion, the most significant, and pertaining to national news stories such as the origins of the COVID-19 pandemic, New York governor Andrew Cuomo's nursing home scandal, the Kyle Rittenhouse self-defense trial, and who is the greatest domestic terror threat in America, among other topics.

THE COVID LAB LEAK—FACT-CHECKERS GOT IT DEAD WRONG ON THE BIGGEST STORY OF 2020

The entirety of the fact-checkers and "disinformation experts" stood in unison against the now strongly argued case that the COVID-19 pandemic was due to the virus escaping from a lab in Wuhan, China, and not something that emerged out of a wet market.

Never afraid to trust a government at its word, PolitiFact produced eight fact-checks in early 2020 that used or relied on data from the World Health Organization for COVID-19 statistics and that were proven to be untrue because China had lied about their data.

Senator Tom Cotton was among the first to sound the alarm and cast doubt on the official narrative that the virus had resulted in a Wuhan wet market.

He wrote in an April 2020 *Wall Street Journal* op-ed, "Beijing has claimed that the virus originated in a Wuhan 'wet market,' where wild animals were sold. But evidence to counter this theory emerged in January. This evidence is circumstantial, to be sure, but it all points toward the Wuhan labs. Thanks to the Chinese coverup, we may never have direct, conclusive evidence—intelligence rarely works that way—but Americans justifiably can use common sense to follow the inherent logic of events to their likely conclusion."[682] That month Donald Trump also began publicly stating that he had evidence COVID-19 started in a lab.[683]

From the beginning of the COVID-19 outbreak, numerous "experts" drove the media narrative that COVID-19 emerged from a wet market in Wuhan, China via a bat or a pangolin. In mid-2021, the journal *Nature* put the final nail in the coffin of that theory when it published the results of an extensive survey of all Wuhan wet markets from May 2017 to November 2019. It documented 47,381 animals from 38 species and found that "no pangolin or bat species were among these animals for sale." The study's authors noted that "vendors freely disclosed a variety of protected species on sale illegally in their shops," and "so we are confident this list is complete."[684]

The early evidence for the lab leak theory included Wuhan having two labs where bats and humans are known to have interacted, one at the Institute of Virology and the other at the Wuhan Center for Disease Control and Prevention. The former is eight miles from a wet market, and the latter is three hundred yards from it. Furthermore, Cotton noted that both labs collect live animals to study viruses, and Chinese state media released a minidocumentary the December prior following around a team of Wuhan CDC researchers collecting viruses from bats in caves—while openly complaining about the risk of infection.

Cotton points out that, in 2018, even the *Washington Post* reported about U.S. diplomats in China expressing concerns about "a serious shortage of appropriately trained technicians and investigators needed to safely operate" the Wuhan Institute of Virology.

Cotton acknowledged that while the evidence was circumstantial, "it all points toward the Wuhan labs."

---

682   Cotton, Tom. "Cotton Op-Ed in the Wall Street Journal 'Coronavirus and the Laboratories in Wuhan.'" U.S. Senator Cotton of Arkansas, April 21, 2020, https://www.cotton.senate.gov/news/press-releases/-cotton-op-ed-in-the-wall-street-journal-and-145coronavirus-and-the-laboratories-in-wuhan-and-146.

683   Singh, Maanvi, et al. "Trump claims to have evidence coronavirus started in Chinese lab but offers no details." *The Guardian*, April 30, 2020, https://www.theguardian.com/us-news/2020/apr/30/donald-trump-coronavirus-chinese-lab-claim.

684   Xiao, Xiao, et al. "Animal sales from Wuhan wet markets immediately prior to the COVID-19 pandemic." *Scientific Reports* 11, 11898 (2021). https://doi.org/10.1038/s41598-021-91470-2.

And in response to this call for open inquiry, Cotton was immediately blasted as a conspiracy theorist in the media, and the fact-checkers joined in too.

On September 16, 2020, PolitiFact gave a "Pants on Fire" rating to what they called the "conspiracy theory" that COVID-19 may have resulted from humans tampering with it in a lab, matter-of-factly claiming that "the genetic structure of the novel coronavirus rules out laboratory manipulation. Public health authorities have repeatedly said the coronavirus was not derived from a lab."

That article has since been taken down and archived, and an editor's note has been added: "Editor's note, May 17, 2021: When this fact-check was first published in September 2020, PolitiFact's sources included researchers who asserted the SARS-CoV-2 virus could not have been manipulated. That assertion is now more widely disputed. For that reason, we are removing this fact-check from our database pending a more thorough review."[685] Still no word yet on how that thorough review panned out.

That update came just three days after the Poynter Institute's "festival of fact-checking," where at one point, PolitiFact's Katie Sanders asked Dr. Anthony Fauci if he was still confident that COVID-19 had developed naturally. He responded, to their surprise, "'No, I'm not convinced of that,' going on to say 'we' should continue to investigate all hypotheses about how the pandemic began."[686]

The tide on the lab leak theory had already been turning, and the support from St. Fauci was the green light that they were allowed to acknowledge that this issue isn't settled science.

Months prior, in February 2021, the World Health Organization (WHO) made a visit to China, and a number of members left with some doubts about the natural origin of the virus, despite a WHO report declaring the lab leak theory "extremely unlikely." As Matt Taibbi explained:

> From there came a procession of scientists demanding that the lab origin possibility be taken seriously, including a letter signed by 18 experts in Science. When the Wall Street Journal came out with a story that a previously undisclosed

685 "Archived Fact-Check: Tucker Carlson Guest Airs Debunked Conspiracy Theory That COVID-19 Was Created in a Lab." PolitiFact, May 17, 2021, https://www.politifact.com/li-meng-yan-fact-check/.
686 Taibbi, "'Fact-Checking' Takes Another Beating."

U.S. intelligence report detailed how three Wuhan researchers became sick enough to be hospitalized in November of
2019, the toothpaste was fully out of the tube: there was no
longer any way to say the "lab origin" hypothesis was too silly
to be reported upon.[687]

While we may unfortunately never know with 100 percent certainty
the origins of the COVID-19 pandemic, that it was a "lab leak" was made
the "conventional wisdom" by decree.

In October 2020, the progressive media watchdog Fairness & Accuracy in Reporting said that the "evidence-free" lab leak theory "boosts
Trump's xenophobic approach to coronavirus."[688] They later doubled
down as more saw the lab leak theory as plausible, in June 2021 claiming
that the media was giving more respect to the lab leak theory, but that
"there remains as little compelling evidence that the virus escaped from a
Chinese lab as there always has been."[689]

Over at Snopes, an article published in April 2020 aimed to address
the "rumor" and expose the so-called "falsehoods and scientific reali-
ties that undermine" the lab leak theory. "It is factual to state that the
Chinese government hid, downplayed, and misrepresented to its citizens
and the world the threat posed by the novel coronavirus. It is speculative,
however, to assert, as U.S. Sen. Tom Cotton did, that these actions were
done to cover up a leak from a lab," they wrote. [690] By June 2021, they
were calling for the lab leak theory to be formally investigated.[691]

The *Washington Post's* Glenn Kessler, in a tweet on May 1, 2020,
criticized Senator Ted Cruz for suggesting the lab leak theory could be
credible, calling it "virtually impossible" that the virus jumped from the

---

687   Ibid.

688   Cho, Joshua. "Evidence-Free 'Lab Leak' Speculation Boosts Trump's
      Xenophobic Approach to Coronavirus." Fairness & Accuracy in
      Reporting, October 6, 2020, https://fair.org/home/evidence-free-lab-leak-
      speculation-boosts-trumps-xenophobic-approach-to-coronavirus/.

689   Cho, Joshua. "US Media Give New Respect to Lab Leak Theory—Though Evidence Is as
      Lacking as Ever." Fairness & Accuracy in Reporting, June 28, 2021, https://fair.org/home/
      us-media-give-new-respect-to-lab-leak-theory-though-evidence-is-as-lacking-as-ever/.

690   Kasprak, Alex. "The Origins and Scientific Failings of the COVID-19 'Bioweapon'
      Conspiracy Theory." Snopes, April 1, 2020, https://www.snopes.com/news/2020/04/01/
      covid-19-bioweapon/.

691   The Conversation. "COVID-19: Why the Lab Leak Theory Should Be Formally
      Investigated." Snopes, June 2, 2021, https://www.snopes.com/news/2021/06/
      02/covid-19-why-the-lab-leak-theory-should-be-formally-investigated/.

lab.[692] On May 25, 2021, Kessler would be tweeting a link to his latest article, captioned, "How the Wuhan lab-leak theory suddenly became credible."[693]

Amazingly, Kessler blamed Trump for the lab leak theory not being taken seriously, claiming that "the Trump administration's messaging was often accompanied by anti-Chinese rhetoric that made it easier for skeptics to ignore its claims." Or, in other words, he's blaming Trump for the hysteria of his critics.

Senator Cruz took note of the change and took the opportunity to blast Kessler as a clown,[694] while former press secretary Sean Spicer chimed in, "What's missing from this timeline is when you carried the water for the Chinese government and dismissed anyone who dared to question them."[695]

In March 2020, Vox published an article to debunk the "conspiracy theories about the origins of the coronavirus," only to later add updates to their "debunking" to acknowledge that "since this piece was originally published in March 2020, scientific consensus has shifted."[696]

In some cases, the "fact-checker" themselves had a vested interest in denying the lab leak hypothesis.

Early on in the COVID pandemic, virologist Danielle Anderson was one of those commonly cited in attempts to refute the lab leak theory.[697] Her work for "Health Feedback" has been cited by other fact-checkers, including PolitiFact, to argue against the lab leak hypothesis.

In Summer 2021, she was heralded in the media as the "last and only foreign scientist in Wuhan." And as has become standard, all criticism of her work was characterized as "sexist" by the media, claims of which made their way into a *Nature Magazine* article that won a journalism award.

---

692   Kessler, Glenn. May 1, 2020, https://twitter.com/GlennKesslerWP/status/ 1256267931220049920.

693   Kessler, Glenn. May 25, 2021, https://twitter.com/GlennKesslerWP/status/ 1397166166590767111.

694   Cruz, Ted. May 25, 2021, https://twitter.com/tedcruz/status/1397180551589728260.

695   Spicer, Sean. May 25, 2021, https://twitter.com/seanspicer/status/ 1397183264150933511.

696   Barclay, Eliza. "The conspiracy theories about the origins of the coronavirus, debunked." Vox, March 12, 2020, https://www.vox.com/2020/3/4/21156607/ how-did-the-coronavirus-get-started-china-wuhan-lab#veNrKw.

697   Thacker, Paul D. "Funding Documents Expose Virologist Danielle Anderson, Once Feted as a 'Conspiracy Buster.'" The Disinformation Chronicle, September 20, 2022, https://disinformationchronicle.substack.com/p/funding-documents-expose-virologist.

Anderson's name has appeared on multiple grants for projects aiming to manipulate coronaviruses, including a National Institutes of Health award to EcoHealth Alliance's Peter Daszak, and another that was rejected by DARPA for risky gain of function research.

Not only were all the fact-checkers and handpicked "experts" wrong on a story that has implications for international relations, they were deputized by Big Tech to shut up anyone proving them wrong.

THE CUOMO COVERUP

As the disastrous consequences of then–New York governor Andrew Cuomo's policy that forced COVID-19 patients into nursing homes became a national scandal, the fraudulent fact-checkers came out of the woodwork to try to downplay it.

Almost overnight, Cuomo went from being heralded in the media as the nation's most competent governor in fighting the virus, to being exposed as the opposite, but the fact-checkers weren't going to let his former image die without a fight.

Appearing on CNN's ironically named *Reliable Sources* with Brian Stelter in February 2021, PolitiFact Editor in Chief Angie Drobnic Holan played defense for Governor Cuomo, arguing that the simple matter is "actually really complicated."

"Certainly, there are things to criticize about how the administration handled data, but the heart of the matter goes back to last year when the state was asking COVID patients who were ready to be discharged from the hospital, [and] we don't see hard evidence that that made a significant difference in COVID deaths,"[698] Holan said, without giving much wonder as to why exactly the Cuomo administration was so secretive with their nursing home data if there was nothing nefarious going on.

"If you look at the statistics, New York is about having the same numbers as other states around the country, and the issue was employees in the nursing homes who didn't realize they were bringing COVID-19 into the nursing homes so it's a really complicated situation," Holan said. "There's no clear-cut answers here." CNN "fact-checker" Daniel Dale can be seen on screen saying nothing as Holan spouted off these easily fact-checkable lies.

---

698   Halon, Yael. "CNN continues to give cover to disgraced Cuomo as guest claims lack of 'hard evidence' in nursing home scandal." Fox News, February 21, 2021, https://www.foxnews.com/media/cnn-cuomo-brian-stelter-politifact-nursing-home-coronavirus.

Simply summarizing the scandal is enough to rebut Holan.

At the center of Cuomo's litany of errors in 2020 was his now infamous "March 25 advisory" issued to nursing home administrators, directors of nursing, and hospital discharge planners.

The order put nursing homes in a position where they'd be forced to treat those infected with COVID-19. With that fact alone, one can immediately see how such a policy would cause mass death. While a sane individual would prioritize the safety of the elderly against a virus that disproportionately kills the elderly, logic was lost on the Cuomo administration.

The rules were simple: if a hospital determined that a patient who could be sent to a nursing home was stable, the home had no choice but to take them. The order states that (emphasis theirs): *"No resident shall be denied re-admission or admission to the nursing home solely based on a confirmed or suspected diagnosis of COVID-19. Nursing homes are prohibited from requiring a hospitalized resident who is determined medically stable to be tested for COVID-19 prior to admission or readmission."*

As many as 4,500 patients infected with the coronavirus were sent to nursing homes.

What could possibly go wrong? Everything.

As ProPublica noted in their report excoriating Cuomo's policy just two and a half months after it took effect:

> In the weeks that followed the March 25 order, COVID-19 tore through New York state's nursing facilities, killing more than 6,000 people—about 6% of its more than 100,000 nursing home residents.[699]

Meanwhile, the Republican county executive of Rensselaer County, Steven McLaughlin, rightly saw Cuomo's order as absurd and defied it. Van Rensselaer Manor was the only nursing home run by the county that saw a total of zero COVID-19 deaths over the same time period.[700]

States that issued orders similar to Cuomo's recorded comparably grim outcomes. Michigan lost 5 percent of roughly thirty-eight thou-

699   Sapien, Joaquin, and Joe Sexton. "'Fire Through Dry Grass': Andrew Cuomo Saw COVID-19's Threat to Nursing Homes. Then He Risked Adding to It." ProPublica, June 16, 2020, https://www.propublica.org/article/fire-through-dry-grass-andrew-cuomo-saw-covid-19-threat-to-nursing-homes-then-he-risked-adding-to-it.
700   Ibid.

sand nursing home residents to COVID-19 since the outbreak began. New Jersey lost 12 percent of its more than forty-three thousand residents. In Florida, where such transfers were barred, just 1.6 percent of seventy-three thousand nursing home residents died of the virus.[701] That contradicts Holan's claim that nursing home deaths were similar in every state. Policy did make a difference—and a major one.

As even noted by a PolitiFact writer less than three months after the advisory was issued:

> …Once the state issued its March 25 advisory, nursing home operators said that they felt they had no choice but to accept residents who were either known to be infected or suspected to be. That's because the March 25 memo did not say anything about making sure that a nursing home can care for a patient before making an admission decision, and said they "must comply with the expedited receipt of residents." In the month following the memo, nursing homes pleaded for relief from the order.[702]

Furthermore, as ProPublica notes in its analysis, "New York was *the only state in the nation that barred testing of those being placed or returning to nursing homes* [emphasis mine]."

It's for reasons like these that the Society for Post-Acute and Long-Term Care Medicine (AMDA) issued a statement on March 26 opposing the order because they found it to be "over-reaching, not consistent with science, unenforceable, and beyond all, not in the least consistent with patient safety principles." Those concerns were reiterated three days later in a joint statement by AMDA, American Health Care Association, and National Center for Assisted Living.[703]

701 Grabowski, David. "U.S. House of Representatives Ways and Means Health Subcommittee 'Examining the COVID-19 Nursing Home Crisis.'" Ways and Means, June 25, 2020, https://waysandmeans.house.gov/sites/democrats. waysandmeans.house.gov/files/documents/David%20Grabowski_Testimony.pdf.

702 Ramos, Jill. "New York's Nursing Home Policy Was Not Fully in Line with CDC." PolitiFact, June 13, 2020, https://www.politifact.com/factchecks/2020/ jun/13/andrew-cuomo/new-yorks-nursing-home-policy-was-not-line-cdc/.

703 American Health Care Association. "State Advisories re: Hospital Discharges and Admissions to Nursing Homes and Assisted Living Communities." PALTC, March 29, 2020, https://paltc.org/sites/default/files/AMDA-AHCA-NCAL%20Statement%20on%20State%20Advisories%20FINAL.pdf.

Holan's claim that it was nursing home staff that infected seniors, not the coronavirus patients they were forced to take, is straight out of the Cuomo playbook.

In July 2020, the New York Health Department released a report attempting to exonerate themselves where they spawned the talking point Holan is touting.[704] The problem with putting blame on nursing home workers rather than the infected patients they treated is ridiculous for two reasons. First, as already documented, nursing homes in New York were barred from testing those entering their facilities. Second, nurses themselves were tested when entering their workplaces. Staff could have only been responsible for getting others sick if they happened to receive false negatives on their daily testing. The Health Department (probably deliberately) got the correlation backward—that it was patients infecting staff, not vice versa.

Buried in a footnote in the Health Department report is that McKinsey & Company analyzed the data for the nursing home study. Previously, the Cuomo administration had relied on projections from McKinsey that New York would need 55,000–110,000 hospital beds and 25,000–37,000 ventilators.[705] Those projections, fortunately, turned out to be massively overstated—but, at the time, they were what led to the disastrous nursing home policy.

So not only did the New York Department of Health produce a study exonerating the New York Department of Health, but they were aided by McKinsey to analyze the data regarding the policies their shoddy projections spawned. Seldom does a study's conflict of interest itself have a conflict of interest.

In August 2020, PolitiFact's Michelle Andrews first tried to defend Cuomo, who rated "Mostly False" a statement from Michael Caputo that Governor Cuomo "forced nursing homes across NY to take in COVID positive patients and planted the seeds of infection that killed thousands of grandmothers and grandfathers?"[706]

---

704 "New York State Department of Health Issues Report on COVID-19 in Nursing Homes." New York State Department of Health, July 6, 2020, https://www.health. ny.gov/press/releases/2020/2020-07-06_covid19_nursing_home_report.htm.

705 Ross, Chuck. "Andrew Cuomo's Report on Nursing Home Deaths Marked By Clear Conflicts Of Interst." The Daily Caller, July 12, 2020, https://dailycaller.com/2020/ 07/12/andrew-cuomo-new-york-nursing-home-deaths-coronavirus-mckinsey/.

706 Andrews, Michelle. "Is Cuomo directive to blame for nursing home COVID deaths as HHS official claims?" PolitiFact, August 24, 2020, https://www.politifact.com/factchecks/ 2020/aug/24/michael-caputo/hhs-official-blames-cuomo-nursing-home-covid-death/.

Andrews rated the claim "Mostly False" on the basis that "it's unclear how many of the deaths the policy might have caused," and an expert is quoted saying that "based on the timeline of the policy and deaths in the city, it is very unlikely that policy contributed to thousands of deaths."

Andrews also decided to add something Caputo never said explicitly: "While the introduction of COVID-19 positive patients into nursing homes no doubt had an effect on infection spread, Caputo's statement suggests it was solely responsible. That's not what the evidence shows." In other words, Andrews looked for the one criticism of Cuomo's nursing home policy that she was able to interpret a caveat onto so she could rate the claim false (as this seems to be an interpretation of Caputo saying that Cuomo "planted the seeds of infection").

Two weeks before this fact-check was published, doubt had already been cast on the reliability of New York's nursing home death numbers. An Associated Press report noted that New York is the only state that only counts residents who died on nursing home property from the coronavirus and not those who were transported to hospitals and died there as nursing home deaths. In other states, nursing home resident deaths make up 44 percent of total coronavirus nursing home deaths, which would imply an additional eleven thousand nursing home deaths in New York if that percent holds constant.[707]

It wasn't until January 28, 2021, that New York AG Letitia James released a report on the nursing home coverup, which found that "nursing home resident deaths appear to be undercounted by DOH by approximately 50 percent."[708]

PolitiFact didn't bother to acknowledge this until February 16, 2021, but added that their "ruling of Mostly False is unchanged by this new information."

---

707   Condon, Bernard, et al. "New York's true nursing home death toll cloaked in secrecy." Associated Press. August 11, 2012, https://apnews.com/212ccd87924b6906053703a00514647f

708   https://ag.ny.gov/press-release/2021/attorney-general-james-releases-report-nursing-homes-response-covid-19.

THE RITTENHOUSE CASE: FACT-CHECKERS BRAZENLY BACK THE MEDIA NARRATIVE ON THE MOST BLATANTLY OBVIOUS SELF-DEFENSE CASE EVER

The trial of the year in 2021 was the trial of Kyle Rittenhouse, who, during the summer of the year prior, had shot in self-defense three far-left rioters who had assaulted him, two fatally.

This happened during a summer when rioters, in the name of social justice, destroyed and looted predominantly minority neighborhoods, causing a record $2 billion in damages (a figure estimated based on insurance payouts). And as Brad Polumbo, an economics writer with a questionably spelled surname, points out, that figure is a major underestimate because 40 percent of small businesses have no insurance at all, and of those who do, 75 percent are underinsured.[709]

There were also at least twenty-five people killed during the protests[710]—and the rioters had killed more unarmed black people in just the summer of 2020 than the police they were protesting did that entire year.[711]

Long before the trial, PolitiFact's Haley BeMiller decided to tackle Donald Trump's objectively true statement about a video of the shooting: "You saw the same tape as I saw. And he was trying to get away from them, I guess; it looks like. And he fell, and then they very violently attacked him. And it was something that we're looking at right now and it's under investigation." Trump added, "I guess [Rittenhouse] was in very big trouble. He would have been—I—he probably would have been killed."

Even before this was all proven in court, it was obvious to anyone who viewed the video of the assault that Trump's description was accurate. Yet discussion of the case, including any mention of the name Kyle Rittenhouse, was banned from Facebook. Even sharing a picture

709   Polumbo, Brad. "George Floyd Riots Caused Record-Setting $2 Billion in Damage, New Report Says. Here's Why the True Cost Is Even Higher." FEE, September 16, 2020, https://fee.org/articles/george-floyd-riots-caused-record-setting-2-billion-in-damage-new-report-says-here-s-why-the-true-cost-is-even-higher/.

710   Beckett, Lois. "At least 25 Americans were killed during protests and political unrest in 2020." *The Guardian*, October 31, 2020, https://www.theguardian.com/world/2020/oct/31/americans-killed-protests-political-unrest-acled.

711   "Police Shootings Database." *Washington Post*, https://www.washingtonpost.com/graphics/investigations/police-shootings-database/.

of Rittenhouse would automatically be flagged and taken down by Facebook's algorithm.[712] GoFundMe prevented Rittenhouse from fundraising for his defense, and the "fact-checkers" were there to enable the crackdown on the truth.

But according to BeMiller, Trump's accurate description of events isn't accurate because it doesn't have added context that she made up. She claims:

> The president [Trump] correctly describes some minor details about that night. But overall, his comments grossly mischaracterize what happened—leaving out that by the time of the events he described, prosecutors say Rittenhouse had already shot and killed a man.[713]

Rittenhouse shooting only after being attacked isn't exactly a "minor" detail here. And that he had been attacked by a mob after shooting someone else who had just attacked him doesn't provide the "context" she thinks it does. All this really proves is just how intent on causing harm to Rittenhouse they were, considering they didn't think twice about assaulting an armed man who had just shot someone else who attacked him.

It was proven in the trial that the first man Rittenhouse shot, Joseph Rosenbaum, a registered sex offender who had just been released from a mental institution, had threatened to murder Rittenhouse and was only shot after chasing him, cornering him, and grabbing his firearm. Video played in court proved that Rittenhouse retreated as much as he physically could before his gun was grabbed, in which case he shot and killed Rosenbaum.

It's also worth noting that as Rosenbaum had been chasing Rittenhouse, another member of the mob fired a gun into the air (which Rittenhouse could've easily mistaken as being at him), not exactly signaling that they were a friendly bunch. BeMiller makes no mention of this.

Rosenbaum was on video from hours later in the night, violently daring someone "shoot me n---a." When Rittenhouse's attorney quoted

712 Levine, Jon, and Eileen AJ Connelly. "Critic blasts 'dangerous' Facebook power after Kyle Rittenhouse verdict." *New York Post*, November 20, 2021, https://nypost.com/2021/11/20/critic-blasts-facebooks-power-after-kyle-rittenhouse-verdict/.

713 BeMiller, Haley. "Trump paints false picture of Kyle Rittenhouse shootings ahead of Kenosha visit." PolitiFact, September 1, 2020, https://www.politifact.com/factchecks/2020/sep/01/donald-trump/trump-paints-false-picture-kyle-rittenhouse-shooti/.

this in court, a number of hack publications presented the incident as "Rittenhouse attorney uses n-word in court" in their headlines[714]—a deliberately misleading narrative none of the fact-checkers saw fit to clarify.

Despite Rosenbaum threatening to murder Rittenhouse, beginning to chase him while someone else fired a gun, cornering him, and then grabbing his weapon, BeMiller described the encounter as follows:

> Joseph Rosenbaum, 36, approached Rittenhouse and a reporter interviewing him that night and began to chase Rittenhouse after he did a "juke" move. Rosenbaum threw a plastic bag at Rittenhouse, but it didn't hit him.
>
> The two ended up in a parking lot, and the reporter told authorities that Rosenbaum tried to grab Rittenhouse's gun. Rittenhouse fired four shots, and Rosenbaum dropped to the ground in front of him.

If that's not the deliberate creation of a bogus narrative, what is? Rosenbaum didn't "try" to grab Rittenhouse's gun—he grabbed it. Yet BeMiller tries to present the situation as if Rosenbaum's only weapon was a plastic bag.

After Rosenbaum was shot and killed, Rittenhouse fled and was attacked by a large mob that knocked him over, forcing him to defend himself while he was on the ground.

BeMiller describes the second shooting incident with a similarly fictitious account of events, claiming:

> Rittenhouse began running slowly down the street as a crowd began to follow him, with some people shouting "get him!" and shouting he just shot someone. Rittenhouse tripped and fell.

A mob chasing Rittenhouse while yelling, "Get his ass!" is described as a "crowd [beginning] to follow him," and him falling after being hit by rioters while running for his life is described as him "tripping."

BeMiller adds that:

---

714   For example: Collman, Ashley. "Kyle Rittenhouse: Defense Attorney Repeats N-Word in Opening Statement." Insider, November 2, 2021, https://www. insider.com/kyle-rittenhouse-trial-opening-statements-2021-11.

> While he [Rittenhouse] was on the ground, police say, he appeared to fire two shots at a man who jumped over him but missed.

The man who "jumped over him" became known as "jumpkick man" during the trial because his identity was unknown, and video shows him kicking Rittenhouse, not "jumping over him." The man was later revealed to be Maurice Freeland, a career criminal with an open domestic violence charge for "throwing his girlfriend to the ground and attacking her." (Or as BeMiller might describe it: she tripped, and he jumped over her).

BeMiller then describes the final shootings as follows:

> After that, Anthony Huber, 26, ran up to Rittenhouse with a skateboard in one hand and appeared to hit him with it before reaching for Rittenhouse's gun. Rittenhouse fired one round that hit Huber in the chest and killed him.

> Rittenhouse sat up and pointed his gun at Gaige Grosskreutz, 26, who had started to approach him. Grosskreutz took a step back and put his hands in the air, but then moved toward Rittenhouse, who fired a shot that hit Grosskreutz in the arm.

> Grosskreutz had a handgun. It is unclear whether Grosskreutz was pointing the gun at Rittenhouse, or if Rittenhouse saw that Grosskreutz had a gun.

Huber, a repeat domestic abuser that has assaulted members of his own family and once threatened to "gut his brother like a pig" and burn down their home, did not "appear" to hit Rittenhouse with a skateboard; he beat him with it; and he did not "reach" for Rittenhouse's gun; he grabbed it.

Grosskreutz putting his hands in the air was a fake-out, and he immediately pointed his gun at Rittenhouse seconds later. By Grosskreutz's own admission during the trial, he wasn't shot until after he pointed his gun at Rittenhouse:

Rittenhouse Attorney Corey Chirafisi: When you were standing 3 to 5 feet from him with your arms up in the air, he never fired, right?

Grosskreutz: Correct.

Chirafisi: It wasn't until you pointed your gun at him, advanced on him, with your gun, now your hands down pointed at him, that he fired, right?

Grosskreutz: Correct.[715]

While Grosskreutz was in the hospital following the shooting, his former roommate and friend Jacob Marshall posted to Facebook, "I just talked to Gaige Grosskreutz. His only regret was not killing the kid [Rittenhouse] and hesitating to pull the gun before emptying the entire mag into him." To avoid incriminating his friend, during the trial, Marshall walked this back on the stand and said he was lying and that his story was "one hundred percent made up."[716]

After her entire narrative was officially destroyed in court a year later and Rittenhouse was acquitted, BeMiller added the following "disclaimer" to her post: "Editor's note: This item was updated to make clear that we are rating whether Trump described what happened accurately, not the separate question of whether what happened amounted to self-defense or, as charged by local prosecutors, homicide and other offenses."

But her entire fact-check was trying to portray Rittenhouse as a murderer who was only accosted by a mob because of that—which is a false narrative. Why she thinks this note changes anything about her delusional work remains a mystery.

Further proof that her fact-check is nothing more than political activism is how she characterizes the police shooting of Jacob Blake that set off the rioting in Kenosha, Wisconsin, that Rittenhouse was present to protect against:

> Jacob Blake, 29, was shot in the back seven times at close range by Officer Rusten Sheskey on Aug. 23, 2020 as he walked away from officers and tried to get into an SUV with

---

715 Associated Press. "Shooting victim says he was pointing his gun at Rittenhouse." Politico, November 8, 2021, https://www.politico.com /news/2021/11/08/shooting-victim-kyle-rittenhouse-520336.

716 Keller, Aaron. "'I Lied' on Social Media: Former Roommate Says Gaige Grosskreutz Never Said His 'Only Regret Was Not Killing' Kyle Rittenhouse." Law & Crime, November 10, 2021, https://lawandcrime.com/live-trials/live-trials-current/kyle-rittenhouse/i-lied-on-social-media-former-roommate-says-gaige-grosskreutz-never-said-his-only-regret-was-not-killing-kyle-rittenhouse/.

three of his children inside. The shooting left him paralyzed from the waist down, according to his family.

Compare that to how else this could be framed: Blake, who had an open warrant for felony sexual assault, "tried to get into an SUV" to grab a knife while resisting arrest. The reason the police were there is that he showed up at the home of his alleged victim.

While this information wasn't available at the time, the DOJ later declined to seek charges against the officer who fired the shots despite this occurring during the post–George Floyd Black Lives Matter hysteria of 2020, and none of the officers involved in the incident were charged.

Blake sued the officer who shot him in the back but ended up dropping the lawsuit. Nothing in the case mentioned a settlement.

PolitiFact Legal Team Derailed by Actual Jurist

The PolitiFact legal team would be served well by employing an actual lawyer or two.

Over a year before Kyle Rittenhouse went to trial, Daniel Funke rated as "False" a claim that "at 17 years old Kyle (Rittenhouse) was perfectly legal to be able to possess that rifle without parental supervision."[717]

The armchair legal analyst claimed that "the Wisconsin Department of Justice honors concealed carry permits issued in Illinois. But Rittenhouse did not have a permit to begin with, and he was not legally old enough to carry a firearm in Wisconsin."

Rittenhouse was charged by prosecutors with a misdemeanor count of possession of a dangerous weapon under the age of eighteen.

Unlike the fact-checkers, I don't pretend to be a lawyer, but I can quote the trial's Judge Bruce Schroeder, who is also the longest currently serving judge in the state of Wisconsin.[718]

Judge Schroeder said he "spent hours" reviewing the Wisconsin gun law and couldn't state with certainty what it meant for Rittenhouse's par-

---

717 Funke, Daniel. "'Perfectly legal' for Rittenhouse to carry a gun? False."
      PolitiFact, August 28, 2020, https://www.politifact.com/factchecks/2020/aug/
      28/facebook-posts/did-kyle-rittenhouse-break-law-carrying-assault-st/.

718 Woodfield, Greg. "Rittenhouse judge - who was put on the bench in 1983 by a
      Democratic governor - brings down gavel on trial after being slammed as a racist
      and weathering a torrent of abusive and menacing messages." *Daily Mail*, November
      21, 2021, https://www.dailymail.co.uk/news/article-10222903/Rittenhouse-judge-
      Bruce-Schroeder-bench-1983-Democratic-governor-brings-gavel-trial.html.

ticular case. "I have been wrestling with this statute with, I'd hate to count the hours I've put into it, I'm still trying to figure out what it says, what's prohibited. I have a legal education," he said, adding that he failed to understand how an "ordinary citizen" could understand what is illegal.[719] The charge was tossed after prosecutors conceded that Rittenhouse's rifle wasn't short-barreled, and there's a carveout in the law that allows minors to possess shotguns and rifles as long as they're not short-barreled.

Despite the fact that Judge Schroeder faced numerous allegations of bias from liberal pundits during the trial, which included allegations that he's a right-winger because his cell phone ringtone was "Proud to be an American,"[720] he's a registered Democrat who was appointed by a Democrat governor in 1983 and has run for office as a Democrat in the past for Kenosha DA (in 1972 and 1973) and for the Wisconsin Senate (in 1975).[721]

In response to the legal system disagreeing with the analysis of the non-lawyer Funke, he doubled down, adding the following editor's note defiantly stating that his "False" rating would remain unchanged: "Judge Bruce Schroeder recently dismissed a misdemeanor charge of possession of a dangerous weapon by a person under 18 against Kyle Rittenhouse. Readers asked us if this made the fact-check below invalid. We don't think so. Here's why."

In the form of an editor's note longer than Funke's original article, PolitiFact desperately tries to explain why they're not wrong, concluding, "These subsequent events show the grey areas of local gun laws—hardly a case of something being 'perfectly legal.' Our fact-check remains unchanged."

Before this botched fact-check, Funke was behind another notably embarrassing fact-check months prior when he attempted to fact-check Biden being captured on video checking his watch during the dignified transfer ceremony for the thirteen U.S. troops Americans killed in the Kabul terror attack during the Afghanistan withdrawal.

---

719 Turley, Jonathan. "Judge questions Rittenhouse gun charge, raising doubts about prosecution's case." Fox News, November 14, 2021, https://www.foxnews.com/opinion/judge-questions-rittenhouse-gun-charge-jonathan-turley.

720 College Fix Staff. "'Outrageous' that judge's ringtone is 'Proud to be an American,' Temple professor says." The College Fix, November 15, 2021, https://www.thecollegefix.com/outrageous-that-judges-ringtone-is-proud-to-be-an-american-temple-professor-says/.

721 "Bruce Schroeder." Wikipedia, https://en.wikipedia.org/w/index.php?title=Bruce_Schroeder&oldid=1102442199.

Funke claimed, wrongly, that Biden had only checked his watch once, and it was after the ceremony.[722]

Two Gold Star fathers, Darin Hoover and Mark Schmitz, who were eyewitnesses at the event, went on the record stating that they saw Biden repeatedly checking his watch during the ceremony, which one of them described as "the most disrespectful thing" he has "ever seen." According to them, it didn't just happen once, but thirteen times overall.[723]

A third Gold Star parent, Shana Chappell, wrote in a Facebook post: "I watched you [Biden] disrespect us all 5 different times by checking your watch!!! What the f*ck was so important that you had to keep looking at your watch????"[724]

Eventually, Funke changed his ruling from "partly false" to "missing context," because he knew he had to issue some sort of correction but was too embarrassed to admit he was 100 percent wrong.

Snopes had similarly poor judgment, initially rating the claim a "mixture" on the basis that there is "no video or photographic evidence to support the claim that Biden checked his watch 13 times during this ceremony." They later revised their rating of the claim to "True."[725]

DUELING TERROR NARRATIVES

To further the bogus narrative that right-wing extremism is the greatest domestic threat facing America, PolitiFact's Amy Sherman examined President Joe Biden's claim that his "own FBI director said that the greatest domestic terrorist threat is white supremacists," which she rated "True."[726]

---

722 Funke, Daniel. "Fact check: Biden honored service members killed in Kabul, checked watch during ceremony." *USA Today*, September 3, 2021, https://www.usatoday.com/story/news/factcheck/2021/09/01/fact-check-biden-checked-watch-after-ceremony-dover-air-force-base/5663427001/.

723 Creitz, Charles. "Fathers of Marines killed in Kabul blast rip Biden: 'He talked more about his son than my son.'" Fox News, August 30, 2021, https://www.foxnews.com/media/gold-star-fathers-marines-killed-kabul-biden.

724 McBride, Jessica. "Shana Chappell: Mother of Slain Marine Kareem Nikoui Slams Biden." Heavy, September 7, 2021, https://heavy.com/news/shana-chappell/.

725 Evon, Dan. "Did Biden Check Watch Multiple Times During Transfer of Fallen Soldiers?" Snopes, September 3, 2021, https://www.snopes.com/fact-check/biden-check-watch-13/.

726 Sherman, Amy. "FBI director warned about white supremacist violence." PolitiFact, October 6, 2020, https://www.politifact.com/factchecks/2020/oct/06/joe-biden/fbi-director-warned-about-white-supremacist-violen/.

The context of the remark, from FBI head Chris Wray, was at a hearing where he testified about the FBI's investigation of terrorism threats. He said that the FBI has roughly one thousand domestic terrorism investigations per year and that they include:

> Everything from racially-motivated violent extremists to violent anarchist extremists, militia types, sovereign citizens, you name it. Of the domestic terrorism threats, we last year elevated racially-motivated violent extremism to be a national threat priority commensurate with a homegrown violent extremists. That's the jihadist-inspired people here and with ISIS.

When asked by Democratic Representative Elissa Slotkin how many of these cases or arrests involve white supremacists, he replied:

> What I can tell you is that, within the domestic terrorism bucket category as a whole, racially-motivated violent extremism is, I think, the biggest bucket within that larger group, and within the racially-motivated violent extremists bucket, people subscribing to some kind of white supremacist-type ideology is certainly the biggest chunk of that.

She followed up by asking, "So the white supremacists are the largest chunk of the racially-motivated domestic terrorists?" to which Wray replied, "Yes."

Sherman rates Biden's statement claim as "True." But with the quotes Sherman provided, it's evident Chris Wray didn't even say what Biden claims he said.

Wray did not say that the greatest domestic terror threat is white supremacists—he said that *of racially motivated domestic terrorists*, the largest chunk are white supremacists. He's talking about a subset of domestic terrorism (racially motivated incidents), not the entirety of it (though Wray's said he "thinks" that racially motivated violent extremism is the "biggest bucket" within the largest group).

While too small a sample to extrapolate from, the FBI's top ten most wanted terror list is composed of two members of the May 19th Communist Organization, two far-left black nationalists, an eco-terrorist, a white member of the Black Panthers, and the leftist who allegedly participated in the 1970 bombing of the University of Wisconsin to protest the Vietnam war. Only three men on the list didn't have a political motive for their alleged crimes, and they were all accused of different hijacking incidents.[727]

As if the bar for what's classified as right-ring extremism couldn't be lower, a whistleblower told Representative Jim Jordan that FBI "agents are not finding enough domestic violent extremist [DVE] cases" and "are encouraged and incentivized to reclassify cases as DVE cases even though there is minimal, circumstantial evidence to support the reclassification." Another whistleblower said that FBI officials "have pressured agents to move cases into the DVE category to hit self-created performance metrics" that are used for promotions.[728]

As for the rest of her case, Sherman reached out to Michael Jensen, an investigator at the National Consortium for the Study of Terrorism and Response to Terrorism, who pointed her to a September 4th article by Politico about a draft report at the DHS that identified white supremacists as the greatest terror threat to the United States. The final report would end up concluding that "racially and ethnically motivated violent extremists—specifically white supremacist extremists—will remain the most persistent and lethal threat in the Homeland."

She also cited the following evidence, claiming that:

– Data sets maintained by think tanks and university researchers match the federal government's warnings about white supremacy. START's Global Terrorism Database shows that from 2015 to 2019, white supremacists were responsible for more attacks in the U.S. than other types of extremists.

– A separate study of terrorist incidents by the Center for Strategic and International Security in June 2020 found "the most significant threat likely comes from white supremacists, though anarchists and religious extremists inspired by the Islamic State and al-Qaeda could present a potential threat as well."

---

727 Rosiak, Luke. "Leftists Dominate FBI Top 10 Domestic Terror List, Despite Warnings About Far Right." The Daily Wire, August 4, 2022, https://www.dailywire.com/news/leftists-dominate-fbi-top-10-domestic-terror-list-despite-warnings-about-far-right.

728 Hajicek, Olivia. "Jordan: FBI Exaggerates Domestic Violent Extremism Cases To Bolster Biden's 'Greatest Threat' Narrative." The Federalist, July 28, 2022, https://thefederalist.com/2022/07/28/jordan-fbi-exaggerates-domestic-violent-extremism-cases-to-bolster-bidens-greatest-threat-narrative/.

Each of these studies and their flaws is worth going through individually.

- The DHS Study: This study was only measuring terrorist attacks from the year 2018–2019. It found that over that time period, violent extremists perpetrated sixteen attacks, and forty-eight people were killed. Half were committed by "white supremacist extremists" and accounted for a majority of the deaths (thirty-nine).[729] More than half (twenty-three) of these are attributable to a single killer, the perpetrator of the 2019 El Paso shooting.

- The START Global Terrorism Database: The time frame here measured is 2015–2019, and while it's at least longer than the prior study, it still isn't much. This study found that of 310 terrorist attacks over that time period, thirty-four (11 percent) were committed by white supremacists, who accounted for sixty-four (20 percent) deaths. Sherman completely ignores the data that contradicts her point—that jihadist attacks killed eighty-six over the same time period.[730]

- The Center for Strategic and International Security: This study examines from 1994 to 2020, correctly notes that Islamists are responsible for the greatest number of fatalities because of 9/11, and then tries to downplay that because it harms their conclusion that white supremacists are a greater threat.[731]

How a "white supremacist" attack is defined isn't as straightforward as you'd think, and these studies don't give us much of a breakdown of what these white supremacist attacks they reference entailed.

A 2017 Government Accountability Office (GAO) study titled "Countering Violent Extremism" has been used by members of Congress

729 "Homeland Threat Assessment." Department of Homeland Security, October 2020, https://www.dhs.gov/sites/default/files/publications/2020_10_06_homeland-threat-assessment.pdf.

730 "Global Terrorism Overview: Terrorism in 2019." National Consortium for the Study of Terrorism and Responses to Terrorism, July 2020, https://www.start.umd.edu/pubs/START_GTD_GlobalTerrorismOverview2019_July2020.pdf.

731 Jones, Seth G., et al. "The Escalating Terrorism Problem in the United States." Center for Strategic & International Studies, June 17, 2020, https://www.csis.org/analysis/escalating-terrorism-problem-united-states.

to bolster the same thesis. Cory Booker cited the study when telling CNN in 2018 that "in American history since 9/11, we've had 85 major attacks in our country, 73 percent of them have been by white nationalist hate groups." In what is the most convenient timeline possible for researchers looking to downplay Islamic extremism, the GAO report begins measuring terrorist incidents as of September 12, 2001.

The fact-less fact-checkers over at PolitiFact rated Booker's claim as "Half True" but supported his underlying premise. Their "Half True" rating was based on Booker claiming 73 percent were "white nationalist" attacks, while the study Booker was relying on was documenting "far right-wing violent extremist groups."[732] The real problem with Booker's statement wasn't him using the term "white nationalist" synonymously with "far-right," but that the GAO study's definition is loose enough on what constitutes a right-wing terrorist attack as to be meaningless.

For example, one of the right-wing terrorist attacks is described as: "White Supremacist member of Aryan Brotherhood killed a man." That's it. No detail as to the motive, the race of the victim, or anything else. Since when does a murder become a terrorist incident just because the murderer also happens to be a bigot? A hate crime, perhaps, but not a terror attack. That same white supremacist killed someone else in later weeks and is counted as a separate "terrorist attack" in the study.

Another right-wing terror attack is described as: "Far rightist murdered a homeless man" with no additional information given as to how this is a terrorist attack. Another example given is described as "White supremacist [who] shot and killed 9 at his community college." That attack referenced was the 2015 Umpqua Community College shooting, carried out by a self-described "mixed race" individual who singled out Christians for his attack. Does that sound like a right-wing terrorist attack to you?

Elsewhere, the study described a "right-wing terrorist attack" involving "six white supremacist inmates beat[ing] another prisoner to death." So rare are far-right attacks that the GAO had to go behind prison walls to find examples.

The GAO is playing a game of "use your own terrorism definition." Nearly every single right-wing terrorist attack on the list are individual

732   Sherman, Amy. "Fact-checking Cory Booker's statistic on attacks by white nationalist hate groups." PolitiFact, January 18, 2018, https://www.politifact.com/factchecks/2018/jan/18/cory-booker/fact-checking-cory-bookers-statistic-attacks-white/.

murders that, at best, could accurately be described as hate crimes, but we aren't provided enough context to make that determination.

Another problem in the study is that they're counting these poorly categorized attacks based on their frequency for the "73 percent" figure, not death toll.

While there were sixty-two instances of right-wing terror in the GAO study, they resulted in "only" 106 deaths. That's a death toll racked up in mere seconds on September 11th. When one Islamic terror attack can result in over thirty times the deaths of an inflated estimate of right-wing terror deaths, who in their right mind would think the right wing is more dangerous?

Meanwhile, the GAO's documented cases of Islamic extremism have only twenty-three incidents but a comparably higher 119 deaths. As already mentioned, they conveniently began their timeline post-9/11. By their logic, Islamic terrorism isn't such a threat if you just happen to ignore the worst Islamic terrorist attack on U.S. soil.

In total, I could only find seven incidents that could accurately be described as right-wing terror incidents, resulting in twenty-two victims dead (excluding perpetrators). They are:

- An anti-government violent extremist flew a small plane into an Austin, TX office building with an IRS office in it to protest the IRS and the government. One dead—only the perpetrator.

- A neo-Nazi killed six at a Sikh temple in Wisconsin, 8/5/2012, Oak Creek, Wisconsin. Six dead.

- An anti-government extremist killed a Transportation Security Administration officer at Los Angeles International Airport, 11/1/2013, Los Angeles, California. One dead.

- A white supremacist shot and killed two at a Jewish Community Center, 4/13/2014, Overland Park, Kansas. Two dead.

- The same perpetrator as the previous attack in Overland Park murdered another person at a Jewish retirement center later the same day, 4/13/2014, Leawood, Kansas. One dead.

- White supremacist Dylann Roof shot and killed nine African Americans in a shooting at an African American church, 6/17/2015, Charleston, South Carolina. Nine dead.

- An anti-government survivalist extremist killed three at a Planned Parenthood clinic, including a responding police officer, 11/27/2015, Colorado Springs, Colorado. Three dead.

If we're to apply these revised figures, that would mean seven right-wing terror incidents compared to twenty-three Islamic terror incidents. Not only is the former much rarer, but also, when such terror attacks do occur, the death toll is far less. Even a single Islamic terror incident, such as the 2009 Fort Hood shooting or the 2015 San Bernardino massacre, racked up death tolls of more than half of all right-wing terror incidents combined. Most importantly, however, it proves that three-quarters of terror attacks are Islamic, not the reverse, as Booker claimed.

And any comparison between "white supremacist" violence and "Islamic extremism" needs to be viewed in the light of the fact that nearly 60 percent of Americans are white, while fewer than 1 percent are Muslim. And despite that, the figures aren't in the favor of the left's narrative, even in nominal terms.

THE FACT-CHECKERS TRY TO REWRITE GEORGE SOROS' SORDID HISTORY

The fact-checkers came to the defense of liberal mega-billionaire George Soros, who the media gleefully brands all criticism of as anti-Semitic. Naturally, video of Soros openly discussing his role in aiding the Nazis in Nazi-occupied Hungary as a child makes it much more difficult to brand any criticism of the man as "anti-Semitic," so the fact-checkers have stepped in to deny what Soros himself said.

While most of this book has followed the format of summarizing a fact-checker's claim before responding to it, on this particular issue, I think it's better to give the background information before showing how the fact-checkers falsely presented objective facts.

Soros was born in Budapest in 1930, and the Nazi occupation of Hungary began in March 1944. In the spring of 1944, the Nazis ordered the creation of a Central Council of Hungarian Jews, which was tasked with communicating the wishes of the Nazis and local collaborating authorities to the Jewish community, which Soros briefly participated in before assuming a new identity.[733]

Soros recalled the experience in an interview with the *New Yorker*: "This was a profoundly important experience for me. My father said, 'You should go ahead and deliver [the summonses], but tell the people that if they report they will be deported.' The reply from one man was 'I am a law-abiding citizen. They can't do anything to me.' I told my father, and that was an occasion for a lecture that there are times when you have laws that are immoral, and if you obey them you perish."[734]

George's father, Tivadar, recalled that after George's second day on the job, he returned home with a summons, to which Tivadar asked if George knew what it meant. George replied, "I can guess. They'll be interned." Tivadar then told him the Jewish Council has no right to give people orders like that, recalling in his memoir *Masquerade: The Incredible True Story of How George Soros' Father Outsmarted the Gestapo*:

> "I tried to tell the people I called on not to obey" he [George] said, clearly disappointed that I wouldn't let him work anymore. He was beginning to enjoy his career as a courier: it was all a big adventure.[735]

Soros' biographer echoed similar sentiments, noting that "George had liked the excitement of being a courier but he obeyed his father without complaint." Soros would later cite this experience as a reason for disliking fellow Jews for being collaborators while exempting himself.[736]

During the Nazi occupation, Soros' father, Tivadar, obtained papers giving his immediate family Christian identities. He decided to split up the family so that if one of them was outed as Jewish, the rest of the family had a chance of surviving.

---

733   Note: All of the information here is largely excerpted from pages 2–4 of my book *The Man Behind the Curtain: Inside the Secret Network of George Soros*. However, I have included the original footnotes from the book in lieu of citing my own book to make the information easier to locate and validate.

734   Mead, Rebecca. "A Soros Survivor's Guide." *New Yorker*, October 7, 2001, https://www.newyorker.com/magazine/2001/10/15/a-soros-survivors-guide.

735   Soros, Tividar. *Masquerade: The Incredible True Story of How George Soros' Father Outsmarted the Gestapo*. New York: Arcade Books, 2011, 12–13.

736   Horowitz, David, and Richard Poe. *Shadow Party: How George Soros, Hillary Clinton, and Sixties Radicals Seized Control of the Democratic Party*. Thomas Nelson Incorporated, 2007, 79.

After the family was split up for their own safety, Soros went to live as Sandor Kiss with a man named Baumbach, as arranged by his father. Baumbach was a friend of Tivadar, an official at the ministry of agriculture, and a Nazi collaborator. Baumbach played the role of Soros' godfather. Soros would never acknowledge the role that Baumbach played in likely saving his life, and he died anonymously in 1999. His identity was later revealed in 2018 as Miklós Prohászka.[737]

The "godfather" had the job of taking inventory of possessions seized from Jewish families—trips that Soros accompanied him on. It's this that Soros was asked about during the aforementioned interview with *60 Minutes*, when host Steve Kroft asked, "My understanding is that you went…went out, in fact, and helped in the confiscation of property from the Jews."[738]

"I mean, that's—that sounds like an experience that would send lots of people to the psychiatric couch for many, many years. Was it difficult?" Kroft continued.

"Not, not at all. Not at all. Maybe as a child you don't…you don't see the connection. But it was—it created no—no problem at all," Soros said emotionlessly.

"No feeling of guilt," Kroft replied.

"No," Soros replied.

When asked how he couldn't sympathize with other Jews being persecuted, Soros sociopathically replied by noting the "humor" in how his behavior then is similar to his behavior in finance and then employed the old "just following orders" defense.

"Well, of course…I could be on the other side or I could be the one from whom the thing is being taken away. But there was no sense that I shouldn't be there, because that was—well, actually, in a funny way, it's just like in the markets—that if I weren't there—of course, I wasn't doing it, but somebody else would—would—would be taking it away anyhow. And it was the—whether I was there or not, I was only a spectator, the property was being taken away. So the—I had no role in taking away that property. So I had no sense of guilt."

737   Simons, Jake Wallace. "Revealed: The Hungarian 'Schindler' who saved George Soros from Nazi Death squads during the occupation by hiding him behind a cupboard." *Daily Mail*, November 26, 2018, https://www.dailymail.co.uk/news/article-6415189/Revealed-Hungarian-Schindler-hid-George-Soros-Gestapo-death-squads.html.

738   "Charlton Heston/50,000 White Farmers/George Soros." *60 Minutes*, December 20, 1998.

And despite the overwhelming evidence here, the fact-checkers argue that Soros was simply taken out of context. Without exception, the fact-checkers spend all their time arguing about interpreting the *60 Minutes* interview while ignoring all the other historical evidence, including from Soros' own father. Other fact-checkers chose to argue against the exaggerated claim that the interview proves that Soros himself was a Nazi.

Reuters opted for the latter tactic, explaining that Soros was simply a "spectator" who felt no guilt over being one—as if aiding and abetting the Nazis is much better.[739]

Vox framed the *60 Minutes* interview as "Soros discussing his experiences living with that Hungarian official—including allegations of confiscating the property of Jews who had already been forced out of their homes." Here, Soros admitting his behavior is framed as "allegations of confiscating property," and any reader who doesn't watch the interview is left with the false impression that Soros was talking about someone else. *Vox* also defends Soros by stating that he was "only a spectator," which is immediately followed by the hilarious sentence, "…though he does say initially that he did help but seems confused by the question."[740]

The *Washington Post*'s Emily Tamkin, who penned a biography of Soros that few people have read, falsely framed the interview as Kroft having asked Soros if he felt survivor's guilt as a survivor of the Holocaust.[741]

PolitiFact ignored the *60 Minutes* interview entirely and decided to debunk some random Facebook post that alleged that Soros was a "Nazi soldier."[742]

Snopes also decided to fact-check an exaggerated claim that Soros was "an SS Officer or Nazi Collaborator During World War II," which

---

739   Reuters Staff. "Fact check: False claims about George Soros." Reuters, September 29, 2020, https://www.reuters.com/article/uk-factcheck-false-george-soros-claims/fact-checkfalseclaims-about-george-soros-idUSKBN23P2XJ.

740   Coaston, Jane. "George Soros is not a Nazi, explained." Vox, July 11, 2018, https://www.vox.com/2018/6/11/17405784/george-soros-not-a-nazi-trump.

741   Tamkin, Emily. "Five myths about George Soros." *Washington Post*, August 6, 2020, https://web.archive.org/web/20210210160614/https://www.washingtonpost.com/outlook/five-myths/five-myths-about-george-soros/2020/08/06/ad195582-d1e9-11ea-8d32-1ebf4e9d8e0d_story.html.

742   McCarthy, Bill. "No, George Soros wasn't a Nazi soldier." PolitiFact, February 10, 2020, https://www.politifact.com/factchecks/2020/feb/10/facebook-posts/no-george-soros-wasnt-nazi-soldier/.

they rated false because they don't think what he did qualifies as being that of a collaborator.[743]

They acknowledge a passage in Tivadar's book where he talks about George Soros' experience with "godfather" Baumbach, who he mistakenly calls "Baofluss." Tivadar wrote, "During the week George passed his time alone in Baufluss' apartment.... The following week the kindhearted Baufluss, in an effort to cheer the unhappy lad up, took him off with him to the provinces. At the time he was working in Transdanubia, west of Budapest, on the model estate of a Jewish aristocrat, Baron Moric Kornfeld. There they were wined and dined by what was left of the staff. George also met several other ministry officials, who immediately took a liking to the young man, the alleged godson of Mr Baufluss. *He even helped with the inventory.*"[744] Snopes says this doesn't make George Soros a "collaborator" because it occurred on only one occasion that there's a record of.

It's ironic that this comes against a backdrop where the threshold to brand anyone on the political right a "Nazi" is a single policy disagreement. The media has branded making the "OK" symbol with your hand a "Nazi" symbol yet draws the line when you call someone who aided and abetted the Nazis a Nazi.

THE "FACT-CHECKERS" GOT IT DEAD WRONG ON HUNTER BIDEN AND CHINA

Among the many Hunter Biden-related stories that the fact-checkers got wrong was one that had to do with his business dealings in China.

While they were happy to ignore his escapades when they could've influenced a presidential election, NBC News apparently decided the year 2022 was a perfect time to actually look at the hard drive from Hunter's laptop and made a startling discovery:

> From 2013 through 2018 Hunter Biden and his company brought in about $11 million via his roles as an attorney and a board member with a Ukrainian firm accused of bribery and his work with a Chinese businessman now accused of

---

743   Emery, David. "Was George Soros a SS Officer or Nazi Collaborator During World War II?" Snopes, September 19, 2017, https://www. snopes.com/fact-check/george-soros-ss-nazi-germany/.

744   Soros, *Masquerade*, 71.

fraud, according to an NBC News analysis of a copy of Biden's hard drive and iCloud account and documents released by Republicans on two Senate committees.

The documents and the analysis, which don't show what he did to earn millions from his Chinese partners, raise questions about national security, business ethics and potential legal exposure.

In December 2020, Biden acknowledged in a statement that he was the subject of a federal investigation into his taxes. NBC News was first to report that an ex-business partner had warned Biden he should amend his tax returns to disclose $400,000 in income from the Ukrainian firm, Burisma.[745]

Specifically, NBC found that Hunter made $5.8 million from two deals with Chinese business interests, which accounted for half his income from 2013 to 2018.

During one of the 2020 presidential debates, Joe Biden told the American public that his son Hunter (who he says is the smartest person he knows—which is probably true) never made any money from China (which is not true).[746]

Hunter's most lucrative relationship was with Ye Jianming, a Chinese businessman who has been under detention on bribery charges since 2018. Jianming's Hudson West III paid Hunter nearly $4.8 million in about a year.

Hunter also did work for one of Ye's associates, Patrick Ho, who was convicted in U.S. federal court of bribing top officials in Chad and Uganda in pursuit of oil deals. He was sentenced to three years in prison in March 2019 and then expelled from the U.S. One $1 million wire from Hudson West to Hunter in March 2018 had the memo line "Dr Patrick Ho Chi Ping Representation."

745 Winter, Tom, et al. "Analysis of Hunter Biden's hard drive shows he, his firm took in about $11 million from 2013 to 2018, spent it fast." NBC News, May 19, 2022, https://www.nbcnews.com/politics/national-security/analysis-hunter-bidens-hard-drive-shows-firm-took-11-million-2013-2018-rcna29462.

746 McCormack, John. "Biden at Last Presidential Debate: 'My Son Has Not Made Money' from China." National Review, December 10, 2020, https://www.nationalreview.com/corner/biden-at-last-presidential-debate-my-son-has-not-made-money-from-china/.

The "fact-checkers" were already on the case years ago, with the *Washington Post*'s fact-checker Glenn Kessler rating the following claims from Trump "Four Pinocchios" back in 2019:[747]

- "When Biden's son walks out of China with $1.5 billion in a fund, and the biggest funds in the world can't get money out of China, and he's there for one quick meeting and he flies in on Air Force Two, I think that's a horrible thing. I think it's a horrible thing." — President Trump, remarks with Ukrainian President Volodymyr Zelensky, Sept. 25, 2019

- "Ask how his son made millions of dollars from Ukraine, made millions of dollars from China, even though he had no expertise whatsoever." — Trump, in remarks to reporters with British Prime Minister Boris Johnson, Sept. 24

- "The son took money from China—a lot of money from China." — Trump, remarks to reporters at the United Nations, Sept. 23

We know for sure that the claims in the second and third bullet points are true, and interestingly enough, the only claim that Kessler actually dissects is the first, which makes reference to $1.5 billion in a fund and then bases the entire fact-check rating around that specific claim.

While Trump characterized Hunter as "walking away with" $1.5 billion in a fund, the fund in question, called BHR Partners, was a fund that aimed to raise $1.5 billion. Hunter received a 10 percent interest in the fund.

"Affiliates of the advisory firm had said they planned to raise $1.5 billion, but it appears the fundraising fell far short of that"—Kessler wrote—which is contradicted by BHR's website, which now claims to manage assets that equal roughly $2.24 billion.[748]

While this could be just written off as Trump misspeaking or being imprecise with language, Kessler uses it as an opportunity to provide more "context" for Hunter's shady business dealings. The main sources Kessler uses for his "fact-check," which aims to assure us that Hunter

---

747 Kessler, Glenn. "Trump's false claims about hunter Biden's China dealings." *Washington Post*, September 26, 2019, https://www.washingtonpost.com/politics/2019/09/26/trumps-false-claims-about-hunter-bidens-china-dealings/.

748 BHR Partners. "About Us." BHRPE, http://www.bhrpe.com/list.php?catid=31&page=1.

Biden in no way profited from a fund he owns 10 percent of, include "the Biden camp," a representative for BHR, and George Mesires, a lawyer for Hunter Biden. So, we're just supposed to take the word of those who have a vested interest in every Hunter scandal being swept under the rug.

What Kessler doesn't include in his analysis is of note. In trying to distance Hunter financially from BHR, he excludes other salacious details that would be damaging to him, such as the fact that the others involved in this venture included Christopher Heinz, the stepson of John Kerry, and the Thornton Group, which is owned by the nephew of notorious mobster Whitey Bulger and son of former Massachusetts state senator Billy Bulger.[749]

Kessler concludes his fact-check with the following:

> One could argue Hunter Biden has been trading off his father's name, and certainly arranging a handshake between a business partner and the vice president in China raises eyebrows. But Hunter Biden did not raise money for the fund; instead, he was on a board that advised potential investors. He did not obtain an equity stake until after his father was no longer vice president — and that investment of less than half a million dollars has not yet yielded a payoff for Hunter Biden, according to his attorney.[750]

In the world of Kessler, one isn't trading off their family name if the said family member stops being vice president at any point during the transaction.

749 Miller, Joshua Rhett. "Mobster Whitey Bulger's nephew played role in Hunter Biden's Chinese business ventures: emails." *New York Post*, April 14, 2022, https://nypost.com/2022/04/14/hunter-biden-laptop-connects-whitey-bulger-nephew-to-china-dealings/.
750 Kessler, "Trump's false claims about hunter Biden's China dealings."

AUTHOR BIO

Matt Palumbo is the author of *The Man Behind the Curtain: Inside the Secret Network of George Soros* (2022), *Dumb and Dumber: How Cuomo and de Blasio Ruined New York* (2021), *Debunk This!: Shattering Liberal Lies* (2019), and *Spygate: The Attempted Sabotage of Donald J. Trump* (2018).